Soham Yoga

Soham Yoga
The Yoga of the Self

Swami Nirmalananda Giri
(Abbot George Burke)

Light of the Spirit Press
Cedar Crest, New Mexico

Published by
Light of the Spirit Press
lightofthespiritpress.com

Light of the Spirit Monastery
P. O. Box 1370
Cedar Crest, New Mexico 87008
OCOY.org

paperback edition:
ISBN-13: 978-0-9985998-7-8

hardcover edition:
ISBN 13: 978-1-955046-02-2

Library of Congress Control Number: 2018948347

Bisac Categories:
• OCC010000 BODY, MIND & SPIRIT / Mindfulness & Meditation
• YAN024090 YOUNG ADULT NONFICTION / Health
& Daily Living / Mindfulness & Meditation

07172023

CONTENTS

PREFACE

Some history

Yoga is an eternal science intended to reveal and manifest the Eternal. Although the identity of the Supreme Self (Paramatman) and the individual Self (jivatman) with Soham is indicated in the Isha Upanishad (16) and the Brihadaranyaka Upanishad (1.4.1) respectively, no one knows exactly when it was that the knowledge of Soham Yoga was revealed in the world, but the following we do know.

A young man was wandering in the mountains somewhere in India–most likely in the Western Himalayas. He had seen no one else for a very long time, but one day he heard the faint sound of a human voice. Following it, he saw from a distance some people seated together near a river. Slipping into the water, he began swimming toward them. All along the river on that side thick reeds were growing so he was not seen as he stealthily made his way closer.

Soon he began to understand what was being said. Fascinated by the speaker's words he came as close as he dared and for a long time remained absorbed in the amazing things being spoken. For the science of yoga was being expounded by a master to his disciples. Then he heard the master say: "There is a 'fish' in the reeds over there, listening to everything I am saying. Why doesn't he come out and join us?" He did as suggested and became a resident of the master's ashram and learned both philosophy and Soham Yoga.

After diligent practice of Soham meditation for quite some time, the master asked him to return to the plains and teach that yoga to whomever would listen. He was given a new name, Matsyendranath. (Matsyendra means Indra Among Fish and Nath means Master. Indra is king of the gods.) We have no knowledge of what the master's name was. Matsyendranath and his disciples only referred to him as Adi Nath–Original/First Master. Some believe Adi Nath was Shiva himself manifested to teach yoga, or perhaps the Bhagavan Sanatkumara about whom the Brihadaranyaka Upanishad says: "To such a one who has his stains wiped away, Bhagavan Sanatkumara shows the further shore of darkness" (7.26.2).

Matsyendra wandered throughout India, teaching those who were awakened enough to desire and comprehend the yogic path. One day in his wanderings he came to a house where the owner's wife gave him something to eat and a request: that he would bless her to have a child. In response he blessed her and gave her some ashes from a sacred fire, telling her to swallow them. Then he left. The woman followed his instructions and soon conceived and gave birth to a male child. Several years later Matsyendra came there again and saw the little boy outside the house. He told him to bring his mother, and when she came he asked if she remembered him, which she did. Pointing to the boy, he said: "That is my child. I have come for him." The woman agreed and Matsyendra left with the boy, whom he named Gorakhsha, Protector/ Guardian of Light.

Goraksha in time became the monk Gorakshanath (usually called Gorakhnath), the greatest yogi in India's recorded history. In every part of India there are stories told of his living in those areas. He also lived in Nepal, Tibet, Ladakh, and Bhutan. There are shrines and temples to him in all those countries, both Hindu and Buddhist. His major temple is in Gorakhpur, the birthplace of Paramhansa Yogananda, whose younger brother, Sananda, was originally named Goraksha. Considering all the lore about him, Gorakhnath must have lived at least two or three hundred years, and there are many who claim that he has never left his body but is living right now in the Himalayas.

Gorakhnath had many disciples, a large number of them attaining enlightenment. They were the first members of the Nath Yogi Sampradaya, which in time numbered in its ranks the great sage Patanjali, founder of the Yoga Philosophy (Yoga Darshan) and author of the Yoga Sutras, and Jesus of Nazareth (Sri Ishanath). For many centuries the majority of monks in India were Nath Yogis, but in the nineteenth century there was a sharp decline in their numbers, which continues today. However there are several groups of "Nath Panthis" that follow the philosophy and yoga of Matsyendranath and Gorakhnath, and therefore are involved with the Soham mantra as the heart of their sadhana.

Soham

Soham (which is pronounced like "Sohum") means: I Am That. It is the natural vibration of the Self, which occurs spontaneously with each incoming and outgoing breath. Through becoming aware of it on the conscious level by mentally repeating it in time with the breath (*So* when inhaling and *Ham* when exhaling), a yogi experiences the identity between his individual Self and the Supreme Self.

There are mantras that change things and others that reveal the eternal nature of things. Soham does both. According to the Nath Yogis (see *Philosophy of Gorakhnath* by Askhaya Kumar Banerjea), Soham has existed within the depths of God from eternity; and the same is true of every sentient being. Soham, then, will reveal our inner being. By meditating on Soham we discover our Self, within which Soham has existed forever. The simple intonation of Soham in time with the breath (see Chapter Two) will do everything in the unfolding of the yogi's spiritual consciousness. For sound and breath are the totality of Soham sadhana. (See Appendix Three: Breath and Sound in Meditation.)

The practice is very simple, and the results very profound. Truly wondrous is the fact that Soham Yoga can go on all the time, not just during meditation, if we apply ourselves to it. The whole life can become a continuous stream of liberating sadhana. "By the mantra 'Soham' separate the jivatman from the Paramatman and locate the jivatman in the heart" (Devi Bhagavatam 11.8.15). When we repeat Soham in time with the breath we are invoking our eternal being. This is why we need only listen to our inner mental intonations of Soham in time with the breath which itself is Soham.

It is my hope that through practice you will experience for yourself the value and benefits of Soham Yoga that is presented in this book. The important thing about Soham Yoga is that it really works. It only takes perseverance. Archimedes said: "Give me a fulcrum and I will move the world." Soham Yoga is the fulcrum.

Swami Nirmalananda Giri (Abbot George Burke)
Light of the Spirit Monastery
OCOY.org

(Please see the Glossary for the definition of unfamiliar words and also for brief biographical information on unfamiliar persons.)

YO

SOHAM YO

Yoga philosophy
The basic tex
Yoga Darsha
India. I
phy

Yoga is a Sanskrit word that mea is both union and the way to that union. What do we join through yoga? First, we join our awareness to our own essential being, the spirit whose nature is pure consciousness. In yoga philosophy this is known as the Atman or Self. Next, we join our finite consciousness to the Infinite Consciousness, God, the Supreme Self (Paramatman). In essence they are eternally one.

The individual Atman-spirit (jivatman) originally dwelt in the consciousness of that oneness. But through its descent into the material world the spirit lost both its awareness of the eternal union and the capacity to manifest it on a practical level. Through yoga the lost consciousness can be regained and actualized in the yogi's practical life sphere.

Regarding this, a yogi-adept of the twentieth century, Dr. I. K. Taimni, remarks in his book *The Science of Yoga*: "According to the yogic philosophy it is possible to rise completely above the illusions and miseries of life and to gain infinite knowledge, bliss, and power through enlightenment *here and now* while we are still living in the physical body.... No vague promise of an uncertain postmortem happiness this, but a definite scientific assertion of a fact verified by the experience of innumerable yogis, saints, and sages who have trodden the path of yoga throughout the ages."

Since rational thought precedes rational action, we should begin with the philosophical side of yoga.

of the Yoga philosophy is the Yoga Sutras (also called
na), written by the sage Patanjali, a Nath Yogi of ancient
contrast to other philosophical systems, Yoga is a philoso-
which stimulates its investigators to engage in yoga as a practice
through which they will experience and demonstrate its truth and
worth. What begins as theory develops into practice which culminates
in realization. Yoga is philosophy, discipline, and experience—a revelation
of consciousness.

In the Bhagavad Gita, Krishna the teacher tells Arjuna the student:
"Truly there never was a time when I was not, nor you, nor these lords
of men—nor in the future will there be a time when we shall cease to
be" (Bhagavad Gita 2:12). We are eternal beings, without beginning
and without end. Originally we were points of conscious light in the
infinite ocean of Conscious Light that is God—gods within God. And
so we still are, for it is not possible to be outside of Infinity. Yet we are
also here in this ever-changing world, the experience of which blinds
us to the truth of our immortal life within God. As Blavatsky wrote
in *The Voice of the Silence*: "Heaven's dew-drop glittering in the morn's
first sunbeam within the bosom of the lotus, when dropped on earth
becomes a piece of clay; behold, the pearl is now a speck of mire."
Each one of us is a dew-drop of heaven, but for countless life-cycles
we have forgotten that.

God the Lord—Ishwara

In the Yoga Sutras the word for God is Ishwara: the Lord, Ruler,
Master or Controller possessing the powers of omnipotence, omnipresence, and omniscience. It is toward this Ishwara that our life is to
be directed if we would attain perfection in yoga. In Yoga Sutra 1:23,
Patanjali says that samadhi, the state of superconsciousness where absoluteness is experienced, is produced by Ishwarapranidhana: the offering
of one's life to God. This is not merely dedicating our deeds and thoughts

to God, but consciously merging our life in the greater life of God and making them one. Yoga is the way to accomplish this.

Since yoga is a practical matter, we need some workable, pragmatic understanding of the nature of God. For how will we seek and recognize him if we have no idea who he is? Patanjali supplies us with exactly the kind of definition we need: "Ishwara is a particular spirit who is untouched by the afflictions of life, actions [karma] and the results and impressions [conditionings] produced by these actions" (Yoga Sutras 1:24).

A particular Spirit. God is a special, unique, conscious Being, not just abstract existence. God is a particular Spirit in the sense that God can be distinguished from among all other things or beings.

Untouched. Though Ishwara is within all things and all things are within him, yet he stands apart. This is stated several times in the Bhagavad Gita: "Know that [all] states of being proceed from me. But I am not in them—they are in me…. [This world] does not perceive me, who am higher than these and eternal" (7:12-13). "[I am] sitting as one apart, indifferent and unattached in these actions" (9:9). "[I am] outside and inside beings—the animate and the inanimate—incomprehensible because of its subtlety, far away and also near" (13:15). "All beings dwell within me, but I do not dwell within them" (9:4).

God is unique in the sense that he is *Ekam Evam Advityam Brahman*: the God who is one, only, without a second. He is not one of many, nor is he even one of two. He is one in every sense of the term. God is neither conditioned nor confined in any manner. Therefore he is not touched or tainted by the afflictions or faults of life (relative existence), in contrast to us who live within them as though they were the air we breathe and the basis of our existence. Nor is Ishwara bound or in any way conditioned by actions; therefore he is ever unchanging.

It should be noted that Ishwara is considered to be male in contradistinction to the divine creative power, Prakriti or Shakti, that is female. Consequently Ishwara is referred to as "he." Brahman the

3

Absolute is referred to as "it" because Brahman transcends such dualities as male and female, positive and negative. Since the English word "God" almost always implies Ishwara, in this book God will be referred to as "he."

Infinite Consciousness: Omniscience

God is the essence and the apex of consciousness, so Patanjali further says: "In him is the highest limit of omniscience" (Yoga Sutras 1:25). Commenting on this, Shankara says: "The all-pervading mind of the supreme Lord is in simultaneous contact with every object." The omniscience of God is total and absolute, for in truth God *is* Omnipotence, Omniscience, and Omnipresence.

In this sutra Patanjali introduces a significant fact, for he does not just say that omniscience (*sarvajña*) is in God, but that the *seed* of omniscience (*sarvajña bijam*) is in him. Within God is the seed or potentiality of omniscience for those who are united with him through their practice of yoga. Omniscience is not just objective knowledge, but infinity of consciousness, the Being of God himself.

The two Selfs

The age-old question asked along with "Who is God?" is "Who am I?" The true "I" of each sentient being is the spirit-Self. But there is more. God is the Self of the Self as the ocean is the "self" of every wave. The illumined know that they are the immortal Self whose ultimate Self is the Immortal Itself. We are spirits within Spirit, in a wondrous way both ourselves and Brahman, both finite and infinite.

"Two birds, companions [who are] always united, cling to the self-same tree. Of these two, the one eats the sweet fruit and the other looks on without eating. On the self-same tree, a person immersed [in the sorrows of the world] is deluded and grieves on account of his helplessness. When he sees the other, the Lord who is worshipped and his greatness, he becomes freed from sorrow" (Mundaka Upanishad 3.1.1-2).

The key

Meditation is the key to knowledge of both the Self and the Self of the Self. Knowing one, both are known, so say the sages.

Dr. I. K. Taimni, in *The Ultimate Reality and Realization*, says this: "It is only when the realization of being a pure spirit or atman has been attained that it is possible to achieve the final goal of union of the atman with the Paramatman, the Supreme Spirit which exists eternally beyond the manifested universe and from which the manifested universe is derived. When this final realization has been attained and union of atman with Paramatman has been brought about there is not only a complete sharing of consciousness between the two but also of the infinite Power which is inherent in the Universal Consciousness.... It is necessary to distinguish between the powers which are acquired on the realization that he is a pure spirit or atman and those which are attained when he is able to destroy the last vestige of egoism and his consciousness becomes united with that of Paramatman. The former, though tremendous in some respects, are still limited, while the latter which are really the Powers of the Supreme Spirit are infinite and can manifest through the center of consciousness of a Self-realized individual because there is fusion of the individual consciousness with the Supreme Consciousness and the channel between the two is open."

God and gods

We are gods within God, finite spirits within the Infinite Spirit. But what is spirit? Yoga philosophy tells us that spirit is *consciousness*. We are eternal consciousnesses, each of us individual and distinct. Yet we are more. Each of us takes our being from God as the wave takes its existence from the ocean.

God is the eternal root, the ground, of our being, our greater Self. We are not God, but in some ineffable manner God is us: the Self of our Self, the Spirit of our spirit. God is all, and we are the parts, each of us possessing an eternal and irrevocable distinction. That is why Krishna told Arjuna: "Truly there never was a time when *I* was not, nor *you*, nor *these* lords of men—nor in the future will there be a time when *we* shall cease to be" (Bhagavad Gita 2:12).

"There are two selves that drink the fruit of Karma in the world of good deeds. Both are lodged in the secret place [of the heart], the chief seat of the Supreme. The knowers of Brahman speak of them as shade and light" (Katha Upanishad 1:3:1).

God and creation

God, the infinite Spirit, is pure consciousness, but has extended or emanated himself as the cosmos: physical, astral, and causal. "Brahman, indeed, was this in the beginning. It knew itself only as: 'I am Brahman.' Therefore it became all" (Brihadaranyaka Upanishad 1:4:10). This seemingly dual nature of God as Light and Power, as Consciousness and Matter, has puzzled the minds of even the wise.

God, the Original Being, projects himself as the ever-changing dance of creation, as the evolving Light that is the cosmos. God projects the creation, evolves it, and withdraws it back into himself in a perpetual cycle. The creation can be thought of as God's body: that God becomes incarnate in creation again and again. And as parts or reflections of God we do exactly the same through our personal reincarnation.

There is a law that governs the place and kind of our embodiment. That law is karma, the principle of exact and inevitable reaction to our own actions and mental states, resulting in a seemingly endless domino effect of continual birth and death. Yoga offers us the possibility of evolving our consciousness and ending this chain of embodiments by the awakening-transformation from time and mortality into eternity and immortality.

And us...

All conscious beings have existed eternally within the Being of God, one with him, distinct though not separate from him. Rooted in the infinity of God, they have within themselves an innate impulse to transcend their finitude and attain the boundlessness of their Origin. This is impossible, since they are as immutable as God, the only infinite being. They can become godlike, but they cannot become God. Yet the urge for transcendence is part of their nature. (See *Robe of Light*.)

The solution to this dilemma is simple. The individual consciousnesses cannot alter their natural state of finitude, but they can come to share and participate in the infinite consciousness of God. Even though they cannot become infinite themselves, they can experience the infinity of their divine Source, just as a psychically sensitive person can experience the thoughts and feelings of others without becoming them. In the same way, spirits can evolve to experience the consciousness of God while remaining in their naturally limited state. They do not become God the Absolute, but they enter into that Absolute Life and are one with it.

As Shankara explains in his Yoga Sutra commentary: "When the light of several lamps appears simultaneously, it cannot be made out which is the light of which." Consequently, liberated spirits experience the infinite Being of God, infinite consciousness, as their own being. Krishna has described it this way: "Know this, and you shall not again fall into delusion. By this you shall come to see all creation in your Self and then in me" (Bhagavad Gita 4:35).

When the spirits are unshakably established in that consciousness the goal has been attained. All they need do is develop the capacity for such a state of awareness. This is done by learning to fully experience the state of existence of a being completely different from themselves while retaining the awareness of their true identity. They can put on the costume of a consciousness utterly different from theirs, and not just experience that other mode of consciousness, but become able to function as that other kind of being.

Evolutionary creation

To enable the spirits to enter into this process, God breathes forth his own Self as the Power from which is manifested all the realms of relative existence, from the most subtle worlds of perfected beings to the most objective worlds of atomic matter. They can then enter into relative existence by taking on coverings, or bodies, of varying grades and patterns of vibratory energies. They descend into this material world and begin working their way up the ladder of ever-evolving forms and consciousness. Beginning with forms whose scope of consciousness is vastly less than theirs, they work their way upward, entering into higher and higher levels of awareness until they can surpass their original breadth of consciousness and begin to partake of a life of awareness much beyond their own. This then culminates in their developing the ability to share in the Divine Consciousness itself.

There are seven worlds (lokas) or main divisions of relative existence. These worlds are the rungs of the evolutionary ladder. They correspond to the seven levels of consciousness that determine which of the worlds the individual spirit incarnates in. Keeping in mind that "world" in this list does not mean a planet, but a great division that includes within it many levels of existence, many planes of consciousness, here is a list of the seven worlds:

1. Bhur Loka, where the dominant consciousness is that of matter.
2. Bhuva Loka, where the dominant consciousness is that of feeling: emotion, instinct, and lower intuition.
3. Swar Loka, where the dominant consciousness is that of sensory experience.
4. Maha Loka, where the dominant consciousness is that of thought and reflective perception.
5. Jnana Loka, where the dominant consciousness is that of fundamental causation and spiritual intuition.
6. Tapa Loka, where the dominant consciousness is that of mastery of all the lesser elements and levels.
7. Satya Loka, where the dominant consciousness is that of spirit-consciousness itself.

Bhur Loka is purely material; Bhuva and Swar Lokas are astral; Maha Loka is a mixture of astral and causal; Jnana and Tapa Lokas are completely causal; and Satya Loka is a mixture of extremely subtle causal and pure consciousness.

Incarnating spirits move upward and downward in the three lower worlds of Bhur, Bhuva, and Swar, but once they attain the level of Maha Loka they are never reborn in the three lower worlds unless they will to do so. Spirits may move between the two worlds of Maha and Jnana, but once they reach Tapa Loka they remain there until they evolve into Satya Loka which is the world of the perfectly liberated spirits and the spirits that have evolved beyond Tapa Loka and are so close to liberation that they can arise to such a rarefied spiritual atmosphere as Satya Loka. Those fully liberated spirits who return to lower worlds for the benefit of others do so as avatars, incarnations of God-consciousness.

In the intervals between embodiments the spirit spends time in the astral regions where awakening and growth also take place. (This is best explained in the forty-third chapter of *Autobiography of a Yogi* by Paramhansa Yogananda.) Upward and upward they evolve until their capacity for awareness is developed to such a perfect state that they can experience and participate in God's all-embracing consciousness, thenceforth to live in his infinity.

As Shakespeare wrote, "all the world's a stage" with the individual spirits wearing their body-costumes and playing their karmic parts. Just as actors begin with small parts and progress to bigger roles by demonstrating their skill in those smaller parts, so also do the spirits advance to higher and more complex forms of existence and consciousness, at last returning home to God. The Sufi poet, Rumi, wrote:

> A stone I died and rose again a plant.
> A plant I died and rose an animal;
> I died an animal and was born a man.
> Why should I fear? What have I lost by death?

As man, death sweeps me from this world of men
That I may wear an angel's wings in heaven;
Yet e'en as angel may I not abide,
For nought abideth save the face of God.
Thus o'er the angels' world I wing my way
Onwards and upwards, unto boundless lights;
Then let me be as nought, for in my heart
Rings as a harp-song that we must return to him.

Oliver Wendell Holmes, one of many great Americans whose belief in reincarnation is overlooked, wrote in his poem, *The Chambered Nautilus:*

Build thee more stately mansions, O my soul,
As the swift seasons roll!
Leave thy low-vaulted past!
Let each new temple, nobler than the last,
Shut thee from heaven with a dome more vast,
Till thou at length art free,
Leaving thine outgrown shell by life's unresting sea!

That is the purpose of creation and our place in it.

The religion of Yoga

The Nath Yogi Gorakhnath, considered the greatest yogi in the history of India, wrote: "By birth I was a Hindu, but through maturity I became a Yogi." It is commonly said that Yoga is not a religion. But since religion is derived from the Latin word *religere*, which means "to bind back," and yoga means "joining," practically speaking yoga is the *only* religion. The many systems of dogmas and doctrines are by their very nature not really religions at all, and in most instances are systems of superstition, either by the nature of their ideas or practices or by the attitudes of their adherents toward their beliefs and disciplines.

Only when Yoga and Self-realization are the matrix around which a philosophy has been formulated for their furtherance is it worthy of our consideration. Other philosophies only produce confusion and distraction from the goal.

Regarding this, in his commentary on the twenty-second sutra of the Kaivalya Pada of the Yoga Sutras, Taimni says: "The student will have noticed that in the ideas set forth in the above pages no effort has been made to link up the facts of Yogic philosophy with doctrines which are considered to be religious. But this does not mean that there is no relation between them. In fact, a religious man can see, if he studies the subject of Yoga with an open mind, that all the ideas of Yogic philosophy can be interpreted in religious terms, and the consciousness which the Yogi seeks to uncover within the folds of his mind is nothing but that Supreme Reality which is commonly referred to as God. God is recognized by every religion with any philosophical background to be a Mighty Being whose consciousness transcends the manifested Universe. He is considered to be hidden within every human heart. He is supposed to transcend the mind. Basically, these ideas are the same as those of Yogic philosophy. The main difference lies in the assertion by Yogic philosophy that this Supreme Reality or Consciousness is not merely a matter for speculation or even adoration but can be discovered by following a technique which is as definite and unfailing as the technique of any modern Science. Yoga thus imparts a tremendous significance to religion and places the whole problem of religious life and endeavor on an entirely new basis and it is difficult to understand how any religious man can reject its claims without giving them due consideration."

It is yoga alone which reunites the consciousness of the individual to its infinite source, restoring the lost unity. Earlier I quoted a paragraph from I. K. Taimni's book *The Science of Yoga* about the purpose of yoga, but omitting his preceding words regarding the relation of yoga to religion, or rather, their difference. Here they are now, for I think you will find them relevant:

"The Orthodox religious ideal which requires people to be good and moral so that they may have a happy life here and hereafter is really a concession to human weakness and the desire to prefer the so-called happiness in life to enlightenment.

"In this respect the philosophy of yoga differs fundamentally from most of the orthodox religions of the world which offer nothing better than an uncertain and nebulous happiness in the life after death. They say in effect 'Lead a good life to ensure happiness after death, put your faith in God and hope for the best.' According to yogic philosophy death no more solves your spiritual problem than night solves your economic problem. If you are poor you do not expect on going to bed that your economic problem will be automatically solved next day. You will have to get up the next day and begin where you left off the previous night. If you are poor economically you do not expect to get rich overnight and if you are poor spiritually, bound by illusions and limitations of all kinds, you cannot expect to become enlightened [by simply being reborn] or, if you do not believe in reincarnation, in the vague and unending life which is supposed to follow death."

Yoga is the way we answer for ourselves the prayer:

> Lead me from the unreal to the Real.
> Lead me from darkness to the Light.
> Lead me from death to Immortality.

The Conscious Universe

The ancient yogi-sages of India directly experienced the truth that the entire universe is a manifestation of divine consciousness—of God. All creation is really spirit, not matter at all. More to the point, it is the infinitely complex and perfect thought of God. Just as we create worlds and live in them when we dream or daydream, in the same way the cosmic dreamer is dreaming the cosmic dream of this evolutionary creation, and we are dreaming our personal dream within it. Therefore it all has a meaning and a purpose and is absolutely perfect and consistent with itself. We must keep this in mind at all times, but especially when considering our life-dream within the greater dream.

As yogis aspiring to infinite consciousness through the self-evolution produced by our yoga practice, we should understand every step of the way, and this requires a comprehension of the specific laws governing our presence within creation and our way out of relativity back into the Absolute.

The two oldest Upanishads on Soham

The Isha and the Brihadaranyaka are the oldest of the Upanishads, giving us the earliest record of Soham that we know.

The Isha Upanishad concludes with four mantras that are to be recited by a dying person to ensure his ascension to the solar world upon leaving his body. (These mantras are also recited by those who attend the cremation of the body.) The sixteenth verse says: "O Pushan, the sole seer, O Controller, O Sun, offspring of Prajapati, spread forth your rays and gather up your radiant light that I may behold you of loveliest form. I am that Purusha [Spirit-Self]: I AM SOHAM." (The Sanskrit text is: *Yo sav asau purushah; soham asmi*.) At the core of every sentient being Soham exists as the Self—*is* the Self. *Soham asmi* literally means "I AM THAT I AM," which is exactly what God told Moses was his Name (Exodus 3:14; Soham: I am that; Asmi: I am).

The Brihadaranyaka Upanishad (5.15.2) repeats the identical words. It earlier says: "In the beginning this [world] was only the Self [Atman], in the shape of a person. Looking around he saw nothing else than the Self. He first said, 'I am Soham' [*Soham asmi*]" (1.4.1) Thus Soham is the "first speaking" of the Absolute Itself: the expression of the knowledge and knowing of the Self. As said earlier, Soham is the Name (Embodiment) of the Primeval Being, the Self of the Universe and the Self of our Selfs. Soham is the Consciousness of Brahman and of the Self of each one of us. We, too, are Soham.

In the section of the Yoga Sutras (1:27) dealing with Ishwara, the Supreme Lord, Patanjali makes this statement: *Tasya vachakah pranavah*–"His vachaka is the Pranava." Although universally believed to refer to the monosyllable Om, "Vachaka" means speech, speaking or spoken form, and "Pranava" means Life, Life-Giver and Breath Principle–the Breath Word. Integrating this with the Brihadaranyaka verse we see that the Pranava, the Breath Word, is Soham. For "he first said: 'Soham.'" Ishwara "speaks" Soham as the inner foundation of the universe, as the evolutionary life force within the cosmos and every individual being. Soham is the Self of the Universe and the Self of our Selfs.

Thus Soham is the Pranava in two ways: 1) As the Breath Word since it accompanies every breath–*So* on inhalation and *Ham* on exhalation, and 2) As the Life Word since it has been inherent in us from eternity and in every relative form we have taken on in our evolutionary journey. Soham is at the core of every living thing.

Patanjali continues regarding Soham: "Its constant repetition and meditation [is the way]. From it [result] the disappearance of obstacles [to enlightenment] and turning inward of consciousness" (1:28-29). Soham is the Breath and Life Word. We invoke our lower self when we simply say "I [*aham*]" but we invoke our higher, divine Self when we say "Soham," joining it with the breath.

The Adi Pinda

From eternity there has existed in the depths of Brahman and every spirit-Self potential for expansion and manifestation. When the time for expansion/manifestation is to begin, this potential awakens and comes into play, at first only internally. Although it is internal it is symbolically called a pinda, a body, known as the Adi Pinda, the Original Body. Actually it is not really a body, a kosha or sharira, but a foreshadowing, a kind of blueprint, of what will in time manifest as the causal, astral and material body of the cosmos. Further the Adi Pinda is the source of all other bodies or individual existences. It is also the eternal link and meeting-ground between the transcendent and the phenomenal planes of existence–between the Transcendent Spirit and Its phenomenal cosmic self-manifestation.

According to Akshaya Kumar Banerjea in *Philosophy of Gorakhnath*, the Adi Pinda has five elements that are actually five forms of spiritual consciousness: Paramananda or supreme bliss; Prabodha or Manifestation; Chidudaya or Self-arising of Transcendent Consciousness; Prakasha or Illumination; and Soham Bhava. (See *Philosophy of Gorakhnath* for a more complete analysis of the Adi Pinda.)

Soham Bhava: the beginning and the end

A Brief Sanskrit Glossary defines bhava: "Subjective state of being (existence); attitude of mind; mental attitude or feeling; state of realization in the heart or mind." Soham Bhava is an eternal element in the essential being of both God and each one of us. Though essentially consciousness, it is also the original (and originating) potential of both the cosmos and each individual sentient being. At the beginning of creation, it becomes an internal movement within Brahman, a stirring, a fecundity, the seed of relative existence, though itself beyond relativity. Soham Bhava is the Original Face which is reflected in each individual spirit. The Soham Bhava is itself Self-knowledge, the Atmajnana. This is because Soham Bhava is the pure consciousness of the Self: Atma Chaitanya. It is the Self whose essential nature is Consciousness. Therefore Soham Yoga is the direct means to Self-realization.

The Soham Breath

To realize its own potential the Soham Bhava becomes the Soham Breath within all. The Rig Veda (hymn 129) says that in the beginning the One "breathed breathlessly." The Soham Breath is the archetypal breath within God and within all beings and is the uniting principle of the Supreme Being and individual beings.

The Soham Breath is itself Yoga and Yogi. On the cosmic level it is the root or seed that is the beginning of all things, the Holy Breath, the *Agia Pneuma*, the Holy Spirit, the Holy Light, from which all things proceed and into which all things are ultimately resolved. It is the Primal Breath within all beings that enables them to manifest, evolve and return to their Origin. Throughout eternity Soham is the unfolding story of every one of us, including God. Soham is the root of the breath, the life within each sentient being, ripened and changed from potential to actual, the impulse that is both creation and entry into creation, that which expands and evolves until it manifests in many stages from most subtle to most objective as the physical breath.

First it is the force that impels the individual onto the path that leads into involution (relativity), into experience and identity with increasingly complex forms of manifestation; and it is also the impulse that moves the spirit onto the path of evolution—of growth out of relativity. Second, it is the beginning of duality: a vast chain of constant cycling between two poles—negative and positive—that makes relative existence possible, both as evolving consciousness and evolving organism.

The spirit travels along the path of involution until it reaches the experience of self-awareness and self-reflection (self-analysis) within a human body sufficiently developed to permit and produce that awareness. Then it begins the path of evolution back to infinity. Of course, the two paths are really one; it is only a matter of the direction being taken. The point where involution becomes evolution is a kind of watershed or continental divide. All this is a direct production of the original breath, the Soham Breath which takes place both macrocosmically and microcosmically. This has a profound yogic significance, as the dedicated Soham yogi will perceive.

In yogic treatises we find it stated over and over that the breath is the essence of our existence. Prana means both life and breath in Hinduism and Buddhism. In fact, the word Atman (Self) comes from the root-word *at*, which means "to breathe." Other religions also use the same word for both spirit and breath: in Judaism, *ruach*; in ancient Greek religion and Eastern Christianity, *pneuma*; in ancient Roman religion and Western Christianity, *spiritus* which comes from *spiro*, "I breathe."

Soham Bhava is the root and Soham Breath is the flower. "So" is the inhalation and "Ham" is the exhalation. In the original stage, "So" produces the inhalation and "Ham" produces the exhalation. But after a few stages along the path to relativity, inhalation produces "So" and exhalation produces "Ham." Then in the heights of evolution things go back to the original mode. For the breath itself is an extension-manifestation of Soham.

Total and simultaneous effect from the beginning

From the beginning of our yoga practice we must work in the physical, psychic and spiritual levels at the same time. This of course requires the appropriate methodology, and not just a bundle of theories. It is essential to begin purifying and evolving our total makeup, physical, astral and causal, from the very first. Otherwise no lasting change can be effected by us.

Some methods start at the top and work downward, like drilling for water or oil. Until the bottom is reached nothing much really happens, though there can be a lot of phenomena throughout. Other methods start deep down and work upward, like water or oil breaking up through the earth as in a "gusher." But the yogi has to wait and wait for the result. In both approaches the yogi has to wait for the end. But from the beginning Soham sadhana works throughout the yogi's entire makeup, physical, astral and causal. It does not move either up or down, but rather expands outward, increasing to the final limits. From the very beginning the Soham sadhaka experiences Reality which continues to expand until perfect realization is attained.

Discovering Yoga

The ancient yogis of India found after intense and extensive self-examination that the mind, the instrument of the spirit-consciousness, was fundamentally affected by two factors, breath and sound, and that all other elements were quite secondary to these two things. Investigating the breath in its subtler and subtler (higher and higher) levels, they found that breath and sound were inseparable, really two manifestations of a single factor: an impulse that came directly from the spirit-Self. In the highest level they found that the breath is a unitary-yet-dual impulse manifesting in a circular motion or pattern that is single yet possessing two halves which appear in the body as two parallel movements: inhalation and exhalation.

They further discovered that the root impulse of inhalation makes the subtle sound of *So*, and the root impulse of exhalation makes the subtle sound of *Hum* (written as *Ham* in Sanskrit). Since all creation is the thought or ideation of God, meaning is inherent in everything, including the breath: "That [*So*] I am [*Ham*]." In this way every living being is perpetually intoning Soham ("Sohum") at the core of their being, saying: I AM THAT–the spirit-Self which is a divine part of the Divine Infinite. Since Soham is eternally flowing within us without volition it is known as ajapa japa, automatic, involuntary repetition.

No matter how many ages we wander in forgetfulness of our divine origin and nature, we are always affirming "I am That" without ceasing at each breath. But we have lost the awareness of that sacred thread of inmost knowledge and are now wandering without direction or discernment. But by mentally intoning Soham in time with the breath–*So* when inhaling and *Ham* when exhaling–we consciously take hold of the thread and begin moving in the right direction.

Through constant, silent mental repetition (intonation) of Soham in time with their breath, those primeval yogis united their outer and inner consciousness and will. In this way they brought their physical, astral and causal bodies back into alignment with the evolutionary vibrations of Soham, for Soham is the keynote of the evolving universe. Repeating it in a constant flow turns the mind inward and produces spiritual awareness in an ever-increasing degree, in time putting us in touch with the cosmos as well as our Self and God. And that is what this book is all about, for this tradition has been handed down even until today, though often obscured and nearly lost.

The religion of yoga is the way to restore the original evolutionary pattern on the individual level, enabling the yogis to go from darkness to the light of God which will fill the horizon of their consciousness completely in the realization-experience that is the ever-increasing awareness of God as the prime reality and our individual spirit as a divine atom of that divine light, drawing on the infinite life for its finite life. Since God is our own inmost reality, through Soham japa and meditation we will become increasingly ourselves until we become fully-realized gods within God. That is the glory of yoga. The experience of separation from God is an illusion, but the experience of union with God through yoga is reality. Soham is the force that impels us ever onward and upward.

Mantra

Yoga is based on the science of spiritual sound, or mantra. A mantra is a series of sounds whose effect lies not in an assigned intellectual meaning, but in an inherent sound-power that can produce a specific effect physically or psychologically. The word mantra itself comes from the Sanskrit expression *manat trayate* which means "a transforming thought," that which produces an objective, perceptible change. When joined to the breath, Soham is the supreme mantra of Self-awareness and Self-knowledge culminating in liberation.

For a mantra to produce its effect it must be pronounced correctly. Soham is pronounced like our English words *So* and *Hum*. The short a in Sanskrit is pronounced like the u in *up* or *hunt*, so we say "hum" even though we write it as "ham."

It is most important to pronounce the *O* correctly. It should be pronounced like the long *o* in the Italian or common American manner—as in home and lone. In England, Canada, and parts of the American South, the long *o* is sometimes pronounced as a diphthong, like two vowels jammed together: either like "*ay*-oh" or "*eh*-oh." This is not the correct manner of pronouncing the *O*, which should be a single, pure vowel sound.

The same is true of the *U* in *ham* (hum). As already pointed out, it is pronounced like the u in *up* or *hunt*–not like the u in *truth* or *push*, as is done in parts of Great Britain.

A mantra is most effective if it is mentally intoned–that is, mentally "sung"–on a single note. (The pitch does not matter–whatever is spontaneous and natural.) This makes the repetition stronger and of deeper effect, because intoning unifies the mind and naturally concentrates it.

The way to receive the benefit of a mantra is japa, the continual repetition-intonation of the mantra. In this way the invoker is constantly imbued with the power and consciousness inherent in the mantra. So whenever we intone Soham in time with the breath, we align and link our consciousness with its origin: both our spirit and Divine Spirit.

God is the guru of all

Without any doubt it is greatly beneficial to have a personal teacher (acharya) who can instruct the aspirant in meditation practice and answer any questions that might arise. But the true guru of every one of us is God. "You are the worshipful Guru" (Bhagavad Gita 11:43).

"The Lord dwells in the hearts of all beings" (Bhagavad Gita 18:61). Dwelling in the hearts of all, God empowers and guides the questing souls. Gorakhnath, the greatest of all yogis, asked his teacher, Matsyendranath: "Who is the Primal Guru [Adiguru]?" And Matsyendranath answered: "The Eternal Beginningless One [Anadi] is the Primal Guru" (Gorakh Bodha 21-22). He continued: "Realization of that Guru gives us immortality" (Gorakh Bodha 24).

Since God is eternal, it is from him that all knowledge has come, especially the revelation of spiritual truth. And as we have just seen, that Guru's first utterance was "Soham" (Brihadaranyaka Upanishad 1.4.1). As Vyasa observes: "His purpose is to give grace to living beings, by teaching knowledge and dharma [righteousness]." "There is no other but God to give the teaching which is a boat by which they can cross over the sea of samsara, and he teaches knowledge and dharma to those who take sole refuge in him.... For all the kinds of knowledge arise from him, as sparks of fire from a blaze or drops of water from the sea," says Shankara. This does not mean that qualified spiritual teachers are not helpful to us, but dwelling in the hearts of all God continues to be the Guru of questing souls. All others are really only teachers (acharyas), valuable though they may be.

Yogiraj Shyama Charan Lahiri Mahashaya wrote to a student regarding the guru: "No one does anything; all is done by God. The individual [that seems to be the guru] is only an excuse; remain abidingly focused on that Divine Guru; in this is blessing."

Swami Yatiswarananda, Vice-president of the Ramakrishna Mission, wrote to one of his students: "We bring the message of the guru of gurus.... please turn to him for light and guidance, for peace and blessedness.... The Lord, the guru of gurus, alone can give us the shelter, the illumination and the bliss we need."

Sri Ramakrishna himself said: "Satchidananda [Existence-Consciousness-Bliss] alone is the Guru; he alone will teach" (1.2.8; also: 4.2.1, 5.1.2, 5.5.1). "There is no other Guru except Satchidananda. There is no other refuge but him. He alone is the ferryman who takes one across the ocean of relative existence" (1.12.8). "The more you will advance, the more you will see that it is he who has become everything and it is he who is doing everything. He alone is the Guru and he alone is the spiritual ideal [ishta devata] of your choice. He alone is giving jnana, bhakti and everything" (4.26.2). "Do you pray to Satchidananda Guru every morning? Do you?" (4.9.2).

These citations are taken from the Majumdar translation of *The Gospel of Sri Ramakrishna*. From Nikhilananda's translation: "'I am a guru...'–that [thought] is ignorance" (p. 307.). "A man cannot be a guru" (p. 616). "If somebody addresses me as guru, I say to him: 'Go away, you fool! How can I be a teacher?'" (p. 633). He was also fond of

21

a devotional song addressed to God, which said: "Thou art my ever-gracious Guru" (p. 207).

God is the guru of humanity because he has implanted in us the Soham mantra. In the depths of our being, God is perpetually stimulating–actually teaching–Soham as the agent of the spirit's evolution and perfection. In this way God is the guru of each one of us. The aspiring yogi can then feel safe and assured, for God will be his guru, just as he has been for all the enlightened throughout the ages. "He is guru even of the ancients," affirmed Patanjali (Yoga Sutras 1:26). In the sixth edition of Paramhansa Yogananda's *Whispers From Eternity*, on page 263 there is this declaration-vow to God: "Thou art my Guru-Preceptor; I am Thy disciple."

Divine discipleship

The first American disciple of Paramhansa Yogananda was Dr. M. W. Lewis, who perfectly assimilated the wisdom imparted to him by Yogananda. In a talk given in San Diego, California, in 1955, he said these inspiring words:

"To me the real meaning and understanding of discipleship is that a disciple, a true disciple, is 'one who follows God.' Many times the Master said that. In spite of his realization and his oneness with God, which he had and does have now, he said when leaving Boston, 'Never mind what happens to me. That Light which you see is far greater than I am. That is God himself.' And so, there is only one Guru, and that is God, and the greater the saint, if we can classify them that way, the surer they are to say, 'I am nothing, God is all.' And so, the Master said that. God alone is reality. He is with you. He is the One Great Guru. And the Master was most humble, because the more you realize there is One Reality, God himself, the more humble you become, because the ego cannot stay. If you have realization of God, the ego has left.

"And so, realize: who may become a disciple? Anyone; anyone who knows the Presence of God, and follows God. Master often said that someone said to him in India, 'I hear so-and-so is your disciple in

America.' He said, 'They say so.' And seeing the confusion on the face of the inquirer, he said, 'I haven't any disciple. They're all disciples of God.' How wonderful that is. And so, just realize, he who knows God may be called a disciple. Now that means you must have contact with God. There must be a relationship between you and God, an understanding, a realization that God is in you, you are in God, there is one consciousness—God alone. Now if you have that, you may be called a disciple."

(Dr. Lewis himself was the disciple spoken of in India.)

You are also the guru

All spiritual life is self-initiated from within; we are both guru and disciple as Krishna and Arjuna symbolize in the Bhagavad Gita. Ultimately the yogi must be guided by the Divine from within his own consciousness. The God-illumined mind becomes our guru. "The mind is itself guru and disciple: it smiles on itself, and is the cause of its own well-being or ruin," wrote the great poet-saint Tukaram (*Tukaram's Teachings*, by S. R. Sharma, p. 19). He also wrote: "The guru-disciple relationship is a sign of immaturity" (*ibid.*, p. 20) "The mind will eventually turn into your guru," said Sri Sarada Devi, the consort of Sri Ramakrishna (*The Gospel of the Holy Mother*, p. 340). Swami Brahmananda, a major disciple of Sri Ramakrishna, said: "Know this! There is no greater guru than your own mind. When the mind has been purified by prayer and contemplation it will direct you from within. Even in your daily duties, this inner guru will guide you and will continue to help you until the goal is reached" (*The Eternal Companion*, p. 120).

Yogiraj Shyama Charan Lahiri Mahashaya wrote to a student regarding the guru: "Guru is the one who is all; guru is the one who is merciful. You are the guru within yourself" (*Garland of Letters (Patravali)*, Letter 45). In *Purana Purusha* by Dr. Ashoke Kumar Chatterjee it is recorded on page 224 that Yogiraj made these two statements: "I am not a guru. I do not hold the distinction of 'guru' and 'disciple.'" "The Self is the guru... the immortal, imperishable guru."

23

The great fourteenth-century yogini, Lalla Yogeshwari, sang about finding her inner guru, her Self:

> With passionate longing did I, Lalla, go forth.
> Seeking and searching did I pass the day and night.
> Then, lo, saw I in mine own house a learned man [pandit],
> And that was my lucky star and my lucky moment
> when I laid hold of him. (*Lalla Vakyani* 3)

This is the authentic viewpoint of the yogi. Devanath, a renowned yogi-saint of Western India, wrote in one of his hymns: "I alone know that I myself am the guru and also the disciple."

One of the greatest yogis of the nineteenth and twentieth centuries was Paramhansa Nityananda of Ganeshpuri. He stated that attaching oneself to a human guru was the trait of a second class aspirant, and desiring initiation was the trait of a third class aspirant. (See the *Chidakasha Gita*, section 89).

Sri Gajanana Maharaj, whose life and teachings inspired this book, said the following:

"If you really enter inside, your real guru who is inside will automatically lead you to the right path. Otherwise you will not be able to understand clearly who is leading you on."

"With firm faith, having turned back the course of thoughts from the outward world to inside himself, a sadhaka has to carry on the japa and meditation for a long time. As he progresses, he gradually reaches perfection and realizes that his own Self has been his sadguru. This state is known as oneness of jiva (the individual Self) and Shiva (the Supreme Self). It is also called sakshatkara. A sadhaka then naturally enjoys the bliss of the Self and becomes devoid of desire for anything else."

"Consider atmic experience as your real sadguru. Then there will be no necessity of relying upon the words of others, however great they be.

I would never tell you to place your blind faith in anyone, as I consider that to do so leads to self-ruin."

"Practice is the most important means of controlling the mind. Thus we become our own guru. 'The guru should turn away our mind from the various vices to which we are addicted. Everything is in the hands of a guru. If he means it, he alone will be able to develop good tendencies in my mind.' Such thoughts are weak and misleading and would be of no use to anyone. The Gita says, 'We alone are our friend and we alone are our enemy.'"

"A sadhaka reaches the stage when his own Atman (Self) becomes his guru."

"I alone know that I myself am the Guru and also the disciple." (Quoting the saint Devanath.)

Another teacher

According to Vyasa there is another teacher: our yoga practice itself. He says: "It is yoga that is the teacher. How so? It has been said: 'Yoga is to be known by yoga. Yoga goes forward from yoga alone. He who is not careless [neglectful] in his yoga for a long time, rejoices in the yoga.'"

The experience gained from yoga practice itself teaches us the reality and value of yoga. But even more, it opens our intuition and enables us to comprehend the inner workings of the subtle levels of our being and the way to its mastery. Yoga truly becomes our teacher, revealing to us that which is far beyond the wisdom of books and verbal instructions. Moreover, it is practice of yoga that enables us to understand the basis and rationale of its methods and their application. The why and wherefore of yoga become known to us by direct insight.

In his commentary on Yoga Sutra 2:28 Vyasa says: "From practicing yoga, illusion [ignorance] is destroyed and perishes. When it is destroyed, there is manifestation of right vision. In proportion to the practice done, illusion is dispelled. In proportion to its destruction, the light of [spiritual] knowledge increases correspondingly. This increase is an experience of increasing refinement [subtlety] up to the realization of the true nature of the purusha [spirit]." The Yoga Vashishtha says it clearly and truly: "God consciousness is not achieved by means of the scriptures, nor is it achieved by the grace of a teacher. God consciousness is only achieved by your own subtle awareness."

When Gorakhnath asked: "Who is the guru that leads to the goal?" Matsyendranath told him: "Nirvana itself is the guru that leads to the goal." That is, the liberated condition of the Self, though presently buried beneath the debris of lifetimes of ignorance, is itself the inspirer and guide to the revelation of our eternal liberation.

Nevertheless, it is virtually impossible to find the Goal without at least basic advice and guidance from someone with experience. Self-awakened yogis such as Sri Ramana Maharshi are those who attained realization in a previous birth.

Initiation?

It is commonly believed that an aspiring yogi must be empowered for yoga practice through some kind of initiation or transference of power. There are many exaggerated statements made about how it is impossible to make any progress, much less attain enlightenment, without initiation. But the truth is that Brahman has already initiated us into Soham and is always maintaining the presence, the flow, of that mantra within us. Soham Yoga is based squarely on the eternal nature and unity of the jivatman and the Paramatman, and is the demonstration of the eternal, single nature of God and man.

CHAPTER TWO:

THE PRACTICE OF SOHAM YOGA MEDITATION

The Bhagavad Gita tells us more than once that our divine Self and God, the Self of our Self, lives forever in our hearts (10:20; 13:17; 15:15; 18:61). Yet if we do not possess direct experience of our Self and God, simply believing that does us no good at all. We all, and always, have the Divine within us, but we must experience that for it to mean anything. Yoga is the key to that blessed experience.

The supreme master of yoga, Gorakhnath, said: "He who aspires to any attainment without the practice of yoga meditation cannot succeed in hundreds of years" (Gorakh Rahasyam 4).

Meditation is the process of centering our awareness in the principle of pure consciousness within which is our essential being. As the Gita says: "He whose happiness is within, whose delight is within, whose illumination is within: that yogi, identical in being with Brahman, attains Brahmanirvana" (Bhagavad Gita 5:24).

Normally we lose awareness of our true Self through consciousness of external objects. Since we are habituated–if not actually addicted–to objective consciousness, we can use that very condition to our advantage. Rather than disperse our consciousness through objects that draw us outward, away from the source of our being, we can take an object that will have the opposite effect, present it to the mind, and reverse our consciousness.

Such an object must have three qualities: (1) it must be something whose nature it is to turn our awareness inward and draw it into the most subtle depths of our being, (2) it must be something that can continue to be perceived even in those most subtle areas of our awareness, (3) it must already be present in our inmost being awaiting our discovery of it. Therefore it must be an object that can both impel and draw us, accompanying our questing consciousness inward, not being transcended when the mind and senses are gone beyond, but revealing itself as the Self.

That object is the mantra Soham. By sitting with closed eyes and letting the mind become easefully absorbed in experiencing the inner mental repetitions of Soham in time with the breath, we thereby directly enter into the *state of consciousness* that is Soham, the state of consciousness that is both Brahman the Absolute and our Self. What takes time is becoming permanently and absolutely established in that consciousness.

Sound and consciousness are, practically speaking, the same. Since the individual spirit (jivatman) and God (Paramatman) are essentially one, we can conclude that Soham, repeated within the mind in japa and meditation, will produce the consciousness of both Atman-Selfs and restore their lost unity.

Meditation is the process of restoring our consciousness to the center—our eternal spirit-Self—and keeping it there so our evolution will proceed exactly according to the divine plan without any more delays or deviations. Here are some statements of the upanishads regarding meditation: "The Self, though hidden in all beings, does not shine forth but can be seen by those subtle seers, through their sharp and subtle intelligence" (Katha Upanishad 1:3:12). "When one's [intellectual] nature is purified by the light of knowledge then alone he, by meditation, sees Him" (Mundaka Upanishad 3.1.8).

Knowing this, Lalla Yogeshwari also used to sing: "An ascetic [yati] wanders from holy place to holy place to seek the union brought about by visiting himself" (*Lalla Vakyani* 36).

Paramatman and jivatman

So yoga is a very real union of the absolute with the relativ divine alchemy that erases all difference between jivatman and Param man while ineffably retaining and revealing their distinction from one another. Therefore our yogic practice must be an invocation of both the absolute and the relative. This is accomplished through Soham: we are moving toward that union every time we intone Soham with the breath.

Kashmiris are known for their excellent food, as I well know from my days of starving in the Himalayan foothills while looking forward to the time when I would stay with my Kashmiri friends in Delhi and enjoy good food. Consequently Lalla Yogeshwari used the simile of cooking onions and garlic when speaking of the power of Soham to unite the jivatman with the Paramatman. Considering the Paramatman as "onion" and the jivatman as "garlic" she said:

> I came to know that onion and garlic are the same.
> If a man fry onion he will have no tasty dish.
> If a man fry garlic, let him not eat a scrap thereof.
> Therefore found I the flavor of Soham.
> (*Lalla Vakyani* 90)

The Paramatman and the jivatman are eternally united, but if we meditate on Brahman alone we will not attain realization, "will have no tasty dish." On the other hand, if we meditate on our individual Self alone, ego may intrude as a false self, so we should "not eat a scrap thereof." Instead we must link them together in the ideal "flavor" attained through the sadhana of Soham in which the two are experienced and known as one.

The Practice of Soham Yoga Meditation

1. Sit upright, comfortable and relaxed, with your hands on your knees or thighs or resting, one on the other, in your lap.

ghtly downward and close them gently. This
ractions and reduces your brain-wave activity
ive percent, thus helping to calm the mind.
your eyes may move upward and downward
own accord. This is as it should be when it
usly. But start out with them turned slightly
downward without any strain.

3. Be aware of your breath naturally (automatically) flowing in and
out. Your mouth should be closed so that all breathing is done
through the nose. This also aids in quieting the mind. Though
your mouth is closed, the jaw muscles should be relaxed so the
upper and lower teeth are not clenched or touching one another,
but parted. Breathe naturally, spontaneously. Your breathing
should always be easeful and natural, not deliberate or artificial.

4. Then in a very quiet and gentle manner begin *mentally* intoning
Soham in time with your breathing. (Remember: Soham is pronounced like our English words *So* and *Hum*.)

Intone *Soooooo*, prolonging a single intonation throughout each
inhalation, and *Huuummm*, prolonging a single intonation throughout each exhalation, "singing" the syllables on a single note.

There is no need to pull or push the mind. Let your relaxed
attention sink into and get absorbed in the mental sound of your
inner intonings of Soham.

Fit the intonations to the breath—not the breath to the intonations. If the breath is short, then the intonation should be short. If
the breath is long, then the intonation should be long. It does not
matter if the inhalations and exhalations are not of equal length.
Whatever is natural and spontaneous is what is right.

Your intonation of *Soooooo* should begin when your inhalation begins, and *Huuummm* should begin when your exhalation
begins. In this way your intonations should be virtually continuous, that is:

SooooooHuuummmSooooooHuuummmSooooooHuuummmSooooooHuuummm.

Do not torture yourself about this—basically continuous is good enough.

5. For the rest of your meditation time keep on intoning Soham in time with your breath, calmly listening to the mental sound.

6. In Soham meditation we do not deliberately concentrate on any particular point of the body such as the third eye, as we want the subtle energies of Soham to be free to manifest themselves as is best at the moment. However, as you meditate you may become aware of one or more areas of your brain or body at different times. This is all right when such sensations come and go spontaneously, but keep centered on your intonations of Soham in time with your breath.

7. In time your inner mental intonations of Soham may change to a more mellow or softer form, even to an inner whispering that is almost silent, but the syllables are always fully present and effective. Your intonations may even become silent, like a soundless mouthing of Soham or just the thought or movement of Soham, yet you will still be intoning Soham in your intention. And of this be sure: *Soham never ceases*. Never. You may find that your intonations of Soham move back and forth from more objective to more subtle and back to more objective. Just intone in the manner that is natural at the moment.

8. In the same way you will find that your breath will also become more subtle and refined, and slow down. Sometimes the breath may not be perceived as movement of the lungs, but just as the subtle pranic energy movement which causes the physical breath. Your breath can even become so light that it seems as though you are not breathing at all, just *thinking* the breath (or almost so).

9. Thoughts, impressions, memories, inner sensations, and suchlike may also arise during meditation. Be calmly aware of all these

things in a detached and objective manner, but keep your attention centered in your intonations of Soham in time with your breath. Do not let your attention become centered on or caught up in any inner or outer phenomena. Be calmly aware of all these things in a detached and objective manner. They are part of the transforming work of Soham, and are perfectly all right, but keep your attention centered in your intonations of Soham in time with your breath. Even though something feels very right or good when it occurs, it should not be forced or hung on to. The sum and substance of it all is this: It is not the experience we are after, but the effect. Also, since we are all different, no one can say exactly what a person's experiences in meditation are going to be like.

10. Soham japa and meditation can make us aware of the subtle levels of our being, many of which are out of phase with one another and are either confused or reversed in their polarity. The japa and meditation correct these things, but sometimes, especially at the beginning of meditation, we can experience these aberrations as uncomfortable or uneasy sensations, a feeling or heaviness or stasis or other peculiar sensations that are generally uncomfortable and somehow feel "not right." When this occurs, do not try to interfere with it or "make it better." Rather, just relax, keep on with the japa/meditation, calmly aware and let it be as it is. In time the problem in the subtle energy levels will be corrected and the feeling will become easy and pleasant. Simple as the practice is, it has deep and far-reaching effects, as you will see for yourself.

11. If you find yourself getting restless, distracted, fuzzy, anxious or tense in any degree, just take a deep breath and let it out fully, feeling that you are releasing and breathing out all tensions, and continue as before.

12. Remember: Soham Yoga meditation basically consists of four things: a) sitting with the eyes closed; b) being aware of our breath

as it moves in and out; c) mentally intoning Soham in time with the breath; and d) listening to those mental intonations: all in a relaxed and easeful manner, without strain.

Breath and sound are the two major spiritual powers possessed by us, so they are combined for Soham Yoga practice. It is very natural to intone Soham in time with the breathing. It is simple and easy.

13. At the end of your meditation time, keep on intoning Soham in time with your breath as you go about your various activities, listening to the inner mantric sound, just as in meditation. One of the cardinal virtues of Soham sadhana is its capacity to be practiced throughout the day. The *Yoga Rasyanam* in verse 303 says: "Before and after the regular [meditation] practice, the repetition of Soham should be continuously done [in time with the breath] while walking, sitting or even sleeping.... This leads to ultimate success."

Can it be that simple and easy? Yes, because it goes directly to the root of our bondage which is a single—and therefore simple—thing: loss of awareness. Soham is the seed (bija) mantra of nirvanic consciousness. You take a seed, put it in the soil, water it and the sun does the rest. You plant the seed of Soham in your inner consciousness through japa and meditation and both your Self and the Supreme Self do the rest. By intentionally intoning *So* and *Ham* with the breath we are linking the conscious with the superconscious mind, bringing the superconscious onto the conscious level and merging them until they become one. This is what the Bhagavad Gita (6:29) means by the term yoga-yukta—joined to yoga. It is divinely simple!

To sum it all up: Soham Yoga sadhana is the difference between divinity and humanity, between liberation and bondage. Compared to other yoga practices, it is the avatar and they are all only men. Other yoga methods are part of the ocean of samsara, and the yogi's feet often trail in the water as he attempts to fly across. But this practice takes the yogi far above the ocean, flying upward to the Infinite with no obstacles whatever in between.

Soham Yoga Sadhana in three sentences

The two supreme yogis of India's history, Matsyendranath and Gorakhnath, and the Yoga Chudamani Upanishad have each made three identical statements that are most important for the yogi, for they present the essence of Soham Sadhana.

1. The inhalation comes in with the subtle sound of *So*, and the exhalation goes out with the subtle sound of *Ham*.
2. There is no knowledge equal to this, nor has there ever been in the past or shall be in the future any knowledge equal to this.
3. There is no japa equal to this, nor has there ever been in the past or shall be in the future any japa equal to this.

The implication is that the unequaled, and therefore supreme, knowledge and the unequaled and supreme yoga practice are the mental intonations of *So* throughout the inhalation and *Ham* throughout the exhalation. And therefore that intoning *So* and *Ham* in time with the breath is the totality of Soham Yoga practice.

And it is *japa*: the deliberate intoning of Soham in time with the breath—not a passive listening to a sound supposed to be the ajapa japa breath sounds. (Those sounds may be heard, but only peripherally, while Soham is still being deliberately and continuously intoned inwardly in time with the breath.)

What makes the japa of Soham in time with the breath the unequaled japa? All other mantras by themselves produce a particular, intended effect. And this is of great value. But the Soham mantra does not just contain the seed-consciousness of "I Am That," the Soham Bhava. Its ajapa repetition has been going on within the yogi from eternity, before he entered into relative existence—and was then propelled along the evolutionary path by the inner power of Soham. Therefore, when repeated in time with the breath it directly joins the yogi's consciousness with his original condition, his transcendental nature. It does not just make a change in his consciousness, it moves his consciousness into its original state. Right from the start the process of Self-realization begins and moves steadily toward complete revelation of Atmabhava–Atmajnana which is the same as Brahmajnana: liberation.

Such gimmicks as thinking the breath is going up the spine with the intonation of *So* and down the spine with the intonation of *Ham*, or intoning Soham at the chakras, are not Soham Sadhana. Consequently, the Soham yogi's attention should be only on the movement of his breath and his mental intonations of *So* and *Ham* in time with it.

These three statements of Matsyendranath, Gorakhnath and the Yoga Chudamani Upanishad also imply that the difference between Soham Yoga and other yogas is the difference between lightning and a lightning bug.

How is this? Because, as we have seen in the previous chapter, according to the Isha and Brihadaranyaka Upanishads both the individual Self and the Supreme Self say: "I am Soham" (Soham asmi). That is, "Soham" is the fundamental nature of both the Supreme Self (Ishwara) and the Individual Self (Jiva) of each one of us. The intonations of Soham in time with the breath are direct invocations of both. Therefore Soham Sadhana takes us directly and immediately into the consciousness of the Self and the Supreme Self, simultaneously. Other yoga practices do not do this, but go about it in a roundabout manner, taking many years (if not decades or lifetimes) before even beginning to do what Soham Sadhana starts doing from the very first.

In Soham Yoga only the sufficient time to experience the full range of Self-experience and become permanently established in that experience is necessary for the Soham yogi to become liberated. As soon as he truly knows: "I am Soham," the Great Work is complete. For Ishwarapranidhana not only means offering the life to God, it also literally means offering the breath (prana) to God. This is done by intoning *So* during inhalation and *Ham* during exhalation, both in meditation and the rest of the day and night. In this way Soham Bhava, God-consciousness, is attained.

Soham: both a Mantra and the Eternal Name of God and Man

A mantra is any sound formula that by its own inherent vibration creates a change, either inner or outer. Soham is therefore a mantra–the supreme mantra. But the secret of its supremacy is the fact that it is also the Divine Name of both God, the Paramatman, and the individual Self, the Jivataman. This is indicated by the two oldest Upanishads–the Brihadaranyaka Upanishad the the Isha Upanishad.

The Brihadaranyaka Upanishad says: "In the beginning this [cosmos] was only the Supreme Self [Paramatman], in the shape of the Purusha. Looking around he saw nothing else than the Self. He first said, 'I AM SOHAM' [*Soham asmi*]" (1:4:1). Thus we see that Soham is the original, primal Name of Brahman the Absolute, the Supreme Self.

And since the Self (Atman) of each sentient being is one with the Absolute, it is also the Name of each one of us: we, too, are Soham. In the sixteenth verse of the Isha Upanishad at the time of death the departing Self of each human being says: "I am that Purusha [Spirit-Self]: I AM SOHAM" [*Soham asmi*].

The great yoga master, Sri Gajanana Maharaj of Nashik, said: "[Aspirants] should try to obtain ever-lasting peace by the mantra of Soham.... This simple method of Nama Smarana [Remembrance of the Divine Name] surely and certainly leads to the same goal."

What can you expect?

Yoga and its practice is a science and the yogi is the laboratory in which that science is applied and tested. At first the aspirant takes the word of a book, a teacher or other aspirants that a yoga method is worthwhile, but eventually it is his personal experience alone that should determine his evaluation of any yoga practice. Because each person is unique in his makeup there can be a tremendous difference in each one's experience of yoga. Nevertheless, there are certain principles which can be stated.

If a yogi is especially sensitive or has practiced the method in a previous life, he may get obviously beneficial results right away. Yet for many people it takes a while for a practice to take hold and produce a steadily perceptible effect. One yogi I knew experienced satisfactory effects immediately. Then to his puzzlement for some days it seemed that absolutely nothing was happening, that his meditation was a blank. But he had the deep conviction (no doubt from a past life as a yogi) that Soham sadhana was the right and true way for him. So he kept on meditating for hours at a time. Then one morning during the final hour of meditation results began coming in the form of experiences that he had never had before. All doubt was dispelled, and he knew he was on the right track. From then onward everything was satisfactory, though there were alternating periods of active experiences and simple quiet observation of inner rest.

Experiences, as I say, can be different for everyone, but certainly peace and refinement of consciousness can be expected. Many things will occur that simply cannot be described because ordinary human language has no words for them. The real test is the yogi's state of mind outside meditation. This he should watch carefully. And he must make sure that he is always practicing correctly. Fortunately, Soham sadhana is simple and easy to do.

Effects of practice

Although the practical focus of our attention in meditation is on our intoning of Soham in time with the breath, we of course will be aware of some of the effects the practice produces. For the goal of meditation is perfect awareness of the spirit within Spirit, and our meditation experiences are steps in the ladder taking us onward/upward to the supreme Goal. We experience subtler and higher levels of awareness until we reach the Subtlest and Highest.

We are not obsessed with meditational phenomena, but we are keenly aware of them. We need not analyze them, only observe them in a calm and relaxed manner, understanding that they come and go and are not to be held on to, but perceived like the signs we pass by as we travel on a highway. Actually, we are indifferent to them as phenomena, but intent on them as messages from the spirit and evidences of the transforming power of Soham. We should let awareness of them arise and subside spontaneously during the japa and meditation of Soham. Otherwise we confine and limit its effects within us. The two sound-syllables of Soham joined to the breath produce the evolutionary current of expanding consciousness, affecting all the bodies of the sadhaka. This takes time and requires daily meditation of sufficient length, but that is the purpose of life.

After some time, the sushumna and thousands of nadis (subtle channels) in the body are activated and the subtle energies flow upward through them into the head, the Sahasrara chakra. This leads in time to the yogic state known as urdhvareta, in which the pranas always predominantly flow upward.

The various processes of purifying, refining, straightening out and establishing the correct polarity throughout the yogi's bodies are called "kriyas." The kriyas produced by Soham Yoga awaken hitherto dormant faculties and levels of the yogi. This itself is evolution, enabling the yogi to reach and hold on to increasingly higher levels of consciousness and being. And all this is accomplished by the simple intonation of *So* during natural inhalation and *Ham* during natural exhalation. How can this be? By the inherent power of sound brought into the deepest levels of the mind through the japa and meditation of Soham.

The kriyas produced by Soham can be amazing experiences in themselves, eventually resulting in the wonderful serenity of *sthirattwa*, the steady tranquillity born of meditation, and profound feelings that arise from, and are, the Self: peace, blessed and calm contentment and happiness, the "mellow joy" that Yogananda wrote about in one of his chants.

Warning: Do Not Interfere!

We are used to directing and controlling as much of our life as possible. But what applies to the external life as wisdom is not necessarily so in the internal life of meditation. The very simple twelve points given previously in this section when followed exactly in a relaxed and calm manner will produce the inner environment in which Soham can do its divine work of revealing itself as the consciousness that is the yogi's true Self. If there is any interference in the form of trying to change something or direct the meditation or experience in any way, the process is interrupted and will produce little or no results.

Naturally, since the practice is so incredibly simple and we have read all kinds of propaganda about "powerful" yogas and the chills and thrills they produce and the "profound insights" and even visions of higher worlds, etc. and etc. that supposedly result from them, we wonder if there surely is not "more than this to it" and consider trying out such previously-mentioned gimmicks as intoning Soham at the chakras, integrating it with some artificial form of pranayama, concentrating on the spine while visualizing/imagining currents moving up and down the spine, and other "enhancements" that may entertain but will only be obstacles to success in Soham sadhana.

The truth is that Soham intoned in time with the breath immediately begins producing a tremendous number of yogic kriyas, but kriyas that are so subtle and natural that they are sometimes not perceived. It takes real refinement of the mental energies to experience much of what Soham effects in the entire being of the yogi. I have been astonished at how profound the effects of Soham sadhana are, and some of my experiences have been really incredible, but I have had decades of yogic practice behind me to enable me to experience and understand the workings of Soham. I am not describing any of these experiences lest when you encounter them yourself you wonder if your experience is only autosuggestion based on my description.

Breath (natural breathing) and sound (mantra) are the sole components of authentic yoga. But when confronted with propagandists who expound their complex yoga methods, many initiations, outline their exalted "enlightenment" experiences and list their wonderful attainments, we can feel very much like the following.

Be wise and just breathe and intone Soham in time with the breath with eyes closed during meditation and open during the rest of the day's activity. Nothing else, but just being aware of that process and listening to the inner intonations of Soham, is the secret and the assurance of success. And that is all. Soham must not be interfered with–it really cannot be, so any attempt will interrupt and spoil the practice and drag you back on the path of samsara, however "yogic" it may seem to you.

Simplicity of practice

The simpler and more easeful the yoga practice, the more deeply effective it is. This is a universal principle in the realm of inner development and experience. How is this? In the inner world of meditation things are often just the opposite to the way they are in the outer world. Whereas in the outer world a strong aggressive force is most effective in producing a change, in the inner world it is subtle, almost minimal force or movement that is most effectual–even supremely powerful. Those familiar with homeopathic medicine will understand the concept that the more subtle an element is, the more potentially effective it is. In meditation and japa the lightest touch is usually the most effective. This being so, the simple subtle intonations of Soham are the strongest and most effective form of mantric invocation.

An incident that took place during one of the crusades illustrates this. At a meeting between the leaders of the European forces and Saladin, commander of the Arab armies, one of the Europeans tried to impress and intimidate Saladin by having one of his soldiers cleave a heavy wooden chair in half with a single downstroke of his broadsword. In response, Saladin ordered someone to toss a silk scarf as light and delicate as a spider's web into the air. As it descended, he simply held his scimitar beneath it with the sharp edge upward. When the scarf touched the edge, it sheared in half and fell on either side of the blade without even a whisper as he held it completely still. Such is the power of the subtle and simple practice of Soham Yoga meditation.

Subtlety of practice

Soham sadhana is extraordinarily powerful, yet until we become attuned to it by some time of practice it may seem very mild, just a kind of yogic sitting-up exercise. But it is a mighty tool of yoga alchemy. The secret of its power and effectiveness is its subtlety–the very thing that may cause it to be disregarded and not recognized for its intense value–for it is the subtle energies that are able to work lasting changes in our awareness. The more evolved consciousness or energy become, the more refined and subtle it becomes–truly spiritual. Thus it is the highest level of spiritual powers alone that are able to effect our ascent in consciousness.

One of Yogananda's direct disciples, Brahmacharini Forest, told me that she and many others were puzzled at the great difference they experienced when blessed by Yogananda and by his most advanced male disciple, James Lynn (Rajasi Janakananda). "When Rajasi blessed us, it nearly blew the tops of our heads off," she said. "Sometimes people almost fell over backwards. But when Master blessed us we did not feel anything at all." This was often discussed by the various disciples, but they could not arrive at any conclusion. Forest went to Sister Meera, one of the senior monastics, and asked her about the matter. "Sister Meera explained to me that Rajasi had a great deal of power, but did not know how to direct it. So he just threw it at us and literally bowled us over. Master, on the other hand, had perfect control, and when he blessed us he directed the currents deep into our physical and astral brains, cleansing us from our negative subconscious habit patterns. We did not feel anything, because the currents moved into the astral channels without any resistance, and we were benefited by it."

This was my experience in relation to two of Yogananda's advanced disciples. When one touched me on the forehead I would feel tremendous spiritual force entering the "third eye" and flowing through the brain and spine. It was not violent, but it was very dramatic. In contrast, when one of Yogananda's seniormost disciples touched me in blessing I would feel nothing whatsoever. But in a few minutes, as I sat quietly, I would experience an indescribable elevation of consciousness and a deep inner awakening. It was when I referred to this in a conversation with Brahmacharini Forest that she told me her experience and Sister Meera's clarification.

The situation is very much like running a strong current of water through a hose and through an open window. If the hose is pinched there will be a buildup and eventual explosion–impressive but not beneficial. If the window is closed or the hose aimed at the nearby wall, then the water will spray back into our face–also impressive, but not the intended result. On the other hand, if the hose is straight, the window opened, and the aim correct, the water will pass through the window with no resistance at all.

Tension of any kind interferes with these subtle energies. It is important, then, to keep in mind that often when things seem stuck in meditation and not moving as they should, or when the mind does not calm down, it is often because we are not relaxed sufficiently and are not allowing our inner intonations of Soham to become as subtle as they should be. For the subtler the intonations, the more effective and on target they are.

Even so, I do not mean to give you the impression that your inner intonations of Soham should become feeble or weak in the sense of becoming tenuous—only barely within your mental grasp and liable to slip away and leave you blank. Not at all. The inner sound of the intonations may become subtler and subtler, but they do not at all become weaker—only gentler and more profound and therefore more effective.

Repetition of a mantra is fully effective only when it is extremely subtle and an act of the Self within the buddhi or intelligence.

Not placing the awareness on points in the body

Brahman and the Self being formless, so also is our meditation. And since Brahman is everywhere and the Self pervades the body, we do not deliberately put our mind on any particular place or point in or outside the body. Rather, we fix our attention on Soham which is both our individual spirit (jivatman) and the Supreme Spirit (Paramatman). Soham is also at the core of every cell, of every particle of every atom in our body, so every intonation of Soham vibrates throughout the entire body, as well as the astral and causal bodies.

Sometimes during meditation you may spontaneously become more aware of some point or area of the body, and that is all right, but keep the focus of your attention on the breath and your intonations of Soham, letting whatever happens, happen, letting the subtle energy (shakti) of Soham move where it will and energize and awaken whatever needs energizing and awakening at that moment. Since everything is formed of prana, the essence of breath, intoning Soham in time with the breath effects every part and aspect of our being, physical, astral, and causal.

There is an exception to this. On occasion, such as at the very beginning of meditation or when during the rest of the day you find your attention drifting from the breath and Soham, it can be helpful to make yourself very gently (lest you give yourself a headache from tension) aware of your entire brain (Sahasrara) area, feeling that the breath and Soham intonations are taking place there.

A short time of this awareness (which can arise spontaneously as well) is sufficient—even for just a few breaths—because correct practice will result in Sahasrara awareness naturally.

It is also important to not let the mind wander outside the body. Gorakhnath asked Matsyendranath: "How can a yogi have meditation that goes beyond the physical?" The answer: "He should meditate within his body to rise above the body" (Gorakh Bodha 99-100). Later Matsyendranath told him: "To destroy deception or duality one should reside within" (114). This is why in Soham meditation we do not aspire to leave our body and fly away to some higher worlds, but rather to find the Highest right within ourselves, at the core of every atom of our being.

Increasing experiences and effects

Through the regular and prolonged practice of Soham Yoga there are higher experiences and effects that will open up for the meditator. As time goes on the efficiency of the practice and the resulting depth of inner experience will greatly increase, transforming the practice into something undreamed-of by the beginning meditator–for the change really takes place in the yogi's consciousness. Practice, practice, practice is the key.

We have earlier noted Shankara's statement that the practice of yoga "has right vision alone for its goal, and glories of [external] knowledge and power are not its purpose." Spirit-consciousness alone is true and real.

The path of liberation is a very simple path–the japa and meditation of Soham–and the result is simple: realization of one's own Self (Atman) and ultimately of the Supreme Self (Paramatman). First there is the establishment in the pure consciousness that is our essential being as individuals, and then establishment in the Infinite Consciousness that is the Essential Being of all beings: God.

The Katha Upanishad makes this very clear. First it speaks of what God (Brahman) really is, saying: "Not within the field of vision stands this form. No one soever sees Him with the eye. By heart, by thought, by mind apprehended, they who know Him become immortal" (Katha Upanishad 2:3:9). Brahman is pure spirit, beyond all phenomena, beyond all relative existence or relative experience (objective consciousness). Brahman is not perceived by the senses, inner or outer ("no one soever sees Him with the eye"), yet he is revealed in the core of the yogi's being in meditation. "They who know Him become immortal" because they experience their identity with the immortal Brahman. Next the upanishad describes the nature of meditation in which Brahman is realized. "When the five senses together with the mind cease [from their normal activities] and the intellect itself does not stir, that, they say, is the highest state. This, they consider to be Yoga, the steady control of the senses. Then one becomes undistracted" (Katha Upanishad 2:3:10-11).

Here are the characteristics of meditation which the upanishad calls the highest state: 1) the senses are stilled, 2) the mind is at rest, 3) the intellect wavers not. Then the idea is really driven home by the upanishad: "This, they consider to be Yoga, the steady control of the senses." Shankara affirms that the seeker of spiritual freedom is seeking nothing from meditation "other than the special serenity of meditation practice." This state is also called *sthirattwa* by the yogis. He who attains it is freed from delusion. An incident from the life of Yogiraj Shyama Charan Lahiri Mahasaya give us his perspective regarding sthirattwa as the essence of meditation and realization.

A group of spiritual leaders from Calcutta once conspired against Lahiri Mahasaya. They invited him to join in an evening discussion on spiritual matters. Lahiri Mahasaya accepted the invitation and accordingly attended the meeting.

The conspirators had well prepared themselves to trap Lahiri Mahasaya. For example, if Lahiri Mahasaya were to express his preference for a particular deity, or *ishta devata*, then a particular leader would find exception to that choice. In fact, each member of the group selected a particular *devata* (deity) such as Lord Vishnu, Lord Krishna, Lord Shiva and the Goddess Kali, and prepared to debate and challenge Lahiri Mahasaya's choice.

As soon as Lahiri Mahasaya arrived, he was received in the traditional manner and shown proper courtesy.

After a while one of the members of the group asked Lahiri Mahasaya, "Upon which deity do you meditate?" Lahiri Mahasaya looked at him but did not reply.

Then another gentleman asked him, "Who is your *ishta devata?*" Lahiri Mahasaya turned his head towards him and looked at him in the same way, while keeping his peace.

Finally, a third gentleman asked him, "Can you tell us upon which deity you usually meditate?" Lahiri Mahasaya faced him and said very gently, "I meditate on *sthirattwa* (tranquility)."

The gentleman replied that he did not understand what was meant by this. Lahiri Mahasaya continued to observe silence.

After some time, another gentleman asked him, "Could you please explain this? I do not understand exactly what you are saying." Lahiri Mahasaya, as before, continued to maintain silence.

Another gentleman asked, "Can you enlighten me as to what you mean by that? I do not understand at all!"

Lahiri Baba told him, "You will not be able to understand, and also I will not be able to make you understand (realize) through words."

The group was at a loss. All of their preparation and conniving had come to naught. Only silence prevailed. All kept silent.

After a long time Lahiri Mahasaya got up and silently prepared to leave the meeting. All showed him the traditional courtesy as he left.

So when Yogiraj Lahiri Mahasaya was asked: "On which deity do you meditate?" he simply replied: "I meditate on sthirattwa"–the serenity produced by meditation in which he ever dwelt, and of which he was the embodiment.

It should be the same with us, and Soham sadhana is the way to be established in sthirattwa, which is itself the Soham Bhava.

The mantra of evolution

Mantra is the foundation of yoga sadhana, and the purpose of yoga sadhana is the purpose of the universe and existence itself: our Self-realization. The mantra used in yoga sadhana must be a mantra whose primary purpose and effect is to lead the yogi's consciousness directly to experience of the Self. There are innumerable mantras that purify and uplift the atmosphere when they are recited, but evolutionary force or shakti is not part of their effect, nor is it intended to be. Those mantras elevate, but do not evolve.

So where does that leave–or lead–us? To Soham, the mantra that is not merely an affirmation or producer of the intellectual conviction "I Am That," but the sound formula of the evolutionary power which transmutes the finite consciousness of the Soham yogi into the Infinite Consciousness which *is* That, to actualize what presently is only a potential within the yogi. This is why regarding Jesus, a Nath Yogi well conversant with Soham Yoga, his disciple John wrote regarding himself and his fellow disciples: "To them gave he power to become the sons of God" (John 1:12).

Adhyatmic yoga

The purpose of yoga sadhana is to realize the Self, both the individual and cosmic, the jivatman and the Paramatman. Therefore it must be exclusively adhyatmic in nature. *A Brief Sanskrit Glossary* defines adhyatmic: "Pertaining to the Self (Atman), individual and Supreme (Paramatman)." A practice centered on anything other than our individual and the Supreme Atman-Self, no matter how sacred or beloved to us, cannot by its nature be adhyatmic and so cannot lead to Self-realization and liberation in the Infinite.

For example, Om is the root vibration of the projected cosmos, of samsara (relative existence) itself. Therefore it cannot lead to or reveal the atman or the Paramatman that are beyond samsara. Ishta mantras relate to the symbolic forms, such as Shiva, Vishnu or Durga, that are only aspects of God, and by their very nature are partial in their effect and are not adhyatmic in nature, having no connection with the Self.

Soham is not just a mantra or designation of God; it *is* God. When we repeat Soham in time with the breath we are invoking our eternal being. It is not a state or level of consciousness, it is Consciousness Itself. We and God are nothing else in essence. Soham Yoga is the direct means to Self-realization and God-realization. This is why we do nothing but mentally intone Soham in time with the breath and listen to our intonations.

Jesus prayed: "O Father, glorify thou me with thine own self *with the glory which I had with thee before the world was*" (John 17:5). The glory he had with God before the world (the relative creation) existed is the Soham Bhava from which the world proceeded as Jesus, being a Nath Yogi, knew.

Since Soham sadhana is absolutely adhyatmic and nothing but adhyatmic, Soham Yoga leads to the one and only goal: to realize our eternal Self within the Infinite, the Self of our Self.

The words of the Masters

As both Matsyendranath, the founder of the Nath Yogi Sampradaya, and his disciple, Gorakhnath, wrote about Soham mantra sadhana: "There has never been, nor shall there ever be vidya [yogic knowledge] such as this, and there has never been, nor shall there ever be japa [mantra repetition] such as this."

One of the most amazing things about this sadhana is its marvelous simplicity and self-sufficiency. There is just the simple joining of mental intonations of *So* and *Ham* to the naturally flowing breath, letting the attention become centered in the increasingly subtler sound of the inner intonations, letting them accomplish their work of revelation. By this easy process the yogi will discover the marvel of Soham, because it will spontaneously open his awareness and transform his inner and outer being. Then he will experience that which he could never imagine possible—that "eye hath not seen, nor ear heard, neither have entered into the heart of man, the things which God hath prepared for them that love him" (I Corinthians 2:9).

But first...

But before this happens, or at least before the yogi is established in this state, there are some things that must be experienced.

One effect of Soham sadhana is purification which may involve the tossing up from the lower, subconscious mind refuse, which can also include visual imagery. A yogi I knew used to say: "Meditation can be the real 'confession.'" And he was right. But it has also been my experience that very often such an experience indicates that things are being cleared out. And at other times it is our higher mind telling us to work on what is tossed up.

By calmly keeping on meditating the purification will be completed.

Some reflections on Soham Sadhana–Soham Yoga

Various yogic texts inform us that both Soham and the breath arise directly from our spirit-consciousness. For this reason in Soham Yoga we join intonations of Soham to the breath. Experiencing our inmost consciousness to greater and greater degrees within meditation is the the beginning of cosmic consciousness. The more we meditate the higher and further we penetrate into the Infinite Consciousness of which we are an eternal part. Those who through Soham Yoga continually attune and merge their consciousness in this way will in time become totally identified with the individual spirit-Self and with the Supreme Spirit.

In Dharana Darshan (p. 74), Swami Niranjanananda Saraswati wrote: "There are certain practices in yoga which introvert the mind and bring about an automatic suspension of breath. The difficulty here is that the aspirant becomes extroverted after a short time because the capacity of his lungs is not adequate. This difficulty is experienced by many aspirants. In the practice of ajapa japa, however, this difficulty is eliminated because of the continuous rotation of the breath. Secondly, the ajapa practice is complete in itself and through it one can have direct experience of samadhi. In order to attain samadhi in all other yogic practices one has to control the breath. Whenever the breath is suspended kumbhaka takes place. However, the breathing remains continuous throughout the practice of ajapa japa, and even in samadhi there is no change."

Soham sadhana stands in contrast to many yoga practices which attempt to bring about suspension of the breath (kumbhaka). The problem with these attempts is simple: they are virtually impossible, and when they do occur they are seen to do little if any lasting good, as Buddha discovered when he became able to suspend his breath for hours at a time. As has been pointed out previously, it is not the breath but the condition of the breath that is detrimental and problematic. However long the breath might be suspended, it must be resumed eventually–often in a very short time to the frustration of the aspirant.

In Soham sadhana the breath itself becomes the vehicle of realization, and therefore a precious commodity. In Soham meditation the breath becomes exceedingly refined and is revealed as a movement of consciousness, an evolutionary movement, essential to the yogi. Some meditation teachers claim it is necessary to suspend the breath for a long time in order to experience samadhi, but in Soham yoga it is the uniting and refining of the breath that leads to samadhi–in which the breath continues, though so subtle and refined that it often seems to have stopped.

The power of a mantra is not in its intellectual meaning, but in the effect its vibrations have on our body, mind, and deep inner consciousness. As previously pointed out, Soham is not an intellectual affirmation of our oneness with Brahman, but is an effecting, a revealing, of that oneness. Every time we join Soham to our breath we are moving our awareness closer to that revelation, linking our little Self with the Supreme Self.

Earlier in Chapter One I wrote about the ancient yogi-sages: "They further discovered that the root impulse of inhalation makes the subtle sound of *So*, and the root impulse of exhalation makes the subtle sound of *Hum* (written as *Ham* in Sanskrit)." In the highest levels of the human being the mantric sounds of *So* and *Hum* are alternately vibrating, being literally "spoken" by the Self. That is why the Isha Upanishad says the departing spirit says *Soham asmi*–"I am Soham." And the Brihadaranyaka Upanishad (1:4:1) tells us that the Self "first said, 'I am Soham' [*Soham asmi*]" when it entered into relative existence and began to evolve. Because of this, when the yogi observes his breath and mentally intones *So* and *Hum* in time with his inhalations and exhalations he links up directly with the Self and therefore unites his lesser awareness with his highest consciousness, the spirit. And this is the process of Self-realization.

Soham is perpetually present in the core of our being, perpetually vibrating throughout our various levels or bodies. Therefore the conscious, subconscious, and superconscious minds are united in the repetition of Soham in time with the breath–which itself is proceeding from Soham. Thus the three are perfectly harmonized and in time made one.

The very word Atman (Self) comes from the root *at*, which means "I breathe." Because of this Pandit Shriram Sharma, who will be cited extensively later on, wrote: "The savants of spiritual knowledge opine that in the innermost centre of the soul, its sense of self-recognition–as a fraction of Parabrahman–is eternally reflected and gives rise to the continuous cycles of the self-existing (ajapa) japa of Soham (meaning 'I am That: Brahman'). While discussing the meaning of 'Soham' one should not be confused with respect to the precision of the liaisons in this Sanskrit word (according to the Sanskrit grammar: *sah* (that) + *aham*=Soham), because Soham has not been a word derived from the Sanskrit grammar. Rather it is a Nada that is self-existing because of the eternal linkage of *'so'* (That, the Supreme Consciousness) and *'aham'* (the consciousness of the individual Self).... Soham represents the oneness of the soul and Brahman."

Meditation on God in his true nature is meditation on Formless Reality. This is done by meditating on sound and breath in order to return to the original state where we, too, are formless. Soham is a sound formula that reveals the Formless by bringing our mind into its pure state in which God can be perceived as he really is.

Experience shows us that when we try to control and still the mind it wanders and jumps about in reaction. But if we quietly watch what is happening, especially in relation to the breath and Soham, the mind in time becomes calm and begins to move inward steadily. Then everything goes or stops as it should, and awareness keeps increasing.

Sound

Sound is the basis of all that is, and the way to the realization of the All That Is, including our true Self and the Supreme Self, God.

"By sound one becomes liberated [*Anavrittih shabdai*]" (Brahma Sutras 4.4.22). Sound joined to the breath is the beginning, middle, and end of our meditation practice. Consequently, listening to and experiencing the effects of our inner intonations of Soham in time with the breath is the heart of Soham Yoga.

Inwardly listening to the mental intonations of Soham is a major key to success in meditation because listening to the mantra makes the yogi responsive to its vibrations. In that way the maximum benefit is gained. It is essential that we become centered in the etheric levels of our being, from which sound arises, and this is done by inwardly intoning Soham and listening to those intonations. During meditation, whatever happens, whatever comes or goes, relax and keep *listening* to your inner intonations of Soham. It is the sound of Soham joined to the breath that accomplishes everything. And by listening to it you become totally receptive and responsive to it so it can work its transforming purpose to the maximum degree. The Soham yogi should be totally absorbed in both the inner *intoning* and the inner *hearing* of Soham.

If things do not feel or seem to be going right, it may mean that you are not fully listening to the sound of Soham, that your attention is somewhat divided. At such times I have had everything feel and go right immediately when I relaxed and easefully recentered my awareness totally on the sound of Soham.

We must master both the energy (shakti) and the sound (shabda) aspects of a mantra. The energy aspect brings about certain experiences, from simple feelings to visual and auditory impressions. The sound aspect is mastered by making sure we pronounce the mantra exactly correctly, never "losing" it in an abstract state, and following it through all its subtle permutations and entering into the consciousness it embodies.

Shabda and Nada

Shabda and Nada are both usually translated in yogic texts as "sound" and in many philosophical texts are used interchangeably, but in yogic usage they have a very important distinction. Shabda is sound of any kind made by any means proceeding from any medium: for example, the sound made when a drum is struck or the wind blows. Shabda encompasses the entire range of natural sounds, including the inherent sound-vibration of physical objects and processes. Nada, however, is very specialized. It is exclusively sound emanated by Divine Impulse, sound that comes directly from Universal Consciousness with no intermediate stages or secondary causes. In a very real sense Nada is the voice of God. According to the yogis, Soham is Nada in this precise, technical sense. It is, therefore, the voice of the Self as well as the voice of God.

Putting the awareness on mere shabda—which includes the sounds of the chakras and other inner sounds, even though they emanate from very subtle levels—leads only to their relative source and not to Reality. Only that Nada which comes directly from the Source will lead to the Source, and it must be a dual source, both the Absolute and the relative, Brahman and the jivatman. That Nada is Soham.

Inner psychic sounds

It may be that sometimes you will hear various inner sounds such as a gong, bell, harp, flute, bee, waterfall, vina, bagpipes, and suchlike. These are often mistaken for genuinely spiritual phenomena when in reality they are only the astral sounds of the bodily functions. For example, the bee sound is the astral sound of cellular division, the flute sound is the astral sound of the lymphatic circulation, the bell sound is the astral sound of the cardio-pulmonary functions, and so forth. They are purely physical and have no true yogic value whatsoever.

The so-called "Cosmic Motor" sound heard by some yogis who plug their ears and listen for it is only the astral sound of the cosmic fire element from which the body and the material plane emerge and into which they are dissolved. That this is so is shown by the following upanishadic statement: "This *fire* which is within a man and digests food that is eaten is Vaisvanara. *Its sound is that which one hears by stopping the ears*" (Brihadaranyaka Upanishad 5.9.1). So that sound is nothing more than the astral sound of our metabolism and our food being digested. It, too, is psychic, not spiritual. Buddha described how during his intense practice of various yogas he became adept at hearing this astral sound, assuming that it was a spiritual experience, until after examining its effects he realized it was just a psychic distraction that led nowhere, and he abandoned it.

In short, all such astral sounds should be ignored. Stay with your inner, mental intonations of Soham.

Prana and Mahaprana

In the lesser levels of the individual and the cosmos, prana moves as the force of life, but in the higher levels Mahaprana moves as the unalloyed Divine Life, one aspect of which is Soham. Because of this, Soham sadhana both lifts the yogi up to and invokes the Mahaprana, enabling the yogi to truly live the Divine Life.

Soham is not the sound of the physical breath, but the sound (Nada) of the Mahaprana as it manifests as inhalation and exhalation. As just explained, there are two kinds of sound: ahata (shabda) and anahata (nada). Ahata occurs in nature, is material sound even when subtle, but anahata is Divine Sound (Divya Shabda) and is spiritual, conveying spiritual opening and insight. Such is Soham. Only the proficient yogi whose perceptions have been refined can hear these subtle sounds of Soham–Sat Nada–during his practice. For Soham sadhana opens the yogi to the inflow of Mahaprana and increases the inflow the longer it is practiced.

Pandit Shriram Sharma says: "In the Soham sadhana, as stated earlier, the Nada of the mantra Soham is 'heard' (experienced) with each breath by the 'ears' of the subtle body.... hence it is also defined as the ajapa japa of Gayatri: that which arouses and liberates the prana (in the ocean of Mahaprana). This is also called sadhana of Prana Gayatri."

Understanding the problem

Why are there so many yoga methods? It is because of differing diagnoses of the root problem of human beings. Buddha said that it was important to ask the right questions to get the right answers. In the same way we must know the real problem of humanity if we are to formulate the solution. If we accept secondary problems as the primary ones, our answers will be secondary ones and unable to clear up the fundamental problem whose solution will bring about the solution of all other troubles. For example, our problem is not restlessness of the mind, the pull of negativity, unawakened kundalini or not knowing one of the symbolic forms of God mistakenly called gods, or an avatar or master. There are many symptoms, but we have only one actual problem: we do not know and experience our individual being (jivatman) within the cosmic being (Paramatman).

All kinds of yoga gimmicks have been invented, but the only true yoga is that which immediately puts us in contact with the Self, even if only to a minimal degree at first. For that practice will keep on increasing our awareness until it is perfect. And that is the simple intonation of Soham in time with the breath. Because of the release of Self-awareness and the harmony produced by this simple practice, profound processes (kriyas) do take place in the physical and subtle bodies, but even they are only themselves symptoms of the process of Self-awakening.

The root cause of our ignorance and its attendant miseries is forgetfulness of our true Self and of God, the Self of our Self. Since the two are really one, it follows that our meditation must consist of that which is common to both the Self (Atman) and the Supreme Self (Paramatman). And that is Soham.

The words of Sri Gajanana Maharaj of Nashik regarding saints and faith in saints apply equally to yoga methods: "If you want to attain the goal of human life and therefore want to put your faith in some saint, remember that if that saint shows you the path of Self-experience, then only should you put your faith in him. If, however, you put your faith in a saint on account of the miracles performed or reported to be performed by him, you may perhaps obtain the fulfillment of some of your worldly desires but you will never thereby attain the real aim of human life." We should look at all yoga methods in this context.

The right approach

When we want to swim in the ocean, we do not dive into a particular wave, but into the ocean itself. A wave, being only a manifestation on the surface of the ocean, must be left behind if we are to sound the depths of the ocean. If we stay with the wave, we will find ourselves being thrown onto the shore and out of the ocean. It is the same with meditation on names and forms–whether of gods, avatars or liberated masters. We need to dive down where name and form cannot go or arise.

We must meditate on the Self, not on external beings or forms. As Sri Ma Sarada Devi said: "After attaining wisdom one sees that gods and deities are all maya" (*Precepts For Perfection* 672). Sri Ramana Maharshi said: "Since the Self is the reality of all the gods, the meditation on the Self which is oneself is the greatest of all meditations. All other meditations are included in this. It is for gaining this that the other meditations are prescribed. So, if this is gained, the others are not necessary. Knowing one's Self is knowing God. Without knowing one's Self that meditates, imagining that there is a deity which is different and meditating on it, is compared by the great ones to the act of measuring with one's foot one's own shadow, and to the search for a trivial conch [shell] after throwing away a priceless gem that is already in one's possession" (*Collected Works*, section 28).

Since we must realize the individual Self (jivatman) and the Supreme Self (Paramatman), we do japa of Soham which includes both. That is why Sri Gajanana Maharaj also said: "Some people say that meditating upon Nirakara [the Formless Reality] is difficult. But in my opinion it is very easy and in addition it is natural. A man easily gets into the state of samadhi by meditating upon Nirakara. The path of doing so is, however, concealed and secret. Once you get it you can be in that state although outwardly you may be talking, laughing, playing, or sleeping. This power is concealed like the river Saraswati [which flows underground and unseen]. As some people have not understood this secret path, therefore, they say that it is difficult, and that it would require the passing of various lives to obtain success in it."

In effective meditation the mantra and the Self of the yogi should be actually one–the mantra must proceed from the Self. The Shiva Sutras say: "If the mantra is kept separate from the repeater of the mantra and its goal, one cannot attain the fruit of the mantra" (Shiva Sutras 1:4). The divine Self is both the origin and the goal of Soham.

The solar path of liberation

"The sun, indeed, is life.... assuming every form, life and fire who rises [every day]. Who has all forms, the golden one, the all-knowing, the goal [of all], the sole light, the giver of heat, possessing a thousand rays, existing in a hundred forms–thus rises the sun, the life of all creation" (Prashna Upanishad 1:5, 7-8).

All plant, animal, and human life on this planet depend upon the sun. Human beings, especially, are solar creatures. It is the subtle powers of sunlight which stimulate growth and evolution. Sunlight particularly stimulates the activity of the higher centers in the brain, especially that of the pineal gland. Even in the depths of the earth sensitive people can tell when the sun rises and sets above them. The sun truly awakens us in the deepest sense. As the germinating seed struggles upward toward the sun and out into its life-giving rays, so all higher forms of life reach out for the sun, which acts as a metaphysical magnet, drawing them upward and outward toward ever-expanding consciousness.

The Amritabindu Upanishad (verse 26) refers to "the gate of liberation which is known as the open orb"–the sun. When the individual comes into manifestation on this earth he passes from the astral world into the material plane by means of the sun, which is a mass of exploding astral energies, not mere flaming gases. And when the individual has completed his course of evolution within this plane, upon the death of his body he rises upward in his subtle body and passes through the sun into the higher worlds, there to evolve even higher until he passes directly into the depths of the transcendent Brahman.

To ensure that this would take place, a verse of the Rig Veda (3.62.10), the Savitri Gayatri, was repeated at sunrise and sunset by spiritual aspirants in ancient India. However the yogis and the scriptures spoke of another Gayatri–the Ajapa Gayatri, Soham–which bestows liberation on those who invoke it constantly, in and out of meditation.

The Surya Upanishad says that Soham is the seed-mantra, the essence, of the Sun. At the beginning of the Maha Vakya Upanishad, Brahma the Creator is said to have declared: "The personal knowledge that this Sun is Brahman is got by chanting the Ajapa Gayatri: Soham." At the end of the upanishad Brahma says that those who invoke this Gayatri will have the realization: "I am that sun who is the ethereal light. I am that Shiva who is that sun of Knowledge. I am the supremely pure [vishuddha] light of the Atman. I am all the light that we know."

The Taittiriya Upanishad says: "He who is here in the person and he who is yonder in the sun–he is one. He who knows thus, on departing from this world reaches to the Self which consists of bliss" (Taittiriya Upanishad 2:8:1).

The Chandogya Upanishad says: "Even as a great extending highway runs between two villages, this one and that yonder, even so the rays of the sun go to both these worlds, this one and that yonder. They start from the yonder sun and enter into the nadis. They start from the nadis and enter into the yonder sun." (Chandogya Upanishad 8.6.2). The solar energies and the breath are also intimately connected. Our life depends on the light of the sun, so the japa and meditation of Soham in time with the breath aligns us with the solar powers and greatly increase our life force and the evolution of all the levels of our being.

The solar rays do not just flow into this world, they also draw upward through the sun and beyond. In the human body the process of exhalation and inhalation is related to solar energy, and much of the solar power on which we subsist is drawn into the body through our breathing. The solar rays do not just strike the surface of our body, but penetrate into the nadis, the channels in the astral body that correspond to the physical nerves. Just as the electrical impulses flow through the physical nerves, the subtle solar life force, or prana, flows through the subtle nadis and keeps us alive and functioning. And as we have already seen, the breath, as it flows, is always sounding Soham. The breath, then, is a vehicle for the solar energies that produce evolution, and we increase its effect through the japa and meditation of Soham.

The continual intonation of Soham, both in and outside of meditation, conditions our subtle levels so that at the time of death we will be oriented toward the solar powers and can ascend within them–especially if we continue our intonations of Soham in the astral body after the physical body has been dropped. Those intonations will guarantee our ascent into the solar world. Those who have imbued themselves with the mantric vibrations will enter through the solar gate and not be compelled to return to earthly rebirth.

Those who continually invoke and meditate upon Soham during their lifetime will remember Soham at the time of death, and by means of Soham will ascend to the sun and beyond into the real Beyond. "Whatever he [the yogi] fixes his mind on when he gives up the body at the end, to that he goes. Always he becomes that" (Bhagavad Gita 8:6).

True spiritual experience

The yogi's aspiration is to experience the Real, the Truly Existent (Sat) which we call Brahman, the Paramatman. So immediately he is confronted with the crucial question: What is true spiritual experience? This must be answered lest he wander in this and future lifetimes through delusional experiences and byways he mistakes for spiritual realities. Fortunately the masters of yoga have given us clear information as to the nature of real spiritual experience.

When Gorakhnath asked Matsyendranath: "What is the abode of knowledge [jnana]?" the Master replied: Consciousness [chetana] is the abode of knowledge" (Gorakh Bodha 21-22). Shankara defines correct meditation as "meditation established in the perception of the nature of spirit alone, pure consciousness itself." Yoga Sutra 3:55 tells us: "Liberation is attained when the mind is the same as the spirit in purity." That is, when through meditation we are permanently filled with nothing but the awareness of pure consciousness, liberation is attained. "That is the liberation of the spirit when the spirit stands alone in its true nature as pure light. So it is." This is the conclusion of Vyasa. Pure consciousness alone prevails. True spiritual experience, then, is the experience of pure, unalloyed consciousness that is the nature of spirit and Spirit, of the individual and the cosmic Self.

Non-dual consciousness

True spiritual experience is the non-dual experience of Spirit. The Brihadaranyaka Upanishad says: "For where there is duality as it were, there one smells another, there one sees another, there one hears another, there one speaks to another, there one thinks of another, there one understands another. Where, verily, everything has become the Self, then by what and whom should one smell, then by what and whom should one see, then by what and whom should one hear, then by what and to whom should one speak, then by what and on whom should one think, then by what and whom should one understand? By what should one know that by which all this is known? By what, my dear, should one know the knower?" (Brihadaranyaka Upanishad 2:4:14). The Chandogya Upanishad tells us: "Where one sees nothing else, hears nothing else, understands nothing else, that is the infinite. But where one sees something else, hears something else, understands something else, that is the small [the finite]" (Chandogya Upanishad 7.24:1).

The Atman-Self is never anything but consciousness, yet it, like God, has extended itself outward as the many levels of our present state of being. Unlike God, we have lost control over just about everything, and by becoming absorbed in experience of our external being have caused it to take on a virtually independent existence, dragging us along with it. Conversely, by keeping ourselves centered in pure awareness, the witnessing consciousness that is our real Self, we will begin the process of turning all those levels back into pure spirit.

Our intention in meditating is to center our awareness permanently in the consciousness of who we really are—in the spirit whose nature is itself pure consciousness. We center or merge our awareness in the breath and Soham because they arise directly from the Atman and will lead us into the consciousness which is the Self.

Soham Bhava—the Goal

In Chapter One we briefly looked at Soham Bhava and are now ready for a second look at it as the true spiritual experience the yogi seeks. Gorakhnath gave a great deal of attention to the subject of how the many worlds were projected by God within his own infinite Being. He did this because each one of us is a miniature universe reflecting that primeval process, and in time the reversal of that process, as a ladder of divine ascent, will lead us back to our Source.

He wrote that many stages or processes take place within the Divine Consciousness even before the beginning of creation. The final preparatory stage which Banerjea (*Philosophy of Gorakhnath*) describes as "the eternal link and meeting-ground between the transcendent and the phenomenal planes of existence, between the Transcendent Spirit and his phenomenal cosmic self-manifestation," consists of five aspects or potentials—foreshadowing the five elements, five senses, etc. of our present mode of existence. One of them is Soham Bhava—the state of being and awareness which is not just "I am" but "I am THAT." In other words, God does not just know he exists, he knows exactly Who he is. He is not just a dot of consciousness, he is the infinite expanse of Consciousness in which all the divine glories (aishwarya) are present and active. Soham is the bhava of Brahman/Ishwara and of the jivas within him. "Soham"–I Am That–is the bhava of both to a total degree.

Gorakhnath says that Soham Bhava includes total Self-comprehension (ahamta), total Self-mastery (akhanda aishwarya), unbroken awareness of the unity of the Self (swatmata), awareness of the unity of the Self with all phenomenal existence (vishwanubhava), knowledge of all within and without the Self–united in the Self (sarvajñatwa). It is the purpose of our entry into the cosmos, and our evolution into and out of it, to attain Soham Bhava on the individual level by rising into and uniting with God in his infinite, universal Soham Bhava. In this way we become gods within God, perfect reflections of–and participants in–the Divine Life. Because of this, at the moment of our entry into relativity God implanted within us–initiated us into–the mantric power of Soham, which will carry us onward to the union with the divine Soham Bhava and the perfection and divinization of our own Soham Bhava. This is why the Jnanarvana Tantra says: "Know this [Soham] to be the Paramatman."

Arthur Avalon sums it up quite well in *Shakti and Shakta*: "It is the actual experience of this declaration of 'Soham' which in its fundamental aspect is Veda: knowledge (Vid) or actual Spiritual Experience, for in the monistic sense to truly know anything is to be that thing. This Veda or experience is not to be had sitting down thinking vaguely on the Great Ether and doing nothing. Man must transform himself, that is, act in order to know. Therefore, the watchword is Kriya or action" in the form of Soham sadhana.

Soham Bhava is inherent in Soham as an aspect of divine consciousness. The attainment of Soham Bhava is liberation, for it is not an intellectual concept or a conviction or a feeling, but a total state of Consciousness-Being: Satchidananda.

Hamsa Yoga

In *A Dictionary of Hinduism: Its Mythology, Folklore, and Development 1500 B.C.–A.D. 1500*, Margaret and James Stutley write: "The Hamsa [Swan] symbolizes knowledge and the life-force or cosmic breath (prana), 'ham' being its exhalation, and 'so,' its inhalation which is regarded as the return of the individual life-force to Brahman, its cosmic source."

Kabir wrote the following song:

> Tell me, O Swan, your ancient tale.
> From what land do you come, O Swan? to what shore will you fly?
> Where would you take your rest, O Swan, and what do you seek?
> Even this morning, O Swan, awake, arise, follow me!
> There is a land where no doubt nor sorrow have rule: where the
>   terror of Death is no more.
> There the woods of spring are a-bloom, and the fragrant scent
>   "Soham" is borne on the wind:
> There the bee of the heart is deeply immersed, and desires no
>   other joy.

The swan (hamsa) is the individual soul (jivatman) flying in the Chidakasha, the Sky of Consciousness, which itself is the Supreme Soul (Paramatman). The swan wings its way through eternity, going from birth to birth until at last it rests at home in the Divine from which it originally came. When Gorakhnath asked his teacher Matsyendranath: "When form dissolves and the Formless remains, where does the hamsa dwell?" he was told: "When the form becomes Formless then the hamsa resides in the Supreme Light [Parama Jyoti]" (Gorakh Bodha 43-44).

Because the breath goes out with *ham* and comes in with *so*, the path of ajapa japa is also called Hamsa Yoga–Yoga of the Swan, for in Sanskrit hamsa means swan. But as we see from the large amount of material cited in this book, the sadhana mantra is Soham. That is why Pandit Shriram Sharma entitled his book on Soham sadhana *Hamsa*

Yoga: The Elixir of Self-Realization. There, on page eighteen, he explains: "The continuous japa of 'Rama–Rama…' sounds like 'Mara–Mara….' Similarly, if the sound of Soham is enunciated repeatedly without a pause, it generates a cycle and echoes in the reverse order as 'hamso…hamso' and thus sounds like 'hamsa–hamsa…' because of its continuity. This is why the Soham sadhana is also called hamsa yoga sadhana." Further on: "The repeated pronunciation of 'ham–sah'…'ham–sah' in a continuous manner is heard in the reverse cyclic order as 'Soham'… 'Soham'–this is what the yogis have experienced."

The two syllables So and Ham are the two wings by means of which the swan-spirit flies back to Spirit. "The Supreme Swan is Soham" (Nirvana Upanishad 2).

Why Soham and not Hamsa?

How is it that the sadhana mantra is Soham and not Hamsa? Certainly the breath goes out with the sound of *Ham* and in with the sound of *So*. It is like the tick-tock of a mechanical clock: which comes first? But for yoga practice, the mantra is Soham. This has been the consensus of yogis for centuries. It was also made very clear to me after some months of Soham Yoga practice during prolonged meditation, and will also become known to those who persevere.

The only authoritative text that is mistakenly believed to teach differently is the *Vijnana Bhairava*, a text of Kashmir Shaivism. Some quote what is supposed to be verse 155a: "Air is exhaled with the sound *Sa* and inhaled with the sound *Ham*. Then reciting of the mantra Hansa is continuous." However this verse is not found in any of the published facsimile or standard print texts of the *Vijnana Bhairava*. Rather, it is found only in a commentary by Kshemaraja on the Shiva Sutras and attributed to the *Vijnana Bhairava*. It is sometimes included in modern editions of *Vijnana Bhairava*. But even if it was really part of the *Vijnana Bhairava*, why base a yoga practice on the statement of a single book when dozens say otherwise? There is a profound rationale behind the use of Soham instead of Hamsa by the yogis. It is not a matter of which syllable comes first, but which is dominant in the awakening yogi.

Why Soham instead of So-aham?

Since it is said that the mantra means "I am That," why isn't the mantra pronounced "So-aham" instead of "Soham"? Two reliable scholars have answered that.

First, from the grammatical and philosophical standpoint Dr. Chaman Lal Raina says: "Soham is the combination of two words viz. Sah + Aham. According to the rules of the Sanskrit grammar Sah + Aham becomes Soham. It is the principle of joining consonant with vowel to form a varna/alphabet. Sandhi means the joining of two words, under the grammatical rules of the 'Sandhi' in the Sanskrit language. The joining of Sah + Aham is governed by the principle of Visarga Sandhi. What is Visarga in Sanskrit language? It is Nirvana or final liberation/ beatitude…, it is represented by two dots, written in the manner as ':' to represent Jivatman/individual soul and Paramatman/Absolute. The word Sah means that some person different from first person and second person. The first person word is Aham, which in Sanskrit means I am, I exist. When this I merges with That, the ego of 'I' identity merges with THAT, who is Ishwara of the Vedas, Brahman of the Upanishads, Bhagavan of the Puranas."

Next, Pandit Shriram Sharma writes from the context of both grammar and yoga: "The savants of spiritual knowledge opine that in the innermost centre of the soul, its sense of self-recognition–as a fraction of Parabrahman–is eternally reflected and gives rise to the continuous cycles of the self-existing (ajapa) japa of Soham (meaning 'I am "That"– Brahman'). While discussing the meaning of 'Soham' one should not be confused with respect to the precision of the liaisons in this Sanskrit word (according to the Sanskrit grammar: *sah* (that) + *aham*=Soham). Because Soham has not been a word derived from the Sanskrit grammar, rather it is a nada that is self-existing because of the eternal linkage of '*so*' (That, the Supreme Consciousness) and '*aham*' (the consciousness of the individual Self).... Soham represents the oneness of the soul and Brahman....

"Soham is the sandhi form of sah + aham, the nominatives of the third and first person singular pronouns. Sah can be prefixed to other pronouns for emphasis, as in Soham: 'I myself;' 'I, that very person' or satvam: 'Thou thyself;' 'Thou, that very person.' But in a literal reading, the phrase means 'That–I' or 'he–I.'" Therefore Soham is the sadhana mantra.

The yoga of the Self

Authentic yoga brings about everything spontaneously from deep within, from the Self. The yoga tradition says that the contemplation of Soham is the contemplation of our own true nature. It is the knowledge of our own Self.

If our spiritual practice (sadhana) is to bring us to our eternal, natural state of spirit-consciousness, it, too, must be totally natural. Therefore the term *sahaja* is often found in yoga treatises, meaning that which is natural, innate and spontaneous. Soham Yoga is the sahaja, spontaneous, yoga, for the prana/breath movement occurs in every evolving being, and that movement is inseparable from the vibration of the subtle sound of Soham. Though seemingly two, the movement of the breath and the vibrating of Soham are the same thing, like fire and heat. Not only that, this is the only characteristic common to all forms of existence, from the atom to the perfectly liberated individual. Nothing, then, is more natural than intoning Soham in time with the breath. It is the key to our inmost, true Self and its revelation.

That is why Vasuguptacharya said that through Soham one becomes aware of the true nature of one's Self. In the Self everything is to be found, for everything exists in the Self of the Self: the Supreme Self, Brahman. Soham Yoga is the Yoga of the Self and also the way to worship the divine Self: not with words but with direct experience of the Self. This is the supreme meaning of Ishwarapranidhana: the offering of the breath (prana) to God by means of the breath-mantra Soham: I am That. Therefore Lalla Yogeshwari sang:

> He who has recognized the Brahmarandhra as the shrine of the Self-God,
> He who has known the Unobstructed Sound   borne upon the breath unto the nose,
> His vain imaginings of themselves have fled far away,
> And he himself [recognizes] himself as the God.
> To whom else, therefore, should he offer worship?
> (*Lalla-Vakyani* 33)

The best aspect of all this is that everything happens naturally and spontaneously at just the right time, simply through the Soham breath. When the breath and Soham are perfectly merged it is the major force of inner transformation-transmutation. The Soham breath is the inner secret of the yogi. Saint Paul wrote: "We all, with open face beholding as in a glass the glory of the Lord, are changed into the same image from glory to glory, even as by the Spirit of the Lord" (II Corinthians 3:18). In Soham Yoga meditation we sit with closed eyes, looking into the mirror of our breath joined to Soham. Eventually in that mirror we see reflected the Archetypal Soham Breath of the Cosmos, the Breath of God himself. This it is which changes us from glory to glory into perfect image-reflections of Ishwara, the Lord.

Soham is a fundamental fact of the universe, a basic theorem of spiritual mathematics. Soham vibrates in every atom of every world–and in every atom of our astral, causal, and physical bodies as well. Although it was discovered by the sages of India, it is not the exclusive property of any religion or philosophy. It is not a sectarian mantra; it belongs to all without distinction or exclusion. Although it was perceived by the Indian yogi-rishis, it is not a creation or formulation as are many other mantras. Rather, it is swayambhu: self-begotten, self-existent and self-sufficient. It arises spontaneously within, from the Self. It does not have to be artificially implanted or empowered in us by any kind of external initiation. This mantra is going on in every one of us, but as long as we are outward turned we do not become aware of it. It is only during meditation, when we enter into our own depths, that we become aware of Soham, which has always been going on within us.

The universality of Soham Yoga practice is shown in the Garbha Upanishad which describes the various phases of the child's development in the womb. In the seventh month after conception, the soul receives knowledge of its past and future. It knows who it has been and who it will be, what it has suffered and what it will suffer. This profoundly disturbs and even frightens the child, so it begins calling on God for help. Since God is the indweller in all beings, he has all along been aware of the child's dilemma, and when it calls out to him he calms it by revealing the Atma Mantra, Soham, to it as a trait of its eternal being. When it takes refuge in that mantra, repeating it in time with its internal breath which after birth will produce the lung-breath, it remembers its nature as part of God, from whom it is inseparable. In this way God has become its guru even in the womb. As Kabir said: "The Guru awakened me within by imparting just one word." Immersed in Soham awareness, the awareness of its true nature, it becomes calm and serene. But it loses this awareness in the trauma of birth and begins crying, making the sound Kwanh, Kwanh, or Ko'ham, Ko'ham: Who am I? Who am I? forgetting the insight it had gained. It loses the memory of Soham and begins to identify with the body and its characteristics. Plunged into ignorance through forgetfulness, it begins to live out that ignorance, unaware of the Self. Later if he comes to learn about Soham, he can regain his lost identity.

The inner repetition of Soham

The effectiveness of Soham sadhana lies in the fact that we are actively generating the subtle, mental sound of Soham to link up with the already-occurring sound in the highest levels of our being. It is a uniting of our conscious awareness with the inner psychic and spiritual awareness. Further, our intentional intonations of Soham begin to radiate throughout our entire being, increasing and strengthening the primal impulse toward higher evolution. In this way we take charge of our development and ensure that it keeps going on at all times.

Regarding this, Pandit Shriram Sharma wrote: "Even the self-inspired, continuous ajapa japa of Gayatri performed naturally (along with each respiration cycle) without any effort is said to provide complete protection to the prana and offer spiritual knowledge and siddhis equivalent to that of the other yoga sadhanas. *Then think about the impact of this ajapa japa if it is performed as a sadhana with ascetic disciplines, sankalpa and shraddha!* Indeed, this sadhana (of Soham) then becomes the highest kind of spiritual sadhana because no branch of knowledge and science is found superior to the Gayatri-vidya and no japa better than the japa of the Gayatri (mantra). The shastras therefore sing great paeans on the Soham sadhana."

Soham is the seed of transcendence, pushing us onward, but our outer and inner bodies have become obscured and confused and no longer reflect or vibrate to that divine seed. Because of this our evolution has been greatly retarded, halted or even reversed. So our bodies must be set right and brought into alignment with Soham by the conscious, intentional japa and meditation of Soham.

Two mistaken approaches

There are two mistaken approaches to Soham sadhana that I would like to mention here.

Because of the notoriety of Kriya Yoga through *Autobiography of a Yogi* and others of Yogananda's writings, various people have tried to make imitations that incorporate their own ideas. One of these is the idea that when inhaling the yogi should feel and hear *So* ascending in the spine and when exhaling should feel and hear *Ham* descending in the spine. This has no basis at all in the Nath tradition and is just a distraction. Soham sadhana takes place in the sahasrara and does indeed profoundly affect the spine and the yogi's entire body. But only when done as I have outlined it.

The other mistake is to simply breathe and try to hear the physical breath itself making the sounds of *So* and *Ham*. The breath does indeed produce these sounds, but on the subtle astral level, not on the physical auditory level. In genuine Soham sadhana we mentally produce the sounds in order to link our awareness with the inner subtle pranic sounds which our mental intonations will in time reveal to us. But we even then keep right on intentionally intoning Soham in time with the breath. Otherwise we will wander off in byways that end eventually in a mental and psychic swamp.

CHAPTER THREE:

SOHAM ACCORDING TO THE SCRIPTURES AND THE MASTERS OF YOGA

An important point to keep in mind in this chapter

In this chapter, as well as others, you will find expressions such as "repetition of Soham," "japa of Soham" or "remembrance of Soham." This never means just saying Soham over and over like an ordinary mantra. Rather, it is always intoned mentally in time with the natural breath. When we breathe in naturally we mentally intone "So" and when we exhale naturally we mentally intone "Ham." This is because the movement of the subtle, inner breath produces those sounds during our inhalation and exhalation. By intoning those syllables in time with the breath we begin linking up with the eternal process that is at the center of our very being, both immanent and transcendent. Then we become established in the Soham Bhava which is the Consciousness which is us. And that is Self-realization, which is also liberation (moksha).

The Vedic Gayatri Mantra–the Savitri Gayatri–is a prayer for enlightenment recited at dawn and sunset, and is considered the most important verse in the entire Vedas. The yogis, however, say that there is another Gayatri, the Ajapa Gayatri, which also relates to enlightenment. Being "ajapa" it is repeated spontaneously by the subtle levels of our existence in time with the breath. That Gayatri is "Soham," whose conscious japa in time with the breath is considered a direct means to enlightenment. So whenever mention is made of ajapa japa it means the japa of Soham joined to the breath.

The teaching that the incoming breath makes the sound of "So" and the outgoing breath the sound of "Hum" is found in: Shiva Swarodaya, 51; Yoga Shika Upanishad 1.5, 6:53; Dhyana-Bindu Upanishad 61(b)-63; Yoga Chudamani Upanishad; Kularnava Tantra; *Mahanirvana Tantra;* Niruttara Tantra; Goraksha Shataka, 42; and in: T. N. Rao, *Vedanta: The Knowledge Supreme;* Swami Parmeshwarananda, *Encyclopaedic Dictionary of Upanisads;* L. R. Chawdhri, *Secrets of Yantra, Mantra and Tantra;* Yogi Pranavananda, *Pure Yoga;* Margaret and James Stutley, *A Dictionary of Hinduism: its Mythology, Folklore, and Development 1500 B.C.-A.D. 1500. It is also found in many of the books written by Swami Sivananda of Rishikesh.*

Here are some quotations regarding ajapa japa–Soham Yoga. I apologize for not having noted the exact verse numbers of some citations.

Isha Upanishad

In the oldest upanishad, the Isha Upanishad, we find Soham in the sixteenth verse which concludes: *Yo sav asau purushah; Soham asmi:* "I am that Purusha [Spirit-Self]: I AM SOHAM."

In Sanskrit Soham means "I Am That," but at the core of every sentient being Soham exists as the Self–*is* the Self. Therefore the seer of the upanishad concludes: "I am Soham." *Soham asmi*–"I am That I am"–is exactly what God told Moses was his Name (Exodus 3:14).

Brihadaranyaka Upanishad

In the next oldest Upanishad, the Brihadaranyaka Upanishad, we are told:

"In the beginning this (world) was only the Supreme Self [Paramatman], in the shape of a person. Looking around he saw nothing else than the Self. He first said, 'I am Soham' [*Soham asmi*]" (1:4:1).

Thus, Soham is the "first speaking" of the Absolute Itself: the expression of the knowledge and knowing of the Self. We, too, are Soham.

Later in the Upanishad (5.15.2), the identical words are found as in the verse cited previously from the Isha Upanishad.

Maha Vakya Upanishad

At the beginning of the Maha Vakya Upanishad, Brahma the Creator is said to have declared: "The personal knowledge that this Sun is Brahman is got by chanting the Ajapa Gayatri: Soham." At the end of the upanishad Brahma says that those who invoke this Gayatri will have the realization: "I am that sun who is the ethereal light. I am that Shiva who is that sun of Knowledge. I am the supremely pure [vishuddha] light of the Atman. I am all the light that we know."

Narada Parivrajaka Upanishad

Solely by the mantra Soham joined to the inhalation and exhalation, the jiva perceives the supreme Brahman (6:4).

Nirvana Upanishad

The Supreme Swan [Paramhansa–the Self] is Soham (2).

[The two syllables So and Ham are the two wings by means of which the swan-spirit flies back to Spirit.]

Surya Upanishad

Soham is the seed-mantra, the essence, of the Sun.

Yoga Chudamani Upanishad

This mantra [Soham] which is called Ajapa Gayatri will give salvation to all yogis. Just mental repetition of this mantra will help one get rid of all sins.

There are no practices as holy as this, no japa which is equivalent to this, and no wisdom equivalent to this and in the future there shall be nothing equivalent to it.

This Ajapa Gayatri which rises from the Kundalini supports the soul. This is the greatest among the sciences of the soul (33-35).

Yoga Shikha Upanishad

The breath goes out with the sound "ham" and goes in with the word "so".... This chanting of the mantra "Soham, Soham," [in time with the breath] is called Mantra Yoga (1.5).

Garuda Purana

The Gayatri called Ajapa is the giver of liberation to the sages; by merely repeating it mentally one is released from all sin (15:70).

Jnanarvana Tantra

Know this [Soham] to be the Paramatman.

Kularnava Tantra

The body is the temple of God. Let the jiva worship with "Soham."

Yoga Vashishtha

The living soul knows itself to be "Soham" (Utpatti Khanda 3:64:9).

Gheranda Samhita

The breath of every person in entering makes the sound of "sah" and in coming out, that of "ham." These two sounds make Soham. Throughout a day and a night there are twenty-one thousand and six hundred such respirations. Every living being performs this japa unconsciously, but constantly. This is called ajapa gayatri (5:84).

All jivas are constantly and unconsciously reciting this ajapa mantra, only for a fixed number of times every day. But a yogi should recite this consciously (5:90).

Yogavishaya of Minanath [Matsyendranath]

One constantly meditates: "Soham" (29).

Sharda Tilaka

Every human performs the japa of Soham in each cycle of breathing. One who does not realize this is like a blind man because he lives in the darkness of worldly illusions and he can never get moksha. The Ajapa Gayatri bestows moksha on the yogis. Anybody can get rid of all sins and evils by attaining its knowledge and realizing its power. There is no knowledge equivalent to it. No punya [meritorious action] comparable with the prodigious benefits of this sadhana has ever existed in the past or is likely to exist any time in the future.

Tirumantiram

In yoga practice Soham is chanted. The yogi who silently chants it while breathing surely attains the Holy Way (3:731).

Arthur Avalon

[With] the mantra "Soham" the sadhaka infuses his body with the life of the Devi, the Mother of all (*Shakti and Shakta*, chapter 26).

With the mantra Soham the sadhaka leads the jivatman into its place in the heart (*The Serpent Power*, p. 243).

The Kularnava Tantra [9:32] says: "The body is the temple of God. The jiva is Sadashiva. Let him give up his ignorance as the offering which is thrown away (nirmalya) and worship with the thought and feeling, 'I am That' [Soham]."

On page 185 of *The Garland of Letters*, Arthur Avalon speaks of "the Soham Atman."

Akshaya Kumar Banerjea

Every jiva continually repeats this mantra Soham. This is called Ajapa-Gayatri and is the best form of Gayatri-mantra. Gayatri means a sacred song, by the singing of which one is delivered from all bondage. By the wonderful Divine design this great mantra pregnant with the highest spiritual truth is being constantly sung by every jiva with every breath day and night without any effort. A sadhaka has only to pay deep attention to the inner meaning of his natural breath, in order to realize the identity of the individual self and the Cosmic Self and attain liberation (*Philosophy of Gorakhnath*, p. 166).

This Gayatri named Ajapa is the giver of moksha (liberation from bondage) to the Yogis (who concentrate their attention upon this natural japa). By mere concentration of attention upon this Ajapa-Gayatri a man becomes liberated from all kinds of sins.

He [Gorakhnath] sings the glory of this Ajapa-Gayatri in various ways and instructs all spiritual aspirants to make the best use of this natural device for their spiritual self-realization (*Philosophy of Gorakhnath*, p. 166).

This natural Gayatri-mantra has its origin in Kundalini Shakti and is the sustainer of the vital system. The knowledge of this is called Prana-vidya (true insight into the vital system), and it is mahavidya (great wisdom). He who attains the knowledge of this Ajapa-Gayatri is truly the knower of Yoga. Wisdom equal to this, japa equal to this, knowledge equal to this, have never been and will never be.

This is a magnificent conception of our natural breathing process. The highest enlightenment is associated with it. The cultivation of this conception and constant remembrance of the essential identity of the individual Self and the Self of the universe with every breath occupies a very important position in Gorakhnath's system of yoga sadhana. It is known as Ajapa-Yoga (*Philosophy of Gorakhnath*, p. 166-167).

Helena Petrovna Blavatsky

In the first volume of The Secret Doctrine, Stanza III, Section 8, Helena Petrovna Blavatsky gives an explanation of the words: "Where was the germ, and where was now darkness? Where is the spirit of the flame that burns in thy lamp, oh lanoo [disciple]? The germ is that, and that is light; the white brilliant son of the dark hidden Father." In other words: What is that Essence which is both the individual's Self and Ishwara, the Emanation-Son of Brahman, and therefore Brahman Itself? Here is her explanation:

As in the Hebrew Bible, many a mysterious sacred name in Sanskrit conveys to the profane ear no more than some ordinary, and often vulgar word, because it is concealed anagrammatically or otherwise.... "So-ham," "That (am) I"–Soham being equal to Sah, "he," and aham, "I," or "I am That." In this alone is contained the universal mystery, the doctrine of the identity of man's essence with god-essence, for him who understands the language of wisdom.

Brahmananda

O sadhus, O noble people, contemplate the mantra Soham. Become aware of the mantra Soham.... As you contemplate this mantra, you will attain the supreme state." *(I found this in a writing of Swami Muktananda, but did not note its name.)*

Dharam Dass

One of Kabir's disciples, Sri Dharam Dass, composed the following which are often recited by devotees of Kabir in their devotional gatherings (satsangs). In essence they are the teachings of Kabir, also.

In the hymn beginning *Puran Brahm Daya*, Kabir twice refers to God within as "the Soham Guru" about which he says: "The liberated soul finds refuge in the Soham Satguru, and realizing Soham becomes sinless."

The incomprehensible God is present everywhere, and meditation on sound is the way to realize him.… Kabir has explained this [Soham] gayatri, and whoever recites it always will be free of karmas and doubts.

Plant the flag of God between two mountains: the individual Self and the Universal Self.… This is indeed a marvelous experience. The Self remains fully conscious, endowed with noble and deep intelligence. It realizes the Eternal Name and will not perish, because it is Soham.

His consciousness soars to the house of Ida and Pingala, and remains steadfast in Sushumna, and realizes the Reality: I AM SOHAM, and controls his consciousness in this channel of God realization. Subduing the mind, the soul soars to spiritual heights, and bathes in the serene lake of meditation. In that state of consciousness, the soul worships the Divine Sound, and realizes that there it is no other God than the supreme unattached Absolute.

The essence of the four Vedas and six philosophies is Soham. Soham is the eternal essence expressing "I am That." (*Brahm Nirupan* 12).

The first gayatri [Adi Gayatri: Soham] is the essence of all the recitations, and the person reciting it attains liberation. On the path to liberation there are 880 million places to cross (obstacles) where Yama blocks the way. Reciting the gayatri the soul overcomes sorrow.… The soul realizes, "I am Soham" and goes forward to dwell in eternal Sat Lok [the highest world of the Siddhas]. Reciting this gayatri this soul becomes free of grief and goes onward.

The first gayatri represents the eternal abode and the soul realizing Soham enters it. Kabir says that by its silent recitation the soul resides in the eternal abode. Truth is eternal and void, and beyond the duality of sin and virtue Kabir teaches to proclaim this gayatri to others.

Make the breath into your rosary, and meditate upon the Supreme Reality, and know that this Reality of Soham Shabda resides in you as the Self. Soham pervades the breath. The beads of the rosary are tied in a knot. Use the breath to tie the knot of God in your heart. This is the proper rosary for you.

The rosary is your own breath. There is a rare devotee who can use the rosary of the breath in this way.... he is always conscious of Soham Shabda as non-duality.

God is ever present from the beginning. He is present now, and will be present to the end. But if you seek him in the fathomless depths, you will not find Him there. How can one get hold of God? He is the Soham Shabda, the all pervading Brahman that is changeless.... I am Soham Shabda which is unutterable and steadfast, and beyond description.

Soham is my support. The Self within repeats "Soham, Soham" melodiously.

O Brother! Listen to the eternal Word.... You will easily cross the ocean of birth and death. Be in love with Soham Shabda, and win the fearless and eternal abode.

As long as there is life in the body, this instruction brings pleasure. The soul then recites Soham silently.

The soul remains fully conscious, endowed with noble and deep intelligence. It realizes the Eternal Name and will not perish, because it is Soham.

The soul then rejoices in meeting its Beloved, who never becomes separated from its gaze. The soul is freed from the bondage of time and death.... The soul then recites Soham silently.

In *Brahm Nirupan,* Dharam Dass wrote about meditation on the formless Brahman (nirakara or nirakshar) in this way: "As said before, Nirakshar cannot be written about. It is eternal and can only be experienced. Thus the person, who, with a concentrated mind and devotion and love, recites it continuously with understanding is wise. All doubts and illusion are removed from him, and he overcomes death. He indeed realizes Soham Shabda" (*Brahm Nirupan* 11).

Eknath

When the "I"-sense, giving up its identification with the body, identifies itself with the Self as Soham, the Supreme Being, pure consciousness, is revealed in the heart. The mind, giving up all thoughts and fancies, transcends itself. The intellect becomes firmly centered in the Absolute Brahman.

Sri Gajanana Maharaj (Gajanana Murlidhar Gupte)

Sri Gajanana Maharaj of Nashik in Maharashtra was one of the great yogis of the Nath Yogi tradition in the twentieth century.

O my mind, be always repeating the japa of Soham.

The Soham mantra has great powers, and owing to its powers a man is sure to have the goal of human life fulfilled. Meditate and repeat this mantra Soham in your mind.

Simply go on repeating the mantra Soham. That will take care of everything else.

The taking in of the breath generates the sound "So" and the giving out generates the sound of "Ham." Thus the sound of "Soham" is being continuously generated in every creature, although very few are conscious of it.

Soham means "I am That." Soham therefore, is the sign show-ing the oneness of the jiva (human soul–atman) and Shiva (Supreme Self–Paramatman).

All knowledge has been centered in Soham. All the four Vedas, the Gita and the Gayatri Mantra tell us nothing except "Soham."

One can accomplish anything by meditating upon Soham. Disgust for sexual pleasures, the ending of all karma, release from the cycle of birth and death, the realization of the Self–in short everything can be obtained through Soham. This is the real Dhyana Yoga or Raja Yoga.

The reason why Shabda (Vak or Word) is called Brahman is that Shabda is a means leading to Brahman and hence it is desirable to look upon Shabda as Brahman. It is a sort of sentiment or feeling. Sri Vidy-aranya also says similarly. Carry on the repetition of Soham. It will be sufficient for you.

When the power of breath gets an upward turn, the breath proceeds upwards through the Sushumna and... proceeds to the brahmarandhra at the centre of the brain. The Soham consciousness then merges in the unknowable Supreme Self and the sadhaka attains perfection.

I do not ask you to put your faith in me but I earnestly ask you to put your faith in the Soham mantra and in your Self-experience. Try to get Self-experience and be assured that the whole world will appear to you as nothing else but Brahman, if you practice Dhyana Yoga with intensity.
Even though you may be in the world, you will be as it were out of it and you will be beyond pleasure and pain and the equanimity of your mind will never be disturbed. All your bodily diseases will disappear of their own accord. When you realize Brahman, the stage of a sadhaka is over. After that you may remain in the world enjoying the full bliss of

Self-realization, a devotee in the real sense of the word of the all pervading Omnipotence. It has been said, "One can really worship God only after becoming one with him."

I am always taking the "wine of Soham" and thus I have been spoilt. If any one wants to spoil his life as I have spoiled mine, he should with open eyes and confidence in himself take this dose of the Soham wine and then live in the bliss of his own Self.

A person should day and night repeat Soham in his mind and direct all his senses towards it. He will then become one with it.

He alone is a true saint who has thoroughly realized the truth of Soham [I am That]. His mind, intellect and his senses and even the hair on his body are full of the true meaning of Soham. He may or may not do any outward actions. Even though he may do certain actions, he is detached from them. He is videhi [apart from the body] like King Janaka. He looks upon worldly and spiritual things equally and goes beyond the states of pain and pleasure. He knows the only true Being and is always experiencing the state of unlimited joy.

I therefore, say that if you have learnt Dhyana Yoga it is all well with you. If not, try to learn it. Strictly speaking God is none else than our own Self. Every one should try to see this Self by the torch of Soham and obtain the internal sight. Saints have said, "Persons who have obtained the internal vision are saved while those who have only the external vision are drowned."… If you really enter inside, your real Guru who is inside will automatically lead you to the right path. Otherwise you will not be able to understand clearly who is leading you on.

Kabir has said, "If you want to know the Eternal, you will not find him in the Vedas, the shastras or in the Koran, in the temples or in the mosques. Penance, pilgrimage, breath-control, or living on nothing but neem leaves, will not lead you to him. You can find him only in your breath." (Soham: "So" when taking in and "Ham" when giving out the breath)."

All human beings on this earth are really gods themselves, but those who know themselves enjoy peace and joy.... If your life is not pure, what can soap do? Your mind must be internally merged in the divine joy.... Do not entertain evil thoughts. If, however they arise in your mind, check them then and there by the mantra Soham. Then your mind gradually will become void of thoughts.

I wish to say with all the earnestness at my command that every person should internally repeat the mantra Soham and should bear in mind that he himself will be able to fulfill his desires. Only it must be borne in mind that he must keep his conduct pure, should have at least a little vairagya and should have firm faith in Soham. When once a person obtains this self-confidence, he is sure to get Self-experience and will meet with his real guru–his Self. Evil thoughts will then cease to rise.

One thing regarding this japa must be remembered. This japa of Soham must be repeated continuously in the mind. It should not be allowed to be known to others that you are repeating the japa. This japa should be so continuously and incessantly repeated that it must be heard internally even in our sleep. Thus the japa becomes one with the mind. When this stage is reached, if a person then prays to this God of internal light to grant his desires, he should be absolutely sure of his prayers being granted. This method is a hundred times superior to that of praying for favors to God who is outside ourselves. Not only will the desires be granted, but either in this or in the next birth according to the person's present efforts and previous karma, a person is sure to attain the highest bliss of the Self.

If all my brothers and sisters will do as I have just said, they will be able to enjoy real happiness and would never fall into the clutches of false saints.

This [Self in the form of] "I" is present in each and everything, even in the minutest atom of dust. It is your Self. Know it. Through continuous meditation on the idea of Soham [I am That] be one with that Self which itself is the Supreme Self. I cannot tell you anything beyond this. This God is in my heart, similarly he is in your heart also. When through the grace of Guru and through the japa of Soham you will get the internal sight, you will be able to understand everything.

Through the grace of my guru I got the Soham mantra and I am at present in the sadhaka state. My sadguru told me to repeat Soham internally and then to get the awareness of the japa of Soham merged into the Supreme Self and enjoy eternal peace and joy. If this was done I myself will become one with the self-existent, eternal and blissful Principle and experience the presence of that Supreme Self everywhere. I will then become perfect, leave off all egoism and realize the real "I." In the end even this would be forgotten.

The ignorant human spirit takes birth and questions, "Who am I?" But originally this human spirit was full of knowledge and was one with the Supreme Self. The answer to the human spirit's question "Who am I?" is the mantra Soham (I am That), which having thoroughly convinced the human spirit that it is one with the Supreme Self, takes the human spirit back to its original state of knowledge and bliss.

You have only to get Self-experience by carrying on the practice of meditation steadily. I have got full experience in this very body of the power of Soham. I therefore never tell any of my friends to bring the forms of deities before their mind's eye, but give them the mantra Soham and turn their minds inwards, owing to which all ideas become merged in the sahasradala. After some time all these merge into the spirit and the aspirant gets for at least a short time into the state of samadhi, and experiences great joy.

Those who repeat Soham with very great intensity become at once merged in the sound. Hence they are unconscious of any visions of light. Some of my friends, therefore, who get merged in sound do not see any visions. If you do not see any visions, you should not on that account entertain any doubts regarding the efficacy of Soham.

Among all the different stages of the powers of Shakti, the power of Soham is the most exalted.

My sadguru had me drink the nectar of Nama (Name of God) and I tell you the same Nama, being ordered by my sadguru to do so. I am approaching the stage of perfection. If you also wish to come with me, you should repeat that Nama "Soham" in your heart with firm faith. Your deep-rooted mental tendencies will vanish and the dirt of desire accumulated in previous births and in this birth will be washed away and your individual spirit will be merged into the Universal Spirit and you will always remain in your real original state and thus attain everlasting peace.

A sadhaka comes to realize the power of the Self and ultimately to grasp that there is one everlasting and all-pervading Being which is present in everything and which is the only thing that exists. He then becomes one with Soham. He obtains everything which is to be obtained, to him nothing remains unattained, all his doubts are solved and he is merged in everlasting bliss. He becomes one with Brahman and never falls from this state.

Take this torch of Soham to light you through the dense darkness of ignorance; and having safely crossed the ocean of worldly existence, remain in the world in a spirit of detachment. This torch will lead you safe to your destination and once you reach there, you will be merged in your real Self and be full of bliss and joy. I am showing you the path leading to the Infinite and if you follow it you are sure to realize the real nature of Brahman.

If a sadhaka practices Dhyana Yoga with intensity, I am sure in this very life he will reach the state of perfection through the power of the Soham mantra.

Now let us see the real significance of Soham. All creatures are taking in and giving out breath. The taking in of the breath generates the sound So and the giving out generates the sound of Ham. Thus the sound of Soham is being continuously generated in every creature, although very few are conscious of it. To be conscious of this sound is the real "Sudarshana [Chakra]" of "Soham," which means "I am He." "Soham," therefore, is the sign showing the oneness of the jiva (human soul) and Shiva (Supreme Soul).

The ignorant human soul takes its birth and questions, "Who am I?" But originally this human soul was full of knowledge and was one with the Supreme Self. A sadguru gives the answer to the human soul's question, "Who am I?" by telling him the mantra Soham, "I am That," which thoroughly convinces the human soul that it is one with the Supreme Self and takes the human soul back to its original state of knowledge and bliss.

Carry on the repetition of Soham. It will be sufficient for you.

Repeat without a break the mantra Soham internally.

I do not know anything else except the two letters. [The Soham mantra is considered as having two letters—that is, syllables.]

As this Soham Mantra is the mantra of all the Nine Nathas and as it is also the mantra signifying the action of breathing of all creatures, an aspirant who takes to it is sure to make some progress in this very birth and to get experiences showing his progress.

The mind must be internally immersed in Soham and become full of bliss. While carrying on this practice it is all one to me whether people hail me as a great saint or place me on a donkey and take me round through the streets, as was once done in the case of Sri Tukaram. I do not in the least care about this. If my mind is absolutely clean and full of the bliss of Soham, entirely devoid of egotism and concentrated in the internal sound of Soham even when outwardly doing worldly actions, I shall consider myself as extremely fortunate. My practice is going on in the direction of obtaining this eternal bliss and I can say from experience that I feel that I have ascended some steps on the steep path leading to the temple where eternal peace and happiness have been enshrined.

He alone is able to explain the real nature of Soham who has himself experienced its power.

This Soham will in course of time remove the dirt of bad thoughts and make the mirror of the mind clean. As soon as the mirror becomes clean, the blissful nature of Soham will be realized. Hence we should direct all our efforts towards keeping our attention fixed on Soham without any break. If we do so we shall surely attain complete peace and happiness and life will be full of bliss.

Soham is the real path of knowledge (Jnana Marga). Owing to this, egotism disappears. In the path of knowledge, the sadhaka's consciousness becomes more and more comprehensive, until it becomes all-pervading. Thus, in the path of knowledge one becomes all-pervading and one with the universal Being.

The Dhyana Yoga of the Nath Pantha which has been handed down from Matsyendranath acts like a light which clearly shows the right path. I say this from my own experience. As the sadhaka has to repeat the japa and also to meditate, this path is known as Dhyana Yoga. With firm faith, having turned back the course of thoughts from the outward world to inside himself, a sadhaka has to carry on the japa and meditation for a long time. As he progresses, he gradually reaches perfection and realizes that his own Self has been his Sadguru. This state is known as oneness of jiva (the individual Self) and Shiva (the Supreme Self). It is also called Sakshatkara. A sadhaka then naturally enjoys the bliss of the Self and becomes devoid of desire for anything else. This path is also known as Dhyana Yoga or Karma Marga, because a sadhaka gets Sakshatkara after progressing through many steps. He also attains complete knowledge, hence it is called Jnana Yoga. I therefore again and again say that people should have recourse to this simple path of self-deliverance.

The Soham mantra is the real savior.

My brothers and sisters, I am merely a traveller on the path of the light of Soham and a disciple of my sadguru, still a student learning saguna dhyana. Having experienced certain things myself I tell the things to you through the grace of my divine sadguru. Awaken and kindle the flame of Soham in this dense darkness of ignorance, practice Dhyana Yoga and obtain Self-realization. Your whole worldly existence will be full of bliss. Great spiritual powers will be generated in you and no evil-minded person would ever dare to cast an evil eye towards you. When your meditation will attain intensity, friends and foes alike will begin to behave like brothers and sisters towards you. You may then carry on your ordinary social and worldly life. You will be happy spiritually as well as in your worldly life. This is what is meant by attaining spiritual greatness while at the same time leading a worldly life. This is the real grace of the guru, which is the same as the grace of our real Self. Knowledge of spiritual things does not conduce to weakness of mind. It teaches how to give a blow for a blow, but with the proper mental attitude. Instead of merely saying that all these spiritual things are false and chimerical, people should first try to get actual experience and then call these things false if they find them so.

I wish to emphasize that he who has no attachment for worldly objects, who is perfect, has completely controlled his senses, and whose mind is entirely devoid of any desire of sensual pleasures, who remains in the world but is, as it were, out of it—because of his entire detachment—he alone obtains the sovereign kingdom of everlasting atmic bliss. He becomes one with Soham, and obtains the real grace of his sadguru. His mind is pure like the water of the Ganges, which moves in its course purifying all who come in contact with it. All bad thoughts entirely disappear, and his actions are quite naturally done. He is externally, as well as internally, quite calm and at peace.

In this stage he sees Brahman in all things; in other words, he is entirely immersed in the experience that everywhere there is nothing but all-pervading joy and bliss. His joy and peace are not dependent upon anything else, and hence they are everlasting. They are not disturbed under any circumstances, however adverse. His experience tells him that he himself has taken the form of the biggest as well as the minutest things. This is the real meaning of Soham. This is the real Atmajnana. Without this Atmajnana, all actions are useless.

Now there is the question: Is there any use in carrying on the japa of Soham without faith in its efficacy? The answer to that is that the repetition of the japa will always be useful, even though done without faith. It will never do you any harm. No doubt all the shastras and saints lay stress on faith, and hence the above statement will appear contrary to their teachings. However, if you go deep into the matter and observe minutely, you will easily be able to reconcile the two statements. Without having faith—although it may be in the subconscious mind—no one will be induced to practice the japa. As soon as a person begins to repeat the japa, faith is there accompanying the japa like its shadow. If we carefully follow this argument the seeming contradiction will cease to trouble us. A real mumukshu or devotee will never be deceived by the seeming contradiction, and will never allow his mind to be disturbed and turned away from the path.

This mantra Soham is the inner, subtle sound produced by the incoming and outgoing breaths. Everyone is breathing and producing this sound, but no one is conscious of it. Hence no one practices this japa. If anyone carries on the practice by fixing his attention upon this japa, he will be sure to obtain its fruit. I carried on the japa with perseverance and firm faith, and later this practice became my nature.

Oh God, all these things come to pass through your grace alone. There is not the slightest doubt about this. You yourself gave me the mantra of Soham. Through the power of this mantra you shower your grace upon sadhakas and bless them with real knowledge. But I only pray to you to save all those who put their faith in the mantra of Soham, each according to his aptitude.

My brothers and sisters. If you also carry on the practice with firm faith and assiduity, you too will get experience in a greater or lesser degree. From amongst all who thus try, only those whose practice reaches perfection will get Self-realization. Faith, perseverance and continuous effort lead to success and realization of the Self. If your efforts are weak, or if you abandon the practice in the middle and ask why you do not get experiences which others get, it will be a senseless question not deserving any answer. "There is no firm conviction and the mind is wandering everywhere." If such is the state, abhyasa (practice) will be useless and will be of no avail. Hence you must have firm faith and realize your oneness with Brahman through the power of the mantra.

The sadhaka will develop a liking for this practice leading to oneness with Brahman, and he alone will ultimately enjoy everlasting bliss. All dross is sure to be swept away from the heart of a sadhaka by the constant japa of Soham. If the seed of Soham is sown in such a field, it is sure to sprout into a beautiful tree which will be laden with the fruit of the bliss of Self-realization. Such sadhakas will be enjoying unchanging bliss and will very easily cross the river of worldly existence. When a sadhaka reaches this stage he can very easily control his mind, intellect and ahankar. The power generated by the constant repetition of the Soham mantra is sure to lead to the complete liberation of the sadhaka. "Your treasure is within you, only you have forgotten the place where it is hidden."

If we want to make our whole worldly life full of bliss, we must meditate on the Self through the mantra of Soham. Such has been my own experience and I have reached this stage entirely through meditating on Soham. I cannot say that I have attained this stage through my own efforts. This Soham which has come out of the Avyakta (the Unmanifested) has brought the shakti (power) of the Avyakta with it, and owing to this shakti everything of mine has become Krishnarpana (one with the Godhead). Hence, Maya does not trouble me. I have become one with Soham and I have realized my Self by meditating on it. I am enjoying unchanging bliss.

The mantra Soham is the sole savior. I am absolutely sure of this, not merely intellectually but through self-experience. All saints have resorted to this very mantra, and when their thoughts become entirely merged in the Supreme Self they become one with Brahman and shine forth in this world. Through their grace and through meditation on Soham I am enjoying the same bliss which they enjoy. But I am following in their footsteps and taking draughts of the supreme bliss. These saints have boldly declared in their imperishable words that they have been saved by Soham, and that others will also be saved by the same mantra. Future saints also will preach the same principle.

The mantra Soham was hidden in the Avyakta in the deep recesses of my own soul. This treasure was with me but I had forgotten the place where it was hidden. The saints pointed out to me that place and from that time I have been continuously contemplating on the Self. This Soham which has come out of the Avyakta is ever present in the hearts of men. Saints become one with this Soham which is in their own hearts and then the Soham merges itself again into the Avyakta.

I therefore think that Soham is the real Karma [action leading to liberation], it is the true "I." This Soham is the real secret. It is God, it is Karma, that makes us realize this.

Just as the child never has any doubt that its mother will fulfill all its desires, similarly sadhakas should have firm faith in their sadguru who is none other than Soham, and have not the least doubt that this mother Soham will deliver them from all troubles and difficulties.

My dear brothers and sisters, this Soham japa is like an ocean which is full of unlimited bliss.

The repetition of Soham may be sakama (action with expectation of fruits), or nishkama (action without expectation of fruits). As Soham is based on the workings of nature, its japa, though it may be carried on with the object of fulfilling earthly desires, will ultimately be united with the real Soham which is enshrined in the innermost core of our being, and thus bring into awakening the power of the Paramatman. Objects of earthly desires are not permanent. The joy which is felt in their attainment is evanescent. But the effect of even the sakama japa of Soham is not altogether lost. It retains its force and awakens the power of the Self.

This "I" [the true Self] is Soham, and eternal peace is its nature. A person might say that he does not want all this bother about God, dhyana, devotion, faith and concentration. All right; but let him say whether he wants peace, calmness and happiness or not. Even if he thinks that these ideas about God, etc., are false and illusory, still he must admit that there is somebody inside him who thinks them false and illusory. This knower inside us is the Self and that Self is Soham.

If an aspirant carries on the continuous meditation on the sound of Soham, he will become one with Soham. If he happens to die in this state he can be sure of attaining sadgati (everlasting happiness; final beatitude) after his death. It is very difficult to bring our mind to bear upon the contemplation of God at the time of our death. The force of desires is very great at that time, a person becomes a prey to them, and owing to this has to go through the cycle of various lives. If, however, he gets himself accustomed to the continuous intense contemplation of the sound of Soham, his mind at the time of death will not be entangled in the meshes of worldly desires, but will be merged in Soham and hence he will be sure to go to a higher state after his death. I therefore say to you all: commence the japa of Soham and carry it on ceaselessly.

What is necessary is that we must devote our attention to this Soham. The more your attention is directed towards Soham the greater will be the change in your mind and thoughts. The speaker, the doer, the action itself, and in fact everything, will be one with Soham. I am at present experiencing the bliss of such a state, and anyone else who will do as I have done will attain similar bliss. As long as the "I" dwells in this body, we must get into the habit of repeating Soham. Ceaseless repetition will make the trend of all thoughts full of Soham.

Soham is always present as a witness in everybody's mind. As soon as a man gains consciousness of the ever-existing presence of this "I" he attains the goal of human life. This state is known as sakshiavastha (the state where the "I" is consciously felt to be the ever-present witness). This Soham is ever present in every being in the form of his own Self. This Soham is continuously going on, it never stops. This Soham which is seen in all animate and inanimate things is my Jani Janardan (God present in all human beings), and wherever I use the word "Jani Janardan," I mean by it this Soham that is present in all.

The japa of Soham should be repeated in as natural a manner as possible. There is no necessity of assuming any particular posture (asana). It should be carried on even while doing worldly actions. No misgiving should be entertained regarding its effect even though there may be absence of concentration. Such doubts are groundless. Even when we feel that our mind is concentrated, that state of concentration is only apparently so. The mind is in its very nature extremely fickle, and we cannot be sure when it will dart away and throw us into a whirlpool of thoughts. Everyone knows that this state of concentration is generally momentary. It is no doubt true that in the state of samadhi the mind is concentrated for a longer duration, but that state of samadhi also is not permanent; it lasts only for some time. After that the person again descends into consciousness of surrounding worldly objects, the play of good and bad desires generating pleasure or pain is resumed, and the body carries on its usual activities.

Some people think that if they carry on the japa of Soham they may get into a state of [continual indrawn or abstract] concentration, and then it will be difficult for them to carry on their worldly duties easily. This idea also is false. Soham is our real nature. If we become one with it we will, on the contrary, be able to carry on our usual worldly duties more efficiently.

"All possible troubles beset the worldly life." Keeping this truth firmly in mind, it is necessary to get deliverance from samsara (worldly existence) by the internal repetition of Soham. The seeing of many visions is not a sure sign of progress. Real progress lies in the continuous meditation on the sound of Soham going on without a break, after the visions have stopped. If a person carries on the continuous practice of the Soham japa, his mind will in course of time get concentrated upon it, and he will then experience the state of samadhi.

Attaining the state of samadhi is not the final goal of our life. In the state of samadhi there is no consciousness of the external world, and there is experience of bliss. But this state lasts only for a short time. As soon as the normal consciousness is gained, the world makes its presence felt as before and the old play of desires, full of pleasure and pain, commences. Thus it will be seen that it is a mistake to suppose that we have reached our final goal when we reach the state of samadhi. What is necessary in this stage, is that even while we are conscious of worldly objects our meditation on Soham must be ceaselessly going on, and the worldly objects and events should produce no reaction on our mind, making it unsteady. Hence it is necessary to carry on the meditation of Soham ceaselessly. When this practice is carried on continuously, a state is reached when the presence of the Paramatman is felt in all the three states: the waking, the dreaming and the sleeping. Thus, the state of ajapa-japa is reached, and when this is reached we experience the state of samadhi even while we are doing worldly activities. The mind itself becomes one with Soham and the truth of the following words is realized: "The mind has become fixed and motionless in one place. Atmic bliss has, therefore, been realized to the full. Nothing remains lacking."

The object of the above discussion is not to make aspirants despondent and abandon the practice through a sense of frustration if they find that their efforts are not crowned with success in a short time. They are sure to realize the real power of Soham after some days if they carry on the practice continuously, with great intensity. There is absolutely no doubt about this. I say this from my own experience. The aspirant should have the firm determination that he will carry on the practice of Soham intensely in the future, although he might have failed to do so in the past.

This "I" inside the body may be called by any name. It may be called God or Nature or any other name. The knowledge of this "I" leads to peace and happiness. Is there anyone who does not want this peace and happiness? Our mind is like a mirror. Various thoughts are always arising in the mind. It is a mistake to think that we are sinners, and hence will not be able to concentrate upon Soham. Who is it that thinks we are sinners, and hence would not be able to concentrate on Soham? It is our own Self which is inside us. Various thoughts are always having their play in the mind. According to the different thoughts, the mind is plunged in sorrow or in joy. We should think about the "I" inside, who is the witness of all these thoughts. That is Soham.

If we sit quiet and at ease divesting the mind of all disturbing thoughts, we shall get a glimpse of this witness inside. The mirror of our mind has been covered over with the dirt of innumerable impressions left by bad thoughts entertained through the course of innumerable previous lives. The dark soot of kama (desire) and krodha (anger) is lying in thick layers on the surface of this mirror. It is our duty to try to wash away all this dirt and soot by means of good desires, and by increasing the flow of good thoughts.

Sri Tukaram says, "Wherever I go you are always with me to bear me company." The companion here referred to is none other than Soham. Wherever you may be, in whatever condition you may be, this Soham, this witness, this Paramatman, is always your companion. You have never been or will ever be separated from Him because you and He are one. Only you are not conscious of His nearness and presence. You must first become fully conscious of His nearness and presence and then lose the sense of this consciousness also by becoming one with Him. Then you will be bliss incarnate, everlasting, unchanging bliss.

I am telling all this from my own experience. If you put forth strong efforts in the direction I have mentioned above, you are sure to attain success.

While carrying on the contemplation of Soham, an aspirant should always be carefully observing whether his worldly desires are gradually dropping off. The gradual dropping of worldly desires, and the capability to perform worldly actions solely from a sense of duty and not with a view to achieve some object, are sure signs of spiritual progress. If an aspirant makes it a point to see that his attention is continuously fixed on Soham, that his mind is growing more and more detached, and that he is continuously carrying on the practice with firm faith in the path of Soham sadhana, I am sure that he will certainly reach the goal. Whether a person is a mumukshu (aspirant), sadhaka, or a siddha (a person who has obtained siddhi or power), if all his desires have completely disappeared and he has attained a complete sense of detachment, then he attains a state in which the Supreme Self is always with him wherever he stays. There is no necessity for him to go anywhere. I therefore urge all people, whether ignorant or learned, mumukshus or sadhakas, to carry on the japa of Soham with their attention continuously directed towards it.

Some people say that the present age is the age of material enjoyment. That the present Yuga is Kali Yuga, and in this Yuga it is extremely difficult to attain the highest goal of Self-realization. Naturally, men in general will be always striving to obtain material happiness. I, however, think that it is not proper to be complaining about external conditions. A little consideration will, on the contrary, convince us that external conditions are almost the same in all Yugas. The change lies in the mind, the attitude it adopts. According to the attitude of your mind you will feel that the age is Satya Yuga or Kali Yuga. Everything thus depends on your mind. Hence I say that you should get your mind immersed in the ceaseless contemplation of Soham and then you will find that the difficulties created by troublesome external conditions will automatically disappear.

Some persons carry on the japa for some time, but owing to lack of intensity on their part, when they find that they are not making marked progress, or when they do not see any visions, they give up the practice, thinking that fate is against them. Or if they carry on the japa, they do it merely mechanically without any heart in the matter.

If our mind is unsteady, if it does not feel any joy in the contemplation of Soham, we should ask ourselves the question: Why do we not experience pleasure in doing the japa? The obvious answer is that it is our own lack of faith that comes in the way and bars us from getting this joy. There is also another thing. Thousands of bad impressions have been accumulated in our mind through the course of previous births. How can all these impressions disappear at once?

In the case of those whose bad impressions have been cleared away to an appreciable extent, if they carry on the practice they will get some spiritual experiences sooner or later according to their merit. If any bad desires have beset their mind in this life, the continuous contemplation of Soham will gradually destroy all those desires in this very life. In the next life the remaining bad impressions and bad desires, and kama (desire or lust), krodha (anger) and lobha (greed), generating them or generated by them, will surely disappear. You should have no doubt regarding this in your mind. You may have no faith in me, but you must have faith in Soham.

I therefore say again and again, that the real power lies in the mantra Soham. This power is also centered in you. If you thoroughly realize this power, and become one with it, you will easily attain atmic bliss, even though you may be leading a worldly life. You will be thoroughly happy internally, as well as in your worldly life.

My brothers and sisters should remember that a liking for and devotion to God is the result of the accumulation of great merit in previous lives. If you have this liking, God in the form of Soham who has His dwelling in the outgoing and incoming breath of every human being, will be realized by you. I say this from my own experience.

There are stone idols of gods and there are portraits or pictures of gods. Looked at from the point of view of our senses, they are merely lifeless stones or pictures. Is there any movement in them? But do we not superimpose the presence of Rama, Vitthala, Krishna or Dattatreya on these lifeless things by the force of our faith? And when this emotion of devotion generated by faith reaches its climax, these idols of stone are actually perceived as full of chaitanya. They talk with us and walk with us and behave with us as if they are our friends and companions of long-standing. We should carefully consider within ourselves how we fixed our faith in these stone idols in the beginning. We so fixed our faith owing to the teachings of saints and devotees. That is, our faith was generated owing to the words of others in whom we had faith. For some days, months or years we maintained this faith and ultimately this faith culminated in the above-mentioned realization.

Similarly, you should entertain firm faith in the power of Soham. Do not allow your faith to be shaken although in the beginning you do not get any experiences. If you give this consideration to the matter of Soham in the same manner, you will find that having faith in Soham is a matter solely depending upon your own mind. Even if owing to bad impressions of past lives doubts assail your mind, it lies with you to drive away these doubts with assiduous efforts, remembering that therein lies the successful fruition of your life. When the mind is concentrated and becomes one with the mantra, all thoughts disappear. Only you must have a true and firm determination. We can be said to have a true and firm determination only when we are able to translate our ideas into action. Hence saints have said, "God grants the fulfillment of true and firm determination, and the desires entertained by the devotees are crowned with success" (Tukaram).

The path which leads to the true knowledge of this "I" and to the realization of oneness with it, is the path of spiritual progress. He who desires to go by this path must naturally practice self-restraint and keep himself detached from material pleasures. Abandoning of material pleasures outwardly, or abandoning them by merely forcibly curbing the mind, is of very little use. The renunciation must be mental—the mind must gradually develop a dislike for these material pleasures. If you will try to immerse your mind in the continuous contemplation of the sound of Soham, this renunciation becomes easy. The mind becomes one with Soham, and then the ajapa japa begins. In this state our whole worldly existence becomes full of happiness. The mind of a person who attains this state goes beyond pleasure and pain. It becomes full of universal love, and he feels nothing but love in this material world which to others is full of pleasure and pain.

When will a sadhaka reach the ultimate goal of human life? My friends, doubts are bound to assail the mind. To entertain various doubts and misgivings is quite natural to the mind. As long as a person is alive, his mind will always be full of thoughts, good or bad. Hence it is futile to wait till the mind abandons all mistaken thoughts and doubts. People who think that they will not be able to make any progress in spiritual matters until this inflow of thoughts is stopped should pay particular attention to the following illustration.

There are bound to be innumerable waves on the sea. If a person thinks that he will swim in the sea when all these waves are stopped, will he ever be able to swim in the sea? He will surely come to know that the waves will never stop and he will never be able to swim. Similarly, every person who wants to follow the spiritual path should not wait for the disappearance of all thoughts, but should start the contemplation of Soham and try to keep his mind fixed upon it. He should not allow his mind to be diverted from it by the waves of thoughts.

As long as a person identifies himself with this body, these doubts and thoughts are sure to assail him and cause disturbance. A sure way to escape from the clutches of these thoughts is to develop a feeling that we are not the body. It is the nature of the mind to carry on the continuous play of thoughts. The mind (manas), the intellect (buddhi), and the chitta (consciousness) are all inside us. Buddhi is the power which enables us to determine something. The mind is always fickle and moving from one idea to another, and when the mind concentrates upon something it is called chitta. A sadhaka, therefore, should concentrate upon Soham and thus turn his mind into chitta. If he continues this practice for some time, his mind will gradually gain in calmness and ultimately will become one with Soham and with the inherent, everlasting bliss which is the real nature of Soham, and thus his chitta will become chit (consciousness). Once this state is attained, that person will experience unlimited joy. Such a person is easily able to identify himself with all persons with whom he comes into contact, and with all circumstances in which he finds himself placed. His peace of mind is never disturbed, and he is always immersed in everlasting and unchanging bliss. He attains the goal, and the real purpose of human life is fulfilled.

Kabir says: "Rama Nama is repeated by almost all people—by thieves, by licentious people, and by rich people. But that Nama by which

Dhruva and Prahlada were saved was something different." I boldly tell you with firm assurance that the "different" Nama referred to by Kabir in these lines is none other than Soham. He who makes that Nama his own becomes one with the universal power. His words acquire the force of truth, and hence are full of power.

One must remember that the Siddha Name of Soham alone will be useful in easily crossing this ocean of worldly existence and ending the cycle of births and deaths. This Siddha Nama is a power; it is like a mother to the universe, and it is the entity that is calling itself "I" in the body. It is a flame of love.

A mumukshu is terribly afraid of this panorama of worldly existence and, not being able to know who he really is, becomes full of bewilderment and misery. Then Soham is shown to him. His bewilderment disappears, he begins to enjoy constant and everlasting peace and ultimately obtains moksha.

If you repeat the Soham mantra in your mind, by continuous practice your mind gets concentrated upon it. The concentration is dhyana. If this force is uninterruptedly stored up in your heart, be sure that you have obtained the goal of human life.

Somebody might say, "We have carefully listened to what you have told us. But what will be the use of all this for solving the practical difficulties of our actual life in this world?" No doubt this question is very important.

If your difficulties remain as they are, all this effort of japa and concentration will be useless and good for nothing. But I say this with all emphasis, that once you get the experience of the Avyakta [the Divine Unmanifest], the power of the Avyakta is such that it will more than suffice for solving all possible difficulties in your worldly life. There is no necessity of your trying anything else for that purpose.

You should only try your best to obtain the experience of the Avyakta. Once that is done, you will get such a power that it will either drive away all possible difficulties which beset you, or all difficulties will automatically disappear.

True karma [yoga] lies in remaining absolutely calm and undisturbed by fixing your abode in the all-pervading Chaitanya. I have said something about karma [yoga] before. Here I put it in the shortest way and the fewest words: To remain indifferent to pleasure and pain, and to perform actions from a sense of duty supported by the basis of Self-knowledge, is the real karma [yoga]. Lord Krishna describes himself as "Aham," that is, "Soham," which is the real power of Avyakta.

If a man carries on the japa of the saving mantra Soham, he will thereby surely succeed in gradually obtaining peace of mind. Sometimes doubts and fears will assail him. He should not mind them, but carry on the practice with greater and greater intensity. If this is carried on till the time of death, he will find that at the time of death his mind is not centered in worldly matters. Even if his mind is slightly disturbed and attracted a little towards these things, he should still carry on the japa, and then at the time of death his mind will be engrossed in the contemplation of Soham.

I have explained this point as clearly as I could. Only you must have the lighted torch of Soham with you, and must try to obtain peace in its light. I have said what I know from my own experience. Everybody should try to realize it by his own experience. He must only remember that love is the Self, and the Self is love. Soham is the Self, and the Self is love. Soham is the Self, and there is everlasting peace in the Self. That itself is the Avyakta, the Unmanifested, in which everything lives, moves and has its being. Obtain everlasting peace by the mantra of Soham, which surely and certainly leads to the goal.

I say that through his experiences a sadhaka comes to realize the power of the Self, and ultimately to grasp that there is one everlasting and all-pervading Being which is present in everything and which is the only thing that exists. He then becomes one with Soham. He obtains everything which is to be obtained, to him nothing remains unattained, all his doubts are solved, and he is immersed in everlasting bliss. He becomes one with Brahman, and never falls from this state.

If once you know the real path leading to this Self-experience, you can enjoy the bliss of the Self even though you may be leading a worldly life.

You should repeat the Soham mantra. You will, owing to it, obtain internal sight.

Although the mind has always a tendency to leave the object of meditation and run away to other things, the only remedy is to bring it back again and to fix it on the object of meditation. If we try to give a bend to the branch of a tree, in the beginning as soon as we remove our hand from it, it again becomes straight and assumes its original position. But by continuous efforts of bending it and also by tying the bent parts by means of a rope etc., we succeed in giving it a permanent bend. Similarly, if a person while repeating his japa finds that his mind has wandered away, the only remedy is to forcibly bring it back and to fix it again on the japa.

This path of meditation has been shown to you by me. But the result or success will depend upon everyone's keenness in practicing, and his faith in the Self. Consider atmic experience as your real sadguru. Then there will be no necessity of relying upon the words of others, however great they be. Hence I say there is nothing secret in this path. What little I have told you has been told freely and with frankness.

Every step in this path of yoga should be minutely scrutinized by the inner sight and tested by experience and reasoning. Where you cannot understand, shastras may be referred to. I would never tell you to place your blind faith in anyone, as I consider that to do so leads to self-ruin. Awaken your discriminating power, test every thing in the light of your experience as you test gold in fire and on the touchstone. If you think that there is some sense in what I say, try to realize it in your experience. There is no cause of fear in this path. Truth can be proclaimed in broad daylight to thousands of people. There is no danger to it.

O my mind, be always repeating the japa of Soham. Through faith in Soham external worship has been left behind. The soul has been realized in the form of Soham. Through the sound of Soham the guru has been beheld—that guru who saves people by the principle of Soham. The guru has been clearly manifested through the sound of Soham: that guru who saves all the poor, troubled souls by the truth of Soham.

Concentrate upon the mantra Soham and the result will inevitably follow.

As long as the breath goes on, life goes on, and the activities of the body go on. The saints have explained the meaning of the incoming and outgoing breath, and Soham is the sound which is produced by the incoming and outgoing breath. This Soham sound is ceaselessly being repeated in our body whether we are conscious of it or not. If we become conscious of this internal Soham, we shall experience peace of mind. If we fully understand this Soham, we shall attain complete bliss, which is the real nature of Soham, and become one with it.

Various doubts and misgivings assail the mind. This is the natural result of evil impressions left on our mind by bad thoughts in previous lives. But there is no reason why we should feel discouraged.

Our present duty is to get ourselves accustomed to the entertaining of good thoughts.

Every mumukshu should ceaselessly put up strong efforts to meditate upon Soham. It does not matter even if the japa is sakama. He should not give any thought as to when the japa will lead to the final attainment of the goal. His efforts should be directed towards trying to keep his attention fixed on the sound of Soham. He should try to fix his attention on Soham even while doing worldly actions. This Soham will in course of time remove the dirt of bad thoughts and make the mirror of the mind clean. As soon as the mirror becomes clean, the blissful nature of Soham will be realized. Hence we should direct all our efforts towards keeping our attention fixed on Soham without any break. If we do so we shall surely attain complete peace and happiness and life will be full of bliss.

I therefore tell you with all the emphasis I can command that you should at once begin to repeat the japa of Soham with firm faith. It does not matter if you place no faith in me. Have firm faith in Soham and you will attain the same bliss that I am enjoying.

Those who have read some religious books and those who have listened to religious discourses must have often heard the words: Jivatma, Shivatma, and Paramatman. Jivatma is the individual soul who experiences pleasure and pain in this worldly life. Shivatma is the Paramatman who is the root cause of all the activities in the Universe. The absolute Being who pervades all things and is also beyond them is the Paramatman, otherwise known as Brahman. One and the same Being has been given these different names according to the different aspects in which He has been looked at.

Thus there is one absolute principle on which the ideas of Jivatma, Shivatma, and Paramatman have been superimposed. We get superficial, wordy knowledge of these terms from religious books and discourses, and our mind is confused. Now, where is he located who gives these different names and utters these words? He is located in this body, in the heart. This "I" located in the heart of all human beings, conceives these different aspects and gives utterance to these different names. If you search for this "I," you will come to know it is an absolute principle having no form, no attributes, and which cannot be described in words. If it is without attributes and without form, can it ever be perceived by the eye? No.

Then if you ask about the nature of this principle, for an answer you should see what all saints have said about it. They say that the real nature of this "I" is unchangeable bliss. The everlasting bliss residing in our heart is the sign by which the absolute truth can be traced. Every human being is ceaselessly trying to get happiness. Nobody is needed to tell him to do so. The reason why every human being ceaselessly tries to find happiness is because unchanging bliss is the real nature of the "I" inside him. When a person realizes the nature of this bliss, he has nothing more to do. All his activities stop.

When the "I" has been seen by the "I," that is, the real "I" has been realized by the egoistic "I," the duality between the seer and the seen disappears and now nothing further remains to be seen. When this stage is reached one realizes that the "I" pervades everywhere, and that nothing has existence except this all-pervading Self. In this stage the phenomenal world has no existence. Referring to this stage, Sri Ramdas has said, "Why are you asking about the cause, etc., of this world, which, in fact, has no existence and was never born?" This state is indescribable in words. All words, therefore, are meaningless, and silence is the only eloquence regarding it.

In order to attain this natural stage, saints have prescribed a certain practice. The Soham which is in the hearts of all saints who have obtained Self-realization helps the saints to realize the blissful nature of the Self. In this connection Sri Tukaram has said that the body is the real Pandharpur and the soul is the real Vithal.

I, too, told myself, my mind, to contemplate ceaselessly on Soham. The mind is pliable and turns towards that to which it is made to turn. When the mind, therefore, was made accustomed to the japa of Soham, the mind became one with Soham, and thus became merged in the Paramatman. Through the ceaseless contemplation of Soham, the mind became one with the Paramatman, and began to enjoy the everlasting and unchanging bliss which is the nature of the Self.

All actions that one does in this stage naturally become dedicated to God (Krishnarpana), and therefore are nishkama. There being absolutely no egotism, the idea that "I am doing the actions" is altogether absent, and therefore the karma becomes nishkama, and the apparent doer is all the while immersed in his natural bliss, and is thus absolutely detached, although leading a worldly life.

I have therefore to request you all to carry on the practice of japa continuously. Do not care to see whether your actions are sakama or nishkama; only take care to see that your attention is continuously directed to the japa. It does not in the least matter if you do not have recourse to any other sadhana. You are sure to be successful in the end.

Lord Krishna has said in the Gita that the mind, which by nature is fickle and hence difficult to be controlled, can be brought under control by constant practice (abhyasa). Thus, practice is the most important means of controlling the mind. Thus we become our own guru. "The guru should turn away our mind from the various vices to which we are addicted. Everything is in the hands of a guru. If he means it, he alone will be able to develop good tendencies in my mind." Such thoughts are weak and misleading and would be of no use to anyone. The Gita says, "We alone are our friend and we alone are our enemy."

If we carry on the japa with firm faith, we clearly realize after some time the power of the mantra. If we train our mind to entertain only good thoughts, not only are we ourselves benefitted, but our conduct produces good effects upon others also. This light of love in the form of Soham inside us sheds its luster on our whole life and makes it full of happiness. Its beneficial influence is also felt by the whole external atmosphere around us. The first thing required is firm faith without any doubts and misgivings, and the second is the continuous practice of the mantra japa.

If therefore you continue the practice steadily, the tendency of the mind towards good thoughts and actions will be more and more increased, and owing to the ceaseless contemplation of Soham there will gradually be the realization of your own inherent blissful nature, and the mind will be enjoying complete peace and happiness.

Brothers and sisters, if you carry on the practice of japa with full faith, and ultimately realize your oneness with Soham you, too, will become full of bliss like myself.

Instead of wasting valuable time, you should utilize it in the contemplation of Soham. While carrying on the practice, you should try to drive away from your mind doubts and misgivings which assail it, and try to concentrate on Soham and to become one with it. I say from my own experience that if you do so, your efforts will surely be crowned with success.

Pleasure and pain come out of the Avyakta. That is, their source lies hidden in the Supreme Being, which has no form and which is beyond comprehension. To say that the Avyakta can be seen is meaningless. Then how can the experience of it be described in words?

Pay, therefore, no heed to the pains and pleasures which befall you, but carry on the practice of Soham with a heart full of faith and determination. The manifest (Vyakta) and the unmanifest (Avyakta) are not really different from each other. The manifest is nothing but the unmanifest assuming form, and has the unmanifest as its basis. Persons who have attained Self-realization will tell you that what we call karma is nothing but the manifestation of the unmanifest.

The real use of shastric treatises is to train and prepare the mind and the intellect in such a manner that they can grasp the ultimate truth. The discourses of pundits well-versed in shastras may be very interesting to hear, but they will be of no use in getting the real experience and the everlasting peace which dwells in Soham. All sense of past, present and future is absolutely absent in that stage. That is the Avyakta. There is no past and present in it. It only exists. As to the Sun there is no night and day, similarly, there is no past and present in the Avyakta.

Paramartha (spirituality) is a subject regarding which various misconceptions hold full sway in our present-day society. Sri Ramdas has said: "There is a bazaar of shastras, various gods and deities are crowding in it, and people are performing various religious ceremonies for securing the fulfillment of their desires. Various tenets and opinions clash with each other. Everybody thinks his own view to be correct, and anybody else's wrong. There is no agreement anywhere, and all are contradicting each other." Under these circumstances, how to find out the truth is a very difficult question. Sri Tukaram says: "There are so many gods. Where should I place my faith?"

No doubt this is all true. But it must be remembered that Paramartha is a thing which is to be achieved by one's own efforts. There is a very easy method which should be followed by someone. He should remain quietly where he is, and at once begin the japa of Soham. He should repeat the japa with a pure mind, and should have firm faith that the Soham japa will fulfill all his wishes. The Soham mantra is the real savior. If it is repeated with intense faith, accompanied with a sense of detachment from all worldly objects, it will itself make him understand what is true and what is false. Our salvation really lies in our own hands. I therefore advise my mind to always get immersed in the contemplation of Soham, and thus to free itself from the snares of all such doubts.

Some persons do not understand the difference between meditation (dhyana), and concentration (ekagrata). It is a common idea with aspirants that as soon as they begin the mantra Soham their mind should become concentrated and they should enter into the state of samadhi. It is a laudable wish, no doubt, but it is out of place at the time. Because when the aspirant is told to meditate upon Soham, he is not told to get concentrated at once. He is told to repeat the japa of Soham in order that he may be able to meditate properly.

The main idea in meditation is that while the japa is going on there should not be the flow of other thoughts disturbing the repetition of the mantra. The experience is, of course, only temporary because our mind is naturally fickle. It is very difficult for it to concentrate itself upon one idea.

In the case of some aspirants, however, owing to some practice done in the previous life they get concentrated as soon as they begin meditation. They also see some visions. But this only shows that they must have practiced to some extent in their previous life. They therefore get all those experiences almost at once. But this does not mean that they have, owing to this, got everything which is to be obtained. They too must not stop there, but carry on further practice until they reach the final goal of human life.

To find out the "I," a person must have firm, unswerving faith. Once he obtains this, he will be able to see clearly the path before him. This is known as Anugraha. When this Anugraha is obtained, he must carry on the japa of the mantra Soham, which is the answer to the question, "Who am I?" The meaning of the mantra is: "I am He," "I am God." Keeping this in mind, the sadhaka must carry on the japa with firm faith.

The continuous repetition and meditation of this mantra, Soham, is known as abhyasa (practice). This japa will not interfere with any of your worldly duties. As the contemplation proceeds, the broom of Soham will sweep off the dirt of the innumerable desires entertained through the course of previous lives from the heart, and the heart will then become pure. Owing to this, a sense of detachment will grow and the mind will be entirely free from desires. As soon as you reach this stage, you will be immersed in the bliss of the Self, and then there will be no further necessity of carrying on the search for the "I."

The aim of all yogas is the realization of the Godhead. The state is known by various names such as Sayujyata, Soham, Aham Brahmasmi, or Sakshatkar. To reach this goal, firm faith, persevering effort, complete devotedness, concentration and a capacity to persevere are necessary. If a sadhaka carries on practice in this manner, he is sure to reach the goal of Self-realization sooner or later, according to the merit acquired by him in previous lives. If a sadhaka does not carry on the practice for a sufficiently long time with firm faith, but leaves it in the middle, being tired of waiting, he will never attain Self-realization.

The sadhaka alone, who has gained this aptitude for spiritual knowledge in his previous life, will develop a liking for this practice leading to oneness with Brahman, and he alone will ultimately enjoy everlasting bliss. All dross is sure to be swept away from the heart of such a sadhaka by the constant japa of Soham. If the seed of Soham is sown in such a field, it is sure to sprout into a beautiful tree which will be laden with the fruit of the bliss of Self-realization. Such sadhakas will be enjoying unchanging bliss and will very easily cross the river of worldly existence. When a sadhaka reaches this stage he can very easily control his mind, intellect and ahamkar. The power generated by the constant repetition of the Soham mantra is sure to lead to the complete liberation of the sadhaka.

Let us consider the subject of the Unmanifested (Avyakta). We have to designate all things by some word. This necessity of using some word to designate things is felt by all, whether saints, learned persons or ignorant people. When a child is born, it does not say that it should be called by a particular name such as Govinda or Gopal; but people give it some name. The same is the case with the Unmanifested. A child was born from the Unmanifested and the saints called it Maya. From time immemorial saints have come out of the Unmanifested, assuming a saguna form and having bodies–embodiments of light–in order to teach human beings and to spread spiritual knowledge in the world.

Every human being is sent into this world for the purpose of enjoying the bliss of the Self, while doing worldly actions in a detached spirit, and of realizing the Godhead. We must not get entangled in the nets of sex and money [lust and greed: materialism]. Thus, our ahamkar will be sattwic and not tamasic. It is the tamasic ahamkar that makes the world so full of misery. If we want to make our whole worldly life full of bliss, we must meditate on the Self through the mantra of Soham.

Such has been my own experience and I feel that this body is not mine. I have reached this stage entirely through meditating on Soham. I cannot say that I have attained this stage through my own efforts. This Soham which has come out of the Avyakta (the Unmanifested) has brought the shakti (power) of the Avyakta with it, and owing to this shakti everything of mine has become Krishnarpana (one with the Godhead). Hence, Maya does not trouble me. I have become one with Soham and I have realized my Self by meditating on it. I am enjoying unchanging bliss.

Every religion has got its own saints and prophets. If a person of whatever religion has firm faith and meditates on the Self, he is sure to go beyond pleasure and pain and to attain everlasting bliss. The mantra Soham is the sole savior. I am absolutely sure of this, not merely intellectually but through self-experience. This does not mean that I have become a saint or that I deserve to take my seat along with the great saints. I only say that all saints have resorted to this very mantra, and when their thoughts become entirely merged in the Supreme Self they become one with Brahman and shine forth in this world. I have not reached that stage as yet, but I am sure that through their grace and through meditation on Soham I am enjoying the same bliss which they enjoy. I have not as yet arrived at the stage of such great saints as Jnaneshwar, Tukaram, or Ramdas. But I am following in their footsteps and taking draughts of the supreme bliss. These saints have boldly declared in their imperishable words that they have been saved by Soham, and that others will also be saved by the same mantra. It is they who handed over to me the mantra Soham which was hidden in the Avyakta in the deep recesses of my own soul. This treasure was with me but I had forgotten the place where it was hidden. The saints pointed out to me that place and from that time I have been continuously contemplating on the Self. Future saints also will preach the same principle.

I am telling others to repeat Soham not on my own initiative, but the saints are speaking with my mouth. This Soham which has come out of the Avyakta is ever present in the hearts of men. Saints become one with this Soham which is in their own hearts and then the Soham merges itself again into the Avyakta.

I therefore think that Soham is the real Karma [action leading to liberation], it is the "I" and the saints have made me realize this "I." This Soham is the real secret. It is God, it is Karma, that makes us realize this through their grace. Through continuous practice and meditation on the Self a person attains a stage in which actions become automatic. Such actions may be called sakama or nishkama. Just as saguna and nirguna are one, similarly in that stage sakama and nishkama are one. He does not look to the result and is indifferent whether the actions result in loss or gain. He is ready to endure both. He is sure that the body, this earthly tenement, is not his own. Hence he does not not care whether pleasure or pain is the result of that action.

I therefore say that people should pay careful attention to what I have said above and keep firm faith in the mantra Soham. This faith should be such as the child has in its mother. Just as the child never has any doubt that she is its mother and that she will fulfill all its desires, similarly they should have firm faith in the sadguru who is none other than Soham, and have not the least doubt that this mother Soham will deliver them from all troubles and difficulties.

My dear brothers and sisters, devote all your energies to acquire this love which is pervading the whole world but of which we are not conscious. By the japa of Soham you will establish this love in your hearts and become blessed. This Soham japa is like an ocean which is full of unlimited bliss.

The repetition of Soham may be sakama, or nishkama. As Soham is based on the workings of nature, its japa, though it may be carried on with the object of fulfilling earthly desires, will ultimately be united with the real Soham which is enshrined in the innermost core of our being, and thus bring into awakening the power of the Paramatman. Objects of earthly desires are not permanent. The joy which is felt in their attainment is evanescent. But the effect of even the sakama japa is not altogether lost. It retains its force and awakens the power of the Self.

An atheist might say, "I cannot understand all this. God and the Paramatman are all ideas and guesses. What have I to do with them?" Let us for the sake of argument admit that what he says is true, that these are all ideas. Now let him answer the following question: "You know that these are all ideas. Who is it that knows about these ideas and is conscious of their being mere ideas?" A person sometimes says, "I am ignorant." Let him consider who is the knower of his ignorance. A person sometimes says, "I do not want this, I do not want that." Even though he might say that he does not want anything, still the "I" would always remain. This "I" is Soham, and eternal peace is its nature. A person might say that he does not want all this bother about God, dhyana, devotion, faith and concentration. All right; but let him say whether he wants peace, calmness and happiness or not. Even if he thinks that these ideas about God, etc., are false and illusory, still he must admit that there is somebody inside him who thinks them false and illusory. This knower inside us is the Self and that Self is Soham.

As long as the breath goes on, life goes on, and the activities of the body go on. The saints have explained the meaning of the incoming and outgoing breath, and Soham is the sound which is produced by the incoming and outgoing breath. This Soham sound is ceaselessly being repeated in our body whether we are conscious of it or not. If we become conscious of this internal Soham, we shall experience peace of mind. If we fully understand this Soham, we shall attain complete bliss, which is the real nature of Soham, and become one with it.

Aspirants should not become despondent and abandon the practice through a sense of frustration if they find that their efforts are not crowned with success in a short time. They are sure to realize the real power of Soham after some days if they carry on the practice continuously, with great intensity. There is absolutely no doubt about this. I say this from my own experience. The aspirant should have the firm determination that he will carry on the practice of Soham intensely in the future, although he might have failed to do so in the past.

What is necessary is that we must devote our attention to this Soham. The more your attention is directed towards Soham the greater will be the change in your mind and thoughts.

If you realize that Soham is the real nature of "I" in the body–and that this Soham is ceaselessly going on, you will thoroughly understand that "I" is the Soham inside. The speaker, doer, the action itself and in fact everything will be one with Soham. I am at present experiencing to some extent the bliss of such a state, and anyone else who will do as I have done will attain similar bliss. As long as the "I" dwells in this body, we must get into the habit of repeating Soham. Ceaseless repetition will make the trend of all thoughts full of Soham.

This Soham is ever present in every being in the form of his own Self. This Soham is continuously going on, it never stops. This Soham which is seen in all animate and inanimate things is my Jani Janardan (God present in all human beings), and wherever I use the word "Jani Janardan," I mean by it this Soham, present in all.

While carrying on the contemplation of Soham, an aspirant should always be carefully observing whether his worldly desires are gradually dropping off. The gradual dropping of worldly desires, and the capability to perform worldly actions solely from a sense of duty and not with a view to achieve some object, are sure signs of spiritual progress. If an aspirant makes it a point to see that his attention is continuously fixed on Soham, that his mind is growing more and more detached, and that he is continuously carrying on the practice with firm faith, I am sure that he will certainly reach the goal. Whether a person is a mumukshu (aspirant), sadhaka, or a siddha (a person who has obtained siddhi or power), if all his desires have completely disappeared and he has attained a complete sense of detachment, then he attains a stage in which God is always with him wherever he is.

These words are the expressions of my internal intuition. The expressions used may not be polished and beautiful, but I humbly request that on that account people should not be indifferent to what I say. I have first practiced what I preach. Hence people should also translate these precepts into practice, and then see whether they are true or not. I therefore urge all people, whether ignorant or learned, mumukshus or sadhakas, to carry on the japa of Soham with their attention continuously directed towards it.

It is the nature of mind to carry on the continuous play of thoughts. The mind is always fickle and moving from one idea to another, and when the mind concentrates upon something it is called chitta. A sadhaka, therefore, should concentrate upon Soham and thus turn his mind into chitta. If he continues this practice for some time, his mind will gradually gain in calmness and ultimately will become one with Soham and with the inherent, everlasting bliss which is the real nature of Soham, and thus his chitta will become chit (consciousness). Once this stage is attained, that person will experience unlimited joy. His peace of mind is never disturbed, and he is always immersed in everlasting and unchanging bliss. He attains the goal, and the real purpose of human life is fulfilled.

A person should should with firm determination follow the path of truth and keep firm faith in the final goal by following that path. He should not allow any scope to doubts regarding the length of time which will be required to attain the goal. He should firmly believe that sooner or later he will certainly attain the state of everlasting bliss, and fearlessly carry on the practice. While carrying on the practice, he should try to drive away from his mind doubts and misgivings which assail it, and try to concentrate on Soham and to become one with it. I say from my own experience that if you do so, your efforts will surely be crowned with success.

God has innumerable names, and people are calling out His various names according to their individual liking. But one must remember that the Siddha Name of Soham alone will be useful in easily crossing this ocean of worldly existence and ending the cycle of births and deaths. This Siddha Nama is a power; it is like a mother to the universe, and it is the entity that is calling itself "I" in the body. It is a flame of love.

If you repeat the Soham mantra in your mind, by continuous practice your mind gets concentrated upon it. The concentration may be called dhyana. If this force is uninterruptedly stored up in your heart, be sure that you have obtained the goal of human life.

[An aspirant] should carry on the japa of the saving mantra Soham. He will thereby surely succeed in gradually obtaining peace of mind. Sometimes doubts and fears will assail him. He should not mind them, but carry on the practice with greater and greater intensity. If this is carried on till the time of death, he will find that at the time of death his mind is not centered in worldly matters. He will still carry on the japa, and then at the time of death his mind will be engrossed in the contemplation of Soham.

I have explained this point as clearly as I could. Only you must have the lighted torch of Soham with you, and must try to obtain peace in its light. I have said what I know from my own experience. Everybody should try to realize it by his own experience. He must only remember that love is the soul, and the soul is love. Soham is the soul, and the soul is love. Soham is the soul, and there is everlasting peace in the soul. That itself is the Avyakta, the Unmanifested, in which everything lives, moves and has its being. Try to obtain everlasting peace by the mantra of Soham.

God sends real saints into this world with the mission to save sincere aspirants and devotees of sattwic disposition. False saints, however, deceive and mislead other people–ignorant as well as educated. Real aspirants should not be led away by miracles performed through the force of siddhis, because as Sri Krishna has said, "All actions are useless without the real knowledge of the Atman."

People should quietly and persistently carry on the japa of Soham on their own initiative, instead of running after every saint, true or false, whom they happen to hear about. In this way they will not be deceived, or misled.

The world is like a big jail, and people are born into it to serve out their sentences. Have therefore a wholesome fear of this jail, and try to purge away your sins and evil desires by the japa and contemplation of

Soham. You need not do anything else for the purpose of your deliverance. Keep firm control over your mind, and then you will easily get control over your life. Pay, therefore, no heed to the pains and pleasures which befall you, but carry on the practice of Soham with a heart full of faith and determination.

Samadhi is of two kinds. A mumukshu who had made some preparation of mind in his previous life, resorts to pranayama and the various practices of hatha yoga, gets internal vision, and his mind is then merged in the light which is seen internally. This is one kind of samadhi. There are others who are quite unconscious of their body. They see no visions, so that they are not conscious of anything either outside or inside. They are always merged in the Supreme Being, and entirely unconscious of their surroundings. This is the second kind of samadhi. Both of these kinds of saints are of very little use to the world.

There are, however, other saints like Sri Jnaneshwar, Tukaram, or Eknath who, while conscious of this world and its implications, are always enjoying the bliss of the Self. They are in what is known as sahajawastha. They see unity in diversity, deal with worldly matters in a worldly way, and still inwardly are immersed in the bliss of Self-realization. Such saints alone are useful to the world, and they alone can lead others to the supreme goal by a method which people can easily follow.

Hence I say that everyone should repeat Soham. It surely and certainly leads to the knowledge of the Self, and the attainment of everlasting peace One's actions then in the worldly life are automatically done, and one is absolutely detached from them, just as a lotus leaf is from water.

"It must be remembered that Paramartha [Self-realization—the highest goal of human life] is a thing which is to be achieved by one's own efforts. If anyone, therefore, has a sincere desire to obtain it, there is a very easy method which should be followed by him. He should remain quietly where he is, and at once begin the japa of Soham. He should repeat the japa with a pure mind, and should have firm faith that the Soham japa will fulfill all his wishes. Once he gets this firm faith, he will come to know the Soham mantra is the real savior. If it is repeated with intense faith, accompanied with a sense of detachment from all worldly objects, it will itself make him understand what is true and what is false. There will then be no occasion to find fault with the reputed saints, or to fall into the clutches of false saints. Our salvation really lies in our own hands. I therefore advise my mind to always get immersed in the contemplation of Soham, and thus to free itself from the snares of all such doubts."

Through faith in Soham external worship has been left behind. The soul has been realized in the form of Soham. Through the sound of Soham the guru has been beheld—that guru who saves people by the principle of Soham.

The final goal of Soham is Self-realization.

I say that a sadhaka comes to realize the power of the soul, and ultimately to grasp that there is one everlasting and all-pervading Being which is present in everything, and which is the only thing that exists. He then becomes one with Soham. He obtains everything which is to be obtained, to him nothing remains unattained, all his doubts are solved, and he is immersed in everlasting bliss. He becomes one with Brahman, and never falls from this stage.

D. D. Bhave, a disciple of Sri Ganajana Maharaj

On 10-12-37, Sri Gajanana Maharaj conferred his grace upon me by giving me the mantra Soham.

One day when I had been to Maharaj in the evening as usual for his darshan, Maharaj said that one must worship Shakti. Then one gets all the siddhis (powers) of the yoga path. Only care must be taken of not utilizing those powers for oneself. There must not be a single thing in the yoga path which one does not understand.

Next day when I sat for meditation early in the morning, the goddess having six arms, whom I had once seen before, stood before me and told me to make japa of the stotra beginning "Namo Devyai, Mahadevyai…." [This is a hymn to the Goddess, part of the Sri Durga Saptasati, also known as the Chandi.] She said that by that japa one can acquire the whole power of the universe in oneself, and saying which she disappeared. After I had repeated the japa for about a week or fortnight, the goddess again appeared before me and said, "I have not got six arms, I have only two. But I showed six arms to you as I had to put down your six enemies (the six passions) and for that purpose I had equipped myself with six arms. But now there is no necessity for me to put down your six enemies as they are being slowly conquered by you without effort by the japa of the mantra Soham. I have originally only two arms and one should meditate upon me in that form because my form of two arms represent dwaita (duality) and through this dwaita you have to go into adwaita (oneness)."

[In Hindu theology, the Six Passions, Arishadvarga, are the six enemies of the mind, which are: kama (lust), krodha (anger), lobha (greed), moha (delusive, often emotional, attachment or temptation), mada (pride), and matsarya (jealousy): the negative characteristics of which prevent man from attaining moksha or salvation.

The two syllables of Soham are the two "arms" of the devi which take the sadhaka from duality to non-duality.]

I narrated this incident to Sri Gajanana Maharaj. He said "You have acquired so much power that the goddess has of her own accord given you her grace although you had not asked or begged for it. Among all these different stages of the powers of Shakti, the power of Soham is the most exalted."

V. K. Mahegaonkar, a disciple of Sri Gajanana Maharaj

Be attentive and understand the six centers (or plexuses) in which the Sudarshana Chakra. is revolving twenty-one thousand and six hundred times. You should take the Sudarshana Chakra of Soham in your hand and conquer the six enemies (the six passions). ...and the Paramatman will bless you with His darshan.

You should at once begin to tread the path of Soham and Sushumna. This is the path of real devotion, which everyone who is born as a human being should follow.

Concentrate your mind. If you steadfastly stick to the mantra Soham, you will yourself be one with the Paramatman.... Soham tells you how to acquire the nirguna state. ...Soham shows that everything is Brahman.

Soham is the Shabda Brahman (Brahman manifested in the form of sound). It itself is the Paramatman, It Itself is the Megha-Shyam (God). It is nothing but the "I" pervading everywhere.

The real greatness of Pandharpur [the famous Vithoba (or Vithala) Temple of Lord Krishna] resides in Soham.

The four Vedas are nothing but Soham, which is the expression of Brahman in words. Soham is the pure Sudarshana, which removes all distinctions and gives the experience of Unity in diversity.

Soham is the Nirguna Brahman, Soham is the Saguna Brahman.

If a person obtains Soham samadhi, he gets complete Brahmajnana. Death itself bows before it. It is the original seed of Shunya (void). God Brahma and God Vishnu worship really this Deity. You should meditate upon this Soham Brahman. Thereby you will be one with it and will attain perfection.

Soham gives Salvation (Mukti). Soham is the Brahman described in Maha Bharata and the Bhagawata. Soham gives Brahmajnana and the main teaching of the Gita is nothing but Soham.

Soham is Punya (Virtue).... When the mind becomes Unmana (loses consciousness) in the contemplation of Soham, the Unmani state is reached. Shiva, Vishnu and Brahma have obtained the samadhi state through this very meditation. All troubles cease when this stage is attained. So this Soham is the secret test of all.

By the contemplation of Soham attachment to sensual objects is destroyed, the effect of karma (actions) is nullified, the chain of births and deaths is cut off and a person becomes immortal.

Soham is the Atma–tattwa (the principle of the Self). To obtain realization of this Soham, great merits accumulated in many lives are required. Rishis, Munis, Siddhas, Sri Dattatreya, Gorakshanath and others always contemplated upon this Soham.

The nine Nathas contemplated upon this Soham and transmitted their knowledge to the eighty-four Siddhas.

Soham is the seed which later on sprouts into the tree of samadhi, oneness with, and the realization of, God. All the Siddhas meditate upon this, which is obtained only through great merit. They become holy owing to this and obtain final absolution.

The ajapa japa is automatically going on in the breath (So in taking the breath in, and Ham in giving out). When one repeats this japa of

Soham consciously then it is called ajapa japa. If one fixes his attention on the sound produced by the breath, the three nadis—Ida, Sushumna, and Pingala—become free in their actions.

The yogi as it were plays a game in the Turiya in the company of the three Nadis, Ida, Pingala, and Sushumna, to the accompaniment of the sound of Soham.

The yogi hears the sound of Soham and gets merged in it.

The Soham seed was first obtained in its Vaikhari Speech (the outward expression); it was sown in the field on the tableland of the Para. The Pashyanti speech gives birth to Jnana (knowledge) and a bumper crop was reaped in the Madhyama.

The six Chakras (centers) can be gone through by means of the Soham sound. When the six centers are thus gone through, great merit is acquired by the sadhaka and through that merit the realization of Brahman is accomplished.

The practice should be continuously carried on keeping the attention fixed on Soham. Complete and unchangeable bliss then envelopes the sadhaka quite naturally of its own accord.

Gorakhnath

Through the ajapa japa [Soham] the mind rids itself of restless thoughts (*Gorakhbodha* 102).

The gayatri called ajapa [Soham] is the giver of liberation to yogis; simply with the resolve [sankalpa] to recite this [Soham] is he freed from all demerit (*Goraksha Sataka* 44).

Knowledge like this, repetition [japa] like this, insight like this neither was nor shall be (*Goraksha Sataka* 45).

The gayatri [Soham] is sprung from Kundalini and supports the prana. Knowledge of the prana is the great knowledge. Who knows this is an adept (*Goraksha Sataka* 46).

Self-knowledge is the light [of the mantra] Soham. [It belongs to] neither earth nor sky nor sea (*Gorakh Vani* 18:5).

Practice mental recitation with such an intensity that the mantra of "Soham," "Soham" is pronounced mentally, produced without your doing so out loud. Sit firmly in the asana and meditate. Contemplate day and night on the Divine.... then the divine Sound is perceived automatically, the Sun rises in the Sushumna, and the current of consciousness comes to dwell in the Sahasrara lotus and the bhramargufa [brahmarandhra] is illuminated with the radiance of the Self. (*Unfortunately I have lost track of the source of this. I only know that it is the sixth verse of one of his writings.*)

Janabai

One whose intellect is centered in equanimity and who has attained inner knowledge through the japa of Soham, recognizes God [Hari] is his inner heart.

Jnaneshwar

Soham japa or Soham awareness is the state of total peace, of complete rest.

Contact between the senses and their objects of perception is ended through Soham japa.

When one experiences or becomes aware of Soham, the body consciousness is dissolved and the senses turn inward, away from their objects.

Just as light pervades everywhere, from the sun to its reflection in water, the Soham consciousness extends from the embodied Self to the Supreme Self. When man becomes fully immersed in the Soham vision, he, along with it, spontaneously merges with the Supreme Being.

As soon as I approached the mantra Soham, I entered the turiya state.

Jnaneshwar Bharati

The Soham mantra is a natural mantra because it is already part of your nature. *So* is the sound of inhalation, and is remembered in the mind along with the inhalation. *Ham* is the sound of exhalation, and is remembered in the mind along with the exhalation.

The Soham mantra has been called the universal mantra because of the fact that its vibration is already a part of the breath, and everybody breathes. (*Soham Mantra Meditation*)

Attention is required: There is one skill that is of utmost importance to meditation, and that is training the attention. It means developing a steady, unbroken relationship with the Soham of the breath, regardless of the other activities of the mind. It is not about repressing thoughts, but is more like listening intently to the whisper of a beloved friend in a crowded room. It is your conviction to attention that makes the voice clear, not the elimination of the other people. So too, the thoughts of the mind are allowed their life, as you listen passionately to the Soham, Soham of the breath ebbing and flowing through the gross and subtle bodies, and the mind.

Kabir

You should take a dip in the Manasarovar [of the Divine Absolute] and perform the japa of Soham. The japa of Soham is beyond the limits of sins or sacred virtues.

His password is Soham. [Soham is the password which admits us into liberation, into the Being of Brahman.] (Quoted in *The Impact of Sufism in India*.)

The Supra-Causal Realm (Bhanwar Gupha) is vibrating with Soham.

There is a land where no doubt nor sorrow have rule: where the
    terror of Death is no more.
There the woods of spring are a-bloom, and the fragrant scent
    "Soham" is borne on the wind:
There the bee of the heart is deeply immersed, and desires no
    other joy.

If you want to know the Eternal, you will not find him in the Vedas, the shastras or in the Koran, in the temples or in the mosques. Penance, pilgrimage, breath-control, or living on nothing but neem leaves, will not lead you to him. You can find him only in your breath. [*So* when inhaling, and *Ham* when exhaling.]

Lalleshwari (Lalla Yogeshwari)

One of the greatest saints of Kashmir, Lalleshwari (Lad Ded) lived and wrote her inspired poetry in the fourteenth century.

The anahata sound… mounts the horse of the breath and rides in and out in the form of Soham. (*Lalleshwari*, Section 71)

Everything is contained in Soham. (*Lalleshwari*, Section 73)

Become the close companion of the inhalation and exhalation. By combining Soham with them, you can sail across [samsara]. (*Lalleshwari*, Section 74)

Day in and day out pursue Soham in your breath. Then you will become what you really are–the perfect and supreme light. (*Lalleshwari*, Section 75)

If you want to christen your body, name it after the formless God. Repeat that Name and remember it: Soham–I am That.... Your I-ness will flee from you, and only Shiva will remain. (*Lalleshwari*, Section 78)

As long as I failed to see my Self, I could not see the ocean even though I was drowning. When I held aloft the torch of Soham, I saw that I was the ocean itself. O Lalli! Do not let the light of Soham be extinguished, not even for a moment. (*Lalleshwari*, Section 83)

Everything has become new for me. My mind is new, the moon is new, the sun is new. The whole world appears fresh and new as if rinsed with water. Since I washed my mind and body with the soap of Soham, I have become like new. I am transformed. Now Lalli has become the great Shakti which leaps with bliss. (*Lalleshwari*, Section 103)

It is easy to compose scriptures, but very difficult to follow them. The scriptural methods for seeking the Truth are complex and subtle. I forgot the scriptures in my practice of Soham. I forgot the texts in my yogic techniques. Still, I attained perfection, the bliss of Consciousness. O Lalli! Now the goal of life is fulfilled. (*Lalleshwari*, Section 131)

The mantra Soham, "I am That," consists of So, "That," and Aham, "I." I renounced Aham in the form of my pride and expanded to become perfect. I expanded into Shiva and became Shiva. (*Lalleshwari*, Section 149)

I read and study only one word, and that word is Soham. When I seized that word I caught Lord Shiva himself. In the fire of that word all my dross was burned to ashes, and I became pure gold. (*Lalleshwari*, Section 152)

Swami Maharaj of Akalkot (Swāmi Samarth Mahāraj; Akkalkot Swami)

The person who repeats 'Soham Soham' [in time with the breath] accomplishes the liberation from personal existence and gets absorbed in the divine substance, with the realization that he is the Self.

Swami Muktananda Paramahansa

Perhaps the best-known twentieth-century teacher of the Nath Yogi tradition was Paramhansa (Bhagavan) Nityananda of Ganeshpuri. His most renowned disciple was Swami Muktananda who came several times to America on his world tours, and founded many yoga centers.

Soham is the gateway to meditation. (*From the Finite to the Infinite*, p. 179).

Soham is the highest meditation. (*From the Finite to the Infinite*, p. 120).

Concentrate on the mantra, and the mantra will take you to the formless One. As you pursue Soham more and more, it will take you to the formless One. As you meditate continually, there comes a point when you forget what is outside and what is inside. You also forget yourself completely. It is at this point that you are meditating on the formless One (*From the Finite to the Infinite*, p. 168).

Soham is a very well-respected mantra. Soham japa is called aja-pa-japa.... It is constantly repeating itself within you. If you become aware of it, it has the power to destroy all your sins. This is a fact. The

Soham mantra is ancient and without beginning (*From the Finite to the Infinite*, p. 189).

Keep repeating Soham, Soham. Give up "I" and take up Soham (*From the Finite to the Infinite*, p. 323).

You cannot serve others with ego; you can serve them only with the Soham awareness. Soham awareness means awareness of your identity with the inner Self.... If aham or ego goes, what remains is Soham. Soham means "I am That," and it can do infinite work (*From the Finite to the Infinite*, p. 348).

When the ego vanishes and Soham fills the heart, then there is pure bliss (*Satsang With Baba*, Vol. 2, p. 229).

The repetition of Soham is most effective. Soham is usually repeated by those seekers who have already attained a very high state.

All mantras finally dissolve into ajapa-japa—into Soham (*Satsang With Baba*, Vol. 3, p. 185).

Kabir says that the natural movement of Soham is this: the breath comes in with the sound *So*, and it goes out with the sound *Ham*.
Soham goes on within every creature spontaneously, and if one becomes aware of it one reaps sublime fruit. Concentration on Soham awakens the Kundalini instantly (*Satsang With Baba*, Vol. 4, p. 282).

For an intelligent, perceptive person, this mantra [Soham] is very effective. The aham or sense of self is not the artificial ego. It is the natural, pure ego, the self-sense without any false identification. The glory of this mantra is described in a commentary on the Guru Gita (*Satsang With Baba*, Vol. 4, p. 282).

Soham is a divine technique. Jnaneshwar says: "Soham japa or Soham awareness is the state of total peace, of complete rest." He adds, "Contact between the senses and their objects of perception is ended through Soham japa" (*Satsang With Baba*, Vol. 4, p. 281).

Describing the plight of the child in the womb as it goes through various phases of development according to the Garbha Upanishad, Muktananda says:

When the fetus in the womb is seven months old, the soul receives knowledge of its past and future. It knows who it has been and who it will be. When the movie of its lives passes before its mind, it becomes frightened and begins moving restlessly here and there.... Finally, the fetus becomes desperate and begins to call out to God for help.

Now God, the Self, is right there. He has been watching all of this, and when at last the soul starts crying out and taking refuge in Him, God bestows His grace upon it. He gives it instruction in Soham, which means "That am I."

As the fetus repeats the mantra, it begins to understand its identity with the supreme Principle. It becomes immersed in the Soham awareness, the awareness of its true nature, and becomes calm and serene. However, when nine months are over, the fetus is forcibly ejected from the mother's womb. The moment it comes out, it begins crying, making the sound "Kwanh, kwanh," or "Ko'ham, Ko'ham." It forgets God's instructions and the understanding it has attained. It forgets the awareness of Soham, and cries, "Ko'ham—who am I?" It begins to identify itself in different ways, saying, "I am this body," "I belong to a particular class," "I am a woman," "I am a man," "I am a sinner." It becomes established in this kind of understanding and lives its life accordingly (*I Am That*, pp. 34, 35).

Shaivism says that the contemplation of Soham is the contemplation of your own true nature. It is the knowledge of your own Self. Therefore, you should realize this japa in all your activities (*I Am That*, p. 40).

If ego can be replaced by Soham, there will be nothing left to renounce. (*Selected Essays*, p. 134).

Soham is everyone's own mantra (*Soham Japa, A Meditation Technique For Everyone*, p. 13).

Harmonize the repetition of mantra with the breathing as follows: With "So" take it in and with "ham" bring it out.... When one's mind is fixed on "So" with the incoming breath and on "ham" with the outgoing breath it is mantra-japa.... Your beauty, your energy, your duty, your religion, your Guru and guide; your study, worship and prayer–all lie in engaging yourself to the remembrance and repetition of "Soham," "Soham." This is my instruction, this is my precept. This is to be followed or practiced, and reflected upon devoutly. (*From a letter written on April 23, 1968*)

[The Guru Gita] speaks of a mantra in the sahasrara, at the crown of the head. Inside there is a triangle [trikuti] and there are two syllables, *So* and *Ham*, and the mantra Soham arises from there. Right in the center of this triangle the guru dwells. For this reason, you don't have to continue to search for a Guru. If you see that Guru, you will receive messages from him. If you experience this relationship between a Guru and a disciple, even for a moment, it is more than enough. (*From the Finite to the Infinite*, p. 307)

You should repeat Soham until you become completely absorbed in meditation.... Soham is the gateway to the kingdom of meditation. Keep repeating Soham as much as you can. (*From the Finite to the Infinite*, p. 168)

Soham is the final japa. It is meant for Siddhas, for free beings.... Soham is the most natural mantra. It is the true mantra. (*From the Finite to the Infinite*, p. 190)

Every part of your body reverberates with this mantra. Every blood cell reverberates with it. You don't always realize this, but when you meditate and become very quiet and look within, you experience that every blood cell contains the Soham mantra; it reverberates in this body. And not only in this body–it permeates the entire universe. (*From the Finite to the Infinite*, p. 192)

Make [the monkey mind] dance on the stage of Soham. For that, meditate and repeat the mantra. (*From the Finite to the Infinite*, p. 407)

Discard aham or ego, and grasp Soham. (*From the Finite to the Infinite*, p. 323)

The awareness of Soham, "I am That," is the best way of worshiping the Self. (*From the Finite to the Infinite*, p. 241)

Jnaneshwar Maharaj describes his own experience in this manner: He says that the seeker,… takes refuge in Soham and finds inner rest. Kabir says that Soham is the japa that goes on automatically, and if one is aware of it, one goes beyond sin and virtue. Kabir has written a large number of verses on this theme. Then, take the case of Vasuguptacharya, who was also a Siddha. He says it is by means of Soham that we explore our inner nature, that we become aware of the inner Self. Janabai, a Siddha yogini, writes in one of her poems that when one becomes aware of Soham within, one becomes aware of the inner Self, one recognizes Lord Hari within. (*Satsang With Baba*, Vol. 1, p. 200)

In fact, *So* and *Ham* comprise the entire universe in their scope. *So* is the supremely pure changeless Shiva, and *Ham* is the inner Self or Shakti… *So* is God and *Ham* is the inner soul. (*Satsang With Baba*, Vol. 1, p. 200)

It signifies a very high state when Soham arises within. That is the true vibration of the inner Self. (*Satsang With Baba*, Vol. 1, p. 281)

He who is repeating Soham with intense faith cannot be harmed by any power in this universe. (*Satsang With Baba*, Vol. 2, p. 102)

Man takes so much pride in his petty name, he subjects himself to so much suffering, he fights and he gets caught up in so much unpleasantness, in spite of the fact that by repeating Soham, the True Name, the Divine Name, he could attain the divine state.

Soham is not a sectarian mantra. There is nothing artificial or imaginary about it. It is self-begotten. It has arisen itself. It is the mantra for all renunciants, for all sadhus, for all holy beings. Soham is vibrating within by itself. It doesn't have to be artificially created. This mantra is going on in every one, but as long as we are outward turned we do not become aware of it. It is only during meditation, when we plunge into our own depths, that we become aware of Soham, which has always been going on within us. Therefore a poet-saint says, "Soham is ajapa-japa. Do japa of it. Then you will get beyond both sin and virtue."

Soham is enormously helpful for attaining perfection…, because when this mantra is repeated, Kundalini is awakened much more quickly than it would be in any other way. Kundalini begins to work with much greater force and experiences come far more easily.… He who becomes Soham while repeating Soham, becomes the Lord.… The highest state is gained.…

Soham is a symbol of the highest attainment. Soham is the final goal of man. Every being should grow into Soham awareness. (*Satsang With Baba*, Vol. 3, pp. 183, 184)

Soham is in fact the mantra of meditation. Soham is not the exclusive property of any particular sect or school of philosophy. It belongs to everyone because Soham is without beginning, it is self-existent. Every human being has the right to do Soham because Soham goes on by itself within everyone. Therefore, repeat Soham. You should continue to do Soham because Soham is ideally suited for meditation. The scriptures also say that within every creature the mantra Soham is going on by itself. In certain higher stages of meditation you will discover that what you are now repeating deliberately has always been going on within you involuntarily. You can continue to do Soham. (*Satsang With Baba*, Vol. 4, pp. 49, 50)

Soham is meant for one who is very highly evolved, who understands what truth is, one who is enlightened. (*Satsang With Baba*, Vol. 4, p. 280)

Soham japa is ajapa japa; that is, Soham japa takes place within spontaneously. There is nothing higher than this [Soham japa]. You should make yourself aware of this japa, and that will lead you to the supreme state. (*Satsang With Baba*, Vol. 4, p. 281)

Soham is called ajapa japa. You shouldn't try to force anything. Follow the natural movement of your breath. While inhaling repeat "So," while exhaling repeat "Ham." In the course of doing this you will attain spontaneous inner kumbhaka which is of great significance because during this kumbhaka the inner Shakti is unfolded completely. Vasuguptacharya says that through Soham one becomes aware of the true nature of one's Self. This ajapa japa is one of the greatest secrets of Siddha Yoga, the sahaja or spontaneous yoga. This pranayama combined with the repetition of these two syllables is extremely useful....

One saint says that through ajapa japa all sins and virtues fall away. Another says that ajapa japa draws liberation to one's own home. Hans Raj, a saint, composed about 250 couplets in Sanskrit while commenting on Shankaracharya's verse on Soham.... Great saints, such as the nine Naths, retired into solitude and in the end they concentrated on Soham. Through this they attained the highest realization.

Lord Shiva, while revealing the secret of mantra japa to His consort, says, "Only he gets the full benefit and reward of japa who regards his own Self to be Bhairava, who regards his own Self to be the Supreme Lord, who achieves the awareness of Soham, 'That am I.' Only to such a one do all realizations come." ...Lord Shiva says that the very moment one realizes that the Self is pure consciousness, that the Self is the highest consciousness (and this is what aham refers to), he attains the highest realization. (*Satsang With Baba*, Vol. 4, pp. 282, 283)

You do not hear that word which the saints have heard and spoken of: *Soham shabdachi thanim pahudat jhalom*–"I found rest in the word Soham." (*Play of Consciousness*, p. 9)

O Yogini Kundalini, you are the supreme deity of spiritual aspirants. O Guru, O abode of love, dynamic energy, You are the grace that came from Nityananda. You are the two-syllabled Soham, his gift to me. (*Play of Consciousness*, p. 28)

If aham, the individual ego, is destroyed and replaced by Soham, "I am That," what is left to renounce? (*Play of Consciousness*, p. 226)

Soham is the meditation mantra you gave, which stabilizes the flow of concentration.... I became peaceful, I became satisfied, I became Soham. (Praise of Nityananda in *Play of Consciousness*, p.22)

The pranayama of this [Siddha] path is the repetition of "So" on the incoming breath and "Ham" on the outgoing breath. (*Play of Consciousness*, p. 40)

Kabir wrote: "The ajapa japa, Soham, destroys all your sins and virtues." The Soham awareness is also described as the awareness, "I am the Absolute [aham Brahmasmi]," or "Thou art That [tat twam asi]." It is the understanding of your identity with the supreme Principle, and the understanding has the power to destroy all of your accumulated karmas and past impressions [samskaras]. Not only does it destroy the effects of millions of sins, it also cuts the bondage which arises from your good action. Most people want to eliminate the effects of their bad actions, not realizing that their virtues are just as binding as their sins. Your sins bind you with an iron chain and your virtues with a golden one. That is the only difference between them. If you want liberation, both sin and virtue must be wiped out, and that is what happens when you attain the awareness of Soham. This awareness puts an end to the cycle of birth and death, killing the notion of duality. (*I Am That*, p. 49)

This mantra [Soham] has the power to transform you completely. (*I Am That*, p. 54)

Instead of repeating "I am, I am, I am" all the time, why don't you repeat "Soham, Soham, Soham," which means "I am That," in other words, "I am God, I am He." (*Selected Essays*, p. 27)

The Siddhas residing in Siddhaloka repeat this spontaneous mantra [Soham] without stop, thereby remaining in the state of Siddhahood.

The true Siddha mantra, Soham, is unique because it is not man-made. ...the Siddha mantra is natural and was not composed by anyone.... The mantra of which I speak goes on spontaneously in all living creatures. In the beginning it was imparted by the Lord himself....

In Vedic literature, the fetus is said to receive knowledge of the past and future in the seventh month. It remembers the sufferings of its previous lives and learns of the suffering to come. It becomes restless and begins to kick and move about, but wherever it moves, the heat and secretions of the surrounding internal organs press against it, causing it to feel pain. A description of these effects is found in the Garbhopanishad which is part of the Vedas. The supreme Lord takes pity on the child's suffering.... From his seat in the heart, he instructs the child, "Why do you move about unnecessarily? Sit peacefully in one place, remember God and repeat the mantra Soham, Soham, Soham." For all of us, therefore, the supreme Lord himself was the Guru in the beginning. Many learned people don't know this simple truth though they talk about mantras and initiation. Once I met a scholarly master who said, "You tell me that God is your Guru. But when did he initiate you, and when did you receive a mantra from him?" I told him to read the Garbhopanishad, and he would know what I meant. After that he wrote me a long letter saying that in all of India no one else had given him a proper explanation of this passage.

God initiated us with the Soham mantra when we were in the uterus of our mother. At the end of the ninth month, a vital air called the prabhanjana vayu (the same vital air which consumes the entire universe in the process of dissolution) projects us out into the world. The shock of this experience is so great that as soon as we emerge we start crying "ko'ham, ko'ham, ko'ham: Who am I? Who am I?" forgetting the underlying mantra we learned in the womb. Later, if we meet a mantra seer, he reminds us of what the primal Guru had taught us before birth.

According to the Upanishads, when we inhale, the first part of the mantra, So, is pronounced, and when we exhale, the second part, Ham, is pronounced.... The mantra also speaks its own natural language. The letter So denotes the supreme Lord, source of all religions and philosophies; the exhaled Ham denotes the "I," thereby establishing an identity between the supreme Self and the individual soul.

The Soham mantra has nothing to do with religions, castes, colors, or creeds. It belongs neither to the Hindu nor to the Christian.... The Lord whose body is the universe appears in the form of sound. By indwelling with us, he gives us different kinds of experience through his subtle mantra.

…Soham is so powerful that it awakens the inner Kundalini immediately…. Therefore, in all your activities, all the time, repeat the mantra Soham, Soham, Soham. Try it…. To experience the Self constantly, use the mantra Soham…. Your entire being is made up of Soham. By remembering the mantra Soham without stop, your very body will be converted into Soham. (*Selected Essays*, p. 98-101)

Kabir, the great poet, says, "The Guru awakened me within by imparting just one word." (*Selected Essays*, p. 91)

Ajapa-japa is realized by the conscious repetition of Soham. With ajapa-japa there is effortless pranayama and effortless meditation. The mantra is the easy and triumphant way of Siddhas. It is the ladder to be climbed to liberation, the boat that sails across samsara. It leads, finally, to sahaja samadhi (the natural state). (*Soham Japa, A Meditation Technique For Everyone*, p. 12)

A man is his mind. He becomes exactly what his mind dwells on. Japa of Soham is a mysterious process by means of which a worthy seeker can swiftly experience his identity with the Self. (*Soham Japa, A Meditation Technique For Everyone*, p. 14)

Namdev

The mind will acquire the nature of God [Rama] only when the seeker constantly practices "Soham… Soham."

Nisargadatta Maharaj

So'ham is endless, limitless, measureless, and is the messenger of Truth, who is Self-evident. The message and the messenger are not separate in him. This messenger is himself the joy that is the enjoyment of the endless. (From his preface to *Master of Self-Realization: An Ultimate Understanding*).

Sri Ramana Maharshi

Someone asked Bhagavan Sri Ramana Maharshi: "What is the purport of the teaching that one should meditate, through the 'I am That' thought, on the truth that one is not different from the self-luminous Reality that shines like a flame?"

Bhagavan replied: "The purport of teaching that one should meditate with the 'I am That' thought is this: *sah-aham*: So'ham; *sah* the supreme Self, *aham* the Self that is manifest as 'I.' If one meditates for a long time, without disturbance, on the Self ceaselessly, with the 'So'ham–I am That' thought which is the technique of reflection on the Self, the darkness of ignorance which is in the heart and all the impediments which are but the effects of ignorance will be removed, and the plenary wisdom will be gained…. The body is the temple; the jiva is God (Shiva). If one worships him with the 'So'ham–I am That' thought, one will gain release" (*Collected Works* [Section] 29).

Bhagavan Sri Ramana Maharshi was shown the Sanskrit text of Devikallotara Jnanachara Vichara Padalam (A Study of the Exposition of Supreme Wisdom and Conduct to Goddess Ishwari by Lord Shiva) written on palm leaves. He said that this writing was very, very important, and himself translated it into Tamil with his commentary. Sri T. K. Jayaram then translated it into English, including the following:

[Shiva said to Parvati:] The means by which this mind, which is restless and moves about quicker than the wind, can be brought under control, is indeed the means to obtain liberation; is indeed what is good for those who seek permanent Reality; it itself is pure Consciousness and the state of firmness; moreover, it alone is the righteous duty to be followed by discerning aspirants; it alone is the pilgrimage to holy waters; it alone is charity; it alone is austerities. Know that there is no doubt about this. (8-9)

Bhagavan's comment: Now all your pilgrimages are over. Soham Sadhana is the last pilgrimage.

Repeatedly say thus: I am That, the eternal, Omnipresent Reality which is Brahman. Meditating thus for a long time, whoever abides imperturbably, will become the Supreme Brahman, thereby attaining immortality. (60)

Bhagavan's comment: This is the secret of the Nath Panth. Here comes "I am That" or "That Am I"–Soham. Our system also says this. Meditate thus for a long time on the Self. You have to say repeatedly: "That I Am"–Soham. This sixtieth verse is very important.

Satya Sai Baba

It is said: *Ishwarah Sarva Bhuthanam*–God is the indweller of every living being (Bhagavad Gita 18:61). But with what form? How can one contemplate on God with an invisible form? What is the use of such contemplation? Divinity is the very life breath that can be perceived and heard. How can one recognize and experience the sound of this Divine breath? The Upanishads have given the names of "Brahman" and "Atman" for this invisible Divine breath in human beings. But one cannot understand these abstract concepts with any amount of explanation.

What is the meaning of Ishwara Tattwa (Divinity)? *It can be understood as the Divine, auspicious breath of Soham that emanates from a human being.* Soham means 'I am that' (Divinity). The sound of the breath in the human being, i.e., Soham, establishes the nature of Divinity. If one tries to contemplate on the form without recognizing the sound, he will not be able to understand the nature of Divinity. Soham is sattwic in nature. This sattwa guna is Ishwara Tattwa.

The principles of Brahma, Vishnu and Maheshwara are emanating from the Soham Tattwa in each human being. In this trinity, Shiva is the Soham Tattwa. Thus, Divinity is permeating the entire human body.

It is said: *Shabda Brahmamayi*—"Sound is Brahman." In every breath of the human being there is this Soham chanting. Without this Soham sound, the breath cannot exist. Sound is the real Brahma Tattwa (the Principle of Brahma). The Soham principle in the Brahma Tattwa is Atma Tattwa in essence. Therefore, in order to understand Atma Tattwa one has to recognize the nature of the swasa (Divine breath). Thus, Soham means "I am That." What is this "That"? What is it that proclaims "I am That"?

When you sit for meditation on the Soham principle, you will observe that the "So" comes in and "Ham" goes out while inhaling and exhaling. This process has to be watched carefully. (*Soham—The Right Sadhana*, a discourse delivered on the occasion of Dasara Celebrations, October 12, 2002.)

Soham conveys the message of identity between God (So) and the individual (Aham). (Discourse, 6th October 1997, Prashanti Nilayam)

The joy you get by devotional singing and by performing worship is temporary. But you will get eternal joy by experiencing the Soham Mantra…. You should experience it with every breath. (Summer Showers in Brindavan, # 11, 26-05-2002)

Shankara

In the bodies of all beings "Soham" is the japa that is constantly going on. Knowing "Soham," one is liberated from all bondage. (*Sadacharah* 10).

Pandit Shriram Sharma

In Hamsa Yoga: The Elixir of Self-Realization, *Pandit Shriram Sharma quotes the following, saying that it comes from a yogic treatise in the form of instruction given by Shiva to Parvati:*

Ajapa japa of Gayatri bestows moksha on the yogis. A determined commencement of this sadhana itself can eradicate the evils in the sadhaka's character.

The body of an individual is itself a temple in which God resides in the form of the jiva. After cleaning this temple externally and internally by removing the mist of ignorance and evil conduct, the internal God should be worshiped by the sankalpa of Soham.

Hakara [*Ham*] is pronounced when we breathe out and sakara [*So*] when we breathe in. Concentration on this continuous flow of of nada is Soham sadhana.

Later the Pandit says: Even the self-inspired, continuous ajapa japa of Gayatri performed naturally (along with each respiration cycle) without any effort is said to provide complete protection to the prana and offer spiritual knowledge and siddhis equivalent to that of the other yoga sadhanas. Then think about the impact of this ajapa japa if it is performed as a sadhana with ascetic disciplines, sankalpa and shraddha! Indeed, this sadhana (of Soham) then becomes the highest kind of spiritual sadhana because no branch of knowledge and science is found superior to the Gayatri-vidya and no japa better than the japa of the Gayatri (Mantra). The shastras therefore sing great paeans on the Soham sadhana.

In Jap-Tap-Dhyan [Japa-Tapasya-Dhyana], *beginning on page fifteen, Pandit Shriram Sharma writes:*
Research in spirituality shows that in the innermost levels of the human psyche the being (Atman or Self) is always conscious of its true identity with the omnipresent Creator (Atmabodh Pragya), and this superconsciousness (Self-awareness) of primordial identity (Atmabodh) induces the involuntary (automatic) japa (ajapa japa) of Soham. In the Sanskrit language, Soham is a combination of two words, *So* and *Ham*. However, notwithstanding the complexities of grammar, which are irrelevant for the eternally present sounds, let us consider only the concept behind this nomenclature of Soham. "So" means "That" and "Ham" means "I." Spirituality regards "I" as the basic identity of the living being as soul. Thus, taken as one word Soham implies "I am That," *i.e.* "I" the

individual is one with that Cosmic Presence (Omnipresent God). In this way this concept supports the theory of Advaita, the indivisibility of God and creation. In other words, each individual soul is part and parcel of the Whole, the Supreme Soul, *i.e.* God. The omnipresence of God is a concept common to all faiths of the world. In India spirituality uses a plethora of expressions like "Tatvamasi," "Aymatma Brahma" and "Shivoham" to drive home this vision. They advocate the elemental oneness of the Creator (Brahman) and the Creation (the individual).

Pranayama performed in the course of Soham Sadhana is for this very purpose of re-establishing the interface between the Supreme Soul (God) and the individual soul (human being). Through Pranayama during Soham Sadhana, the individual is reminded of that eternal relationship with the Creator.

Man generally identifies himself as his physical body. All his efforts and activities are exclusively confined to making arrangements for convenience of this body, its pleasures, comforts and benefits. He considers only those persons, places and things as his own which are related to his body. His sense of belonging remains confined to this false field of self and everything else is regarded as "not-self." As a consequence, man does not hesitate from harming "others." This is the state of life of common man described by the seers, in which the infatuated soul aimlessly wanders, deluded by the false perspective of physical, mental and emotional attachments (Maya). Constricted by this illusory relationship the individual becomes involved in selfish, regressive and harmful activities. This narrow outlook is also responsible for numerous physical and mental ailments that result in perpetual situations of suffering, grief and distress. It is necessary to avoid and escape from such an unfortunate situation.

The super-science of spirituality is devoted to showing the prodigal man the path back to his true home. Soham Sadhana has been regarded as a means for awareness of truth, fundamental wisdom and realization of God. It shows the true relationship of the individual soul with the Super Soul (Paramatman) and makes the former realize this relationship.

The concept of Soham (I Am That) does not imply identifying this physical human body composed of the five primordial elements and three qualitative attributes (gunas) with God. Such a premise would be counterproductive, providing man with one more basis for inflating the ego and consequently becoming a cause for his retrogression instead of progressive evolution of the soul.

In this automatic japa of Soham during breathing is imbibed an indication of the true nature of the soul which is factually a part of the omnipresence of God. The concept of indivisibility of the Supreme Being and the individual being actually propounds the universality of the individual entity of soul which, in other words, is the same as the omnipresence of God. Masters of spirituality have endeavored to explain this concept in many ways like giving examples of the ocean and its waves, the sun and its rays, the indivisibility of the cosmic life and its numerous living organisms, the unit of life and the Whole, and the pieces of burning ember in a mass of fire. In this way they have pointed out that on casting off the veils of illusory identifications with the body and mind and becoming devoid of the veils of pollutants of vices, the individual living being (soul) attains oneness with the Supreme Divinity. The only impediment to this unity is lack of true wisdom on the part of man. Disregarding his true relationship with God, the individual considers oneself as an independent being, which results in false sense of an inflated ego, the perception of "I and mine" in relation to the transitory names and forms. Consequently, because of his indulgence in narrow selfishness, man degrades his own self by his meaningless ideologies and counterproductive actions.

Sadhana is meant solely for expelling the pollutants of the mind. The highest endeavor of human life is the attempting of communion with God by augmenting purity in all facets of life, in thoughts, words and deeds. Performance of Soham Sadhana does just this. The expression "because of being a part of God, the individual soul is indestructible" (*Ishwar ansha jiva avinashi*) is found in many places in the scriptural literature and is propagated by the teachers of dharma.

Though man is superficially aware of this truth, this does not serve the purpose. The idea must penetrate into innermost depths of the psyche. Only when the firm conviction in this concept is converted into an unwavering faith in God will it become a source of motivation, for the soul to take up in right earnest the cleansing out of the dirt and dross of ignorance lying in all nooks and corners of mental, vital and physical parts of the being and thus make them empty and pure receptacles for receiving the divine nectar of Self-awareness. Having attained this state, the devotee becomes a medium for expression of the will of God. It is like the merger of a rivulet in the sacred river Ganges or dissolution of a drop of water in the ocean. In both cases the water losing its erstwhile individual identity, acquires the character of the vaster entity. Similarly, the thoughts and conduct of an enlightened person conform to those of an angel (deva).

Japa is not merely a ritualistic chanting of words of some mantra. The process must be associated with the force of self-motivation through the words (vak shakti), contemplation on the objective bio-energy (through pranayama) and emotional involvement. With these inputs the japa becomes live and energized. Adopting this discipline of upasana one can surely look forward to rapid spiritual growth.

Swami Sivananda Saraswati

Do Ajapa Japa. The Prana will be absorbed in the Nada. All the Vrittis will perish.... Do Soham Japa and Soham Dhyana along with the breath. This is very easy.... Remember Soham. Feel his Presence everywhere. This will suffice (*Self-Knowledge*).

Soham Dhyana is Nirguna, Nirakara meditation. Soham means "I am That." This is associated with the breath. Repeat "So" when you inhale and "Ham" when you exhale. This is easy. This is known as Ajapa Japa. Feel that you are the all-pervading pure consciousness when you think of Soham. The source for this breath is Brahman or Atman. You are identical with that source and reality (*Yoga in Daily Life*).

Meditation on Soham is also Nirguna meditation [meditation on the Formless Brahman] (*Meditation on Om*).

With the Mantra Soham the Sadhaka leads the Jivatma into the heart (*Kundalini Yoga*).

Concentrate on the breath with Soham repetition (*Mind: Its Mysteries and Control*).

Soham means: "He am I" or "I am Brahman." *So* means "He," *Aham* means "I." This is the greatest of all mantras. This is an abheda-bodha-vakya which signifies the identity of Jiva or the individual Self and Brahman or the Supreme Self. This Mantra comes in the Isavasya Upanishad: "Soham asmi" ("I am Soham")....

Recognize your own swarupa by negating the body-idea and identifying yourself with the supreme Self. Mentally always repeat Soham. Meditate on Sat-Chit-Ananda, the non-dual Brahman. Watch the breath with silent Soham repetition while sitting, standing, eating, talking, etc. This is an easy method for concentration. The Soham bhava must become habitual (*Sadhana*).

Let every breath sing the song of infinity and eternity with Soham! (*Easy Steps to Yoga*).

Soham means: I Am He. The breath is reminding you of your identity with the Supreme Soul.... Negate the body while repeating the Mantra and identify yourself with the Atman or the Supreme Soul (*Practical Lessons in Yoga*).

Sundardas

Some study the Vedas, the Puranas and other scriptures, others study grammar again and again. Some perform their daily prayers and also practice the six purificatory exercises; others reflect on virtue and time. But all work is accomplished only when everything else but the two syllables [So and Ham] is dispelled from the mind. Sundardas says: Listen O learned one, liberation is not achieved without the japa of Soham.

The Self is God, the Self is Consciousness, and the Self is always repeating its own mantra, Soham, Soham.

Day in and day out, the breath comes in and goes out with Soham, Soham. Use the mala of the breath and repeat it all the time. What can you attain by using wooden beads? If you repeat this ceaselessly, it cools down all different kinds of anguish.

With this mantra [Soham], the Self is constantly worshipping itself.

Give up everything else, keep only these two syllables.

Swami Swarupananda of Pavas

One of the most influential teachers of Soham sadhana in the twentieth century was Swami Swarupananda of Pavas in Maharashtra. Here are some of his words on the subject.

By merely remaining in constant and faithful Soham-awareness, the present-life karma (prarabdha) can be brought to its end, and future karma (sanchit) is destroyed before its birth and the karmi (actor–creator of karma) is offered in oblation to the Supreme Lord.

Have total faith and reverence for Soham sadhana.

Practice Soham sadhana sincerely unto the last breath for Self-realization.

Soham sadhana includes jnana as well as bhakti.

For constantly remembering our real Self [Atman] join "So" (Brahman) and "Aham" (I–the jiva)–"I am Brahman"–with our breathing.... This association of Soham bhava with the breath is the key of the Soham sadhana. After some period of our attention on breath, the mind gets completely introverted and remains focused on Soham bhava. While practicing, if the mind drifts away from the Soham vritti (thought), it can be refocused again taking the help of the breath.

Meditation is the shortest, simplest and most efficient method of Self-realization. Experiencing the oneness between the seeker (the individual sadhaka) and the sought (Satchidananda Brahman) is the essential feature of meditation. Soham sadhana is its most potent method (practice).

There are certain Do's and Don'ts, which help in Self-realization. The things that can distract the sadhaka from Soham bhava are all Don'ts, while all those that help him to focus on Soham bhava are the Do's.

Soham Sadhana is a way of life. It is a holistic approach; a synthesis of yoga or the total yoga (purna yoga). It means all the approaches preached by the Bhagavad Gita, namely Karma yoga, Dhyana yoga, Bhakti yoga, and Jnana yoga are to be integrated into our daily spiritual practice, in every moment of our existence.

Keep on practicing Soham Sadhana with great faith and reverence. One is blessed with achievements proportionate to the efforts and importance attached to such efforts.

Soham sadhana is the simple, direct and sure method of attaining Self-realization but it should be practiced arduously, consistently, with devotion and burning aspiration.

Cling to Soham bhava. Soham bhava can be mastered by remembering Soham all the time in the mind, not allowing the drifting of our mind onto any other thought. We must meditate on Soham–ideally, without a break even for a fraction of a second. Such total mastery over Soham bhava is the natural state of existence of all realized souls. Others can also reach this lofty, very distant, seemingly unattainable goal through sincere, consistent Soham sadhana, giving top priority to it in our life.

Practice Soham sadhana with true faith and devotion. Through such ardent Soham sadhana alone one can transcend the present state of existence on the level of body awareness to the ultimate state of pure existence on the level of eternal bliss.

Clinging steadfastly to Soham Sadhana, we can certainly attain Self-realization one day in this life itself.

Tirumantiram

In yoga practice Soham is chanted. The yogi who silently chants it while breathing surely attains the Holy Way (3:731).

Swami Vivekananda

Let them [human beings] all know what they are; let them repeat day and night what they are: Soham. (*Complete Works*, Vol. 3)

This constant thought or dhyana is as oil that pours in one unbroken line from vessel to vessel; dhyana rolls the mind in this thought day and night and so helps us to attain to liberation. Think always "Soham, Soham;" this [japa] is almost as good as liberation. Say it day and night; realization will come as the result of this continuous cogitation. (*Inspired Talks*. Monday, July 8, 1895)

So'ham–I am He. Repeat this constantly, voluntarily at first; then it becomes automatic in practice. (*Notes of Class Talks and Lectures. Notes taken down in Madras,* 1892-93)

Hearest not thou? In thine own heart, day and night, is singing that Eternal Music–Sachchidânanda: Soham, Soham. (*Discourses on Jnana Yoga*)

CHAPTER FOUR:

THE YOGI'S SUBTLE ANATOMY

Esoteric science

Esoteric science is a necessary factor of all viable spiritual traditions: those that truly open the way to higher consciousness, which is the essence and the purpose of evolution. A major part of that science is the knowledge of our spiritual anatomy, our subtle energy levels through which spiritual consciousness can be invoked and expressed. Those levels are like rungs on a ladder leading to higher degrees of consciousness when understood properly.

Yoga, the supreme esoteric/spiritual science, speaks of special channels and centers of life energy in our subtle anatomy. This knowledge is a major factor in the spiritual life and attainment of the yogi. The ancient yogic seers, including the Nath Yogis who claim that Jesus was one of their most revered gurus (see *The Christ of India*), taught that these channels and centers are means of spiritual realization. The greatest of these yogis, the greatest yogi of all time, was Gorakhnath. Gorakhnath asked his teacher Matsyendranath: "How can a yogi have meditation that goes beyond the physical?" The answer was most relevant to the subject we are considering: "He should meditate within his body to rise above the body" (Gorakh Bodha 99, 100). Later Matsyendranath told him: "To destroy deception or duality one should reside within" (114).

The sole purpose of the cosmos is evolution, and this is especially true of the human body. Though frequently mistaken for an obstacle or distraction by spiritual seekers, the body is a perfect evolution machine when its components are known and worked with. At the same time it is essential for us to know what is significant and what is not, otherwise we can become lost in the complexity of the several energy systems that comprise the human organism. And frankly, although hints of these subtle aspects can be found in several traditions, only the Yoga system is complete in knowledge, understanding and the practical ways of working with them.

The yogic sages have explained the subtle anatomy of a yogi's bodies which he must refine and evolve to assist in his ultimate liberation. In the twelfth chapter of *Autobiography of a Yogi*, Yogananda wrote about his guru Swami Sri Yukteswar Giri: "Master numbered many doctors among his disciples. 'Those who have ferreted out the physical laws can easily investigate the science of the soul,' he told them. 'A subtle spiritual mechanism is hidden just behind the bodily structure.'" The internal alchemy of yoga is a process that occurs when the entire internal mechanism (antahkarana) is perfectly synchronized. Then the transmutation is inevitable and the internal mechanism opens the way into the kingdom of heaven: limitless consciousness.

Just as God is embodied in the multilevel manifestation we call creation or the universe, manifesting himself as the physical, astral, and causal cosmos while yet transcending it, in the same way each sentient being is embodied in a universe of his own, exteriorly finite but interiorly infinite. Neither God (the Paramatman) nor the individual spirit (the jivatman) evolve, for they are eternally perfect and unchangeable, but their "bodies" do evolve over ages beyond calculation. The evolution of the cosmic cosmos is consciously intentional, but the evolution of the individual cosmos is subliminal and therefore unconscious until it reaches a point where the individual spirit can comprehend and take charge of it consciously–in other words, the point at which it becomes a yogi.

Yoga of both body and mind

There are many Sanskrit words with which the yogi must become conversant. Two are Samskara and Vasana. Samskaras are impressions in the mind, either conscious or subconscious, produced by previous action or experience in this or previous lives. They are propensities of the mental residue of impressions–subliminal activators; prenatal tendencies. A Vasana is a bundle or aggregate of similar samskaras manifesting as subtle desire. It is a tendency created in a person by the doing of an action or by enjoyment which induces the person to repeat the action or to seek a repetition of the enjoyment. A Vasana is a subtle impression in the mind capable of developing itself into action, and is the cause of birth and experience in general–the impression of actions that remains unconsciously in the mind.

One of the most renowned yogis of the twentieth century was Swami ("Papa") Ramdas of Anandashram (Kanhangad, Kerala). In *Gospel of Ramdas* he says the following regarding the body, yoga and vasanas.

"Vasanas may be driven out of the mind. But they persist in the body. One whose mind is free from vasanas is said to have *manosiddhi*; one whose body is free from vasanas is said to have *kayasiddhi*. One who has *kayasiddhi* is said to have completely eradicated all his vasanas both from his mind and body. That is perfection in yoga. Some jnanis stop at eradicating the vasanas from the mind and do not care about their ejection from the body. But there are some siddhas who have perfected the body also. By so doing, they say they are divinizing the body. They make the light of the atman permeate the body to such an extent that every particle of the body is made holy and shines with the divine radiance" (p. 374).

"Jnanis stop with the experience of nirvikalpa samadhi and they consider the body and all the universe as illusion or non-existent. Even after the experience of nirvikalpa samadhi, though the mind is free from vasanas, the body is not. Of course, jnanis do not care about it as the body and everything connected with it is unreal. But the yogis are not satisfied with this realization. They make the body also pure and illumined. That is Purna [Full, Complete] Yoga. Then every particle of his body is radiant with spiritual splendor. Now the yogi has attained perfection of the body also, the grandest spiritual experience" (pp. 595, 596).

Chakras and adharas

Just as the outer universe is a complex of many interrelated points such as suns and planets, in the same way the material and subtle bodies of the yogi—which reflect and react on one another—are a network of life energy points known as chakras. Chakras are points in the bodies into which the universal life force (vishwaprana) flows. Without that constant inflow the bodies would become dormant and disintegrate—would die. The chakras are both entrances and exits for the cosmic life power, and points of intelligent direction of the power. There are many subsidiary satellites of the chakras called adharas. Adharas are reservoirs of pranic energies, storage units for the energies that flow into the subtle bodies through the chakras, and therefore can be (and often are) mistaken for a chakra.

In the Bhagavad Gita the human complex is sometimes spoken of as "the city of nine gates" (5:13) referring to the nine major chakras. The Nath Yogi tradition also teaches that there are nine major chakras:

1. The Muladhara, located at the base of the spine
2. The Swadhishthana, located in the spine a little less than midway between the base of the spine and the area opposite the navel.
3. The Manipura, located in the spine at the point opposite the navel.
4. The Anahata, located in the spine opposite the midpoint of the sternum bone.
5. The Vishuddha chakra, located in the spine opposite the hollow of the throat.
6. The Talu chakra, located at the root of the palate (opposite the tip of the nose).
7. The Ajna chakra, located at the point between the eyebrows—the "third eye."
8. The Nirvana chakra, located in the midst of the brain: opposite the middle of the forehead, directly beneath the crown of the head.
9. The Brahmarandhra chakra, located at the crown of the head.

The nature and function of the nine chakras

1. **Base (Muladhara) chakra.** The Muladhara chakra deals with the purely physical, atomic structure of the body. Therefore its energies deal with healing, correcting and empowering the very cells and organs of the body. Positive energies of this chakra manifest as insight into all material phenomena and independence of them; negative energies manifest as totally material perceptions and impulses toward avid attachment to material things and disbelief in anything higher than matter.

2. **Swadhishthana chakra.** The Swadhishthana chakra deals with neurological energies, emotions and desires, including sex/lust. It involves all that is self-centered and egotistical in a person. Through its purification are corrected those areas of our physical and emotional life. It also deals with the fluids in the body including the lymph and blood when there is an abnormality there. Positive energies of this chakra manifest as gentleness, sensitivity to others' feelings, helpfulness and even self-sacrifice; negative energies manifest as negative emotions such as anger, resentment, hatred, jealousy, envy and—most of all–lust.

3. **Navel (Manipura) chakra.** The Manipura chakra deals with the metabolism and the assimilative powers of the body. It, too, relates to desires, especially the desire to acquire, control and encompass. It relates to the digestive system as well. So those are the aspects of a person that correction of this chakra can affect. Positive energies of this chakra manifest as strength of will and purpose and a highly developed sense of order and right conduct; negative energies manifest as greed, possessiveness, negative ambition and materialistic involvements.

4. **Heart (Anahata) chakra.** The Anahata chakra deals with metabolism and controls the cardio-pulmonary system. It too deals with feelings, but feelings of higher affection and altruism. (It is still in the lower levels, so do not mistake its movements for true or

spiritual love or devotion to God.) It also deals with the faculty of sight and therefore basic perception as well as lesser intuition. It has a lot to do with the immune and circulatory systems and controls the thymus gland in the center of the chest. Positive energies of this chakra manifest as loving-kindness, generosity, and unselfish actions for the benefit of others; negative energies manifest as the desire to dominate others and to use them for selfish advantage.

5. **Throat (Vishuddha) chakra.** The Vishuddha chakra deals with intellectual development and the power of speech. The thyroid is controlled by it also. The will is also involved to some extent. Higher intuition comes into play here to some extent, as well. Positive energies of this chakra manifest as wise, uplifting and healing speech, words that have the power to manifest what is being spoken; negative energies manifest as foolish, meaningless words, lies, manipulative and negative, harmful speech.

6. **Talu chakra.** The Talu chakra is a kind of switching station as on a railway. Subtle transmuting energies and the Kundalini move up the spine from the Muladhara to the Vishuddha chakra. Then they need to move forward and reach the Ajna chakra. In the centuries since knowledge of the Talu chakra was almost lost, sadhakas throughout India have expressed frustration with the fact that the energies rise to the Vishuddha and will not move to the Ajna. This is because the way the subtle bodies are constituted the Talu chakra must be prepared and activated before the energies can move forward to the front of the head. But that has usually not been known. I personally have heard of several people making this complaint and known one man who sought advice from many renowned yogis over the years but received no help.

7. **Third eye (Ajna) chakra.** The Ajna chakra controls, coordinates and partakes of all the functions of those beneath it. It particularly deals with spiritual intuition and spiritual will. Positive energies

of this chakra manifest as clear intuition, spiritual perceptions and spiritual will power; negative energies manifest as chaotic or negative psychic experiences as well as whimsical, capricious and negative applications of will.

8. **Nirvana chakra.** The Nirvana chakra is the center in which liberation (moksha) is attained and experienced. Without knowledge of this chakra there is a problem in the liberating energies moving from the front of the head back and upward to the Brahmarandhra chakra through which the yogi's spirit rises to merge with the Absolute. Like the Talu chakra, the Nirvana chakra must be prepared and activated before the energies can so move. The Nirvana Chakra is also called the Jalandhara chakra. Jalandhara means "Holder of the Net" in the sense of perfect mastery of both the subtle energy network of nadis and chakras and of samsara itself, the "net" in which all sentient beings are caught until the Nirvana Chakra is reached in full awareness. Jalandhara also means: "holder of the aggregation," as it also controls the seven chakras beneath it.

9. **Brahmarandhra (Crown) chakra.** The energies of the Sushumna crown chakra are purely spiritual and unconditioned by any influences other than our finite spirit and the Infinite Spirit from which we derive our very existence. So there is never any trouble there. It need only be reached and empowered by the Kundalini to establish the precedence of these holy powers over the lower levels of our existence.

These nine chakras are the actual nine gates of the body spoken about in the ancient scriptures (see Bhagavad Gita 5:13), not the nine openings found in the body. The nine chakras are major factors in the subtle energy system of a human being, the ruling power centers, though there are a great number of minor chakras throughout the gross and subtle bodies of each one of us.

I have presented all the foregoing so you will know that the Nath Yogis are very conversant with the chakras, and if you experience any of them, or the adharas, you will understand what you are perceiving. However there is no need to work with any of them, because during the practice of Soham Yoga, every chakra and nadi is affected and glow with subtle light. As the process continues, they increase in brightness and begin to develop as a seed does when exposed to heat and light. The same is true of every cell and every atom in the yogi's being on all levels, physical, astral and causal.

The Sahasrara Chakra

According to the Nath Yogi tradition, however, the supreme chakra is the Sahasrara chakra, which contains the ajna, nirvana and brahmarandhra chakras, and corresponds to the astral and causal brain, and is the center of Soham Yoga practice.

Although there are numberless chakras, only one, the Sahasrara Chakra, the Thousand-petalled Lotus in the head, need occupy the Soham yogi's attention, because according to the Nath Yogi tradition all the chakras beneath it in the body are only subsidiary reflections of the subtle chakras located in the Sahasrara itself. The Sahasrara chakra contains reflex points that control every aspect of the yogi's physical, astral and causal makeup. Consequently the yogi's attention is naturally and spontaneously oriented toward the Sahasrara by the japa and meditation of Soham.

Since we are essentially consciousness, authentic yoga deals directly with consciousness. And when we speak of consciousness we do not mean "consciousness of spirit," as though spirit were an object and consciousness of spirit only a condition of awareness, but we mean spirit itself which is consciousness, the eternal subject. In yoga treatises we frequently encounter the term "Chidakasha," which means "the Space (Ether) of Consciousness." This is the level of existence and consciousness so pure and subtle, so interwoven with Spirit, that it is indistinguishable from Spirit, which is why the yogis say that the spirit-Self dwells *in* the Chidakasha and *is* the Chidakasha.

The Sahasrara Chakra is the place where individual consciousness and Cosmic Consciousness meet and are one. Everything is there. The individual complex of each person originates in the Sahasrara, and the Sahasrara itself is a map or miniature of the cosmos–physical, astral, and causal. It is the dwelling place of Pure Consciousness: Spirit, both individual and cosmic. Consequently, liberation is experienced in the Sahasrara. The process of Soham meditation takes place throughout the body, but predominantly within the Sahasrara since it is the seat of the spirit-Self. For this reason, even though in Soham meditation we do not usually deliberately put our attention on any particular point in the body, at the beginning of meditation, and sometimes during meditation if our attention drifts, it is good to make ourselves gently aware of the entire brain area for the space of a few Soham breaths, and then let it go and proceed to meditate in the usual manner. We can also do the same outside meditation, as well.

It is the Paradise from which we fell into material consciousness and to which we must be restored through yoga. The Sahasrara is the true Sukhavati, the Pure Land, the abode of the Buddha of Infinite Light (Amitabha), a personification of the Chidakasha. This is why Gajanana Maharaj said that when through Soham the mind is turned inward, "all ideas become merged in the Sahasrara." That is, the yogi's entire consciousness becomes centered there. Gorakhnath described it as when "the current of consciousness comes to dwell in the Sahasrara lotus and is illuminated with the radiance of the Self." In the esoteric writings of both Hinduism and Buddhism we find references to "the jewel in the lotus." The lotus is the Sahasrara and the awakened consciousness of the yogi is the jewel. As Blavatsky wrote in *The Secret Doctrine*: "Each of us has within himself the 'Jewel in the Lotus,' call it Padmapani, Krishna, Buddha, Christ, or whatever name we may give to our Divine Self."

The Bhagavad Gita says in the beginning of the fifteenth chapter that the entire field of relative existence is like a tree whose roots are above and whose branches and leaves are below in the material world. This is not only true of the macrocosm, but also of each one of us that are microcosms—reflections of the macrocosm. Our "roots" are in our brain, the Sahasrara, and our body, limbs, and senses are the trunk, branches, and leaves. The indwelling consciousness of the Sahasrara is literally the taproot into the Infinite, the gateway of higher consciousness, both ascending and descending. The subtle energies of the higher planes flow into the Sahasrara, and through it into the entire body, making it the origin and seat of all supernatural experiences and abilities as well as the point of communication with higher planes and higher consciousness.

Awareness of the Sahasrara is spiritual consciousness itself. From the enlivened Sahasrara the sacred light and power of Spirit will flow into every cell of every level of our being. Soham is the bija (seed) mantra of the Sahasrara Chakra, and directly awakens and develops it. Therefore by intoning Soham in time with the breath we activate literally thousands of channels in the physical and subtle bodies known as nadis, causing the life force to spontaneously, effortlessly, flow upward into the thousand-petalled lotus of the brain (Sahasrara Chakra) and merge into the Divine Light within the Sahasrara that is the essence of Soham. This all happens naturally and spontaneously when we intone Soham in time with the breath. As said before, it can be helpful to sometimes intentionally put our attention on the brain area, the Sahasrara, and feel and hear our intonations of Soham vibrating there. But it must be a very gentle and light attention, because any strain might cause a headache, and after a few breaths it is good to go back to simple awareness of the breath and the sound of inwardly intoning Soham after a while.

As cited in the previous chapter, Swami Muktananda Paramahansa wrote: "[The Guru Gita] speaks of a mantra in the Sahasrara, at the crown of the head. Inside there is a triangle [trikuti] and there are two syllables, *So* and *Ham*, and the mantra Soham arises from there. Right in the center of this triangle the guru dwells" (*From the Finite to the Infinite*, p. 307). The trikuti is also called "the feet of the Guru" who is God, *So* and *Ham* being the two feet. There he also said: "The Guru is always immersed in Soham. When the disciple becomes that Soham, he is a true disciple" (*From the Finite to the Infinite*, p. 285).

Various texts inform us that both Soham and the breath arise directly from our spirit-consciousness. For this reason in Soham Yoga we join intonations of Soham to the breath. Experiencing our inmost consciousness to greater and greater degrees within meditation is the the beginning of Cosmic Consciousness. The more we meditate, the higher and higher and further and further we penetrate into the Infinite Consciousness of which we are an eternal part. Those who through Soham Yoga continually attune and merge their consciousness in this way with the Sahasrara will in time become totally identified with the individual spirit-Self and with the Supreme Spirit. In time every single intonation of Soham vibrates throughout our entire being, within each atom of our existence.

Ida, Pingala, Sushumna and Soham

In the spine there are three major passages or nadis through which life energy and the Kundalini move upward and downward. The one on the left of the spine is known as the Ida, the one on the right as the Pingala, and the one in the center is the Sushumna. Life force, the prana, moves downward in the Ida and upward in the Pingala. Kundalini, however, moves upward in the Sushumna.

We do not awaken Kundalini—it awakens us. In the same way we need not open the Sushumna, for if the Sushumna was not open we would either be a vegetable or dead. Neither is there a need to deliberately "raise" the Kundalini, because the evolving life force of Kundalini always moves upward in the Sushumna, though in many people it is so minimal and slow that it has very little observable effect. But whenever there is creativity or intelligence manifesting in a human being–and most of all when there is spiritual inspiration or insight–it is being produced by the upward flow of the Kundalini in the Sushumna.

The rate of ascent and the volume of the Kundalini's rising is according to the evolutionary development of the individual and the condition of his bodies, gross and subtle. We accelerate the function of the Sushumna and Kundalini through the repetition of Soham in time with the breath. When *So* is mentally intoned, the Pingala, the nadi to the right of the Sushumna, is stimulated, and when *Ham* is intoned the Ida, the nadi to the left of the Sushumna, is stimulated and the subtle life force flows through them continuously. The continual repetition of Soham, even outside meditation, causes these two channels to flow smoothly, fully, and in harmony. When they are in perfect synchronization, the flow of life force in the Sushumna is greatly enhanced and unhindered–so much so that the Yoga Shikha Upanishad says that Soham "is chanted in the Sushumna.... This chanting of the mantra 'Soham' is called Mantra Yoga." Although Soham affects the Ida and Pingala, its main effect and purpose is the stimulation of the Sushumna and the increase of Kundalini activity within it. There is no need to imagine or try to produce or feel or increase the stimulation, because it occurs automatically at the inner intonations of the mantric syllables.

Gorakhnath wrote about it this way: "The Sun rises in the Sushumna, and the current of consciousness comes to dwell in the Sahasrara lotus and the bhramargufa [Sahasrara] is illuminated with the radiance of the Self."

Kundalini and Soham

"The life-sustaining gayatri [Soham] is born from the kundalini. He who knows this knowledge of the life force, the great science, is a knower of the Vedas" (Goraksha Paddhati 1.46). "This cosmic Shakti exists in the individual bodies of all breathing creatures (Prani) in the form of Kundalini (Kundalirupa)" (Arthur Avalon, *The Garland of Letters*, p. 113). According to various scriptures and writings of master yogis, Soham is inherent in all things as the force–the KulaKundalini–that points them to the Goal and moves them along toward the Goal. We intone Soham to put ourselves and our bodies back into harmony with the innate evolutionary impulse of the universe–with Soham–and attune them to the Kundalini that flows in response to our intonations of Soham in time with the breath. In this way we clear the pathway for the rising Kundalini from the Muladhara to the Brahmarandhra.

What is Kundalini? Actually, it is quite a simple thing: it is the evolving power inherent in the universe and in all forms of life: Soham. It is the Kundalini that functions in the chakras and the subtle channels that connect them known as nadis. It is only the mode of movement that varies in them. Kundalini in no way "sleeps" and does not need awakening–only a clearing of the way for its perfect functioning. It pervades everything and is active in everything. Ultimately it is seen to be the universe and that which transcends the universe.

Kundalini is not energy in essence, but consciousness. However, when consciousness moves it is seen as energy. As Gorakhnath explained at length, Shakti (Energy) is really Shiva (Consciousness) acting in a dynamic way. This is a profound and essential truth which must be grasped by the yogi. Kundalini is the Living God in whom we live, move, and have our being. The essential sound-form (vachaka or mantra) of Kundalini is Soham. As the Yoga Chudamani Upanishad says: "This Ajapa Gayatri which rises from the Kundalini supports the soul. This is the greatest among the sciences of the soul" (Yoga Chudamani Upanishad 35). Ajapa is the natural japa (mantric sounds) made by the breath as it flows in and out: Soham. Gayatri is a mantra invoking the powers of evolution and enlightenment.

Soham is the original extension or emanation of Kundalini, which is both mula prakriti, root-energy, and mula chaitanya, root-consciousness. Therefore Gorakhnath says in the *Goraksha Sataka*: "The [ajapa] gayatri is sprung from Kundalini and supports the breath [prana]. Knowledge of the breath is the great knowledge [mahavidya]. He who attains the knowledge of this ajapa-gayatri is truly the knower of yoga. Wisdom equal to this, japa equal to this, knowledge equal to this, have never been and will never be" (46). This is in contrast to those who consider the breath to be an obstacle to realization and the cause of restlessness. It is not the breath itself but the breath in a state of distortion and disharmony that produces the trouble. Certainly, without the breath nothing can be accomplished by the yogi. Correction of the breath through Soham is a fundamental step in yoga practice.

The rising of Kundalini is a matter of consciousness and not energy. When the Kundalini rises the consciousness expands, unfolds, and evolves. Soham japa and meditation remove all blockages in the subtle channels (nadis) of the subtle bodies, and cause the bodies themselves to vibrate to Soham as their fundamental frequency. Just as Soham pervades the physical, astral, and causal creation, so the vibrations of Soham pervade all our bodies, awakening and evolving them. Soham Yoga is Kundalini Yoga, pure and simple.

As already stated, during the practice of Soham Yoga every chakra and nadi is affected and glows with subtle light. As the process continues, they increase in brightness and begin to develop as a seed does when exposed to heat and light. The same is true of every cell and every atom in the yogi's being on all levels, physical, astral and causal. Consequently we may experience these changes in meditation, but we should let awareness of them arise and subside spontaneously during the japa and meditation of Soham. Otherwise we confine and limit their effects within us.

Looking in the wrong place

"Verily, verily, I say unto you, He that entereth not by the door into the sheepfold, but climbeth up some other way, the same is a thief and a robber" (John 10:1). This statement of Jesus, a Nath Yogi, immediately brings up a very serious and crucial matter. Throughout thousands of years, especially in India, it has been seen that many things can produce the same qualities or abilities and powers in those persons that are considered to be indications of genuine realization and teaching authority.

The different experiences that can be mistaken for spiritual progress and even enlightenment can arise from all five of our bodies (koshas). And in each case they are the result of distortion and malfunction in those bodies produced by false yoga practices that delude the aspiring yogi. Despite the claims made by the false yogis who peddle them, these are not spiritual at all, but material, gross and subtle.

Annamaya kosha. Those centered in the physical body produce physical phenomena such as levitation, living without breathing for long periods of time, living without eating or drinking, floating on water in meditation posture, and appearing to die and being buried for long periods of time and then disinterred and seemingly coming back to life.

Pranamaya kosha. Some of these phenomena can manifest by the practices centered in the pranic body by means of intense pranayama falsely called raja yoga. Others are the ability to appear and disappear, going from one place to another in a moment, the ability to impart intense energy (shakti) to others, the ability in this manner to heal some physical ills or to cause cataclysmic changes in the mind and body of others, the ability to appear in different forms and even to penetrate into the physical and subtle bodies–including the minds–of others. Among these are the "shaktipat" gurus.

Manomaya kosha. Those practices centered in the manasic (sensory mind) levels produce visions, ability to read the thoughts and feelings of others, and to produce visions and mental states in others, the ability to fascinate and control others, especially in their feelings (emotions), the ability to create an intense atmosphere around themselves that appears miraculous, uplifting, joy-bringing and (of course) divine. By their touch those adept in these practices can produce amazing experiences in others and seem to be virtually omnipotent and omniscient. These false yogis are especially adored by their victim-disciples whom they control through emotional manipulation of various qualities–all the way from love to profound fear of the guru's omnipotence and omniscience, not to mention the dire things predicted for those who disobey, get "out of attunement," or separate from the guru. For some reason these fakes like to declare what famous figures of religious and secular history their disciples were in past lives. Especially they thrill their dupes by declaring that they have been his/her disciples for many incarnations (which apparently has not had much effect).

Jnanamaya kosha. Those who engage in and teach practices centered in the intellectual (buddhic) levels have tremendous power of speech. Their every word seems to be absolute truth and totally convincing at all times. These false teachers make predictions, especially of the far future, and traffic in New Ideas For The New Age. They either concoct very difficult intellectual gymnastics for consumption or they impart the "secret knowledge" that has been lost or hidden for ages but which now is to be revealed in great secrecy to dozens, hundred or thousands of disciples.

Anandamaya kosha. Practices centered in the etheric body, the particular realm of which is sound (shabda), may produce all the effects listed in the preceding sections through mantra, since sound is the basis of everything and vak (speech)is the chief faculty of a human being. Mantra is virtually omnipotent when intensely applied. The effects, like all those described previously, are eventually found in the passing of time to either be temporary or incomplete in their effects.

Looking in the right place

Patanjali discusses the various means of gaining the appearance of Self-realization and the fact that they are all temporary and even illusory except for one: the actual transformation of the consciousness into Divine Consciousness, the very real transformation of the human consciousness into the consciousness of the fully revealed Self whose essence is Brahman Itself.

Although correct sadhana affects all the koshas, the centering of our sadhana should be beyond the koshas and in the Self. And the way to do that is very easy and simple: the meditation and japa of Soham.

CHAPTER FIVE:

Points For Successful Meditation and Its Purpose and Philosophy

The place for meditation

It will be most helpful to your practice if you have a special place exclusively for meditation. Your mind will begin to associate that place with meditation and will more easily enter a quiet and peaceful state when you sit there. If you can set aside an entire room for practicing meditation, or even a large well-ventilated closet, that is good, but just an area in a room is adequate. The important thing is that the area be devoted exclusively to your meditation.

The room should be moderate in temperature and free from drafts, both cold and hot. It is also important that it be well ventilated so you do not get sleepy from lack of oxygen in the air.

Your meditation place should be as quiet as possible. Do not play music or other kinds of sounds during your meditation, as that definitely interferes with your entering the Silence and perceiving the subtle forms of Soham. As a rule earplugs are not recommended for the practice of meditation since you can become distracted by the sensation of pressure in the ears, or the chirping, cricket-like noises that go on all the time in the ears, or the sound of your heartbeat. But if you need them, use them. Your place of meditation should ideally be a place where you can most easily forget outer distractions, but if it is not, you can still manage to practice meditation successfully.

It should be softly or dimly lighted. (Full darkness might tend to make you go to sleep.) It is also good to turn off any electric lights, as their pulsation, even though not perceived by the eyes, affects the brain waves and subtly influences the mind, holding it to the level that corresponds to the rate of pulsation. If you like having a candle or wick lamp burning when you meditate, they should be a kind that does not flicker.

Some yogis like to burn incense when they meditate. This is a good practice if the smoke does not irritate their lungs or noses. Unfortunately, much incense, including that from India, contains artificial, toxic ingredients that are unhealthy.

It is good to keep some sacred symbols or imagery in your meditation place—whatever reminds you that God is present.

Meditation posture

For meditation we sit in a comfortable, upright position. This is for two reasons: so we will not fall asleep, and to facilitate the upward movement of the subtle life force, prana, of which the breath is a manifestation.

It is important that our meditation posture be comfortable and easy to maintain. Though sitting upright, be sure you are always relaxed. Yoga Sutra 2:46 says: "Posture [asana] should be steady and comfortable." The *Yoga Vashishtha* (6:1:128) simply says: "He should sit on a soft seat in a comfortable posture conducive to equilibrium." Shankara comments: "Let him practice a posture in which, when established, his mind and limbs will become steady, and which does not cause pain." Here relaxation is the key for Yoga Sutra 2:47 says: "Posture is mastered by relaxation."

There are several cross-legged postures recommended for meditation. They are the Lotus (Padmasana), Perfect (Siddhasana), Auspicious (Swastikasana), and Easy (Sukhasana). You will find them described in books on Hatha Yoga postures. I especially recommend *Yoga Asanas* by Swami Sivananda of the Divine Life Society, as it is written from the perspective of spiritual development and also gives many hints to help those who are taking up meditation later in life and whose bodies need special training or compensation.

If you can sit in a cross-legged position without your legs going to sleep and making you have to shift them frequently, that is very good. Some yogis prefer to sit on the floor using a pillow. This, too, is fine if your legs do not go to sleep and distract you. But meditation done in a chair is equally as good. Better to sit at ease in a chair and be inwardly aware than to sit cross-legged and be mostly aware of your poor, protesting legs.

If you use a chair, it should be comfortable, of moderate height, one that allows you to sit upright with ease while relaxed, with your feet flat on the floor. There is no objection to your back touching the back of the chair, either, as long as your spine will be straight. If you can easily sit upright without any support and prefer to do so, that is all right, too, but be sure you are always relaxed.

If you have any back difficulties, make compensation for them, and do not mind if you cannot sit fully upright. We work with what we have, the whole idea being to sit comfortably and at ease.

Put your hands on your thighs, your knees, or in your lap: joined, separated, one over the other, whatever you prefer. The palms can be turned up or down. Really it does not matter how you place or position your hands, just as long as they are comfortable and you can forget about them. There is no need to bother with hand mudras, as they are irrelevant to Soham Yoga practice.

Hold your head so the chin is parallel to the ground or, as Shankara directs, "the chin should be held a fist's breadth away from the chest." Make a fist, hold it against your neck, and let your chin rest on your curled-together thumb and forefinger. You need not be painfully exact about this. The idea is to hold your head at such an angle that it will not fall forward when you relax. Otherwise you will be afflicted with what meditators call "the bobs," the upper body continually falling forward during meditation.

Meditation is not a military exercise, so we need not be hard on ourselves about not moving in meditation. It is only natural for our muscles to sometimes get stiff or for some discomfort to develop. Go right ahead and move a bit to get rid of the discomfort.

Some yogis prefer facing east or north to meditate, but it has been my experience that in Soham Yoga it simply does not matter what direction I face. Yet you might want to experiment on your own.

Whatever your seat for meditation–chair, pillow, pad, or mat–it will be good if it can be used only for meditation. This will pick up the beneficial vibrations of your meditation, and when you sit on it your mind will become calm and your meditation easier. For the same reason some people like using a special shawl or meditation clothing or a robe when meditating. If you cannot devote a chair to your meditation, find some kind of cloth or throw that you can put over the chair when you meditate and remove when you are done.

Reclining meditation

If we lie down for meditation we will likely go to sleep. Yet, for those with back problems or some other situation interfering with their sitting upright, or who have trouble sitting upright for a long time, it is possible to meditate in a reclining position at a forty-five-degree angle. This is a practice of some yogis in India when they want to meditate unbrokenly for a very long time. (I know of two yogis who meditated throughout the entire day this way.) There may still be a tendency to sleep, but we do what we can, when we can. Here is the procedure:

Using a foam wedge with a forty-five-degree angle, or enough pillows to lie at that angle, or in a bed that raises up to that angle, lie on your back with your arms at your side, or across your stomach if that is more comfortable. Then engage in the meditation process just as you would if sitting upright.

When you are ill or for some reason unable to sit upright you can meditate in this way.

Alternating positions in meditation

Those not yet accustomed to sitting still for a long time, or those who want to meditate an especially long time, can alternate their meditation positions. After sitting as long as is comfortable, they can do some reclining meditation and then sit for some more time, according to their inclination.

Relaxation

Relaxation is the key to successful meditation, just as is ease and simplicity. We need to be relaxed in both body and mind to eliminate the distracting thoughts and impressions that arise mostly from tension.

It is only natural that you will find your mind moving up and down or in and out during the practice of meditation, sometimes being calm and sometimes being restless. Do not mind this at all; it is in the nature of things. At such times you must consciously become even more calm, relaxed, and aware. Lighten up in the most literal sense. As already said, when restlessness or distractions occur, take a deep breath through your nose, let it out, relax, and keep on meditating.

It is also natural when we begin turning our awareness inward that we will encounter thoughts, memories, various emotions, feelings, mental states, and other kinds of experiences such as lights, sensations of lightness and heaviness, of expansion, of peace and joy, visual images (waking dreams), and such like. None of these should be either accepted or rejected. Instead we should calmly continue our intonations of Soham. The inner sound of Soham and the states of consciousness it produces are the only things that matter, for they alone bring us to the Goal. We should never become caught up in the various phenomena, however amazing, entertaining, pleasant (or how inane, boring, and unpleasant) they may be, and be distracted from meditation. Experiences must not be held on to, nor should they be pushed away, either. Instead we should be quietly aware of them and keep on with meditation so in time we can pass far beyond such things. This is relaxation in attitude.

Also, feelings of boredom, stagnation, annoyance and inner discomfort may be the resistance of negative energies which will be cleared away by meditation as we persevere, and should not be taken seriously and allowed to influence us or even get us to end a meditation period to get away from them.

Never try to make one meditation period be like one before it. Each session of meditation is different, even though it will have elements or experiences in common with other sessions.

Do not be unhappy with yourself if in meditation it seems things are just not going right or you are just floating on the top rather than going deep. That is what you need at the moment. Keep on; everything is all right. Remember: Soham is not just intelligent, it is Divine Intelligence, and whatever is best for you to experience is what it will produce, either late or soon, but always at the perfect time. And most important: Never let your mind trick you into stopping your meditation with the idea that you will try later and things may be better. These times of feeling dull and inert are little "dark nights of the soul" which if we endure we ensure that we will never go through the long periods of internal darkness that non-yogis undergo.

It is important in meditation to be relaxed, natural, and spontaneous, to neither desire or try to make the meditation go in a certain direction or to try to keep it from going in a particular direction. To relax and be quietly observant is the key for the correct practice of meditation.

Yet, correct meditation practice is never passive or mentally inert. At all times you are consciously and intentionally intoning Soham. It should be easeful and relaxed, but still intentional, even when your intonations become more gentle and subtle, even whisperlike or virtually silent.

Closed mouth and eyes

Breathing through the mouth agitates the mind, so keeping your mouth closed and breathing only through the nose has a calming effect. So also does closing your eyes, for by closing your eyes you remove visual distractions and eliminate over seventy-five percent of the usual brain wave activity.

Eye positions

The Bhagavad Gita speaks of the yogi "holding the body, head and neck erect, motionless and steady, looking toward the origin of his nose and not looking around" (Bhagavad Gita 6:13). Disagreement has existed for centuries as to whether this means the yogi should look downward toward the tip of his nose or upward to between his eyebrows. Since *nasikagram* means literally "the origin of the nose," it depends on where you consider the nose "begins"—at the point between the eyebrows or the tip of the nose. The consensus throughout India is almost unanimous that the tip of the nose is meant. Even Shankara taught that the eyes are to be turned down toward the tip of the nose. Not that the yogi makes himself cross-eyed, but that he gently turns his eyes downward at the angle of looking at his nosetip. To determine the correct angle, just touch the middle of your extended forefinger to the tip of your nose and look down at it. That is it!

However, during meditation it is natural that the eyes turn upward and downward. When it happens effortlessly and spontaneously, that is perfectly all right. This has to do with the condition and movement of subtle energies in the Sahasrara chakra. This is good when it occurs automatically and without any strain. You need only be centered in the awareness of your intonations of Soham. The eyes will take care of themselves.

Easy breathing

In meditation we breathe through the nose, not the mouth. And since meditation is much easier when your nasal passages are open and clear, whenever they are stopped or stuffy, clear them by use of a NeilMed Neti Pot or NeilMed Sinus Rinse bottle, or similar devices. Some nasal inhalers also help clear the nasal passages. If for some reason your nose stays stopped or stuffy, then accept it and do your best. The benefit will still be great.

Be at peace and confident

Be very relaxed about your involvement with Soham and with all your spiritual disciplines. The moment anxiety enters, so does the ego and things are greatly hindered and even reversed. Just do as you do. Do not be careless or casual, but be careful and relaxed, confident in the blessing of God whose consciousness (bhava) is embodied in Soham. It is better to do effective intonations of Soham rather than just stacking up a lot of nervous, artificial intonations.

You are yourself a part of God; nothing can change that. Have no fear or anxiety. Trust in God who will always be looking after you. And stay in tune with him by the constant japa of Soham and the practice of regular meditation so he can silently guide you through your intuition. Live in God and be at peace and in joy.

Immortal and eternal

We are immortal. How do we know that? It is intuited by anyone with an unclouded awareness. For as long as the human race has existed on this earth, our immortality has been part of common knowledge based on intuition and also by various experiences people have had throughout history: near-death experience, actual dying and returning to life, and seeing or receiving communication from departed persons in both the waking and sleeping states. Some have entered the worlds of the departed, observed and spoken with them and returned to tell about it.

But we are more than immortal. We are eternal. That is, we will not just live forever from this point on, we have also existed forever, from eternity. Eternity is not time without end, but that state of being or existence which transcends this realm of time and space. In eternity neither beginning nor end is possible; it is the state of Divine Being, of God, of whom it was long ago said in the Rig Veda: "His shadow is immortality."

178

How is it possible for us to be eternal? Because our very existence is rooted in the eternity of God. We have always existed within God because in some ineffable way we are part of God, one with him yet distinct from him. It is like the ocean and its waves: the waves are not the ocean, but the ocean is the waves. Eternally we have been the parts and God has been the Whole. We are never separate from him, but we are always distinct from him. We are all spirit, but we are finite and God is infinite. God lives in us and we live in God. We are divine; we are gods within God.

Meditation: the key

We must *know* this, not just believe it. How can we know this? We can know it through practice of the spiritual science of Soham meditation. Like mathematics, this science is based on the fundamental nature of relative existence in which we presently find ourselves for the purpose of the evolution of our consciousness. To understand this we need to know a bit of cosmic history.

The basis of yoga

Yoga is based on the fundamental nature of relative existence: the dynamic field of the evolutionary force or impulse manifesting as movement and sound. In the individual human being the root-impulse manifests as breath and the subtle sound vibration that is the root of inhalation and exhalation. This is the force that impels the individual spirit into the realm of evolution and then produces the evolution itself, and by conscious cultivation of which the awakened individual can continue his own evolution to its ultimate perfection: revealed godhood.

Long ago in the hidden mists of earth's history this secret of Yoga was revealed to those developed enough to perceive it within the depths of their own being. Discovering the way to transcendence, they seized it and applied it. Consciously entering into the stream of divine evolution, they became in the truest sense Ascended Masters, no longer gods in potential but in actuality. They passed on their knowledge of Yoga to others who in turn passed it on to succeeding generations, even unto today. Since it works with the yogi's fundamental makeup and nature, there is no need for any external empowerment such as "initiation." The only thing needed is practice.

The essence of yoga

Yoga sadhana consists of a single process that takes place in two modes: within meditation and outside meditation. It also has two elements, just as does the universe of which we are a living, evolving part. The first is awareness of breath, and the second is the production and awareness of the subtle sound which is both the cause and the effect of the breath. This subtle sound is Soham. The subtle sounds of *So* and *Ham* both produce the breath and are made by the breath, because they arise from the Original Being, the Original Cause, of all things: Brahman. Though two, they are really one conscious Soham Bhava, and change duality into unity on all levels of manifestation as the final step in our evolution. The simple yet profound practice of Soham Yoga, of Soham japa and meditation, will be found to correct, heal and restore all the levels of our existence, physical, mental and spiritual.

Meditation requires two things: power and intelligent direction. The yogi is at all times aware of what is going on and directs everything according to his intelligent will. Even if he simply watches and observes the yogic process, still he is willing (directing) that to be so. He is in charge at all times. Those who are not in charge but believe they are being uncontrollably swept along "by the shakti" are deluded and in grave danger.

Spiritual study

The swadhyaya (self-study) prescribed by Patanjali includes spiritual reading. I will never cease to bless the day I first read the Bhagavad Gita. The wise yogi reads the Gita daily and ponders its truths. The more he does so, the more he will understand as his mind is being continually purified and enlightened through daily meditation. Yogiraj Shyama Charan Lahiri Mahasaya required all his disciples to read the Gita each day. The entire scripture is directed to the yogi, so all seven hundred verses speak to him. Without the principles found in the Gita I could never have persevered as a yogi. It is essential reading for those who want to succeed in yoga and avoid the pitfalls of external life. Nothing can substitute for daily Gita study, which should be made the yogi's lifetime companion and guide.

The most beautiful and readable translation is *The Song of God: Bhagavad Gita*, by Swami Prabhavananda and Christopher Isherwood. It conveys the spirit of the Gita as no other translation does. It is, though, an interpretive translation. But the interpretations are according to the great commentators such as Adi Shankaracharya. The supplementary material, including an essay by Aldous Huxley, is extremely valuable in understanding the Gita's subtle philosophy. My own version, as well as my commentary, *The Bhagavad Gita For Awakening*, has some value as well, I believe. However, in time you need to engage in a deeper study of the Gita, and for that you need translations that will give you the original Sanskrit text, a word-by-word translation, and some commentary. Among the best of these are the translations of Swami Sivananda, Swami Swarupananda and Winthrop Sargeant. All of these can be bought from amazon.com.

Since the Gita is a digest of the upanishads, I also recommend that you get *The Upanishads: Breath of the Eternal* by Swami Prabhavananda. This is also available from Amazon. In time you might find it good to obtain and study Radhakrishnan's *Principal Upanishads*. I have used Radhakrishnan's translation as the basis for my commentary, *The Upanishads For Awakening*.

Another book that will help you tremendously is *The Philosophy of Gorakhnath* by Akshaya Kumar Banerjea. For help in understanding technical Sanskrit terms, I recommend my endeavor, *A Brief Sanskrit Glossary*. These, too, can be obtained from amazon.com.

Ashtanga Yoga

"From the practice of Yoga, spiritual illumination arises which develops into awareness of Reality" (Yoga Sutras 2:28). The yoga of the Yoga Sutras written by the Nath Yogi Patanjali is usually called the Eight-limbed (Ashtanga) Yoga. "Yama, niyama, asana, pranayama, pratyahara, dharana, dhyana, and samadhi are the eight limbs" (Yoga Sutras 2:29).

1. *Yama (Restraint).* Yama consists of the five Don'ts of Yoga: 1) Ahimsa: non-violence, non-injury, harmlessness; 2) Satya: truthfulness, honesty–i.e., non-lying; 3) Asteya: non-stealing, honesty, non-misappropriativeness; 4) Brahmacharya: sexual continence and control of all the senses; 5) Aparigraha: non-possessiveness, non-greed, non-selfishness, non-acquisitiveness.

2. *Niyama (Observance).* Niyama comprises the five Do's of Yoga: 1) Shaucha: purity, cleanliness; 2) Santosha: contentment, peacefulness; 3) Tapas: austerity, practical (i.e., result-producing) spiritual discipline; 4) Swadhyaya: self-study, spiritual study; 5) Ishwara-pranidhana: offering of one's life to God. (Yama and Niyama are considered in detail in Chapter Six, The Foundations of Yoga.)

3. *Asana.* In the Yoga Sutras asana does not mean Hatha Yoga postures, but only meditation postures. Asana is both the sitting posture chosen for meditation and steadiness in that posture.

4. *Pranayama.* Pranayama is the refining of the breath, making it subtle and inward. This is accomplished through objective observation of the breath, and is not an artificial breathing exercise.

5. *Pratyahara.* Abstraction or withdrawal of the senses from their objects by turning the awareness inward is known as pratyahara. In Soham Yoga we begin this by the simple expedient of gently closing our eyes and relaxing them. Immediately the awareness begins to withdraw inward. Breathing only through the nose also helps in this.

6. *Dharana.* "Dharana is the confining [fixing] of the mind within a point or area," says Yoga Sutra 3:1. The word that can be translated

either "point" or "area" is *desha*, as in Bangala*desh*–the area where Bengalis live. We accomplish this by gently fixing our attention in the etheric level of inner speaking and inner hearing by our inner intonations of Soham.

7. *Dhyana.* Dhyana is the process of meditation itself. In Yoga Sutra 3:2, Patanjali defines dhyana as "the uninterrupted flow of the mind–the content of the consciousness–in a single and unbroken stream." This we accomplish by inwardly intoning Soham in time with our breath and listening to those intonations. The sutra may also be translated: "Meditation is the unbroken flow of awareness of the object." Vyasa says: "Meditation is continuity of the experience of the meditation-object."

Shankara defines meditation as "a stream of identical vrittis [thoughts] as a unity, a continuity of vrittis not disturbed by intrusion of differing or opposing vrittis. This is dhyana"–a continuous stream of inner intonations of Soham. And he contrasts the beginning stage of meditation, dharana, with meditation itself, saying: "Whereas in dharana there may be other impressions of peripheral thoughts even though the chitta has been settled on the object of meditation alone–for the chitta is functioning on the location [desha] as a pure mental process–it is not so with dhyana, for there it [the object of meditation] is only the stream of a single vritti untouched by any other vritti of a different kind."

By the continual intonations of Soham with the breath we produce a stream of identical waves in the chitta until that stream becomes a continuous unitary flow of rarefied sound, a single object or wave that is untouched or untainted by any other thought or impression.

8. *Samadhi.* The state in which the mind unites with and identifies with the object of meditation is known as samadhi. This is purely a state of the mind (chitta) and has nothing to do with physical phenomena such as the cessation of all outward sensations, breath,

and heartbeat, though awareness of those phenomena certainly does cease in samadhi.

Fundamentally, samadhi is a state in which awareness, breath, and the inner intonations of Soham become one. When the consciousness totally merges into Soham that is the true samadhi. It is the perfect merging of the consciousness of the individual spirit with the Consciousness of the Infinite Spirit, for Soham is both of these.

States of consciousness

Although asana, pranayama, pratyahara, dharana, dhyana, and samadhi are processes of meditation, in a higher sense they are stages of awareness passed through in meditation.

Asana is the initial stage of body awareness as we sit in the chosen posture and arrange ourselves comfortably. Pranayama is the slowing down and refinement of the breath leading to awareness of the pranas moving in the physical and subtle bodies that results from our physical and mental relaxation (asana) and observation of the breath. Pratyahara is the turning inward of the mind resulting naturally from our closed eyes, relaxation, bodily ease, and the calming of the breath. Dharana is the fixing of the awareness in the etheric levels of our being as we mentally intone and listen to the sound of Soham. Dhyana is Dharana in an unbroken stream when the awareness is absorbed in intoning and listening to Soham. Samadhi is the experience of the absolute unity of the breath, Soham, and the meditator.

In asana the awareness is centered in the physical body, the annamaya kosha. In pranayama the awareness is centered in the pranic (biomagnetic) body, the pranamaya kosha. In pratyahara the awareness is centered in the sensory mental body, the manomaya kosha. In dharana the awareness is centered in the intellect-intelligence body, the jnanamaya kosha. In dhyana the awareness is centered in the will-etheric body, the anandamaya kosha. In samadhi the awareness transcends the bodies and unites with the Atman-spirit.

Asana, pranayama, pratyahara, dharana, dhyana, and the annamaya, pranamaya, manomaya, jnanamaya, and anandamaya bodies also correspond to the earth, water, fire, air, and ether elements respectively.

Avoiding the gears

In meditation stay away from the gears of the mind! It is the nature of the mind to dance around producing thoughts, impressions, memories, etc. Therefore we do not at all care what potential distractions may arise during meditation. We ignore them. And if we ignore them they are no longer distractions. So stay with Soham—with God—and forget everything else. Then all will be yours.

Never come out of meditation to note or write down something. If the inspiration, insight, or idea is really from your higher Self or from God it will come back to you outside of meditation.

Also, do not engage the mind-gears with long prayers, affirmations, and suchlike during meditation. And do not let the mind entice you with "insight," "inspiration," or "knowledge" of any kind. According to Shankara the practice of yoga "has right vision alone for its goal, and glories of knowledge and power are not its purpose."

Outside meditation the gears are also there ready to distract and grind you down, making you lose what you gained in meditation. The problem is that the gears become powerful and habitual in many people very early on in their lives and they are very hard to resist. In fact, they seem to have a life and will of their own (but they do not, it is just the will of our corrupted subconscious), and can pull us away from the lifeline of Soham japa without any effort. We just slip into them. So breaking this habit is one of the major labors the yogi must face at the very beginning of his practice if he really wants to make progress.

Here are the biggest gears:

1. Distraction: getting sidetracked in our attention by things going on around us, including people. Sounds, sights, physical sensations, tastes and smells—the mind is used to running after the whole range.

2. Fantasy/daydreaming. This is especially addictive to people of active imaginations. Those who are seriously addicted prefer imagined experiences to actual ones because they are easy and enjoyable and conform to exactly what we want to happen in the theater of our mind.

3. Memories. These come in endless variety, both of actual events in our lives and simple recall of emotions, sensations, reactions, things seen, read or heard, and ideas of all sorts.

4. Inner monologue. We have all seen people walking along talking to themselves. That is overt, but all of us engage in conversations with ourselves without any outward sign. Actually, we can just babble on and on and on.

My paternal grandmother was a great talker. When I was a child there used to be national talking contests to see who could keep talking the longest time. Whenever the reports would come in the newspaper, my aunts would say: "Mom, you have to enter the contest next year. You will win easily." When my grandmother would be taking care of me, she would start talking to me–but really to herself. So I would go in another room or go out and play and be gone quite a long while. But when I came back, grandmother would still be talking.

The mind is like that.

We must avoid these four major gears assiduously. Back in B.Y. (Before Yoga) they were natural and understandable. But now they must be opposed until they go away. The process is simple: every time we get caught, we calmly turn our awareness back again on our inner Soham japa. And we just keep doing it over and over again. Eventually it will work and then we will be truly steady in our mind in the way that counts the most. "Whenever the unsteady mind, moving here and there, wanders off, he should subdue and hold it back and direct it to the Self's control" (Bhagavad Gita 6:26).

The policy we must adopt toward these four and all the smaller mind-gears is to calmly and firmly put our attention back on the japa.

Again and again and again....

But here is the wonderful secret: after a while the mind gets to prefer the japa to the gears. Yet even then vigilance is needed because it is not hard to revert, since the habits of lifetimes are stored up in our subconscious.

Experiences and thoughts in meditation: be indifferent

While meditating, many things—some of them quite dramatic, impressive, and even enjoyable, as well as inane, boring, and uncomfortable—occur as a side-effect. Have no desire to produce or reproduce or avoid any state or experience of any kind, to any degree. Our only interest should be our intonations of Soham in time with the breath. What arises... arises. During meditation much revealing and release take place in both the conscious and subconscious minds—and sometimes even the physical body—and should always be a passively observed process without getting involved in any way.

Thoughts from the subconscious may float or even flood up, but you need only keep on intoning Soham in time with the breath. The states of consciousness that meditation produces are the only things that matter, for they alone bring us to the Goal.

Much phenomena can take place during the process of correction and purification that is an integral part of meditation. When the chakras are being cleansed and perfected, they may become energized, awakened, or opened. In the same way subtle channels in the spine and body may open and subtle energies begin flowing in them. This is all good when it happens spontaneously, effortlessly. But whatever happens in meditation, our sole occupation should be with Soham and the breath.

It should also be understood that boredom, feelings of stagnation, discomfort and even annoyance with meditation are usually the resistance of negative energies, including negative karma.

Sitting like Buddha

When Gautama Buddha sat beneath the bodhi tree he vowed that until he was enlightened he would not get up even if his flesh and bones were to be dissolved. This is why it is said that Buddha got enlightenment because he knew how to sit. His sitting was in the principle of awareness itself. So if you sit in the same way during meditation, you will be safe from all distractions and illusions as was Buddha.

All the forces of the cosmos came to distract Buddha from his inner quest. Even cosmic illusion itself in the form of Mara came to distract him. But he did not move, either in body or mind. Such steadfastness conquered the forces of ignorance completely. Buddha conquered them by simply ignoring them—which was the only sensible course, seeing that they were just illusions. You, too, can conquer distractions not by combatting them, not by killing them, not by seeing through them or any such thing—but by just having nothing to do with them. The true Self does not touch any of these things, so the path to the true spirit involves not touching them in your mind.

By sitting and ignoring the unreal, Buddha found the Real. Therefore many centuries later Jesus simply said: "In your patience possess your souls" (Luke 21:19). To relax and experience is the key for the correct practice of meditation.

Hatching the egg

Each person will experience meditation in a different way, even if there are points of similarity with that of others. Also, meditations can vary greatly for each of us. In some meditations a lot will be going on, and then in other meditations it will seem as though we are just sitting and coasting along with nothing happening.

When nothing seems to be going on at all, we may mistakenly think we are meditating incorrectly or it just does not work. Actually, meditation produces profound and far-reaching changes in our extremely complex makeup, whether we do or do not perceive those changes.

Some meditations are times of quiet assimilation of prior changes and balancing out to get ready for more change. If we are meditating in the way I have outlined, we are doing everything correctly and everything is going on just as it should be—every breath is further refining our inner faculties of awareness.

Very early in the scale of evolution sentient beings, including human beings, are born from eggs, so it is not inappropriate to think of our development in those terms. All eggs hatch and develop through heat. This is absolutely necessary, just as it is for the germination of seeds (the eggs of plants). Yoga is called tapasya, the generation of heat, for that very reason. Our meditation, then, is like the hatching of an egg. Nothing may seem to be going on, but life is developing on the unseen levels.

The hatching of a chicken egg is a prime example. Inside the egg there is nothing but two kinds of goo—the white and the yolk. Both are liquids and have no other perceptible characteristics than color and slimy texture. The hen does nothing more than sit on the egg and keep it warm, yet as the days pass the goo inside the shell turns into internal organs, blood, bones, skin, feathers, brain, ears, and eyes—all that go to make up a chicken—just by being incubated. At last a living, conscious being breaks its way out of the shell. No wonder eggs have been used as symbols of resurrection from death into life.

Another apt symbol is the cocoon. The dull-colored, earth-crawling, caterpillar encases itself in a shroud of its own making and becomes totally dormant. Yet as weeks pass a wondrous transformation takes place internally until one day an utterly different creature emerges: a beautifully colored and graceful butterfly that flies into the sky and thenceforth rarely if ever touches the earth.

The same is true of the persevering yogi and the eventual revelation of his true nature. Through the japa and meditation of Soham, simple as they are, our full spiritual potential will develop and manifest in us. Meditation evolves the meditator, turning the muddle of his present state into a life beyond present conceptions.

Retracing consciousness

Theseus, an ancient epic hero, was condemned to die in a labyrinth. He survived because he had tied a thread at the entrance of the maze. After his wanderings inside he came out of the labyrinth by following the thread back to the entrance. Sound is the thread, the following of which in meditation will lead us out of the deadly labyrinth of samsara. Specifically, Soham is the sound-thread that leads us out, since it leads back to the Origin of all things—That which "in the beginning... first said, 'I am Soham'" (Brihadaranyaka Upanishad 1.4.1).

Soham meditation is the process of retracing discovered by the sages. Tracing Soham back to Its source, experiencing the subtle states of consciousness inherent in Soham, the Soham yogi discovers it within himself as both Power and Consciousness. As he does so, he experiences within the depths of his awareness the subtle states of consciousness, or bhava, inherent in Soham. For this reason the word frequently translated "meditation" in texts relating to yoga is *bhavanam*—the experiencing of the inner states of consciousness called bhavas. Meditation leads us right into the heart of Soham as we trace the thread of Its sound back through Its many permutations to Its original bhava or impulse of consciousness that expanded outward to manifest as Its outermost form of the spoken Soham.

This procedure is spoken of in the Katha Upanishad: "The Self, though hidden in all beings, does not shine forth but can be seen by those subtle seers, through their sharp and subtle intelligence. The wise man should restrain speech into the mind; the latter he should restrain into the understanding Self. The understanding Self he should restrain into the great Self. That he should restrain into the tranquil Self" (Katha Upanishad 1.3.12,13). By "mind" is meant the manas, the sensory mind; by "understanding Self" is meant the buddhi, the intellect; by "the great Self" is meant the will; and by "tranquil Self" is meant the subtlest level, the Chidakasha, the witness-link between our pure consciousness and our perceptions.

In *Viveka Chudamani*, verse 369, Shankara expresses it this way: "Restrain speech in the manas, and restrain manas in the buddhi; this again restrain in the witness of the buddhi [the chidakasha], and merging that also in the Infinite Absolute Self, attain to Supreme Peace." In the subtle sound of Soham the consciousness of the yogi is resolved into its pure, divine state.

This being so, it is crucial for us to continually remember throughout our meditation that the sound of Soham should be the object of our attention. Throughout meditation keep hold of the thread of Soham and you will be led to freedom. Soham is the seed of liberation.

Joining Soham to the breath

"He who breathes in with your breathing in is your Self" (Brihadaranyaka Upanishad 3:4:1). By joining Soham to our breath, each breath moves us onward toward the goal of Divine Unity. "This unmanifest is declared to be the imperishable, which is called the Supreme Goal, attaining which they return not. This is my supreme abode" (Bhagavad Gita 8:21).

The most important aspect of this quote from the Brihadaranyaka Upanishad is that the breath is the direct action with the Self, that is is the primary manifestation of the Self within us. At the beginning of this Upanishad we are told: "In the beginning this (world) was only the Supreme Self [Paramatman], in the shape of a person. Looking around he saw nothing else than the Self. He first said, 'I am Soham' [*Soham asmi*]" (1:4:1). Soham is the name of the individual Self and the Supreme Self. It literally means: "I am That," "I am the Self." But there is much more to that. Many scriptures and texts on yoga declare that when we inhale the subtle sound of *So* is produced, and when we exhale the subtle sound of *Ham* ("Hum") is produced. And at the same time, those sounds produce the breath. So the breath and the sounds *So* and *Ham* are simultaneously the causes and the effects of one another. They are producer and produced, totally interdependent and inseparable. This is the basis of the original yoga, Soham Yoga.

The breath and Soham arise from the very root of our being, the spirit. Joining Soham to the breath extends its transforming vibrations throughout the entire range of our being. It also unites the different aspects of our being and begins effectively and rapidly evolving us, returning us to the Source—but now transformed.

We join intonations of Soham to the breath because on the subtle levels it is always producing the sound of Soham. The spirit-Self *breathes* Soham. So by consciously joining Soham to our breathing we link up with our spirit-consciousness and enter into it. Further, when the habit of intoning Soham with the breath is established, the simple act of breathing will cue the mind to maintain the intonations.

This is necessary because in all relative beings the prana-breath has become corrupted and confused, binding the spirit rather than freeing it. The prana-breath has gotten out of phase, out of tune or off key—out of alignment with Soham, the original keynote of the universe and the breath. By intoning Soham in time with his breath, the Soham yogi takes charge of his prana-breath, realigns and repolarizes it, restoring it to its original form and function. In this way he sets himself squarely in the upward-moving stream of evolution and accelerates his movement within it.

We have been pulled so out of shape that our original nature and form are undetectable. Soham sadhana puts us back into shape and restores us to our true nature and form. Think of a picture puzzle in which all the pieces have become so mixed up that what is seen is nothing but a chaotic, jumbled mess. Soham sadhana puts all the pieces back into their intended order and our true face, our true Self, becomes known.

It is very necessary for us to begin our intonations of *So* when our inhalations begin, and *ham* when our exhalations begin. This is because one object of Soham Yoga is to perfectly synchronize the breath with Soham in case the two have gotten out of phase with one another. The breath therefore should become smooth, united, and continuous. This is referred to in the Bhagavad Gita (4:29) where it speaks of those who "offer inhalation into exhalation, and exhalation into inhalation." The offering of the exhalation into the inhalation and vice versa refers to the smoothing of the breath until there is no significant or marked pause between inhaling and exhaling, but rather there is a smooth transition from one to the other—one seeming to arise from the other, both together being a single organic unity.

Again: we breathe through the nose, not the mouth.

Making the two into one

We are speaking of "the breath *and* Soham," but in reality they are the same thing. The breath is not just a stop and go light, used merely to let us know when to intone *So* and *Ham*. The breath is a form, a manifestation, of Soham. In Soham Yoga we intone Soham in time with the breath so the two will remerge and become one, restoring their essential unity. Therefore it is important that the breath and Soham be perfectly integrated. That is why the intonation of *So* and *Ham* should begin with the breath movements—inhalation and exhalation. We need not exaggerate this and turn our meditation into a torment of anxiety, but reasonable care should be taken.

Soham is the essential sound-energy form that manifests in living beings as the breath itself. Soham is the sound-form of the subtle power of life which originates in the pure consciousness, the spirit, of each one of us and extends outward to manifest as the inhaling and exhaling breaths. Hence, through the intoning of Soham in and out of meditation we can become attuned to the essential Breath of Life and aware of its subtle movements within. Joined to our breath, the mantra Soham will lead us to the awareness of Breath and Life in their pure state. For Soham is both the breath and the Source of the breath. When joined to Soham, the breath becomes a flowing stream of consciousness.

The Cosmic Breath

As has been said, the original impulse toward manifestation and evolution is dual, both sound and movement. On the cosmic level its most objective manifestation is the projection and withdrawal of the universe that is the cosmic exhalation and inhalation of Ishwara. He exhales and inhales the cosmos in a perpetual cycle of Cosmic Breath. The same thing is done by the individual spirit-Self, its most objective manifestation being the physical breath—the dual movements of inhalation and exhalation which arise from the root impulse of the Original Breath that is common to both the creation and each sentient being within creation. It is the movement of the involution and evolution of all within it, the baton by means of which the Cosmic Conductor brings about the unfolding symphony of cosmic and individual perfection: Soham. Soham japa and meditation is the process of becoming freed from the cycle of birth and death and its attendant defects (kleshas) born of ignorance (avidya) and limitation.

Effective attention

Although we tend to think of attention as merely a state of mind, the opposite of inattention, it is really a great psychic force. Quantum physics has discovered that when a human being sets his attention on anything, that object is immediately affected to some degree—so much so that a scientist can unintentionally influence the result of an experiment, however controlled the external conditions may be. Thoughts are indeed things, but attention is the fundamental power of thought.

I have said this before, but I would like to repeat it to make sure these principles are understood:

1. As we calmly fix our awareness on the breath and the sound of Soham, they become increasingly refined. The breath becomes gentler and easeful, often slowing down until our breathing becomes as light as the breeze of a butterfly's wings, and so does the internal sound of Soham become soft and whisperlike, even virtually silent. Since it is natural for them to become increasingly refined as you observe them, you need not attempt to deliberately make this happen. Your attention will automatically refine

them. As we become more and more aware of the subtle forms or movements of the inner breath and sound, it automatically happens that the breath movements on all levels become slower. This is the highest form of pranayama.

2.   The more attention we give to breath and sound, the subtler they become until the breath reveals itself as the mind-stuff (chitta) itself and Soham as the bhava, the state of realization: I Am That. Both breath and sound, like an onion, have many layers. In the practice of Soham meditation we experience these layers, beginning with the most objective, physical layer and progressing to increasingly subtle layers, until, as with an onion at its core, there are no more layers, but only the pure being of the Self. The breath and sound become increasingly refined as we observe them, and as a result our awareness also becomes refined. Our attention focused on the breath and Soham causes their potential to manifest in the way sunlight causes the petals of a flower to open.

We ourselves are waves in the ocean of Consciousness and Sound. We are Soham. So in Soham Yoga practice, especially when we experience the permutations of the subtle sounds of Soham, we are actually experiencing ourselves. The more we meditate, the higher and higher and further and further we penetrate into the Infinite Consciousness of which we are an eternal part. That is our point of origin, and the subtle vibrations of Soham will take us back there.

Yoga Nidra–conscious sleep

The purpose of meditation is the development of deep inner awareness. The *Yoga Vashishtha* (5:78), a classical treatise on yoga, speaks of the state "when the consciousness reaches the deep sleep state" known in Sanskrit as sushupti. The sage Sandilya in his treatise on yoga, the Sandilya Upanishad, also speaks of "when sushupti is rightly cognized [experienced] while conscious." Ramana Maharshi also spoke frequently of this yogic state known as yoga nidra–yoga sleep. Although it is described as dreamless sleep, it is much, much more, for there is a deepening of consciousness in this state that does not occur in ordinary dreamless sleep.

In the *Chidakasha Gita*, section 120, Paramhansa Nityananda, himself a great Nath Yogi, had this to say about yoga nidra: "Harmonizing both prana and apana [inhalation and exhalation], enjoy the subtle sleep. Harmonizing the prana and apana, enjoy the eternal bliss. Enjoy the conscious sleep of bliss.… Enjoy that sleep which must be the aim and end of man.… Perform the natural japa of the inward and the outward breath." Yoga Nidra is the state of conscious sushupti–dreamless sleep. This occurs during the practice of Soham Yoga when the awareness is gathered into the Chidakasha and when the inhaling and exhaling breaths are harmonized by intoning Soham in time with them. The sleep of yoga Nityananda is teaching us about is the true awakening.

Regarding this Sri Gajanana Maharaj said: "Not to see anything in dhyana [meditation] shows a state of concentration. When seeing is turned into non-seeing, then there is the real state of samadhi. The state of complete samadhi is like the state of death but it is a state of life after having conquered death. The state of sleep is also a kind of death and he really knows the secret of dhyana yoga whose sleep is nothing but samadhi."

In deep meditation we enter into the silent witness state, experiencing the state of dreamless sleep while fully conscious and aware. When approaching this state the beginner may actually fall asleep. This is not to be worried about, for such is quite natural, and after a while will not occur. From birth we have been habituated to falling asleep when the mind reached a certain inner point. Now through meditation we will take another turn–into the state of deep inner awareness. Ramana Maharshi said that even if a yogi falls asleep while approaching–or in–yoga nidra, the process of meditation still continues. Yoga Nidra is the state of conscious sushupti, dreamless sleep, and yet much more, for then the awareness is gathered into the Chidakasha, the principle of pure consciousness. And there is a deepening of consciousness that does not occur in any other state.

So when you have this asleep-while-awake state occur, know that you are on the right track—when it is imageless and thoughtless except for your intonations of Soham (for those should never stop). Not that visions cannot occur during meditation, but it is easy to mistake dreams for visions. Therefore it is wise to value only the conscious sushupti experience in meditation, within which Soham continues to be the focus of our awareness. This is the true samadhi.

The workings of Soham

But there is another, seemingly contradictory, side to this. *Yogash chitta-vritti-nirodhah* (Yoga Sutras 1:2). Patanjali here defines yoga as the stopping (*nirodhah*) of the modifications (*vritti*) of the mind (*chitta*). Superficially considered, this seems to mean merely being blank, without thoughts. But if this were so, dreamless sleep would be yoga, and the more we slept the more enlightened we would become. Still, most yogis tend to think that in meditation no thoughts or impressions should arise—that if they do, the meditation is imperfect and reduced in value. But Soham is a transforming-transmuting force, and that implies change, and change is a process. So sometimes you will simply sit in the happy and peaceful silence of pure yoga nidra, intent on the sound of your subtle intonations of Soham, and at other times things will definitely be going on. Both are equally beneficial, and both may occur in the same meditation.

Meditation, then, is not just sinking down into silence and stasis, though that does happen in some meditation periods, but can be an extremely active state. As you meditate, on the subtle levels you may see, hear, feel, and be aware of a great many things—thoughts, visual impressions, memories, inner sensations, and suchlike. All of this is evoked by your practice, and nothing will be a distraction if you simply observe it in a calm and objective manner, keeping your awareness on the breath and intoning Soham in time with it.

Your interest should be in your intonations of Soham, yet you should be aware of what is going on. The key is to remain a calm observer and able to distinguish between the worthless antics of the lower mind and that which is being produced directly by Soham for your betterment. Spending hours in and out of meditation, invoking Soham constantly, produces the most profound changes in the meditator's psychic energy system on the physical, astral, and causal levels. The union of the prana (breath) and the subtle vibrations of Soham produce dramatic repolarization of the consciousness and life force. Sensitive yogis will experience this along with a myriad other transformations.

"With mind made steadfast by yoga, which turns not to anything else, to the Divine Supreme Spirit he goes, meditating on him" (Bhagavad Gita 8:8).

The four elements of Soham Yoga meditation

There are four components of Soham Yoga meditation:

1. sitting with closed eyes;
2. being aware of the breath as it moves in and out;
3. mentally intoning Soham in time with the breathing;
4. listening to the inner, mental intonations of Soham and becoming absorbed in the subtle sound.

These are the essential ingredients of Soham Yoga meditation, and we should confine our attention to them. If in meditation we feel unsure as to whether things are going right, we need only check to see if these four things are being done and our attention is centered in them. If so, all is well. If not, it is a simple matter to return to them and make everything right. Success in Soham Yoga consists of going deeper and deeper into the subtle sound of the Soham mantra as we intone it within. It is the thread leading us into the center of Reality.

Gorakhnath summed up his Soham Yoga practice and its effect in this manner: "The mind is the root and the breath is the branch; the sound [of Soham] is the guru and attention [to the sound] is the disciple. With the essence called deliverance [*nirvana tattwa*–the principle of liberation] Gorakhnath wanders about, himself in himself" (Gorakh Bodha 10).

Invariables

There are certain invariables of Soham Yoga meditation.

1. We always meditate with closed mouth and eyes.
2. We always mentally intone Soham in time with the breath.
3. Our mental intonations of Soham, like the breath to which we are linking them, should be virtually continuous, not with long breaks between them. That is: *SoooooHuuummmSoooooHuuum-mmSoooooHuuummmSoooooHuuummm.* (Basically continuous is good enough.)
4. *Soham never ceases.* Never. We must not let passivity or heaviness of mind interrupt our intonations by pulling us into negative silence. That would be a descent rather than an ascent.
5. The focus, the center of attention, of our meditation is the sound of our mental intonations of Soham in time with our breath. In an easeful and relaxed manner we become absorbed in that inner sound.
6. Our mental intonations of Soham are gentle, quiet and subtle.

Prayer

It is traditional for some brief prayer to be made before and after meditation. Usually before meditation a simple prayer is made asking divine blessing and guidance. Then at the end another brief prayer is made giving thanks, offering the meditation to God, and asking divine blessing for the rest of the day. There is no set form, just words from the heart. This is not essential for Soham Yoga practice, but those who are so inclined may find it beneficial.

Japa and meditation of Soham

Japa and meditation of Soham support each other. Continual japa of Soham during your daily routine will increase the effectiveness of your practice of meditation, and daily meditation practice will deepen the effect of your japa outside meditation.

When doing japa while we are engaged in other activities there is a profound effect, but we are not able to experience the effects of Soham nearly as much as we can while sitting in meditation. The meditation experience is absolutely essential for spiritual progress, just as japa outside meditation is essential to ensure that meditation will be effective to the maximum degree.

Soham should be intoned constantly, throughout all activities, without break or interruption. Naturally this is difficult, even impossible to do, in the beginning, nevertheless it is possible in time. Immediately upon awakening in the morning, begin the mental intonation of Soham and keep on until falling asleep that night.

It cannot be overemphasized that the breath and Soham transfer our awareness into the subject: consciousness itself. Other objects may draw our attention outward, into the experience of them, and perpetuate the loss of Self-awareness which is our root problem. This should not be forgotten.

The bigger picture

Thoughts do not cease the moment they pass from the conscious mind. They spread out around us into our aura, the subtle field of biomagnetic and mental energies around our physical body, and then on into the surrounding creation, ultimately extending to the farthest reaches of the cosmos and then returning back into our aura and mind. This is a process of mental-spiritual karma. By always doing repetition and meditation of Soham, we set up a continuous current of spiritual vibration that in time becomes a perpetual inflow of higher consciousness as it returns to us after having extended throughout creation and benefited all things and all beings therein. In this way we create the highest form of spiritual karma, uplifting and divinizing both ourselves and all that exists. Therefore, throughout the day and night, whatever you are doing or whenever at rest, continually intone Soham mentally in time with the breath and center your awareness in the sound. Since there is no time when you do not breathe, this is possible.

Responsiveness to yoga practice

The bodies, physical, astral, and causal, are the vehicles through which the individual evolves during the span of life on earth, and must be taken into serious account by the yogi who will discover that they can exert a powerful, controlling effect on the mind. If wax and clay are cold they cannot be molded, nor will they take any impression; if molasses is cold it will hardly pour. It is all a matter of responsiveness. Only when warm are these substances malleable. In the same way, unless our inner and outer bodies are made responsive or reactive to the effects of meditation, we will miss many of its beneficial effects. Hence we should do everything we can to increase our response levels, to ensure that our physical and psychic levels are moving at the highest possible rate of vibration.

Yogic diet

A fundamental key to success in yoga is diet. For just as the physical substance of the food becomes assimilated into our physical body, the subtler energies become united to our inner levels, including our mind. The observant meditator will discover that the diet of the physical body is also the diet of the mind, that whatever is eaten physically will have an effect mentally. Here are some statements about the nature and effect of food that are found in the upanishads.

"From food [has arisen] vital vigor, austerity and works" (Prashna Upanishad 6.4). Ascetic discipline (tapasya), mantra and right action are essential to the yogi, and here we see that the food we eat is their basis. Obviously the kind of food we eat will determine the quality of all those things.

"By food, indeed, do all the vital breaths [pranas, life forces] become great" (Taittiriya Upanishad 1.5.4).

"A person consists of the essence of food" (Taittiriya Upanishad 2.1.1). So we *are* what we eat.

"From food, verily, are produced whatsoever creatures dwell on the earth. Moreover, by food alone they live.... From food are beings born.

When born they grow up by food.... Verily, different from and within that which consists of the essence of food is the self that consists of life. By that this is filled. This, verily, has the form of a person. According to that one's personal form is this one with the form of a person." (Taittiriya Upanishad 2.2.1). The spiritual, astral/causal, body is drawn exclusively from food, so diet is crucial in spiritual development.

"Food when eaten becomes threefold, its coarsest portion becomes the faeces; its middle (portion) flesh, and its subtlest (portion) mind. Water when drunk becomes threefold, its coarsest portion becomes the urine; its middle (portion) the blood, its subtlest (portion) the breath.... Thus, my dear, mind consists of food, and breath consists of water...." (Chandogya Upanishad 6.5.1-2, 4).

"That which is the subtlest part of curds rises, when they are churned and becomes butter. In the same manner that which is the subtlest part of the food that is eaten rises and becomes mind. Thus the mind consists of food" (Chandogya Upanishad 6.6.1, 2,5; the same is confirmed in 6.6.1-5).

"When food is pure, the mind is pure, When the mind is pure, memory becomes firm. When memory [smriti—memory of our eternal spirit-Self] remains firm, there is release from all knots of the heart. To such a one who has his stains wiped away, Bhagavan Sanatkumara shows the further shore of darkness" (Chandogya Upanishad 7.26.2).

"In food everything rests, whatsoever breathes and what does not" (Brihadaranyaka Upanishad 1.5.1).

Both meditation and diet refine the inner senses so we can produce and perceive the subtle changes that occur during meditation.

Meat is both heavy and toxic, especially from the chemicals spread throughout the tissues from the fear and anger of the animal when it was slaughtered. So our minds will also be heavy and toxic from eating meat as well as poisoned by the vibrations of anger and fear. And then there is the karma of killing sentient beings. Moreover, the instinctual and behavioral patterns of the animals will become our instinctual and behavioral impulses.

Fruits, vegetables, and grains have no such obstructions. Consequently, our mental energies will be light and malleable, responsive to our spiritual disciplines. Few things are more self-defeating than the eating of meat. From the yogic standpoint, the adoption of a vegetarian diet is a great spiritual boon. By vegetarian I mean abstention from meat, fish, and eggs or anything that contains them to any degree, including animal fats. It is even better to also eliminate all dairy products and their derivatives from the diet.

Our general health also contributes to our proficiency in meditation, so a responsible yogi is very aware of what is beneficial and detrimental to health and orders his life accordingly, especially in eliminating completely all alcohol, nicotine, and mind-altering drugs whether legal or illegal. Caffeine, too, is wisely avoided, and so is sugar.

All of the above-mentioned substances—meat, fish, eggs, animal derivatives, alcohol, nicotine, and mind-altering drugs—deaden and coarsen the mind and body and consequently the consciousness. Thus they hinder or prevent the necessary effects and experiences of subtle Soham meditation.

The sum of all this is that we must do more than meditate. We must live out our spiritual aspirations by so ordering our lives that we will most quickly advance toward the Goal. This is done by observing the Ten Commandments of Yoga (Yama-Niyama.) They are:

1. Non-violence, non-injury, harmlessness.
2. Truthfulness, honesty.
3. Non-stealing, honesty, non-misappropriativeness.
4. Sexual continence in thought, word and deed as well as control of all the senses.
5. Non-possessiveness, non-greed, non-selfishness, non-acquisitiveness.
6. Purity, cleanliness.
7. Contentment, peacefulness.
8. Austerity, practical (i.e., result-producing) spiritual discipline.

9. Introspective self-study, spiritual study.

10. Offering of one's life to God, especially in the highest sense of uniting our consciousness with Infinite Consciousness through meditation.

These are explained in detail in the next chapter, The Foundations of Yoga.

Training for living

Meditation is not an end in itself, but rather the means to an end–to the daily living out of the illumined consciousness produced by meditation. We go into meditation so we can come out of meditation more conscious and better equipped to live our life. The change will not be instant, but after a reasonable time we should see a definite effect in how we perceive, think and live. If the meditator does not find that his state of mind during daily activities has been affected by his meditation, then his meditation is without value. This is especially important for us in the West since meditation is continually being touted as a natural high or a producer of profound and cataclysmic experiences. Such experiences may sound good on paper or in a metaphysical bragfest, but in time they are seen to be empty of worth on any level–ephemeral dreams without substance. Success in meditation is manifested *outside* meditation–by the states of mind and depth of insight that become habitual. The proof of its viability is the meditator's continual state of mind and his apprehension of both reality and Reality.

Many things lighten and purify the mind, but nothing clarifies the mind like the prolonged and profound practice of meditation. The state of mental clarity produced by meditation should continue outside meditation. Meditation should by its nature prepare us for living. At the same time, meditation should establish us in interior life, making us increasingly aware both inwardly and outwardly. This is because reality consists of two aspects: the unmoving consciousness of spirit and the moving, dynamic activity of evolutionary energy.

Reality embraces both, and to be without the awareness of one or the other is to be incomplete.

Meditation enables us to see deeply into things outside meditation. Through meditation we cultivate the ability to be objective–separate from objects but keenly aware of them and thus able to intelligently and effectively function in relation to them. Meditation, then, is the most effective school for living open to us. And it manifests in the simplest of ways: a more compassionate outlook, a deeper self-understanding, an awareness of changelessness amidst change, a taste for spiritual conversation and reading, and experience of inmost peace. One man who had been practicing meditation for a while remarked to another meditator, "I can't figure out what is happening to me. Last night for the first time in my married life I helped my wife do the dishes."

In the practice of the japa and meditation of Soham we are putting ourselves into a totally–even sublimely–different sphere of consciousness and experience from that in which so much phenomena arise. Meditation is done for the development of consciousness–truly pure and simple–whereas it is our active life that is meant for both *seeing* and experiencing. It is all a matter of consciousness–of consciousness that pervades our entire life–not just a wonderful feeling in meditation. It is the fundamental state of consciousness and mind outside of meditation that matters.

Positive resolve

It is important that we be positive and not negative in our resolve to meditate well. Just not thinking about something undesirable is not enough. Rather than thinking: "I will not think about that," we should resolve: "I will constantly remember Soham." Virtue consists of *doing* good, not just not doing evil. At the same time do not be all anxious about meditating "right" or "well," but just relax and experience what happens as you inwardly intone Soham in time with the breath and listen to the inner, mental sound of the mantra.

Restlessness or calmness—whatever happens is right as long as the simple process continues. Meditation can be a revelation, an uncovering, of what is within, and the perception of both good and bad, negative and positive, comfortable and uncomfortable, lightness and heaviness, fullness and emptiness, alertness and dullness, etc. is part of the correction/cleansing process. Meditation sometimes shows you what is going on, both within yourself and outside in the world. That, too, is beneficial, even if unpleasant at times.

Evocation and invocation

In japa and meditation we are not employing Soham as a prayer, an affirmation, or a remembrance, but as effective evocation—a calling forth—of our inherent, eternal Self-consciousness, and as an invocation—a calling into us—of the Consciousness that is the Supreme Self. Because this is so, we do not need to keep in mind an intellectual meaning of Soham or cultivate an attitude or emotion during our practice. Rather, we relax, listen, and make ourselves open and receptive to its dynamic working within us.

Two views on the nature of meditation—and a third

In India there is a long-standing disagreement on the nature and purpose of meditation. One school of thought considers that definite, conscious evolutionary change is necessary for liberation; consequently meditation must be an actively transforming process. The other view is that the only thing needed for liberation is re-entry into our true, eternal nature—that nothing need be done at all in the usual sense of doing except to perceive the truth of ourselves. Obviously their meditation procedures are going to be completely different.

There is, however, a third perspective on the matter which combines both views. It is true that we are ever-free, ever-perfect, but we have forgotten that fact and have wandered in aimless suffering for countless incarnations. No one is so foolish as to suggest to a person suffering from amnesia that he need not regain his memory since he has not ceased to be who he really is.

The memory block from which we suffer is the condition of the various levels on which we presently function, especially the buddhi, the intelligence. It is also a matter of the dislocation of our consciousness from its natural center. Obviously, then, something really does have to be done to change this condition. A dirty window need not be changed in nature, but it needs to be cleansed of that which is not its nature for us to see through it. It is the same with a dusty or smudgy mirror.

There is an example from nature that can help us understand this. Research has shown that the energy field around a salamander egg, and all through the stages of a young salamander's growth, is in the shape of an adult salamander. This indicates that the etheric pattern of a full-grown salamander is inherent even in the egg and throughout the salamander's development. It is as though the egg has only to hatch and grow around this energy matrix, to fill out or grow into the ever-present pattern. Even when there is only the egg visible to the human eye, the adult salamander is there in a very real, potential form. It is the same with us. We are always the Atman, potential divinity, but that potential must be realized. And meditation is the means of our realization.

Shankara puts forth the question, "How can there be a means to obtain liberation? Liberation is not a thing which can be obtained, for it is simply cessation of bondage." He then answers himself: "For ignorance [bondage] to cease, something has to be done, with effort, as in the breaking of a fetter. Though liberation is not a 'thing,' inasmuch as it is cessation of ignorance in the presence of right knowledge, it is figuratively spoken of as something to be obtained." And he concludes: "The purpose of Yoga is the knowledge of Reality."

Vyasa defines liberation in this way: "Liberation is absence of bondage." Shankara carries it a bit further, saying: "Nor is liberation something that has to be brought about apart from the absence of bondage, and this is why it is always accepted that liberation is eternal."

Liberation, enlightenment, is a state that is not produced but evoked or revealed. Liberation is perception of our eternal nature. It is like something revealed by the light: it is not made existent by the light, it has been there all along in the darkness; but now the light has made it known. Soham Yoga, then is a turning, an opening, to Reality, but not attainment of Reality as something not always possessed. It is like a plant turning toward the sun; it is orientation of consciousness. It is *being conscious*(ness). Soham Yoga establishes our consciousness in the true Self.

Focus on prakriti

Soham Yoga affects our energy-bodies, not our inner consciousness; it *reveals* our consciousness rather than changes it. The purpose of Soham Yoga is liberation, and to this end it affects the prakriti (energy complex) which is the adjunct of our purusha (spirit). Because of this, it is only natural and right that thoughts, impressions, sensations and feelings of many kinds should arise as you meditate, since your meditation is evoking them as part of the transformation process. All you need do is stay relaxed and keep on intoning Soham in time with the breath.

The Soham yogi is already in the Self, *is* the Self, so in Soham Yoga he is looking at/into his personal prakriti in the same way God observes the evolving creation. Soham Yoga purifies and evolves the bodies, including the buddhi, and realigns our consciousness with its true state, accomplishing the aims of both schools of meditational thought previously mentioned.

Since we are talking about material things (prakriti), this might be a good place to mention that it is best to meditate without shoes, because shoes (whatever material they are made from) carry the vibration of the dirt they contact each day.

Prana takes on many forms, including biomagnetism, the force which maintains our body and its functions. The body itself is magnetic, and any disturbance in polarity or magnetic flow is detrimental to health. Leather inhibits the natural flow of the life force (prana). Leather shoes block the upward flow of prana from the earth into our bodies, and leather belts interfere with the flow of prana within the body. On the more metaphysical side of things, the use of leather (or any slaughtered-animal-derived substance) in any manner is a violation of the principle of ahimsa, as Yogananda points out in chapter four of *Autobiography of a Yogi*. It is also an infraction of the principle of shaucha.

It has long been my experience that sleeping with the head toward the north and the feet toward the south can cause a magnetic conflict or disturbance in the body, adversely affecting sleep and even causing nervousness and restlessness. This is also the experience of many yogis I have known.

Visions

Most "visions" seen in meditation occur because the meditator has fallen asleep and is dreaming. There are genuine visions, actual psychic experiences, that can occur in meditation. But Ramana Maharshi gives the true facts about all visions when he says: "Visions do occur. To know how you look you must look into a mirror, but do not take that reflection to be yourself. What is perceived by our senses and the mind is never the [ultimate] truth. All visions are mere mental creations, and if you believe in them, your progress ceases. Enquire to whom the visions occur. Find out who is their witness. Stay in pure awareness, free from all thoughts. Do not move out of that state" (*The Power of the Presence*, vol. 3, p. 249).

How do I know it's working?

It is only reasonable to wonder if a practice is really doing what it is supposed to. Through various forms of emotional and spiritual blackmail many cult-type yoga teachers and groups keep their members afraid to either question or come to the conclusion that what they have been taught is worthless—including the teacher and the organization. Some years ago I received a letter from a man who had been practicing "the highest yogic technique with the greatest masters" in one of those groups for over thirty years and had gotten nowhere. Yet he was afraid to even consider that the method was at fault, not him.

Once in Benares I had a very long interview with Sri Anandamayi Ma in which she spoke with me at length about certain meditation practices that actually deceive aspiring yogis into thinking that they are making progress, and then after years of practice they find themselves (in Ma's exact words:) empty.

Certainly the yogi should be experiencing the effects of a yogic practice. They can take many forms, and since people's energy bodies differ in character and quality, everyone will not experience the same things nor after the same time of practice. Yet peace and a feeling of ease and well-being, including a feeling of quiet joy, should start occurring after steady practice. Some people experience this in the very first meditation and others only after some time. However, if after several weeks nothing is happening the yogi must carefully check to make sure his practice is correct. If it is, then the method may be at fault and he should not hesitate to try something else.

Meditating is very much like drilling for oil or water. The effects, like the drill, pass through various layers of the inner mind–the subtle bodies. Some layers are gone through quickly, and other take quite a while. The yogi can experience very positive effects and then after a while nothing seems to be happening in his meditation. This is because he has become acclimated to the practice and is then going through a period of assimilation and inner adjustment. But after some time (it differs for each person) he will again experience very real effects of progress. This can happen many times until the yogi is really adept.

I knew a man who would take up a practice, feel very real effects from it, and then after some time it would seem to go flat. Unfortunately he would decide that he had received all the benefit it had to offer and would abandon it. He never got anywhere as a yogi, because reasonable perseverance is essential.

It is true, though, that if months go by and your meditation is empty and tedious, then something is wrong and you should acknowledge it and question it.

I have been speaking of experiences, and they are important, but the heart of the matter is the actual *effect* of those experiences.

I knew a woman who had supposedly ecstatic experiences in every meditation, yet outside meditation she was a hateful and spiteful person, cruel to others in her words and deeds. The last time I saw her she was disintegrating mentally and eventually became insane. (For years she had been practicing one of the methods Anandamayi Ma warned me against.)

If a practice does not make you a better person on all levels, stable and positive, wiser and deeper in consciousness, then it should be abandoned as worthless and possibly deadly poison.

Therefore you should carefully examine the source and the effects of any practice. Beware, beware, beware: at this point in time many yoga teachers and practices are harming and even destroying the lives and minds of sincere aspirants. Trust your ultimate conclusions regarding all such. If they are based on calm and careful analysis, free from any emotional clouding or fear, then trust them and act accordingly.

Falling asleep in meditation

It is normal for meditators to sometimes fall asleep while meditating, since meditation is relaxing and moves the consciousness inward. Both the body and the mind are used to entering into the state of sleep at such times. After a while, though, you will naturally (and hopefully, usually) move into the conscious sleep state, so do not worry.

At the same time, be aware that falling asleep in meditation can be a signal from your body that you are not getting enough sleep at night. People are different, and some do need more sleep than others. You should consider extending your sleep time or taking some kind of nap break during the day. Falling asleep in meditation can also be a symptom of a nutritional lack, an indication of low vitality.

Please do not do such things as shock your body with cold water, drink coffee, or run around a bit, hoping to force yourself to stay awake in meditation. This is not the way. Listen to your body and take care of it. Yogis are not storm-troopers. We are engaged in peace, not war.

Physical distractions

We have talked about mental distractions, but what about physical ones? Simple: scratch when you itch, yawn when tired, shift or stretch when you have a muscle cramp, and if you feel uncomfortable, shift your position. We are meditating, not torturing or coercing the body. Such distractions are normal and not to be concerned about. If we give them undue attention by being annoyed or disgusted with them, or trying to force our attention away from them, we will only be concentrating on them, and will compound their distracting power. In time most of these little annoyances stop occurring. Until then, just be calm and scratch and rub and move a little, while keeping your awareness where it belongs.

What about noises? Accept them. Do not wish they would stop, and do not try to not hear them. Just accept the noise as part of your present situation. Neither like nor dislike it.

Care only for your meditation, confident that a few itchings, cramping, noises, thoughts, or memories will not ruin your meditation. "Greater is he [the spirit] that is in you, than he [the body] that is in the world" (I John 4:4). It is your *attention* to them, either in rejection or acceptance, that will spoil your meditation. You must guard against that, and relaxation and indifference to them is the way.

Daily meditation

"Verily; that Self is (abides) in the heart. He who knows this goes day by day into the heavenly world [through meditation]" (Chandogya Upanishad 8:3:3).

Meditation should be done daily, and many meditate twice daily—morning and evening, or before and after work, whichever is more convenient.

When your period of meditation is over, do your utmost to maintain the flow of Soham japa in time with your breathing in all your activities. For those who diligently and continually apply themselves, attainment is inevitable.

When you find yourself with some time—even a few minutes—during the day, sit and meditate. Every little bit certainly does help.

Length of meditation

How long at a time should you meditate? The more you meditate the more benefit you will receive, but you should not push or strain yourself. Start with a modest time, fifteen or twenty minutes, and gradually work up to an hour or an hour and a half at a time, perhaps once a week meditating even longer if that is practical. (There is a special value and benefit in meditating three hours.) But do not force or burn yourself out. It is a common trick of the negative mind to have you meditate for a very long time and then skip some days or weeks and then overdo it again. It is better to do the minimum time every day without fail. Remember the tortoise and the hare.

Also, if you go about it the right way and live in the manner which makes you supremely responsive, one hour's meditation can equal several hours of meditation done by an undisciplined and unpurified yogi.

Keep it inside

Do not dissipate the calmness and centering gained through meditation by talking about it to others. Experiences in meditation are not only subtle, they are fragile, as delicate as spun glass, and speaking about them can shatter their beneficial effects. Bragging, eulogizing and swapping notes about meditation experiences is a very harmful activity.

Avoid it. Otherwise you or others may be tempted to force things or imitate one another.

Do not satisfy any curiosity about your personal yogic experiences or benefits except in the most general terms. Naturally you can tell people that meditation helps you, but do so in only a general way unless you really feel intuitively that you should be more specific. When people seem truly interested in spiritual life and serious about it, give them a copy of this book *and if they read it* discuss the general and practical aspects freely.

Concentration

Although in this book you will find the word concentration, it is not used in the sense of forcing or tensing the mind. Rather, we are wanting to become *aware*–that is *attentive*–to the fullest degree. And this is accomplished in Soham Yoga by relaxation in body, mind, and attitude. Our attention on Soham is always gentle, though determined. It is not a spike we are driving into our mind. We are floating in Soham, not crashing into it.

In meditation both the body and the mind must be relaxed. This relaxation is what most readily facilitates meditation. Think of the mind as a sponge absolutely full of water. If you hold it in your hand, fully relaxed, all will be well. But if you grip it or squeeze it tightly, water will spray out in all directions. This is exactly how it is with the mind. If you hold it in a state of calm relaxation, very few distractions in the form of memories and thoughts will arise. But if you try to force the mind and tense it, then a multitude of distractions will arise.

Learning to continually do japa of Soham

By keeping up the inner repetition of Soham all the time, whatever you may be doing, you will be perpetually cultivating supreme aware-ness itself. A good way to get yourself habituated to the constant japa of Soham is to do japa while you are reading–simply looking at or scanning the page rather than verbalizing in your mind. (This is the secret of speed reading.) Once you learn to do that, since reading demands so much attention, you will pretty well be able to keep the japa going in other activities. Another way to establish the continual Soham-breath process is to use a japa mala and move to the next bead at each inhalation.

Inner negativity

Impulses to negativity or foolishness, whether mental or physical, exist in our minds in the form of samskaras or vasanas. (Samskaras are impressions in the mind produced by previous actions or experiences, and vasanas are bundles or aggregates of similar samskaras.) Worries and anxieties about these samskaras and vasanas in the form of "sins," "temptations," and "wrong thinking" torment a lot of seekers uselessly. Even more futile is obsession with "getting rid of the ego." For the Soham yogi who regularly practices meditation and arranges his inner and outer life so as to avoid their counteracting or conflicting with his practice there is no need for such self-torture. Speaking of these negative and troublesome things, Shankara confidently says: "They are dissolved along with the receptacle, the chitta.... Because they have no effect, they are not given attention, for when a thing is falling of itself there is no point in searching for something to make it fall." I. K. Taimni says: "As the object of meditation continues to fill the mind completely there can be no question of emptying the mind."

Too upset to meditate?

I knew a man who frequently refused medication, saying, "I'm too sick right now to take medicine. I'll take it when I feel better." This amazed me, but we tend to do the same thing regarding meditation. It is the only way to real peace, but when our lives are being swept with the storms of grief, disaster, fears, anger, and suchlike, we say the same thing: "I am too upset to meditate. I'll do it later." But meditation has the ability to soothe and eliminate all disturbed thoughts and inner states.

So whenever any distracted or negative conditions arise in our minds and lives, meditation is the key to peace and clear thinking.

Yogic Environment

One of our monks once showed me two containers. In each one was a very small, green plant less than an inch high, consisting of two leaves. "I planted these nine weeks ago," he said. "Really? What is wrong with them?" I asked. "I used the wrong kind of potting soil, so they won't grow," he told me. It is exactly the same with the study of spiritual philosophy and the practice of meditation: if there is not the right environment, inner and outer, nothing at all will come of it. Not only do we need a special place in our home favorable to meditation, our entire environment should be examined to see that it, too, is not mentally and spiritually heavy, toxic, disruptive and agitating. The same is true of our employment and our associates, business, social, and familial.

The most important environment, of course, is the inner one of our own mind: our thoughts. Our dominant thought should be our intonations of Soham. Next to that should be continual thoughts of spiritual matters drawn from our own study of spiritual writings, attendance at spiritual discourses and conversation with spiritually-minded associates. Our minds should naturally move in the highest spiritual planes. This is neither impossible nor impractical, for everything proceeds from and is controlled by the Supreme Consciousness.

Entering the silence

The expression "entering the silence" is usually misunderstood as sitting with a blank mind. One mystery of Soham is its ability to produce silence through sound—sound that is essentially silence. We go deeper and deeper into the sound, the increasingly subtle sound of Soham, until we reach the heart of the sound which is silence. Through our invocation of Soham the *state* of silence is produced in our mind by enabling us to center it in the principle of the silent witnessing consciousness.

Through Soham the yogi leads his awareness into the silence of the spirit which is beyond the clamor of the mind and the distractions and movements of the body. For true silence is not mere absence of sound, but a profound condition of awareness that prevails at all times, even during the noise of our daily life. Silence is also a state of stillness of spirit in which all movement ceases and we know ourselves as pure consciousness alone.

A great secret

"Receive that Word from which the Universe springeth!... How many are there who know the meaning of that Word?" asked Kabir. Soham is the great secret–the secret of enlightenment.

Once a man was taught a mantra by a yogi. "You must keep this mantra absolutely secret, for it is known to only a very few," the yogi told him. But the next day in the morning as the man walked through the town he noticed that a great many people were repeating that mantra aloud, especially as they did their morning ablutions. Indignantly he went to the yogi, told what he had observed, and demanded to know why he had claimed the mantra was a secret known only to a few. The yogi said nothing in explanation, but brought a shining green object from his pocket and handed it to the man with the instruction that he should show it to the people he met in the town and ask them how much they would buy it for–but he was not to actually sell it to them. "When you do this, I will explain about the mantra," he promised.

The first person he met was a woman who sold vegetables; she offered some eggplants for it, wanting it for her baby to play with. He showed it to some merchants in small shops who offered him small amounts of money for it as a curiosity. A wealthy merchant said that it was an excellent imitation emerald and offered him a goodly sum, for he wanted it to make jewelry for his wife. A banker examined it, declared it to be a genuine emerald, and offered him a great deal of money for it. Amazed by this, the man took it to a jeweler who told him that it was the largest and most perfect emerald he had ever seen. "No one in this land, not even the king, has enough money to purchase this emerald," he concluded.

Frightened at having such a valuable in his keeping, the man hurried back to the yogi and returned the emerald. Smiling, the yogi put it back in his pocket. "Now will you tell me why you claimed the mantra was secret, when everybody in town seems to know it?" demanded the man. "I have already done so by your experience with the emerald," the yogi replied. "How many of the people knew what it really was?" "Only the banker and the jeweler," the man admitted. "And the others–did not their offers for it correspond to their opinion of it and their own financial worth?" "Yes." "There you have it. The mantra I taught you is in the memory and on the lips of many in a superficial way. They repeat it a few times and then drop it. Only those who meditate upon it can know it in truth–as they at the same time increase in spiritual status. My friend, that mantra is very little *known*, but I hope you will strive to realize its value by your own Self-realization through its use."

The man understood. And so will those who come to know the secret of Soham through their own practice. For it is Soham that draws us out from the Primal Depths, Soham that evolves us to the uttermost possibilities, and Soham that liberates and returns us to the Source to share eternally in the fullness of the Life Divine.

Go Forward

Sri Ramakrishna often referred to and told the following parable.

"Once upon a time a wood-cutter went into a forest to chop wood. There suddenly he met a brahmachari. The holy man said to him, 'My good man, go forward.' On returning home the wood-cutter asked himself, 'Why did the brahmachari tell me to go forward?' Some time passed. One day he remembered the brahmachari's words. He said to himself, 'Today I shall go deeper into the forest.' Going deep into the forest, he discovered innumerable sandal-wood trees. He was very happy and returned with cart-loads of sandal-wood. He sold them in the market and became very rich.

"A few days later he again remembered the words of the holy man to go forward. He went deeper into the forest and discovered a silver-mine near a river. This was even beyond his dreams. He dug out silver from the mine and sold it in the market. He got so much money that he didn't even know how much he had.

"A few more days passed. One day he thought: 'The brahmachari didn't ask me to stop at the silver-mine; he told me to go forward.' This time he went to the other side of the river and found a gold-mine. Then he exclaimed: 'Ah, just see! This is why he asked me to go forward.'

"Again, a few days afterwards, he went still deeper into the forest and found heaps of diamonds and other precious gems. He took these also and became as rich as the god of wealth himself.

"Therefore I say that, whatever you may do, you will find better and better things if only you go forward. You may feel a little ecstasy as the result of japa, but don't conclude from this that you have achieved everything in spiritual life.... If you go still farther you will realize God. You will see him. In time you will converse with him."

It is important to keep on in regular yoga practice. It is easy to understand that people may mistake delusions for enlightenment, but we must realize that it is also possible to mistake very real stages in spiritual progress as being the final stage, the ultimate enlightenment, when in reality there is much more territory to be traversed before arriving at the supreme goal of perfect union with God.

In the Yoga Sutras (1:30) Patanjali list the various obstacles to enlightenment. One is *bhranti-darshana*: delusion or erroneous view. Regarding this, I. K. Taimni has written: "This means taking a thing for what it is not. It is due generally to lack of intelligence and discrimination. A Sadhaka may, for example, begin to see lights and hear sounds of various kinds during his early practices. These things are very spurious and do not mean much and yet there are many Sadhakas who get excited about these trivial experiences and begin to think they have made great progress. Some think that they have reached high states of consciousness or are even foolish enough to think that they have seen God. This incapacity to assess our supernormal experiences at their proper worth is basically due to immaturity of soul and those who cannot distinguish between the essential and non-essential things in spiritual unfoldment find their progress blocked at a very early stage. They tend to get entangled in these spurious experiences of a psychic nature and are soon side-tracked. It is easy to see that the unhealthy excitement which accompanies such undesirable conditions of the mind will cause great distraction and prevent it from diving inwards."

Therefore the yogi must keep on all the days of his life. After death it will be seen by what world (loka) he rises to what stage he has really reached. Sri Ramakrishna also said: "Even if one has attained Knowledge, one must still constantly practice God-Consciousness.... What is the use of polishing the outside of a metal pot one day only? If you don't polish it regularly it will get tarnished again.... A brass pot must be polished every day; otherwise it gets stained."

And so it is with the mind and heart of the yogi. Buddha is our perfect example. To the very last day of his life he meditated regularly, often withdrawing into solitude for prolonged periods of intense meditation. Further, every day he followed the same routine that all the monks of the Sangha followed. He never slacked off or abandoned any practice. Never did he neglect spiritual practice and discipline under the pretense that he no longer needed it. He diligently followed the counsel of Krishna: "For the maintenance of the world, as an example you should act. Whatever the best of men does–this and that–thus other men do. Whatever the standard that he sets, that is what the world shall follow. I have no duty whatsoever in the three worlds, nor anything that must be attained, nevertheless I engage in action" (Bhagavad Gita 3:20-22).

Go forward.

CHAPTER SIX:

THE FOUNDATIONS OF YOGA

Sri Ramakrishna frequently spoke of some people who planned to travel overnight on a river in order to attend a wedding the next day. When it was dark they got in the boat and rowed the entire night. When it began to dawn, they saw to their dismay that they were still at the place they started! Why? Because they had not hauled in the anchor and so stayed in one spot.

It is the same with religion and yoga. We can work and work at it, doing many spiritual deeds and practices, yet get nowhere–maybe even regress. Why? Because we have not "weighed anchor and cast off from the shore" of samsara and worldliness–especially in the matter of disciplines and purifications. That is why the first limb of Patanjali's yoga is yama and niyama. Without perfect observance of these ten principles no one can succeed in yoga and spiritual life.

Prerequisites for yoga

Toward the end of his comments on the Yoga Sutras, Shankara makes a valuable remark: "There can be no lamplight unless the oil, wick and a flame are brought together." The idea is that the successful practice of yoga is not a haphazard or capricious matter. All the elements must be brought together. When united and complete, success is the result.

Since the classical Indian texts on Yoga are the basis of this chapter, the word "yoga" is used throughout. But it should be realized that the word "meditation" is equally applicable, for in ancient India yoga and meditation were synonymous.

"Yoga is for the purpose of knowledge of truth," says Shankara. Knowledge (jnana) does not come about from practice of yoga methods alone. Perfection in knowledge is in fact only for those who practice virtue (dharma) as well as yoga.

All things rest upon something else–that is, all things are supported by another. This is because a foundation is needed for anything to exist. Being Himself the Ultimate Support of all things, God alone is free from this necessity. Yoga, then, also requires support. As Trevor Leggett says in his introduction to Shankara's commentary on the Yoga Sutras: "This is yoga presented for the man of the world, who must first clear, and then steady, his mind against the fury of illusory passions, and free his life from entanglements." Patanjali very carefully and fully outlines the elements of the support needed by the aspirant, giving invaluable information on how to guarantee success in yoga.

The first Yoga Sutra says: "*Now* the exposition of yoga," implying that there must be something leading up to yoga in the form of necessary developments of consciousness and personality. These prerequisites are known as Yama and Niyama. Shankara says quite forcefully that "following yama and niyama is the basic qualification to practice yoga."

Yama and Niyama

Yama and Niyama are often called the Ten Commandments of Yoga, but they have nothing to do with the ideas of sin and virtue or good and evil as dictated by some cosmic potentate. Rather they are determined by a thoroughly practical, pragmatic basis: that which strengthens and facilitates our yoga practice should be observed and that which weakens or hinders it should be avoided. It is not a matter of being good or bad, but of being wise or foolish. Each one of these Five Don'ts (Yama) and Five Do's (Niyama) is a supporting, liberating foundation of Yoga.

Yama means self-restraint in the sense of self-mastery, or abstention, and consists of five elements. Niyama means observances, of which there are also five. Here is the complete list of these ten Pillars as given in Yoga Sutras 2:30,32:

1. Ahimsa: non-violence, non-injury, harmlessness
2. Satya: truthfulness, honesty
3. Asteya: non-stealing, honesty, non-misappropriativeness
4. Brahmacharya: sexual continence in thought, word and deed as well as control of all the senses
5. Aparigraha: non-possessiveness, non-greed, non-selfishness, non-acquisitiveness
6. Shaucha: purity, cleanliness
7. Santosha: contentment, peacefulness
8. Tapas: austerity, practical (i.e., result-producing) spiritual discipline
9. Swadhyaya: introspective Self-study, spiritual study
10. Ishwarapranidhana: offering of one's life to God

All of these deal with the innate powers of the human being—or rather with the abstinence and observance that will develop and release those powers to be used toward our spiritual perfection, to our Self-realization and liberation. Shankara says quite forcefully that "following yama and niyama is the basic qualification to practice yoga. The qualification is not simply that one wants to practice yoga. So yama and niyama are methods of yoga" in themselves and are not mere adjuncts or aids that can be optional.

But at the same time, the practice of yoga helps the aspiring yogi to follow the necessary ways of yama and niyama, so he should not be discouraged from taking up yoga right now. He should determinedly embark on yama, niyama, and yoga simultaneously. Success will be his.

Ahimsa: non-violence, non-injury, harmlessness

In his commentary on the Yoga Sutras, Vyasa begins his exposition of ahimsa: "Ahimsa means in no way and at no time to do injury to any living being." "In no capacity and in no fashion to give injury to any being," says Shankara. This would include injury by word or thought as well as the obvious injury perpetrated by deed, for Shankara comments: "Ahimsa is to be practiced in every capacity–body, speech, and mind."

Even a simple understanding of the law of karma enables us to realize the terrible consequences of murder for the murderer. As Vyasa explains: "The killer deprives the victim of spirit, hurts him with a blow of a weapon, and then tears him away from life. Because he has deprived another of spirit, the supports of his own life, animate or inanimate, become weakened. Because he has caused pain, he experiences pain himself.... Because he has torn another from life, he goes to live in a life in which every moment he wishes to die, because the retribution as pain has to work itself right out, while he is panting for death."

Ahimsa is not willfully causing any harm or pain whatsoever to any being whatsoever, in any degree whatsoever. Ahimsa includes strict abstinence from any form of injury in act, speech, or thought. Violence, verbal or physical, causing mental injury or pain, and angry or malicious damage or misuse of physical objects are all violations of ahimsa, unthinkable for the yogi.

Vyasa immediately points out that all the other abstinences and observances–yama and niyama–are really rooted in ahimsa, for they involve preventing harm to ourselves and to others through negative action or the neglect of positive action: "The other niyamas and yamas are rooted in this, and they are practiced only to bring this to its culmination, only for perfecting this. They are taught only as means to bring this out in its purity. For so it is said: 'Whatever many vows the man of Brahman [God] would undertake, only in so far as he thereby refrains from doing harm impelled by delusion, does he bring out ahimsa in its purity.'" And Shankara explains that Vyasa is referring to delusion that is "rooted in violence and causing violence."

In his autobiography Paramhansa Yogananda relates that his guru, Swami Yukteswar Giri, said that ahimsa is absence of the *desire* to injure.

In the highest sense ahimsa is a state of mind from which non-injury will naturally proceed. "Ahimsa really denotes an attitude and mode of behavior towards all living creatures based on the recognition of the underlying unity of life," the modern commentator Taimni declares. Shankara remarks that when ahimsa and the others are observed "the cause of one's doing harm becomes inoperative." The ego itself becomes "harmless" by being put into a state of non-function. And meditation dissolves it utterly. But until that interior state is established, we must work backwards from outward to inner, and abstain from all forms of injury.

The aspiring yogi must clearly realize that the observance of ahimsa must include strict abstinence from the eating of animal flesh in any form or degree as well as the use of anything obtained by or derived from the slaughter of animals.

He must do nothing in thought, word, or deed that harms his body, mind, or spirit. On the other hand, he must do whatever benefits the body, mind, and spirit, for their omission is also a form of self-injury, as is the non-observance of any of the yama or niyamas.

It is no simple thing to be a yogi.

Satya: truthfulness, honesty

"Satya is said to be speech and thought in conformity with what has been seen or inferred or heard on authority. The speech spoken to convey one's own experience to others should be not deceitful, nor inaccurate, nor uninformative. It is that uttered for helping all beings. But that uttered to the harm of beings, even if it is what is called truth, when the ultimate aim is merely to injure beings, would not be truth. It would be a wrong." So says Vyasa.

Shankara says that truthfulness means saying what we have truly come to know is the truth–mostly through our own experience or through contact with sources whose reliability we have experienced for our-selves. "Untruthfulness in any form puts us out of harmony with the fundamental law of Truth and creates a kind of mental and emotional strain which prevents us from harmonizing and tranquillizing our mind. Truthfulness has to be practiced by the sadhaka because it is absolutely necessary for the unfoldment of intuition. There is nothing which clouds the intuition and practically stops its functioning as much as untruthfulness in all its forms," says Taimni regarding the most personal and practical aspect of satya.

Bending the truth, either in leaving out part of the truth or in "stacking the deck" to create a false impression, cannot be engaged in by the yogi. Regarding numbers it is said that "figures do not lie–but liars figure." The same is true here. Equally heinous is the intentional mixing of lies and truth. (Some liars tell a lot of truth.) This is particularly true in the manipulative endeavors of advertising, politics, and religion.

Refusing to speak the truth, as well as avoiding speaking or facing the truth, is a form of untruth.

There are many non-verbal forms of lying as well, and some people's entire life is a lie. Therefore we must make sure that our actions reflect the truth. How many people claim to believe in God and spiritual principles, but do not live accordingly? How many people continually swear and express loyalty and yet are betrayers? We must not only speak the truth, we must live it.

Honesty in all our speaking and dealings with others is an essential part of truthfulness. It is absolutely crucial that the yogi make his livelihood only by honest and truthful means. Selling useless or silly things, convincing people that they need them (or even selling them without convincing them), is a serious breach of truthfulness.

Trying to compromise the truth, even a little, making the excuse that "everybody does it" is not legitimate. For "everybody" is bound to the wheel of birth and death because they do it–and that is not what we wish for ourselves. We can lie to ourselves, to others, and even to God; but we cannot lie to the cosmos. Karma, the law of cause and effect, will react upon us to our own pain.

It is interesting that Vyasa considers that truthful speech is informative. By that he means that truthful speech is worthwhile, relevant, and practical. To babble mindlessly and grind out verbal trivia is also a form of untruth, even if not objectively false. Nor is foolish speech to anyone's gain. Sometimes also people lie by "snowing" us with a barrage of words intended to deflect us from our inquiries. And nearly all of us who went to college remember the old game of padding out written assignments, giving lots of form but little content in hope of fooling the teachers into thinking the student knew the subject well and was saying something worthwhile—even profound. This is one of today's most lucrative businesses, especially in the advertising world.

Speaking truth to the hurt of others is not really truth, since satya is an extension of ahimsa. For example, a person may be ugly, but to say, "You are ugly" is not a virtue. "What is based on injuring others, even though free from the three defects of speech (i.e., not deceitful, nor inaccurate, nor uninformative), does not amount to truth," according to Shankara.

Our intention must never be to hurt in any way, but we must be aware that there are some people who hate the truth in any form and will accuse us of hurting them by our honesty. Such persons especially like to label any truth (or person) they dislike as "harsh," "rigid," "divisive," "negative" "hateful," and so on and on and on. We would have to become dishonest or liars to placate them. So "hurting" or offending them is a consequence of truthfulness that we will have to live with. The bottom line is that truth "is that uttered for helping all beings." For non-injury is not a passive quality, but the positive character of restoration and healing.

Silence can also be a form of untruth, particularly in dealing with the aforementioned truth-haters. For truth is only harmful when "the ultimate aim is merely to injure beings." But if some people put themselves in the way of truth, then they must take responsibility for their reactions to it.

Will Cuppy defined diplomacy as "the fine art of lying." Sadly, it often is. So we must be sure that we do not deceive under the guise of diplomacy or tactfulness.

Self-deception, a favorite with nearly all of us to some degree, must be ruthlessly eliminated if we would be genuinely truthful.

"Therefore let one take care that his speech is for the welfare of all," concludes Shankara.

Asteya: non-stealing, honesty, non-misappropriation

Asteya is abstinence from stealing, which Vyasa defines as: "the improper appropriation to oneself of others' things." He then concludes: "Refusal to do it, in *freedom from desire*, is non-stealing."

What constitutes ordinary stealing is well known to almost all, but human beings have thought up countless ways to steal and not seem to be stealing–all the way from putting slugs in pay telephones to getting people to give us things or money which we neither need nor deserve. Theft and untruth are certainly interrelated. So we must analyze Vyasa's definition and apply it to our situation. But we can consider a few "fudges" that have become respectable and prevalent.

Taking credit that really belongs to another.

Plagiarism, especially in academic matters.

Taking what is not ours, while pretending that we either own it or have it coming to us.

Taking what is not legitimately coming to us, even if freely given. People do this continually in relation to welfare benefits and insurance claims.

Demanding more than a just price or a just wage.

No paying debts–including taxes.

Forcing others to give us something we want from them, whether material or metaphysical.

Not giving to others what we owe them or what we are legally or morally obligated to give.

A lot of people (especially churches and religious groups) expect others to continually give them things or services which they are perfectly capable of paying for. (I am not speaking about unsolicited gifts or charity–that is virtuous.) Or they want big discounts given to them.

Once a natural health practitioner–whose financial situation was much worse than mine–told me that she was willing to charge only half her usual fee for my treatment, and would even treat me for free if I wanted. I explained to her that since I could afford the full amount it would be stealing from her for me to either accept a discount or free treatment. And I cited the Yoga Sutras in support of my contention. The law applies to *all*.

The prophet Malachi posed the question, "Will a man rob God?" (Malachi 3:8) That is extremely easy to do and extremely common. We all need to ponder that possibility seriously and see if in some way we are doing that very thing.

But all these forms of stealing are inner or outer acts, whereas Vyasa defines non-stealing as essentially a psychological state of "freedom from desire." This, then, is the goal of abstinence from stealing. What must be attained is the state of mind in which there is absolutely no desire or impulse to steal. "Stealing cannot exist in those whose desire has been cut off," says Shankara.

Brahmacharya: continence

"Brahmacharya is restraint of the sex organ and other senses," says Vyasa. From this we see that brahmacharya has a twofold nature: control and continence.

Control: Spirit has two aspects: consciousness and energy. Consciousness is constant, whereas energy is cyclic. It is the movement of energy that produces (and is) our experience of relativity, and it is the development of energy that is the process of evolution. Therefore the conservation and application of energy is the main determinant of success or failure in spiritual endeavor. Diffusion and dissipation of energy always weakens us.

Hence brahmacharya is a vital element of Yoga, without which we cannot successfully pursue the greater life of Higher Consciousness.

Basically, brahmacharya is conservation and mastery of all the energy systems and powers of our being. This is especially true in relation to negative emotions, for tremendous energy is expended through lust, anger, greed, envy, hatred, resentment, depression, fear, obsession, and the rest. Further, they are both the causes and the symptoms of losing self-control, a major aspect of brahmacharya. Research has shown that persons in the grip of these emotions literally breathe out vital elements of the body. For example, the breath of angry people is found to be laden with copper. So negative emotion depletes us physically as well as energetically. Positive emotions on the other hand actually enhance and raise our energy and physical levels. The cultivation of (true) love, compassion, generosity, cheerfulness, friendliness, and suchlike make us stronger and calmer—essential aspects of brahmacharya. It is noteworthy that the word "virtue" is derived from the Latin word *virtus*–power–which in turn is derived from the Sanskrit word virya, which means both power and strength.

"A place for everything and everything in its place," is not just a maxim of orderliness. When applied to the individual's energy systems it is the root of strength and health on all levels. Every atom of personal energy possessed by us has both a place and a purpose. To ensure correct placement, and expenditure, of energy is the essence of the yogic science. And brahmacharya is its foundation.

Continence: Sexuality is usually considered the main focus of brahmacharya because it has such a powerful grip and influence on the human being. It is considered that if sex is mastered, all the senses will be mastered as well. There is simply no way to convince those addicted to and enslaved by sex that continence is supreme wisdom. But a few facts can be meaningful to the sincere seeker.

The life of the senses stifles the life of the spirit by carrying away the discrimination of the intellect, as Krishna says: "When the mind is led about by the wandering senses, it carries away the understanding like

230

the wind carries away a ship on the waters." (Bhagavad Gita 2:67) The basic life-force, the prana, is dissipated through any intense activity of the senses, thus weakening the inner being. But sexual indulgence is incalculably more destructive of consciousness than any other form of sense experience, for it expends the life-force to a degree far, far beyond that of other sense experiences. Both body and mind are depleted through sexual activity.

The Prashna Upanishad concludes: "To them alone is this brahma world, in whom austerity, chastity and truth are established" (Prashna Upanishad 1:15). The Gita speaks of the worthy yogis as being "firm in the brahmachari's vow." (Bhagavad Gita 6:14)

For practical information on brahmacharya the following books are extremely valuable: *WARNING: Sex May Be Hazardous to Your Health* by Dr. Edwin Flatto, *Science Discovers The Physiological Value of Continence* and *Nutritional Sex Control and Rejuvenation* by the great twentieth century Rosicrucian, Dr. Raymond Bernard, *The Practice of Brahmach-arya*, by Swami Sivananda, and *The Role of Celibacy in Spiritual Life* by Swami Chidananda.

Aparigraha: non-possessiveness, non-greed, non-selfishness, non-acquisitiveness

Aparigraha includes the ideas of non-possessiveness, non-greed, non-selfishness, and non-acquisitiveness. Vyasa's definition is most practical: "Seeing the defects in objects involved in acquiring them, and defending them, and losing them, and being attached to them, and depriving others of them, one does not take them to himself, and that is aparigraha." Here, as in the other foundations, the true virtue or observance is mostly internal, leading to the correct state of mind for successful yoga practice.

Basically, when a person sees all the effort expended on "things" as well as the unhappiness attendant on both keeping and losing them—what to speak of awareness of their inherent defects—he wisely backs away and frees himself from Thingolatry. Of course we all have to obtain and use many kinds of things, but we can do so objectively, not letting ourselves get stuck up in them like the tar baby of the Uncle Remus story. Being possessed by possessions is truly a great misery; and the belief that happiness comes from external things is truly a great folly.

People do literally lose themselves in "stuff," for they adopt a completely false self-concept. To think that we are what we "have" is to forget who and why we are. Aparigraha clears the inner eye and lets us see our true "face."

The Great Vow

After listing ahimsa, satya, asteya, brahmacharya, and aparigraha, Patanjali continues: "These, not conditioned by class, place, time or occasion, and extending to all stages, constitute the Great Vow." (Yoga Sutra 2:31) They are the Great Vow because they require the exercise of will and because of their dynamic effect on us. Even more, they are great because, like the elements, they are self-sufficient, depending on nothing else, and because they cannot be mutated into something else. They are always what they are, and for that reason they are always to be observed with no exceptions whatsoever. They cannot be neglected or omitted for any reason–absolutely. Patanjali lists the possible conditions which do affect lesser observances: class, place, time or occasion, and stages. A brief consideration of each will be helpful.

Class. No one can mitigate or omit the observance of ahimsa, satya, asteya, brahmacharya, and aparigraha because of "who" he "is." In yoga, too, no one is above the law. That is, no one can produce the effects of Yama without their observance. I knew an Archbishop with a quick sense of humor. Once he made a pungent remark about someone, and a woman objected, saying, "That remark is not Christian." He simply smiled and replied, "Madam, I do not have to be a Christian–I am an Archbishop!" This is an attitude of many, springing from the blindness of egotism.

Place. Whatever may be the ways of a particular place or group of people in which we may find ourselves, the observances of Yama are incumbent upon us. "When in Rome do as the Romans" is one of the silliest axioms ever coined. Peer pressure must never be an influence on us. Nor should unjust rules or laws have any effect on us. What is right must always be done. The will or opinion of others cannot change our obligation to observe the Great Vow. Nor can external conditions change it. Not even to save our lives can we turn from what is forever right.

Time or occasion. Human beings have for some reason always thought that "now" abrogates what was right or true in the past. It does not. Nor does a situation effect any change in what must be done by us as aspirants to yoga. Aversion to being "out of step" or "alienated from society" has no place in the mind and heart of the yogi.

Stage. We never "get beyond" the observance of the Great Vow. Those at the very end of the spiritual journey are as obligated to fulfil the Great Vow as those who are at the beginning. Also, we cannot "go too far" or "overdo" our observance of the Vow. It is all or nothing. "Ahimsa and the others are to be maintained all the time and in all circumstances and in regard to all objects without any conscious lapse," declares Vyasa. Shankara points out that the Great Vow must be observed by us in relation to all beings—not just confined to humans.

Once again we see the psychological nature of the five components of the Great Vow and how their observance is based upon the courage, self-respect, and Self-knowledge of the yogi.

Shaucha: purity, cleanliness

Shaucha means purity and cleanliness within the context of attaining unobstructed clarity of consciousness. "He is not grasped by the eye nor even by speech nor by other sense-organs, nor by austerity nor by work, but when one's (intellectual) nature is purified by the light of knowledge then alone he, by meditation, sees Him who is without parts" (Mundaka Upanishad 3.1.8). "When nature is pure, memory becomes firm. When memory [smriti–memory of our eternal spirit-Self] remains firm, there is release from all knots of the heart. To such a one who has his stains wiped away, Bhagavan Sanatkumara shows the further shore of darkness" (Chandogya Upanishad 7:26:2). Which is why Jesus said: "Blessed are the pure in heart: for they shall see God." (Matthew 5:8) And Saint John: "Every man that hath this hope in Him purifieth himself, even as He is pure." (I John 3:2-3)

"Internal shaucha is the washing away of the stains of the mind" according to Vyasa. "Shaucha implies purity in seeing and listening… and washing away the stains of the mind, such as desire and anger, by the waters of meditation," adds Shankara.

Physical cleanliness is important for it eliminates bodily toxins and prevents disease. Inner purification is important for it eliminates mental toxins and prevents inner ills. For the yogi, the most important external aspect of shaucha is purity of diet. This is because the food we eat determines the vibration of our body and our mind. For this reason it is only wisdom to eat a purely vegetarian diet.

Those who carefully–yes, scrupulously–adhere to a vegetarian diet, omitting all meat, fish, and eggs, and avoiding anything that contains them to any degree will perceive how valuable it is to keep such a dietary regimen. (Again, see *Spiritual Benefits of a Vegetarian Diet.*) Not only will their general health improve greatly (assuming that they eat a balanced and nutritious vegetarian diet), they will see how much lighter and intuitive their minds become. A vegetarian diet greatly facilitates the practice of meditation, making very subtle states of consciousness readily attainable and perceptible. Those who have eaten meat, fish, and eggs for a long time may have to wait a while before fully gaining the benefits of vegetarianism, but it will not be long before they begin to see its beneficial effects to some degree.

Vegetarian diet is a crown jewel for the yogi since it embodies the foundations of ahimsa, asteya, aparigraha, shaucha, and tapas and produces purity and clarity of mind and heart.

There is another, far-reaching aspect to shaucha. While discussing the process of evolution, Vyasa and Shankara also speak about the way to infuse ourselves with higher consciousness. They give the simile of terraced fields on a mountainside. The farmer floods the highest field. When it has received enough water, he then breaks the earth barrier between it and the next, lower field, and the water pours down into it and fills it. And so the process goes until all the fields are watered. Vyasa then firmly declares that mere right or good action or external religiosity effect nothing in the way of transformation into a higher grade of consciousness, but that rather it is a matter of the removal of *obstacles* to higher consciousness that is needed. He points out that no effort is needed to get the water into the field—or the higher consciousness into the individual—except that expended in the removal of the barriers. So the secret is to remove whatever blocks the process of evolution, and it will occur as spontaneously as the water pours down into the field.

It is the removal of obstacles that is the highest form of shaucha. To underscore this, Vyasa continues: "Then again, a farmer in his field cannot force the nutrients of water or earth into the roots of his grain. What does he do, then? He removes the obstructing weeds. With these gone, the nutrients enter, of themselves, the roots of the grain." In the same way, when negative karmas, habits, deeds, thoughts, influences, associations, and situations are uprooted from our minds and lives, the higher consciousness and states of evolution will occur naturally. This is exceedingly important for us to keep in mind. For it is purity (shaucha) in this form that enables the divine light to reach us.

Santosha: contentment, peacefulness

Santosha consists of the passive aspect of contentment and peacefulness and the more positive aspect of joy and happiness. Santosha is a fundamentally cheerful attitude based on a harmonious interior condition and an intellectually spiritual outlook. This is possible only through meditation, and is one of the signs of progress in meditation.

This must not be equated with mere intellectual "positive thinking" or a forced external "happiness" which is a camouflage, not a real state. Santosha is an inner-based quality that occurs spontaneously. It need not be cultivated or "acted out" any more than the blossoming of a flower.

Santosha is also contentment with simple living, and relates to aparigraha. Vyasa says that "santosha is being satisfied with the resources at hand and so not desiring more." Shankara says: "As a result of the satisfaction with what is at hand, even though there may be some lack, he has the feeling, 'It is enough.'" Santosha is freedom from the "bigger and more is better" syndrome that grips most of us.

Santosha is also the absence of negative emotions and the presence of positive emotions. In its highest form santosha is the contentment and peace that comes from resting in our own spirit.

Tapas: austerity, practical (i.e., result-producing) spiritual discipline

Tapas literally means "to generate heat" in the sense of awakening or stimulating the whole of our being to higher consciousness. It is commonly applied to the practice of spiritual discipline, especially that which involves some form of physical austerity or self-denial. The sages of ancient India were very conversant with the principles of physics and formulated their symbols accordingly. When an object is heated, its molecules begin to move at a faster rate than usual. Thus, tapas is a procedure that causes all the components of the yogi to vibrate at a much higher rate, and to eventually become permanently established in that higher vibration.

Regarding physical tapas Vyasa writes: "Tapas is endurance of the opposites. The opposites are hunger and thirst, heat and cold, standing and sitting, complete silence and merely verbal silence." ("In complete silence, nothing like hand-signs is allowed, whereas in the limited silence, indications by hands, etc., are permitted and it is only actual speech that is banned," according to Shankara.) Shankara says these opposites may occur naturally or by our own choice through self-denial. And both Vyasa and Shankara say that tapas is always done in the light of the capability of the yogi and is never exaggerated, strenuous, or beyond the yogi's natural ability.

Basically, tapas is spiritual discipline that produces a perceptible result, particularly in the form of purification. Tapas is the turning from the unreal to the Real, from darkness to the Light, from death to Immortality. But it is never a matter of mere thought or desire, it is always *practical action* towards that end. Consequently, whenever tapas is spoken of it always implies the practice of yoga and the observances that facilitate yoga practice.

We are dual in nature: consciousness and energy, spirit and matter. This being so, we need to realize that although we are essentially consciousness (spirit) we are also energy, and therefore we are our bodies and our minds. Or rather, we are the conscious intelligence that manifests as our bodies and minds. Our lives need to be lived in this perspective. For example, when we understand this truth we understand why such observances or disciplines as yama, niyama, vegetarianism, and moral conduct are so beneficial and necessary for us.

Swadhyaya: introspective Self-study, spiritual study

Swadhyaya means "Self-study." This is usually interpreted as the study of the sacred texts which deal with the nature of the true Self (spirit) and its realization. "Swadhyaya is study of works on liberation (moksha)," says Vyasa. "Swadhyaya is study of works on liberation such as the Upanishads," comments Shankara. But it also means keeping a careful watch on the ego-based mind so as to be aware of its delusive and destructive tricks. For it is no external "devil" or "Satan" we need fear, but the "enemy within," the "Dweller at the Threshold" which is our ego-mind complex that has blinded and enslaved us from life to life and has no intention of giving up its domination of us just because we practice a bit of meditation. Therefore we must be wary of its cunning and subtle ways and carefully analyze the debris it casts up into our consciousness in the form of thoughts and emotions. In this way we will see the direction in which it would pull us. We must take our susceptibility to its machinations most seriously. In swadhyaya we look at and analyze the mind in the calmness and intuition born of meditation.

The highest form of Self-study is that which is known as Atma Vichar–inquiry into the Self (spirit). We must never let go of the vital question: Who am I? We must do all we can to find the answer–not from others or from our intellectual ponderings, but by direct experience of ourselves as pure spirit. Taimni puts it this way: "Though swadhyaya begins with intellectual study it must be carried through the progressive stages of reflection, meditation, tapas, etc. to the point where the sadhaka is able to gain all knowledge or devotion from within, by his own efforts. That is the significance of the prefix swa (self) in swadhyaya. He leaves all external aids such as books, discourses, etc. and dives into his own mind for everything he needs in his quest."

Ishwarapranidhana: offering of one's life to God

The final foundation, for which all the others are a necessary preparation, is Ishwarapranidhana–the offering of one's life to God. This is far more on every level than simple religious devotion, and much more than any kind of discipline or self-denial done in the name of spirituality. *It is the giving to God of the yogi's entire life*, not just a giving of material offerings or occasional tidbits of devotion to God, however fervent or sincere. Moreover, as Taimni points out: "The fact that the progressive practice of Ishwarapranidhana can ultimately lead to samadhi shows definitely that it signifies a much deeper process of transformation in the sadhaka than a mere acceptance of whatever experiences and ordeals come to him in the course of his life.… The practice of Ishwarapranidhana therefore begins with the mental assertion 'Not my will but Thy will be done' but it does not end there. There is a steady effort to bring about a continuous recession of consciousness from the level of the personality which is the seat of 'I' consciousness into the consciousness of the Supreme Whose will is working out in the manifest world."

Ishwarapranidhana is total giving. The yogi does not eke out droplets of his life, but pours out his entire life in offering unto God. He gives all that he has–even his very Self. And this is only sensible, for the entire aim of yoga is the reunion of the individual spirit with the Supreme Spirit, the falling of the drop into the Immortal Sea. Ishwarapranidhana anticipates this divine union and ensures its accomplishment. This is why the first law-giver, Manu, says that the highest sacrifice (medha) is purushamedha–the sacrifice of the individual spirit.

Ishwarapranidhana is also mentioned in Sutra 1:23, where Patanjali says that the attainment of samadhi is brought near to the yogi "by offering of the life to God." Vyasa comments: "As a result of Ishwara-pranidhana, which is bhakti [devotion and love for God], the Lord bends down to him and rewards him,… and the attainment of samadhi and its fruit is near at hand." Shankara says: "The Lord comes face-to-face with him and gives His grace to the yogi who is fully devoted to Him…. The grace is effortlessly gained through the omnipotence of the Supreme Lord. By that grace of the Lord, samadhi and its fruit are soon attainable."

It is incontrovertible, then, that yoga is a thoroughly *theistic* endeavor, one which makes God the center of life and its aim, as well.

The results of perfection (siddhi) in yama and niyama

Shankara makes a very bold–and bald–statement about yoga: *"Success in yoga is determined by result alone… observable by direct perception."* As the ever-memorable Dr. Bronner used to say: "Judge only by the amazing results."

Patanjali lists siddhis–psychic powers or effects–that result from the perfect observance of yama and niyama. Since yama and niyama deal with the innate powers of the human being–or rather with the abstinence and observance that will develop and release those powers, the manifestation of the development and perfecting of those powers will be automatic.

Before considering the specific siddhis resulting from perfection in yama and niyama, it should be explained that perfection in these virtues means that the ignorance which causes their opposites such as injury, lying, and stealing, has been completely eliminated from the yogi, and also that their reappearance in his thought, speech, or behavior has become absolutely impossible. So perfection (siddhi) in yama and niyama is not a matter of action or inaction but one of perfected consciousness.

Perfection in ahimsa

"On being firmly established in non-violence [ahimsa] there is abandonment of hostility in his presence." (Yoga Sutra 2:35) The eminently desirable nature of this siddhi is evident. Wherever a yogi perfected in ahimsa may be, there no hostility can arise; and if it is already present somewhere, upon the yogi's entry it will cease. The one perfected in ahimsa is a living fulfillment of the Prayer of Saint Francis, and is truly an instrument of divine peace. This was true of Buddha in Whose presence hired assassins and even a mad elephant became at peace and incapable of doing harm. "This happens with all living beings," says Vyasa. Many times it has been observed that in the presence of perfected sages wild animals become tame, even friendly, not only toward human beings but even toward their usual enemies or prey. "In the presence of that one who follows ahimsa, even natural enemies like snake and mongoose give up their antagonism," says Shankara. Violent human beings, too, have become peaceful and gentle after contact with holy people in whom ahimsa was completely realized.

Perfection in satya

"On being firmly established in truthfulness [satya], the result of action rests upon him alone." (Yoga Sutra 2:36) Luckily, we have quite a few authoritative commentaries to elucidate this obscure language. All are unanimous in saying that when the yogi is firmly established in truth in all its aspects, then whatever he says or wills comes about without any action being needed to produce it. As Vyasa explains: "When he says: 'Be righteous,' that man becomes righteous; told by him: 'Do you attain heaven,' that one attains heaven. His word is infallible." "When truth is firm in him, events confirm his words," adds Shankara. Yoga-nanda gives an example of this in the first chapter of his autobiography. My friend, Sri Abani Lahiri, told me that his grandfather had the same power even as a child. Once he became angry with another little boy and said, "You should die!" Immediately that boy became deathly ill and was declared by the doctors to have only a few hours of life remaining. When his parents were told, "That Brahmin boy told him to die," they called for him and asked him to tell their son to live. He did so, and the boy was immediately well. Jesus, too, had this power as a child and had to learn how to control it, as recorded in the "apocryphal" gospels. By the power of his word Sri Ramakrishna caused hibiscus blossoms of two different colors to grow on the same plant. At the end of his earthly life, anyone who heard Sri Ramakrishna speak of spiritual awakening became spiritually awakened.

Perfection in asteya

"On being firmly established in non-stealing [asteya], all kinds of precious things come to him." (Yoga Sutra 2:37) Another translation of the second half of the sutra can be: "All kinds of precious things *present themselves* to him." All the treasuries of earth not only are open to someone perfect in asteya, their contents actively seek him out. Yet such a one neither desires or seeks them. If he did, they would no longer come to him. Precious things may be given by others to those perfected in asteya, or simply appear from the divine hand of Providence. The former Shankaracharya of Joshi Matt, Jagadguru Brahmananda Saras-wati, refused to allow anyone to donate money either to himself or to the monastery, whose expenses were great. Yet, he had a box which was always filled with money from which he provided for all the monastery's needs. Yogananda had a little box with a slot in the top where he put in or took out money without counting or keeping record. Yet it was always full. Sri Brahma Chaitanya, a Maharashtrian saint who lived into the twentieth century, was known to be without any resources whatsoever and lived in total frugality. Yet he once made a pilgrimage to Benares where he gave away a tremendous amount of money to the poor and the monastics. As he sat on a simple mat, he kept putting his hand under it and producing the money from an inexhaustible supply. Paramhansa Nityananda literally pulled fortunes in rupees from his clothing to pay for projects he was supervising. Some yogis can simply reach up in the air and bring down anything they desire.

Perfection in brahmacharya

"On being firmly established in brahmacharya, vigor [virya] is gained." (Yoga Sutra 2:37) Virya is not ordinary physical strength, but an almost supernatural power that manifests as strength of body, mind, and spirit. When through brahmacharya the yogi's normal bodily power is conserved, a marvellous alchemical change takes place, augmenting and transmuting his energies to a level unknown to others. The truth that those who keep their bodily energies intact can accomplish whatever they will has been demonstrated for thousands of years by celibates of all lands and spiritual traditions.

Regarding the brahmachari possessed of virya, Shankara says: "He brings out great qualities without limit from himself. He has irresistible energy for all good undertakings. The sense is, that he cannot be thwarted by any obstacle." See how great spiritual reformers have changed the lives of untold thousands, their influence reaching over the world and lasting even beyond their physical life span. So great is the virya of some saints that their mere touch can heal. Sometimes the clothing they have worn or objects they have touched heal the sick and work other miracles. Virya also manifests in the brahmachari's words, giving them a power not found in those of others. As Vyasa comments on this sutra: "From the attainment of virya, he draws out invincible good qualities from himself. And when perfected in it, he becomes able to confer knowledge on pupils."

Through the accumulation of virya the powers of the mind develop beyond all bounds. Yogis have often displayed profound knowledge of subjects they had never studied, and on occasion have shown remarkable artistic abilities.

Virya affects the physical body, too. Swami Dayananda, the great Indian spiritual reformer of the nineteenth century, was once mocked by a man to whom he recommended brahmacharya for increase of bodily strength. When the man got into his horse-drawn chariot and told the driver to go on, the chariot would not move. The driver whipped the horses, but to no avail. In disgust and perplexity the man got out of the chariot and discovered Swami Dayananda holding on to its rear axle!

Perfection in aparigraha

"On non-possessiveness [aparigraha] being confirmed there arises knowledge of the 'how' and 'wherefore' of existence." (Yoga Sutra 2:39) Regarding this Vyasa says: "'What is this birth? How does it take place? What do we become [both in this life and after death], who shall we be and in what circumstances shall we be?' Any such desire of his to know his situation in former, later, and intermediate states is spontaneously gratified." Nothing is more bewildering to the human being than his existence in this world–particularly the how and why of his even being here–no matter how much external philosophy in the form of books or teachers may attempt to answer the gnawing questions set forth by Vyasa. The reality of the situation is this: until the individual knows for himself by direct perception gained through his own development, life must remain a confusing mystery for him. Since the yogi is attempting to extricate himself from the bonds of birth and death, it is imperative for him to know the why and wherefore of human embodiment in all its aspects. He does not need more theory, however plausible and appealing; he needs to know. This knowledge comes from within when all blocks to communication with his inmost consciousness are removed. For this birth has been determined solely by him in his nature as a potentially omniscient and omnipotent spirit. Perfection in non-possessiveness bestows the needed insight. "Since he has no attachment to outer possessions, illumination of the field of his own Self appears without effort on his part," explains Shankara.

Perfection in shaucha

"From purity [shaucha] arises disgust for one's own body and disinclination to come in physical contact with others." (Yoga Sutra 2:40) This siddhi certainly will not be thought desirable in a body-and-sex-obsessed society that insists on being touched and hugged (and often more) by all and sundry, but the serious yogi should consider it carefully. After all, his intention is to disengage himself from the grinding gears of samsara–the chief of which is body-consciousness. Not only are human beings obsessed with their own bodies, they compound the problem by incessant contact with those of others. This contact results in the confusion and conflict of their personal energies (prana) by the invasion and admixture of other's prana with theirs–particularly their psychic energies. Losing the integrity of their energies in this way, their life force become unbalanced, weakened, damaged, and–yes–defiled. This condition manifests as an endless series of physical, mental, and spiritual ills. "I am not myself" becomes a truism in relation to them. But for those who carefully observe shaucha it becomes otherwise.

"When by practicing purity and seeing the defects in the body, he becomes disgusted with his own body, he becomes free from obsession with the body; seeing what the body essentially is, he has no intercourse with others," writes Vyasa. The disgust for the body spoken of here is not a hatred or an obsessive aversion for the body, but rather a profound disillusionment with the body springing from awareness of its many defects, not the least of which is its unreliability and inevitable mortality. The body is also seen to be a repository of pain, disease and filth, however fine the present momentary outer appearance may be. It is in fact a treasury of death.

"With the ordinary purification of the physical body we become more sensitive and begin to see things in their true light. Cleanliness is mostly a matter of sensitiveness. What is intolerably disgusting to a person of refined nature and habits is hardly noticed by another person whose nature is coarse and insensitive. So this feeling of disgust towards one's own body which develops on its purification means nothing more than that we have become sensitive enough to see things as they really are." So says I. K. Taimni.

Patanjali is not finished with the matter of shaucha. Since body and mind are inextricably related, he continues: "From mental purity arises purity of the inner nature, cheerfulness, one-pointedness, control of the senses, and fitness for the vision of the Self." (Yoga Sutra 2:41) Nobody has objection to these, I am sure. When the inner bodies are pure they are refined and fluid, capable of the most subtle practice of yoga and reaching the highest states of consciousness. This state of inner purity is particularly accomplished by thought and diet.

For the inwardly pure there is no need for artificial "positive think-ing." Cheerfulness and optimism rise up from within him as a matter of course. And continue arising. Gone forever are mood swings and the "ups and downs" of life. No more valleys or mountaintops: he soars in the sunlit sky of the spirit as naturally as the eagle flies in the air. Whether engaged in outer or inner activity, his mind is intent upon its purpose, no longer scattered or flapping like a flag in the wind. One-pointed meditation becomes effortless for him. No longer does he struggle with the unruly senses and the mind about which Arjuna says, "The mind is truly unstable, troubling, strong and unyielding. I believe it is hard to control—as hard to control as the wind" (Bhagavad Gita 6:34).

Perfection in santosha

"From contentment [santosha] he gains unsurpassed [superlative] happiness." (Yoga Sutra 2:42) This is because santosha is a state com-pletely free from all desire for objects or the compulsion to gain some outer thing not yet possessed. Such desire is itself great pain—as is usually its fulfillment. Taimni says: "There is a definite reason why superlative happiness abides in a perfectly calm and contented mind. A calm mind is able to reflect within itself the bliss [ananda] which is inherent in our real divine nature. The constant surging of desires prevents this bliss from manifesting itself in the mind. It is only when these desires are eliminated and the mind becomes perfectly calm that we know what true happiness is. This subtle and constant joy which is called sukha and which comes from within is independent of external circumstances and is really a reflection of ananda, one of the three fundamental aspects of the Self."

Vyasa has this comment: "So it is said: 'Whatever sex pleasure there may be in the world, whatever supreme happiness may be enjoyed in heaven, they cannot be accounted a sixteenth part of the happiness of destruction of craving.'" Simply being without compelling desires is great happiness and peace. Here is how the Taittiriya Upanishad expresses it:

"Who could live, who could breathe, if that blissful Self dwelt not within the lotus of the heart? He it is that gives joy.

"Of what nature is this joy?

"Consider the lot of a young man, noble, well-read, intelligent, strong, healthy, with all the wealth of the world at his command. Assume that he is happy, and measure his joy as one unit.

"One hundred times that joy is one unit of the joy of Gandharvas.

"One hundred times the joy of Gandharvas is one unit of the joy of celestial Gandharvas.

"One hundred times the joy of celestial Gandharvas is one unit of the joy of the Pitris in their paradise.

"One hundred times the joy of the Pitris in their paradise is one unit of the joy of the Devas.

"One hundred times the joy of the Devas is one unit of the joy of the karma Devas.

"One hundred times the joy of the karma Devas is one unit of the joy of the ruling Devas.

"One hundred times the joy of the ruling Devas is one unit of the joy of Indra.

"One hundred times the joy of Indra is one unit of the joy of Brihaspati.

"One hundred times the joy of Brihaspati is one unit of the joy of Prajapati.

"One hundred times the joy of Prajapati is one unit of the joy of Brahma: but no less joy than Brahma has the seer to whom the Self has been revealed, and who is without craving."(Taittiriya Upanishad 2.8.1)

Perfection in tapas

"Perfection of the sense-organs and body result after destruction of impurity by tapas." (Yoga Sutra 2:43) Tapas is like the fire that refines gold through the burning out of all impurities. In relation to the body, tapas removes its limitations and defects. This has been shown by scientific studies: "Everyone around the water cooler knows that meditation reduces stress. But with the aid of advanced brain-scanning technology, researchers are beginning to show that meditation directly affects the function and structure of the brain, changing it in ways that appear to increase attention span, sharpen focus and improve memory. One recent study found evidence that the daily practice of meditation thickened the parts of the brain's cerebral cortex responsible for decision making, attention and memory. Sara Lazar, a research scientist at Massachusetts General Hospital, presented preliminary results last November that showed that the gray matter of twenty men and women who meditated for just forty minutes a day was thicker than that of people who did not.... What's more, her research suggests that meditation may slow the natural thinning of that section of the cortex that occurs with age." (*How to Get Smarter, One Breath At A Time*, Lisa Takeuchi Cullen. *Time*, January 16, 2006, p. 93.) "There was a study reported at the American Geriatric Association convention in 1979 involving forty-seven participants whose average age was 52.5 years. It found that people who had been meditating more than seven years were approximately twelve years younger physiologically than those of the same chronological age who were not meditating." (Gabriel Cousens, M.D., *Conscious Eating*, p. 281.)

The process is described by Vyasa as follows: "As tapas becomes complete, it destroys the veiling taint of impurity; when the veiling taint is removed, there are siddhis of the body like the ability to become minute, and siddhis of the senses in such forms as hearing and seeing things which are remote." The body is no longer locked into its habitual patterns of size or location. Nor are the senses any longer limited to functioning within the bounds of proximity of objects. The body and senses become as free as the yogi's spirit, and as expanded in their scope.

Perfection in swadhyaya

"From Self-study [swadhyaya] arises communion with the beloved deity." (Yoga Sutra 2:44) This sutra is not speaking of communion with God the Unmanifest Absolute, but with His manifested forms or with powerful beings–gods, realized Masters, and others who have evolved beyond the earth plane. "Gods, sages, and perfect beings to whom he is devoted come before the vision of the man intent on swadhyaya and give him their help," says Vyasa. The help can be in the form of protection, removal of inner or outer obstacles, and even spiritual teaching. His aspiration expressed through swadhyaya and his love and admiration for them of which, through their omnipotence, they are ever aware, draw them to grant him encouragement, assistance, and instruction.

Perfection in Ishwarapranidhana

"Accomplishment of (or success or perfection in) samadhi arises from Ishwarapranidhana." (Yoga Sutra 2:45) Though we can define samadhi in many accurate ways, when we think about it we realize that samadhi is totally coming to rest in spirit, the cessation of all else, and the centering of our being in God. Samadhi is entering into the heart of God, into the Silence that is the only truth. The perfection of that state is samadhi, which therefore is produced by total devotion of our life to God.

A final word on the subject from Vyasa: "The samadhi of one who has devoted [offered] his whole being to the Lord is perfect.... [By] the knowledge [resulting] from that [samadhi he] knows a thing as it really is."

Self-realization: the goal

"This Self within the body, of the nature of light and pure, is attainable by truth, by austerity, by right knowledge, by the constant (practice) of chastity. Him, the ascetics with their imperfections done away, behold" (Mundaka Upanishad 3.1.5).

And I. K. Taimni: "The student of yogic philosophy will see in these unusual developments which take place on practicing yama-niyama the tremendous possibilities which lie hidden in the apparently simple things of life. It appears that one has only to penetrate deeply into any manifestation of life to encounter the most fascinating mysteries and sources of power. Physical science which deals with the crudest manifestation of life touches the mere fringe of these mysteries and the results which it has achieved are little short of miraculous. There is, therefore, nothing to be surprised at in the fact that the yogi who dives into the far subtler phenomena of mind and consciousness finds still deeper mysteries and extraordinary powers."

IT CAN BE DONE

All the theory and eulogy in the world regarding a meditation method mean virtually nothing. *But practice is everything.* In yoga more than anything else, practice certainly does Make Perfect. And the practice is so marvelously simple.

Krishna told Arjuna: "Of thousands of human beings scarcely anyone at all strives for perfection, and of those adept in that striving, scarcely anyone knows me in truth" (Bhagavad Gita 7:3). To enable each one of us to become "one in a million," yoga was given by the sages to the human race. Its sacred methodology ensures that not a moment of our endeavor is wasted or ineffectual. Those who pursue the path of yoga unto the death of ignorance will be crowned with life. Those who cast aside the false life of the ego shall enter into the true life of the spirit. The ego says "aham" but the spirit says "Soham."

Many have heard of the philosophy and practice of meditation, many have enjoyed lectures and books on the subject (some have even given the lectures and written the books), and yet have never taken up the practice to any degree. They simply did not make the connection between the beautiful theory and the actuality of their own lives. This is pretty much the trouble in all spiritual matters: people do not make the connection or transition from the theoretical to the practical. Consequently, as a friend I urge you in every sense of the expression to literally take this practice to heart.

It is essential in yoga, as in ordinary matters, to realize that all goes according to precise laws. Wishing, wanting, hoping, praying, believing–or their opposites–have no effect at all. When speaking of meditation, Patanjali says: "Its application is by stages" (Yoga Sutras 3:6). That is, meditation keeps moving onward in its effect *when regularly practiced*, just like the taking of a journey. It all goes in an exact sequence. Therefore we cannot expect that meditation will produce enlightenment in a random way like a slot machine in its payoffs. Meditation produces steady growth if there is steady practice.

The secret of success is regularity in meditation. "A diamond is a piece of coal that never gave up." Paramhansa Yogananda formulated a more spiritual version: "A saint is a sinner who never gave up." If you meditate regularly, every day, great will be the result. Water, though the softest substance known, can wear through the hardest stone by means of a steady dripping. In the old story of the tortoise and the hare, the tortoise won the race because he kept at it steadily, whereas the hare ran in spurts. He ran much faster then the tortoise, but the irregularity of his running made him lose the race. Meditation keeps moving onward in its effect when regularly practiced, producing steady growth through steady practice. The more we walk the farther we travel; the more we meditate the nearer and quicker we draw to the goal.

"Practice alone will show you where the truth lies," said Ramana Maharshi. Yoga, the spiritual state, is produced by yoga the practice. Those who persevere in their yoga practice find unfailing and abundant happiness, peace, and fulfillment. Certainly the goal is not reached without much practice through the years, but every step of the way is blessed and brings rejoicing to the yogi's heart. Then at last no more steps are needed, and he enters the ocean of Satchidananda. "A tiny bubble of laughter, I am become the Sea of Mirth Itself," wrote Yogananda.

So it really is all up to you. The sane and sober voice of the sages and scriptures of India assures us that through the simple japa and meditation of Soham all possible spiritual attainments will be realized.

Soham.

JESUS, A NATH YOGI

Saint Paul wrote: "Let this mind be in you which was also in Christ Jesus" (Philippians 2:5). The mind of Jesus was the mind of a yogi: a Nath Yogi.

The Nath Yogis claim Jesus–Sri Isha Nath–as a great adept of their order. The Bengali educator and patriot, Bipin Chandra Pal, wrote: "It is also their conjecture that Jesus Christ and this Isha Nath are one and the same person." He published an autobiographical sketch in which he revealed that Vijay Krishna Goswami, a renowned saint of Bengal, told him about spending time in the Aravalli mountains with a group of extraordinary Nath Yogis. They spoke to him about Isha Nath, whom they looked upon as one of the great teachers of their order. When Vijay Krishna expressed interest in this venerable guru, they read to him his life as recorded in one of their sacred books, the *Nathanamavali*. It was the life of him whom the Goswami knew as Jesus Christ! Here is the relevant portion of that book:

"Isha Natha came to India at the age of fourteen. After this he returned to his own country and began preaching. Soon after, his brutish and materialistic countrymen conspired against him and had him crucified. After crucifixion, or perhaps even before it, Isha Natha entered samadhi by means of yoga. [In samadhi yogis often leave their bodies or remain without breath or heartbeat, so it is not amiss to say that Jesus did indeed 'die' on the cross.]

"Seeing him thus, the Jews presumed he was dead, and buried him in a tomb. At that very moment however, one of his gurus, the great Chetan Natha, happened to be in profound meditation in the lower reaches of the Himalayas, and he saw in a vision the tortures which Isha

Natha was undergoing. He therefore made his body lighter than air and passed over to the land of Israel.

"The day of his arrival was marked with thunder and lightning, for the gods were angry with the Jews, and the whole world trembled. When Chetan Natha arrived, he took the body of Isha Natha from the tomb, woke him from his samadhi, and later led him off to the sacred land of the Aryans. Isha Natha then established an ashram in the lower regions of the Himalayas and he established the cult of the lingam [the Shaivite branch of Hinduism] there."

This last assertion is supported by two relics of Jesus which are presently found in Kashmir. One is his staff, which is kept in the monastery of Aish-Muqan and is made accessible to the public in times of catastrophe such as floods or epidemics. The other is the Stone of Moses—a Shiva linga that had belonged to Moses and which Jesus brought to Kashmir. This linga is kept in the Shiva temple at Bijbehara in Kashmir. One hundred and eight pounds in weight, if several people put one finger on the stone and recite the bija mantra Ka over and over, it will rise three feet or so into the air and remain suspended as long as the recitation continues. "Shiva" means one who is auspicious and gives blessings and happiness. In ancient Sanskrit the word *ka* means to please and to satisfy—that which Shiva does for his worshippers. I have met two people who have raised the Stone of Moses. One of them said that the number required to raise the Stone relates to their spiritual development—that he had raised it with only three others. (For more information about Jesus in India, see *The Christ of India.*)

It is no wonder, then, that Sri Isha Natha said: "I and my Father are one," and: "He that hath seen me hath seen the Father" (John 10:30; 14:9), for those words can be summed up in the mantra Soham.

Other yoga teachings of Jesus are recorded in the gospels. He was speaking as a yogi when he said: "I came forth from the Father, and am come into the world: again, I leave the world, and go to the Father" (John 16:28). Yoga is our way of return. The capacity for return is innate in us, just as it was said of Jesus that he "knew that the Father had given all things into his hands, and that he was come from God, and went to God" (John 13:3). He also said: "Behold, the kingdom of God is within you" (Luke 17:21). "God is a Spirit: and they that worship him must worship him in spirit and in truth" (John 4:24). Only yogis say such things, and only yogis realize their full meaning. Yoga is a restoration of our original consciousness, regarding which Jesus prayed: "O Father, glorify thou me *with thine own self* with the glory which I had with thee before the world was" (John 17:5). For before the world existed we consciously knew that we were one with God, part of Infinite Being.

Saint Augustine wrote in the fourth century: "The identical thing that we now call the Christian religion existed among the ancients and has not been lacking from the beginnings of the human race until the coming of Christ in the flesh, from which moment on the true religion, which already existed, began to be called 'Christian.'" Earlier Saint Paul had written that the Christian Gospel was that which had already been taught throughout the whole world, "which was preached to every creature which is under heaven" (I Colossians 1:23). Authentic–original–Christianity is not new, but eternal in essence, embracing the Ancient Wisdom that has existed from the beginning of the world. All master teachers of humanity, including Jesus the Christ, were revivers of that Wisdom, reminders of what was at their time either lost or almost extinguished.

When we consider the foregoing facts it is only reasonable to conclude that the following of Jesus involves the following of Sanatana Dharma and the practice of Sanatana Yoga: Soham sadhana.

Sanatana Dharma–Eternal Religion–is the unanimous spiritual vision and beliefs of the great saints and liberated masters found throughout the world, whatever the religious tradition in which they lived and taught. Because it was first expressed in India it is often considered a synonym for Hinduism, but it is much more, being universal and beyond any cultural conditionings.

For more about Jesus and India I again recommend you read my book, *The Christ of India.*

The Nath Pantha

By An Anonymous Nath Panthi Of The Twentieth Century

Beloved Ones, the Spirit of the Nath Panth is quite different from that of all the sects of the world.

The origin of the Nath Pantha

[*This section in brackets is by the editor, Swami Nirmalananda Giri*

A young man was wandering in the mountains somewhere in India—most likely in the Western Himalayas. He had seen no one else for a very long time, but one day he heard the faint sound of a human voice. Following it, he saw from a distance some people seated together near a river. Slipping into the water, he began swimming toward them. All along the river on that side thick reeds were growing so he was not seen as he stealthily made his way closer.

Soon he began to understand what was being said. Fascinated by the speaker's words he came as close as he dared and for a long time remained absorbed in the amazing things being spoken. For the science of yoga was being expounded by a master to his disciples. Then he heard the master say: "There is a 'fish' in the reeds over there, listening to everything I am saying. Why doesn't he come out and join us?" He did as suggested and became a resident of the master's ashram and learned both philosophy and Soham yoga.

After diligent practice of Soham meditation for quite some time, the master, known as Adiniath, asked him to return to the plains and teach that yoga to whomever would listen. He was given a new name, Matsyendranath. (Matsyendra means Indra Among Fish and Nath means Master. Indra is king of the gods.) We have no knowledge of what the master's name was. Matsyendranath and his disciples only referred to him as Adi Nath–Original/First Master. Some believe Adi Nath was Shiva himself manifested to teach yoga, or perhaps the Bhagavan Sanatkumara about whom the Brihadaranyaka Upanishad says: "To such a one who has his stains wiped away, Bhagavan Sanatkumara shows the further shore of darkness" (7.26.2).

Matsyendra wandered throughout India, teaching those who were awakened enough to desire and comprehend the yogic path. One day in his wanderings he came to a house where the owner's wife gave him something to eat and a request: that he would bless her to have a child. In response he blessed her and gave her some ashes from a sacred fire, telling her to swallow them. Then he left. The woman followed his instructions and soon conceived and gave birth to a male child. Several years later Matsyendra came there again and saw the little boy outside the house. He told him to bring his mother, and when she came he asked if she remembered him, which she did. Pointing to the boy, he said: "That is my child. I have come for him." The woman agreed and Matsyendra left with the boy, whom he named Gorakhsha, Protector/Guardian of Light.

Goraksha in time became the monk Gorakshanath (usually called Gorakhnath), the greatest yogi in India's recorded history. In every part of India there are stories told of his living in those areas. He also lived in Nepal, Tibet, Ladakh, and Bhutan. There are shrines and temples to him in all those countries, both Hindu and Buddhist. His major temple is in Gorakhpur, the birthplace of Paramhansa yogananda, whose younger brother, Sananda, was originally named Goraksha. Considering all the lore about him, Gorakhnath must have lived at least two or three hundred years, and there are many who claim that he has never left his body but is living right now in the Himalayas.

Gorakhnath had many disciples, a large number of them attaining enlightenment. They were the first members of the Nath Yogi Sampradaya, which in time numbered in its ranks the great sage Patanjali, founder of the yoga Philosophy (Yoga Darshan) and author of the Yoga Sutras, and Jesus of Nazareth (Sri Ishanath). For many centuries the majority of monks in India were Nath Yogis, but in the nineteenth century there was a sharp decline in their numbers, which continues today. However, there are several groups of "Nath Panthis" that follow the philosophy and yoga of Matsyendranath and Gorakhnath, and therefore are involved with the Soham mantra as the heart of their sadhana.]

The origin of this Nath Pantha can be traced to Adinath who instructed Matsyendranath in the path of Self-realization. At the time of Sri Matsyendranath all power in religious and social matters was centered in the hands of the followers of the Vedic religion. Sanatanis, who were followers of the ritualistic form of the Vedic religion (karmakhanda), were to be seen everywhere. Temples and maths (monasteries) were entirely under the control of their followers. They used to proclaim that they alone were fit to be the recipients of the highest knowledge and some of them were highly respected in society, as royal preceptorship and religious leadership was centered in them. The distinctions between men and men and between men and women were very keenly observed. The caste system was very rigid. Only a sannyasin (a monk) was considered worthy of receiving spiritual knowledge. Hence knowledge regarding God fell to the lot of extremely few persons. Shudras, the members of the laborer, servant caste, and those outside the caste system were not allowed to enter the temples. A woman was considered as unworthy of being the recipient of spiritual knowledge.

All religion was considered to be centered in the strict performance of different kinds of rituals. Baths, japa and auterities were the order of the day. The cult of hatha yoga sprang from this tendency and ordinary people looked with great awe upon hatha yogis, as they were supposed to possess the power to reduce anyone to ashes by cursing him. This hatha yoga sect gave rise to various minor cults affording great opportunities to hypocritical self-centered individuals to enrich themselves. The Shakta and Bhairava Sects began to flourish.

The early history of the Nath Panth Sampradaya as well as the later one is shrouded in mystery and therefore definite information regarding the luminaries (important personages) of this Sect and other particulars is lacking. Still we get here and there a few glimpses which throw a flood of light on the glory, grandeur, superiority, nobility and utility of the Nath Sect.

There are two notable instances.

1. Adi Shankaracharya, the great exponent of Advaita Vedanta.

2. Jnanadev [Jnaneshwar], the premier poet-saint and prophet of Maharashtra and the author of two most important works:

(1) *Bhavarthadeepika*, the unique and rare commentary on the Bhagavad Gita.

(2) *Amritanubhava*, an independent philosophical work of great merit, a ripe and mature product of this Nath Sampradaya. In his epilogue to the *Jnaneshwari* or *Bhavarthadeepika*, he gives the early history or origin of this Sampradaya.

The later successors of this Sect are not known and we cannot therefore trace an unbroken line down to this day, since it is the way of the Nath Pantha to work in obscurity, outside public knowledge.

The present times may properly be described as the age of progress or the age of determination of truth. New discoveries are being made in every science. What is new today becomes antiquated tomorrow and the human intellect is trying to break all previous records and soar into regions of knowledge hitherto unknown. Modern intellectuals have as it were taken a vow to find out that one principle theat underlies all different sciences and their branches. Books like *The Great Design* assure us that there is a thread knitting together all sciences.

A thinker might say that all these are haphazard efforts to discover the one basic underlying Principle which is true, beautiful and beneficial, and it is a question how far human intellect alone can proceed in this quest and whether it will ever be able to find out that one underlying Principle, knowledge of which would bring certain peace and happiness to all human beings.

Our Aryan culture, however, looks at this question from a unique standpoint of its own. Our prophets and seers say that human intellect alone will never be able to solve the riddle of the universe. The A.B.C. of this science can only be learned in the school of internal intuition and the knowledge or realization of the human spirit. The rise of Self-knowledge will dispel the darkness of Maya or illusion and the path leading to the highest truth will become distinctly visible. On this path peace and happiness are waiting to give a hearty welcome to the human spirit.

Cast a glance at all the philosophical books in the world and you will find that it is only the philosophical and spiritual books of India that boldly call upon spiritual aspirants to come to them, and proclaim that they will show them the path leading to peace and happiness. This is the call of the Nath Pantha to all human spirits and the real power and greatness of this association lies in this.

Sri Matsyendranath

The figure of Sri Matsyendranath stands out with a unique magnificence and greatness against the background of these social conditions. Sri Matsyendranath, through the power of his great personality, dispelled the dense clouds of ignorance and superstition. The divine luster on his face and his persuasive and sweet speech attracted the hearts of all. There were no restrictions in approaching him. Everyone who approached him was absolutely sure that Sri Matsyendranath would show him the path to everlasting joy and happiness. What a shock was this to the Sanatanis, the followers of the path of rituals! Their temples and Maths began to be less and less frequented.

The first doctrine that was preached by Sri Matsyendranath was this: Everyone, whether a man or a woman and of whatever caste, had a birth-right to obtain knowledge regarding God. There was only one condition and that was that his prajna (power of understanding) must be ripened. He used to preach that anyone who understood the instability of all worldly things and who therefore was convinced that realization of God was the only means of acquiring happiness, was one whose prajna could be said to have been ripened. He used to proclaim loudly to all spiritual aspirants, "Oh ye restless human souls, come to me. I will give into your hands the key to everlasting happiness and will fix the seal of eternal joy on your hearts."

The great Nath did not give learned lectures on Vedanta, nor did he ask people to read any religious books. The spiritual power of Sri Matsyendranath was very great. He understood the minds of his disciples and gave impetus to their wills by his own spiritual power and placed them on the path to Light. And then in course of time they attained Self-realization and were submerged in the ocean of joy.

Sri Gorakhnath and his successors

Sri Gorakhnath was the foremost of the disciples of Sri Matsyendranath. Hundreds of anecdotes have been told regarding this pair of guru and disciple. Sri Gorakhnath instructed a peasant who later on became well known as Adbanganath. Sri Gorakhnath instructed also Gahininath, who in his turn became the guru of Sri Nivrittinath, the guru and elder brother of the great Saint of Maharashtra, Sri Jnaneshwar. This was how the Nath Pantha became rooted in Maharashtra and spread its branches in different parts of it. Nivritti, Jnaneshwar, Eknath and other shining lights of the panth spread their beneficent effulgence all over the land of Maharashtra and made it blessed. The mind loses itself in contemplation of the wide-spread influence of this pantha and the far-reaching results achieved by it. It may be considered as a sign of the special divine grace vouchsafed to Maharashtra that its land has been blessed with the sacred imprints of the feet of such great saints and yogis.

Such is the greatness and power of the Nath Pantha. It gave rise to a succession of great personalities to guide humanity in achieving the highest goal of life and in attaining the highest bliss. This tradition of great personalities will be carried on in future to the end of time and pilgrims on the spiritual path will continue to be guided by the cheerful rays of these shining lights. Blessed indeed are they who get instruction from such sadgurus.

WHAT AND WHY IS A SADGURU–THE NATH TRADITION

Some time ago I came across this article written eighty years ago by an anonymous yogi of the Nath Pantha tradition setting forth the Nath Yogi view of the nature and function of a true (sat/sad) guru. Its explanation of what is a sadguru is so valuable that I have decided to present the salient points and comment on them here. The words in quotation marks come from the original article. Editor's note.

There is a tremendous amount of mythology current in the world (including India) as to what constitutes a true guru. In the view of the original yogic tradition of the Nath Panth, the definition is very simple. A sadguru is someone who knows the way to the Real, the Sat, and can teach and guide those who are real mumukshus–seekers for liberation (moksha)–in the practice of the sadhana that leads to freedom in experience of the divine Self. They simply teach and answer the student's questions, if any, and the work is done. That is the simple truth and simple reality of the matter. Anything else is exaggeration, superstition, falsehood and deception.

Tukaram about the aspirant and the guru

"Tuka says it is no use making haste. The proper time must arrive" (Tukaram).

"This proper time in the case of an aspirant on the spiritual path comes when his mind becomes prepared for being the recipient of knowledge.

"When he thus comes of age spiritually speaking, the sadguru merely points out to him the place where his own treasure has been hidden and thus enables him to realize himself. 'Your treasure is very near you. Only you have forgotten the place where it is lying' (Tukaram)."

This proper time in the case of an aspirant on the spiritual path comes when his mind becomes prepared for being the recipient of knowledge. The aspirant's mind is ready for receiving the highest spiritual knowledge only when a marked degree of evolution–intellectual and spiritual–has been reached and stabilized so there will not be in the future either lack of inner growth and development, or future regression from it.

False gurus and false yogis abound, along with guru cults and yoga cults who are ready to recruit and claim the trust and loyalty of whomever they can attract, as we see all the time in the "yoga world." But just as everything else in the world operates according to precise laws, so does the science of yoga. Those who are not evolved to the necessary level will fail–it is in no way their fault. But it is the fault of those who teach them false yoga, so that they often fall into psychological delusions and suffer very real emotional damage. There is great danger for the unaware seeker of which he is never aware until the lightning has struck and the earthquake has destroyed. Rare indeed are those that can survive the ravages brought about by a false guru and false yoga practices.

When he thus comes of age spiritually speaking. The implication here is that a genuine sadguru perceives a person's level of inner development and knows whether he is capable of taking up the yogic path and following it to the end–liberation of his spirit (moksha)–or whether he even truly wants to do so. Fake disciples are as common as fake gurus and fake yoga practices. They often come together in spiritual marriages made in hell. But a genuine sadguru teaches only those who are truly inwardly qualified, and avoids false "seekers" who really want nothing more than some spiritual drama in their life to catch the interest of themselves and others. There are genuine seekers, of course, *but they must come to him.* He never seeks disciples. This principle is an absolute. Those who seek disciples are frauds.

The sadguru merely points out to him the place where his own treasure has been hidden and thus enables him to realize himself. This is how simple it all is. The teacher tells the aspirant the way to go to enlightenment. That is, he gives instruction in the yogic process that will lead to the realization of his Self. He does not do it for the aspirant, nor does he somehow "confer grace" and make him capable of enlightenment. Nor does he claim that his power is working within the disciple when he meditates, or that he "has already done everything" for him. (The false guru slave-takers say a lot about grace, faith in the guru, and especially "surrender.") A genuine guru does not claim to "empower" the disciple—that has already been done by God in eternity before he even came into relative existence. Rather, the true guru instructs him and answers any questions that may arise in the future. He imparts information and the disciple does everything for himself. As Jesus, himself a Nath Yogi, told his disciples: "Whither I go ye know, and the way ye know" (John 14:4).

Nath commentary on sadgurus

"Sadgurus never think that they have given to the disciple anything of their own nor do they consider that they have in any way heaped obligations on the disciple. On the contrary they feel as it were a sense of relief in having safely returned the deposit to the rightful owner, in having been freed from a heavy responsibility placed upon them by the divine will and in having thus done their duty. Sadgurus who fully know the divine laws have these characteristics."

Sadgurus never think that they have given to the disciple anything of their own.... This is because a genuine yogi knows that he has nothing of his own to give: all comes from God, the Sole Source. And he, too, has come from God, as has the disciple. As eternal, immortal Selfs they are absolutely equals. Knowledge is the only thing that marks the guru from the disciple. So the guru immediately gives him that knowledge by which he will attain all further knowledge for himself.

...nor do they consider that they have in any way heaped obligations on the disciple. Actually it is just the opposite. As Sri Ishanath, whom the world knows as Jesus of Nazareth, said, "Ye shall know the truth, and the truth shall make you free" (John 8:32). True sadgurus free the disciple, usually telling the disciple when he no longer has need of further contact with the sadguru. False gurus bind the disciple ever closer and tighter to himself, dominating his life in many ways beyond even the spiritual. They create in the disciple a terrible will-and-soul-destroying dependence on themselves, disempowering them utterly, making them feel that without the guru they are nothing. I personally know of disciples that because of this have committed suicide when their guru died. This is a far cry from the meaning of the upanishadic dictum Thou Art That (Tat Twam Asi), though "advaitic" fakes like to cite it.

On the contrary they feel as it were a sense of relief in having safely returned the deposit to the rightful owner,.... This is a most important statement. A genuine sadguru of the Nath Pantha knows that he is giving to the disciple what already rightfully belongs to him: Soham. For Soham has always been the essence of each sentient being. The dual movement of inhalation (So) and exhalation (Hum) is the very force that was with him in eternity. And that is what brought him into relative existence and which kept evolving him through countless ages by each breath.

Soham is the breath, the life, of each one of us: guru and disciple alike. So a sadguru knows he is simply showing to the disciple what he has possessed all along. He does not "give" him Soham, but *reminds* him of it by teaching him to join it with his breath—to begin doing consciously what he has been doing unconsciously all along throughout creation cycles. Soham is the truth, the Sat, of his being, and he who reveals this to him is a sadguru. Just as a worthy parent looks for the day when his children will become adults and form their own independent lives, so the sadguru anticipates the day when all his obligations will have been fulfilled and the disciple will need nothing whatsoever from him thenceforth.

...in having been freed from a heavy responsibility placed upon them by the divine will and in having thus done their duty. To impart the knowledge of Soham sadhana to a qualified aspirant is the duty of anyone who knows it himself, having received it freely from his own sadguru. And the aspirant in turn becomes the sadguru of those he will likewise teach: not a god or master, but a friend. Jesus the Nath Yogi said to his disciples, "I call you not servants; for the servant knoweth not what his lord doeth: but I have called you friends; for all things that I have heard of my Father I have made known unto you" (John 15:15).

Sadgurus who fully know the divine laws have these characteristics. A sadguru fully knows the divine laws of yoga and Self-realization. Therefore he does not just have one or some of these characteristics, he has all of them. He alone is a worthy sadguru according to the wisdom of the Nath Pantha.

There are other principles of the Nath Pantha regarding the sadguru in the article I have cited. Briefly stated, they are:

1. The sadguru is himself not the means to realize Brahman or the Self. The sadguru is never the means. Rather, the Soham sadhana he teaches to the disciple is the means and Brahman is the Goal. He merely imparts knowledge of the means, the way, to attain Brahmajnana or Brahmanishtha.

   The Brihadaranyaka Upanishad (1.4.1) tells us that the Paramatman, the Supreme Self (Brahman), in the beginning said, "I am Soham [Soham asmi]" (1.4.1). This should sound familiar, because thousands of years after the Brihadaranyaka Upanishad was transmitted to the world, the Gospel of Saint John opened with the words, "In the beginning was the Word, and the Word was with God, and the Word was God" (John 1:1), which itself is a quotation, the original being: "In the beginning was Prajapati, and with him was the Word [Vak]." (*Prajapati vai idam agra asit. Tasya vak dvitiya asit.* Krishna Yajurveda, Kathaka Samhita, 12.5, 27.1; Krishna Yajurveda, Kathakapisthala Samhita, 42.1; Jaiminiya Brahmana II, Samaveda, 2244). Soham is the Word that was with—and is—the Supreme Brahman. In other words, Soham is Brahman in the form of Sound: Shabda Brahman.

2. The sadguru is never to be considered Brahman, as though he and Brahman are the same. They certainly are one, as are all sentient beings since they are part of the very Being of Brahman. But Brahman is infinite and they are finite. One, but not the same. This is an essential understanding.

3. "Now that Brahman, for attaining which so many efforts have to be made and troubles undergone, is pervading everywhere. It is inside as well as outside a human being. If so, then why should the human soul suffer so many agonies? Why should it be smothered in the vicious circle of births and deaths? The reason is that although Brahman is all-pervading, still It is of no use as It remains unknown. Hence moksha is not obtained by means of Brahman but it can be obtained only by the knowledge of Brahman. This knowledge of Brahman is imparted by a sadguru." The knowledge of Brahman is not a matter of discourses on Brahman, but is the revealing of Soham and its requisite sadhana: continual Soham japa in time with the natural, spontaneous breath: intoning "So" while inhaling and "Ham" while exhaling.

4. "If the desire of an aspirant is really keen, the Supreme Self arranges for his meeting with a sadguru." There is nothing wrong with an aspirant seeking for spiritual wisdom, but he should realize that it is the quality and intensity of his desire to find the path to liberation in Brahman which is the key to his success or failure. When his desire is right and his evolution sufficient, then the Absolute Itself brings about his encounter with a true sadguru. Obviously a sadguru is not going to be met with in

some public or commercial enterprise such as a yoga retreat or public classes for which there is a fee. Wherever many people gather there is very little likelihood of even glimpsing a sadguru, much less learning from him.

5. "There are certain obstacles which prevent the attainment of the knowledge of the Self and until these obstacles are removed, there cannot be the rise of self-knowledge." This can be understood in two ways, both of which are correct: a) that there can be no meeting with a sadguru until the aspirant himself has rid himself of all that stands in the way of his learning and successfully following the yogic path to the attainment of Atmajnana; b) if a sadguru is met by one whose life and mind contain these obstacles, the sadguru will either pass him by or will plainly tell him why and how he must correct himself, and the aspirant himself must do everything needed to qualify himself. The sadguru will give him no instruction until he does so.

6. Until the aspirant possesses the necessary qualifications, a sadguru is of no use to him, for the sadguru cannot help the unfit and incompetent.

   "The power of saints is not of this kind. If they had such a power, they would have led the whole world to moksha, as they are full of compassion and cannot bear to see others unhappy.

   "Vaman Pandit says in his *Yathartha Deepika*: 'If the knowledge of Brahman could be granted to persons who are not fit for it, then saints who are full of compassion for all human beings, would have led all the three worlds to moksha.' But such a thing is against the divine law." Sentimentality and emotion simply cannot come into the matter. The law is truly divine, and like the divine cannot be changed or gotten around.

7. The various ways in which these gurus of the Nath Sampradaya are found by their disciples and lead them to the way of perfection are beyond comprehension.

The sum of all this is that "sadguru" means one who knows the way to the Real, the Sat, and who shows that way freely and without obligations to the qualified (adhikari) individual.

Editor's note: Since the only thing the sadguru really does is tell the aspirant how to practice Soham sadhana, in a sense any means by which this knowledge is imparted is his "sadguru," including this book. Furthermore, the Nath Pantha teaches that the ultimate guru is the aspirant's own Self.

Yoga and Its Different Systems

The ultimate goal of human life is to realize God and become one with Him. We may go further and say that it is the birthright of every human being. Swarajya [absolute freedom] is also our birthright no doubt, but the greatest efforts are required to regain the Swarajya which we have lost. Swarajya is really our own, but a great endeavor has to be put up for removing the obstacles in the way, and the endeavor has to be carried on from generation to generation. Similarly, in the case of the human spirit mukti or liberation or perfect independence is not a thing which has to be obtained and brought from outside. It is there all along with the soul itself. But the spirit has lost its independence by faults of its own. It has become the slave of prakriti and entirely dependent upon it. The purpose of Dhyana Yoga is the freeing the spirit from this slavery or bondage. Dhyana Yoga has the power to transform a beast into a human being and a human being into God.

The acquisition of the Four Sadhanas is an infallible weapon for destroying dependence and for attaining liberation or moksha. They are:

1. Discrimination between eternal and non-eternal things; deeply to think over what is eternal and to distinguish it from things non-eternal; to have a clear idea about what is everlasting and what is evanescent; to distinguish between the Self and the non-Self.

2. Disinterestedness regarding enjoyments in this as well as the next world; to look upon all enjoyments in this world and also all enjoyments in swarga or heaven as the means of bondage.

3. Possession of the six virtues:
   a. Internal steadiness;
   b. Control of the external senses;
   c. Detachment;
   d. A tendency to suffer calmly any evil or calamity;
   e. Faith;
   f. Contentedness.

4. A keen desire for liberation (moksha) just as a person who is without food for a week keenly desires food. This mumukshutwa however, cannot arise without the acquisition of the first three sadhanas.

It can be said that the desire to obtain liberation, is possessed by almost everyone to a greater or smaller degree. The reason is that no one likes bondage, because there is misery in bondage and happiness in freedom. Moksha has been defined in the Vedanta as the complete cessation of pain and the acquisition of the highest bliss. He alone acquires this moksha or liberation, he alone acquires this highest bliss, who has a keen desire for it. When will this keen desire be generated? It will be generated only when there will be intense consciousness of the misery brought on by the bondage of worldly existence. When a person keenly feels the pangs of misery, then only will he feel a keen desire to get himself free. This keen desire to be free is known as mumukshutwa.

The human spirit no doubt has a desire to get free from bondage and to obtain everlasting happiness, but finds itself unable to manage the task. Saints come into this world for the uplift of such human spirits. They point them to the summit of Self-realization and the way to attain it. Such saints who have real experience themselves and who can show others how to experience Self-realization are very rare indeed. To meet such saints shows great good fortune and is the fruit of great merit acquired in previous lives. Otherwise even if such saints are near at hand it becomes very difficult to understand and recognize them. There is another reason also which is at present operating to a great extent: the presence in the world of false saints who have been themselves deceived by a false saint or who have deceived themselves into considering themselves saints. Such "gurus" claim to divulge the "secret path" known to them for attaining moksha only to those who make proper submission to them and accept "initiation" at their hands. Such is not the case, however, with teachers of the Nath Panth (Path of the Nath Yogis). If they meet someone who is sincere and willing to make the necessary effort, they lend him a helping hand and lead him to the proper path. They do not consider him a disciple or themselves a guru. Rather, they refer to their students (a proper term) as their friends.

Nearly one hundred percent of the "yoga" taught in India (and now abroad) is not true yoga at all in the definition of the authentic Nath Panthis, the true Nath Yogis. Rather it is nearly all nothing but hatha yoga and tantric practices somehow cobbled together. This is especially true of the breathing methods called "pranayama." Certain of the less physical breathing methods of both hatha yoga and tantra are often presented as Raja yoga or "the subtle Raja yoga," when they are nothing of the sort. Only the meditation on Soham, mentally intoning "So" when inhaling and Ham ("Hum") when exhaling in time with the natural and spontaneous breathing, is true Dhyana Yoga or Raja yoga.

This is demonstrated by the case of Dr. Krishnaji Govind Kurdukar, an Ayurvedic physician who was studied in the early part of the twentieth century. A longtime practitioner of hatha yoga, for three months he lived on only one quart of cow's milk a day. Then for six months he only took syrup of dried grapes, and after that for 108 days he remained only on water. When he sat for meditation, his whole body would rise up a little more than two feet from the ground and remain there without any support. At the end of those 108 days he was examined by Dr. Bhandarkar, a Civil Surgeon, who found that the regimen had produced no adverse effect upon his mental condition or health, although at the same time he had been engaging in physical work according to his bodily strength. This shows that perfect health and wonderful powers can be acquired by the practice of hatha yoga. But there is another thing which becomes very clear from this case. Whatever benefits a person may derive from the practice of hatha yoga as far as bodily fitness or even some miraculous feats are concerned, hatha yoga is of no use in attaining the real bliss of the Self which lies beyond body consciousness.

Various powers are acquired by practicing different forms of concentration. In the Fifteenth Chapter of the Eleventh Skanda of the Srimad Bhagavatam, Sri Krishna has described to Uddhava at full length the various kinds of siddhis (miraculous powers) which can be thus acquired. There is no doubt that these powers can be obtained. But they are obstacles in the path of Self-realization. Sri Krishna says, "He who desires to obtain greatness in the world will undergo the trouble of acquiring these siddhis, while he who has a firm desire to reach Me will never turn towards them. I have described at great length the various siddhis and the methods of acquiring them only to make you understand that siddhis are only obstacles on the path leading to Me" (Sri Eknathi Bhagwata, Chapter XV).

The greatest goal to which the human being can aspire is the realization of the highest bliss in the attainment of Self-realization. The Bhagavad Gita describes it as, "beyond the senses and capable of being grasped only by the intellect." This happiness falls to the lot of saints and devotees alone. It is therefore necessary for a sadhaka to try to obtain Self-realization which is the highest bliss. This is the real aim of human life. Sri Krishna explains the method of reaching this goal in the following words: "A sadhaka who concentrates his pure mind on me, the Brahman without attributes, obtains the highest bliss in which state all desire comes to an end" (Srimad Bhagavatam, Eleventh Skanda, Chapter XV). By contemplating upon Brahman, the sadhaka obtains the highest bliss and all his desires become merged into that bliss. Sri Eknath says:

"When the highest bliss is obtained, all desires become merged just as at the rise of the sun, all the stars and the moon disappear. All the innumerable desires of the sadhaka get merged in the vast ocean of the Supreme Bliss, while all idea of sensual pleasures is ashamed to show itself and instantaneously dwindles away."

The actual experience of this supreme bliss can be obtained by following the instructions of a sadguru. A true sadguru is one who shows the disciple how to realize the Sat: the Absolute Reality–Brahman. For this reason alone should someone be considered as a sadguru. The sadguru merely points out to the aspirant the place where his own treasure has been hidden and shows him how to realize his Self. "Your treasure is very near you. Only you have forgotten the place where it is lying" (Tukaram). Sadgurus never think that they have given to the disciple anything of their own, nor do they consider that that disciple is in any way obligated to them. On the contrary they feel as it were a sense of relief in having safely returned the deposit to the rightful owner, and thus have only done their duty. Sadgurus who fully know the divine laws have these characteristics.

"To say that the guru and Brahman are on the same level or of the same kind is not really true. The idea of the two being similar or on the same level has no foundation to stand on" (Eknathi Bhagwata, Chapter III). Brahman is pervading everywhere–inside as well as outside a human being. Yet the human spirit suffers so many agonies, smothered in the circle of births and deaths. Why? The reason is that although Brahman is all-pervading, still It is of no use as It remains unknown. Hence moksha is not obtained by means of Brahman, but it can be obtained only by the knowledge, the *knowing*, of Brahman. The way to this knowledge of Brahman is imparted by a sadguru. For if the desire of an aspirant is really keen, the Supreme Self arranges for his meeting with a sadguru.

If we look at the original meaning of the word "yoga," it appears to mean the union of two similar things or ideas, so that ultimately the two things or ideas merge into one another and become one. Thus the jiva (the human spirit) and Shiva (the Supreme Spirit) who appear to be separate in the dual state ultimately become one. But if the jiva is considered to be a part of Shiva, then how can the human spirit and the Supreme Spirit become one? To say so will not stand the test of logic and reason. Yogis, however, have written down their experiences in the state of samadhi in which the jiva experiences that he is nothing but Shiva. The duality, therefore, is merely an appearance and not real. Thus they have written down their experiences in order to help seekers of truth.

Yoga, however, is not to be taken to mean the experience of the unity of the jiva and Shiva, but the path which leads to this experience. Hence yoga may be defined as denoting all those actions, mental or physical, which have to be systematically performed in order to know the real internal Principle in man, the jivatman, and then to experience it as nothing else but the supreme spirit, the Paramatman; in other words, to experience the unity between the human and the supreme spirits. According to Vedanta, chaitanya (consciousness) is the real nature of the jiva. It is not really fettered in any way but it falsely feels that it is fettered. If the spirit had not been really free, moksha would have been an impossibility. Hence moksha is verily nothing but its own traditional wealth kept as a deposit. The jiva is nothing but the Supreme Spirit, but owing to illusion created by Maya he feels himself separate. When this illusion is dispelled by real knowledge, one gets the experience that jiva and Shiva are really one.

The word "jnana" or knowledge is used in two senses: (1) the knowledge of the true nature of things, and (2) the knowledge of the actions which are necessary to be done. The ultimate goal of all yoga is to obtain the first kind of knowledge. The second kind of knowledge tells us what particular mental actions are required to be done in order to obtain the first kind of knowledge. To try to get a clear idea of what is Brahman and what is not Brahman, what is atma and what is not atma, then to concentrate one's mind entirely on the spirit or atma and to practice this concentration almost continuously until the aspirant becomes one with Brahman, are the actions meant. This being one with Brahman is known as swarupajnana. That mukti which is obtained by various yoga practices but which falls short of swarupajnana is not real mukti but what is known as kramamukti—merely a progressive stage of mukti. It is also called Ishwarasayujya mukti, liberation through union with Ishwara. In this stage the sadhaka or aspirant gets help from Ishwara and ultimately obtains oneness, with Brahman.

But a human being is not endowed only with intellect. He has faith, devotion and he has also a body. Hence actions, some physical some mental, have been prescribed. The body and mind are necessary in order to get experience in the world and these very experiences leave their deep-rooted impressions on the mind which then assume the form of desire and prevent the human spirit from realizing itself. Hence it is necessary in the first place to remove these obstacles. It is, therefore, incumbent to obtain control over the mind and breath by means of yoga practices, because God will be realized only when the mind and the breath acquire steadiness. The acquisition of this steadiness is what is known as the state of samadhi. A person will be able to experience this state only, when all ideas and doubts will vanish owing to the mind and the breath being entirely controlled.

A person can be said to have realized himself only when in the state of samadhi the distinction between jiva and Shiva vanishes and they become one. Till then the flow of ideas will continue and the perception of "I" and "you" will remain. Just as a pinch of salt, if thrown into water, soon loses its separate existence and becomes one with the water, similarly, in the state of samadhi the jiva (human spirit) loses itself and becomes one with Shiva (the Supreme Spirit).

In the highest developed state of meditation there is no consciousness of space. There is a limitless ocean of light and there is complete quietude. This state has been described by various names. Some call it the state of unity between the jiva and Shiva, some call it immortality, some call it the attainment of the highest goal, some call it the state of oneness, some call it swarajya: self-rule; independence; freedom; absolute freedom, the state of self-dependence (not depending upon anything else), some call it the state of absolute purity (niranjanawastha), some call it jivanmukti (state of moksha while living in the body), some call it sahajawastha (always being as we are: one with the Supreme Spirit) and some call it turiya, the fourth state beyond the three states of waking, dreaming and sleeping. All these different names, however, point to the same meaning: the state in which the flow of ideas and desires is stopped, the mind goes beyond pleasure and pain, joy and sadness and becomes entirely free from all passions. If a person attains this state while he is in this body, then after he leaves the body, he obtains oneness with the Supreme Self which is known as videhakaivalya mukti.

In order to attain this state, four different paths of yoga have been prescribed. They are:

1. Mantra yoga
2. Hatha yoga
3. Laya yoga
4. Raja yoga

Although the goal of all these paths is the same, still the methods followed in each of the paths are different.

You may go by any path but one thing must be firmly borne in mind, viz. that there can be no realization of Brahman unless the flow of ideas has been stopped and control obtained over the breath, because all thoughts, doubts and desires arise from chitta and prana.

Eight different kinds of practices are there in the different kinds of yoga, but the goal of all is the same. This fact has been repeatedly mentioned here because otherwise it is likely to be lost sight of. The samadhi attained in mantra yoga is known as mahabhava, supreme love and yearning for God; that in hatha yoga as mahabodha, the great awakening; that in laya-yoga as mahalaya, total union of the jiva with Shiva; and that in raja yoga as kaivalya mukti, liberation while living in the body.

To attain the state of samadhi, to experience the unity between the jiva and the Shiva, is the highest of all yogas from the point of view of a sadhaka. In raja-yoga predominance is given to buddhi, in mantra-yoga it is given to worshipping and to repeating the mantra with firm faith and devotion, in hatha yoga to certain external (physical) and internal (mental) actions, and in laya-yoga, which is a higher form of hatha-yoga, to dharana and to the awakening of kundalini, the primordial power within the individual. But these different kinds of yoga are not absolutely independent of each other. In each kind of yoga help is freely taken from methods of other yoga paths.

There are certain things which a sadhaka is required to do as a preparatory stage, in order to qualify himself for any kind of yoga. They are called the eight branches or parts of yoga. They are: (1) yama; (2) niyama; (3) asana; (4) pranayama; (5) pratyahara; (6) dharana; (7) dhyana and (8) samadhi.

1. Yama. This includes:

> Ahimsa: non-violence, non-injury, harmlessness
>
> Satya: truthfulness, honesty
>
> Asteya: non-stealing, honesty, non-misappropriativeness
>
> Brahmacharya: sexual continence in thought, word and deed as well as control of all the senses
>
> Aparigraha: non-possessiveness, non-greed, non-selfishness, non-acquisitiveness

2. Niyama. This includes:

> Shaucha: purity, cleanliness
>
> Santosha: contentment, peacefulness
>
> Tapas: austerity, practical (i.e., result-producing) spiritual discipline
>
> Swadhyaya: introspective Self-study, spiritual study
>
> Ishwarapranidhana: offering of one's life to God

These things are absolutely necessary for a sadhaka who wishes to take up the practice of yoga. He must have complete control over his mind, otherwise he will have a downfall. A man who cannot control his mind is not fit to enter the path of yoga.

3. Asana. This is the practice of sitting comfortably in any one posture for a length of time.

4. Pranayama. This includes three processes. To take in a full breath is known as Puraka, then to keep it in for some time is known as Kumbhaka, and then to give it out completely is known as Rechaka. These three things are to be done in a certain limit of time fixed for each. Pranayama, however, has importance only in hatha yoga.

5. Pratyahara. This means to acquire steadiness of mind by controlling the senses in their natural attractions towards external objects. The mind is very fickle by nature. It as it were takes the external objects inside, through the senses and then becomes engrossed in the contemplation of these objects. Hence it is necessary to gradually draw the mind away from the contemplation of these external objects perceived by the senses and to fix it on some small point, and then to direct its attention towards the spirit or Self.

6. Dharana. This means fixing the mind on any mental object or on a part of the body such as a chakra.

7. Dhyana. Meditation itself on a single thing which results in consciousness of the yogi's individual Self within the Supreme Self.

8. Samadhi. The state in which the mind becomes one with the spirit-Self in the same manner as salt is dissolved in water and becomes one with it. The state of complete samadhi is union with Brahman the Absolute.

These are steps on the path leading to complete concentration of the mind. First control must be obtained over the body by means of yama, niyama and asana; then over the breath by means of pranayama and then over the senses with the help of all the four. When dharana, dhyana and samadhi are added to the previous four things, the mind ceases to function and buddhi alone continues to work. Owing to continuous practice, after some time the yogi acquires a firm sense of detachment from the world and then his buddhi also becomes merged and he attains

Self-realization. In that state the jiva (human spirit) becomes free from all dross, becomes full of knowledge and merges in the Supreme Self or Brahman and becomes one with it just as salt is dissolved in water or as camphor is burnt away without a trace.

In the passing of centuries in this land the pure science of dhyana yoga continued to be studied and practiced in the Nath Sampradaya. Every yogi of the Nath Pantha completely knew dhyana yoga–raja yoga–which is the most important of the yogas, but he also knew something about the other kinds of yoga. With the object that aspirants may gather some useful information regarding all the four kinds of yoga, an attempt is made here to describe them in brief.

1. Mantra yoga. The main object in this yoga is to bring under the control of the mind all things in the world having a name and form, by going through certain practices. All things in the world are capable of being understood by the mind–sound, touch, form, taste and smell. The mind quickly becomes one with what it sees–it is carried away. This is what is known as the vritti of the mind.

The mind is never free, even for a single moment, from ideas and sentiments. Whenever an action is done, it is the sentiment which determines its value as high or low, good or bad. That is why it is necessary to have our ideas or sentiments pure. Just as a man who has fallen on the ground takes support of the ground itself in order to rise, similarly in order to sever the bondage of the human spirit, it is necessary to put oneself under certain restrictions and bonds. The mind becomes unsettled through name and form and it is therefore through name and form that it must be brought to steadiness.

In mantra yoga a sadhaka is asked to meditate upon some object having a name and form, care being taken that the object is such as to give rise to pure ideas and sentiments. This is known as meditation on the saguna (made of the five elements) form of deities. In addition to this the sadhaka has to observe six out of the eight sadhanas: (1) Yama; (2) Niyama; (3) Asana; (4) Pranayama; (5) Pratyahara; and (6) dharana.

Besides this he is asked to observe certain rules of conduct and he has to perform the worship of a deity, using some form or depiction as the object of his worship and meditation. The sadhaka has to repeat the mantra while worshipping or meditating upon the form of the deity, etc. This in due course leads to samadhi which is known as mahabhava samadhi. This yoga is easier than other three. In this yoga attention is required to be paid to different forms of worship, to the different duties prescribed to be observed by the sadhaka.

2. Hatha yoga. In this yoga the main efforts are directed towards bringing the physical body under control. But as the physical body is very closely linked with the astral body, if the physical body is controlled it inevitably leads to the gaining of some control over sentiments, desires and reason. This is because the physical body has been so constructed that it is a proper abode for experiencing the fruits of actions done in previous births which the astral body brings along with it in each incarnation. When the astral and the physical bodies join together, there is no doubt that they are interdependent on each other and hence efforts directed towards the physical body have an effect over the astral body. When, therefore, the physical body is brought under control by certain physical practices, the astral body can also be more easily brought under control by certain mental practices.

To bring merely the physical body under control is not yoga, although it may be useful in keeping the health fit. All the different eight branches of yoga, yama, niyama, etc. have to be practiced in hatha yoga. Meditation is, however, practiced upon light or upon the flame of a lamp. The samadhi in hatha yoga is known as mahabodha samadhi. Steadiness of mind is acquired by means of pranayama. The word "Hatha" consists of two syllables, "Ha" and "Tha." They respectively mean the Sun and the Moon or the prana vayu and the apana vayu. The prana vayu which abides in the heart is always drawing towards it the apana abiding in the muladhara, while the apana is similarity drawing the prana towards itself. These two Vayus, therefore, are as it were fighting with each other and obstructing each other in leaving the body. When, however, they become friendly with each other, they help in leaving the body. These two Vayus become one in the sushumna nerve. The prana which is in the individual body is merely a part of the universal prana (vishwaprana). Hence efforts must first be directed towards bringing about the union between the individual prana and the universal prana. This leads to perfect health and brings about steadiness of mind and concentration.

Pranayama has been given great predominance in hatha yoga. In the other three yogas–mantra, laya and raja yogas–it is of secondary importance. To take the prana upwards to the brahmarandhra (the chakra at the top of the head) through the sushumna, and to experience the state of samadhi there is considered as moksha by the hatha yogis.

In acquiring control over the physical body certain practices have to be done. They include restrictions regarding the place of abode, eating, drinking, sleeping, sitting and sexual intercourse.

3. Laya yoga. This yoga is only a higher stage of hatha yoga. This yoga is to be practiced after the practices of yama, niyama, asana, pranayama, pratyahara, dharana and dhyana are completed. In every human being there always dwells the One Existent, Living and Blissful Shiva and His Consort Shakti. But owing to the net of desires accumulated in innumerable births which envelops this pure being, the human spirit is not conscious of its own real nature. In laya yoga the yogi first obtains control over his mind and then he gets the power of matter merged into the power of the spirit, and the five elements in the human body then become united with the five elements in the universe. It is a well-established principle in all yoga philosophy that whatever is found in the universe is also to be found in the human body.

Just as certain actions have to be done in the mantra and hatha yogas for helping the sadhaka in his progress, similarly certain actions have to be done in this yoga also. In laya yoga the extremely minute nature of the organs of knowledge, their position in the body, the effects which they produce on the astral body, their powers and the inner world which is in the human body are all taken into consideration. Different deities dwell in the different plexuses in the body. The sahasradala is the place of Shiva, the Supreme Self, who is self-existent, life and bliss, and of his Shakti, and the muladhara is the place of the kundalini, which is the power of prakriti. The goal of this yoga is to obtain control over this prakriti and to get it merged in the power of the spirit and thus to attain the state of samadhi.

Just as in hatha yoga the state of samadhi is attained by meditation upon light and in mantra yoga by meditation upon some object having a name and a form, similarly in laya yoga, samadhi is attained by meditating upon the reflection of the kundalini in the form of light which appears at the center between the eye-brows, the ajna chakra. This reflection appears only after kundalini is awakened.

In this yoga, kundalini is awakened by taking the help of hatha yoga and of the general eight branches of yoga—yama, niyama, etc. Predominance, however, is given in this yoga to dharana. The kundalini power holds and supports the human body and is the main support of all the practices in yoga. Just as we open a door by opening the lock, similarly a yogi awakens the kundalini by certain practices and thereby opens the door of moksha. In the human body the highest power is represented by the kundalini. In this power all other powers are centered. If strict celibacy is observed, this power instead of producing matter and thereby degrading itself, produces ojas (subtle vital power) which ascends, along with the power of breath, to the abode of Shiva and Shakti situated in the sahasradala. A person who succeeds in obtaining complete control over the sexual energies becomes free from all bondage.

All the seventy-two thousand nadis of the human body start from the Muladhara as the base of the spine.

Kundalini is also called prana shakti (the power of breath) and Shabda-Brahman (Brahman manifested in the form of sound). All mantras are but the manifestations of the kundalini and hence the kundalini is considered as the presiding deity of all mantras.

He who thoroughly knows this kundalini or prana shakti and brings it under his control is a real yogi and such a yogi alone can attain moksha. All others have been tied and caught in the snares of this world for ages together. The kundalini shines like lightning. Mantras are groups of letters and hence the sounds of mantras are but manifested forms of the kundalini. Even the Supreme Self as observed in the dwaita or dual state is a manifestation of the kundalini. Hence the repetition of mantras is necessary in order to awaken the kundalini.

The essence of mantras is full of life. Mere letters are dull matter, but the power centered in them is vital and full of life. Although this divine power dwells in every human being, still in order that it should produce an appreciable effect in the physical world, it is necessary to tread the path of yoga. When the capability of a sadhaka is joined with the inherent power of a mantra, then only does the spiritual power of the spirit become manifest.

Although this kundalini has its abode at the muladhara chakra in every human being, still it throws light on all yogic principles and makes them manifest in the heart of a yogi alone; and the kundalini of a yogi alone then as it were dances with joy. The Vedas, mantras, the sun, the moon and the fire are nothing but the manifestations of this kundalini power. The kundalini is the mother of the whole universe. All the six chakras and the sahasradala are tricks performed by this conjurer. It may be considered as the universal spirit or Shiva himself. Hence the main point is to awaken it by the repetition of mantras, to take it up to the brahmarandhra and to unite it with the power of the Supreme Self there. When this kundalini merges into the power of the Supreme Self, there is real Self-realization. Hence awakening of the kundalini is the first stage, and then taking it upwards and uniting it with the sahasradala is the next stage which is complete Self-realization.

4. Raja yoga. Raja yoga stands supreme among all the yogas. In the other three yogas—mantra, hatha and laya—the sadhaka gradually acquires purity of mind and becomes worthy of attaining the state of savikalpa samadhi. It is only in raja yoga that he attains the state of nirvikalpa samadhi. A yogi who has attained savikalpa samadhi but has not experienced the state of nirvikalpa samadhi has to be born again and again in this world. In the nirvikalpa samadhi which is attained only by means of raja yoga all desire is absolutely rooted out and the yogi feels himself completely detached from the world, and hence he does not come back when he becomes one with Brahman. The first three yogas prepare the ground for raja yoga. Mahabhava is attained by means of the samadhi in mantra yoga. In hatha yoga the sadhaka gets complete control over breath and goes into the state of samadhi. He becomes as it were dead to all external objects. In the samadhi of mantra yoga the sadhaka is unconscious of the external world and experiences a feeling of joy. But the real perfect samadhi is that which is attained in raja yoga. There is only the consciousness of the Divine Existence in that state and the sadhaka then attains complete mukti or liberation.

Vairagya (detachment) is of four kinds: (1) mild, in which there is absence of attachment towards things of the world off and on; (2) middling, in which here is a desire to enjoy worldly pleasures if they are available, but the desire is not keen enough to produce any unpleasant feeling if they are not available; (3) adhimatra, in which a sense of disgust for worldly pleasures is produced owing to experiences of such worldly pleasures often resulting in misery; and (4) paravairagya, in which there is a complete turning away from the world and objects in it. In the mantra, hatha and laya yogas only the first kind of vairagya, the mild, is necessary. It is only in raja yoga that the sadhaka must have complete or paravairagya. Although in every kind of yoga great emphasis is laid on the preparation of the mind, still it is in raja yoga alone that this preparation of the mind is considered as the only essential thing.

To ascertain and know clearly what the truth is and what is not the truth, what the spirit is and what is the non-spirit, what is eternal and what is non-eternal, by reasoning and by the thoughtful and close study of the shastras, the Vedas, the Upanishads and works of philosophy, then to realize that God is self-existent, that he is life and that he is bliss and then to go into the state of nirvikalpa samadhi and to become one with God, the Supreme Self, is in short the aim of raja yoga.

In raja yoga alone all the results of actions done in former births are nullified, karma really comes to an end and the yogi attains complete mukti even though he may be living in this world in the human form.

Dhyana Yoga As Taught By the Nath Panth

Although during the last thousand years or so the human mind has been in a state of degradation, still at least one man in a thousand could be found, who tried to obtain some knowledge, superficial though it may be, of yoga. Perhaps one man among ten thousands actually practiced yoga. Such men, however, who practiced yoga, generally only practiced certain postures (asanas) and breath control (pranayama). They did not observe yama and niyama. Perhaps one man in a million goes through the different stages of yama, niyama, asana, pranayama, pratyahara and meditation on some object. This state of things demonstrates the truth of Sri Krishna's words in the Gita, "Among thousands of men perhaps one makes any efforts to accomplish yoga."

The Nath Panth has certain fixed standards of his own by which to judge the aptitude of any person with whom they come in contact. If an aspirant has the following qualities in him: (1) good moral character; (2) respect for social ties; (3) a sort of disgust of the worldly life and its ways; (4) faith; (5) devotion and (6) belief in God, a Nath Panth teacher blesses him by giving him the ajapa-japa practice of the Soham mantra which has been handed down from the great Sri Matsyendranath himself.

As this Soham Mantra is the mantra of all the Nath Siddhas, and as it is also the mantra signifying the action of the breathing of all creatures, an aspirant who takes to it is sure to make progress in this very birth and to get experiences showing his progress.

Nowadays there are many so-called gurus giving some mantra to others and there are thousands who receive such mantras and become their disciples. Such persons, however, have no real desire to get moksha. They are more or less bent upon obtaining worldly pleasures. Occasionally perhaps one among a thousand is a real aspirant. But it would be difficult to find that a mantra given by a guru whose mission in life is to obtain money from his disciples rather than to guide them on the spiritual path leading ultimately to real peace of mind has contributed towards at least the purification of the disciple's mind. There have been hundreds of cases where persons, being deceived by external appearances and worldly erudition, have continuously kept going to a guru for years together and have made absolutely no progress from a spiritual point of view.

A guru who really takes care to see whether the disciple is spiritually progresssing is very rare. An aspirant's progress can be ascertained by marking whether there has been any change in the tendency of his mind since his receiving instruction from a guru. If he finds that his mind is gaining in calmness and its attraction respecting external things is becoming less and less, he can be sure that he is progressing.

It will be appropriate at this point to give in short the teachings of the Nath Panth regarding dhyana yoga.

Though it is not necessary in dhyana yoga, as it is in hatha yoga, to do certain bodily and mental actions in order to obtain control over the mind, still if a person does the mental repetition of Soham in time with the natural, spontaneous breath—intoning *So* while inhaling and *Ham* while exhaling—he very soon succeeds in acquiring concentration. In hatha yoga control is obtained first over the breath by pranayama and then control over the mind becomes easy. In dhyana yoga mind becomes concentrated by means of the japa and then control over the breath follows automatically.

In hatha yoga, one has first to do purakha (taking in full breath) and then kumbhaka (holding in of the breath), while in dhyana yoga owing to the concentration of the mind kumbhaka results without the necessity of purakha. This kumbhaka is known as kevala kumbhaka. In that state of deep concentration, the action of breathing is there but it is very subtle and slight. It is so subtle and imperceptible that if a piece of cotton is held close to the nostrils no motion can be perceived. That means that there is the action of breathing only sufficient to carry on the functions of the living body, but otherwise there is kumbhaka. Thus one important stage of hatha yoga is naturally acquired in dhyana yoga without any special efforts directed towards it.

The most important thing in yoga, however, is to awaken the kundalini which is really the pranashakti, and having opened the entrance to the sushumna nadi, to "inhale" and "exhale" prana in the sushumna. The yogi should not try to bring this about according to his imagination of it, but to wait and experience this in time by his simple and direct practice of Soham sadhana. It will occur spontaneously.

By Soham japa in time with the breath the yogi forms the habit of concentration and will be able eventually to remain in that state continuously. This helps the sadhaka a good deal in obtaining the stage of samadhi without making strenuous efforts. The concentration of the mind leads automatically to the control of breath. The sadhaka can sit in any easy posture. The mental japa of Soham should be done without moving the tongue, but only in the mind. Through the internal, mental repetition of the mantra there is natural control of the breath. The breath then begins going up through the sushumna. The mind and the breath then become united and begin to work in harmony. This is a very subtle experience and has nothing to do with the violent and dramatic "awakening of the kundalini" in tantric practices that is only neurological and profoundly pathological, leading to both physical and mental illness.

These things written so far on this subject are possible only through the yogi's practice in this life or his previous lives. Some sadhakas begin experiencing these things quite soon, and others after some weeks or months. Much depends on how thoroughly the sadhaka is observing yama and niyama, and the total and permanent elimination of meat, fish, eggs, alcohol, nicotine and mind-affecting drugs.

During the practice of Soham sadhana the sadhaka may see light inwardly. This seeing is not done through natural faculty of seeing, but is the internal sight of the subtle energies of the mind and the subtle bodies. Its meaning should not be overestimated or exaggerated, but it is a sign that the mind has become calm and concentrated. In time the divine light is perceived and is a sign that the sadhaka is practicing correctly. But it does not mean he is enlightened–just on the right path to enlightenment. I mention this because the ego is always around waiting to lead the sadhaka astray by delusion and pride. The sadhaka should just keep up Soham sadhana and keep moving toward the Goal without distraction.

The sadhaka can experience many things through the internal senses such as sights, sounds, smells, sensations of lightness, heaviness, rising and falling and suchlike. They are only the experiences of subtle materiality, the subtle energies of the astral and causal bodies and senses. They are like signs on a highway. They indicate that the traveler is moving toward his destination, but not that he has arrived there.

Some Nath Panth teachers have the student sit in front of him and practice Soham sadhana. During the time they may have many kinds of experiences such as those listed above or the experience of seeing deities, siddhas, astral worlds, chakras and lights of many colors, or hearing many internal sounds such as bells, waterfalls, flutes, harps, and suchlike. All of these can be distractions from true sadhana and give rise to delusions and illusions–especially of counterfeit enlightenment. Therefore they are real dangers to the sadhaka. The teacher may have the student sit before him one or many times. After all this, the teacher tells him that all these were gateways to delusion, mere distractions from experience of the Real, of the Self and Brahman, and that from then on he will be able to make genuine progress in safety. Sometimes the teacher tells him that he no longer needs to visit him, that he can now proceed onward on his own. This is the way of freedom, of the true Nath Panthis who never make anyone dependent on them. This is why they refer to their students as friends and not disciples. For they are no one's "master."

Now let us see the real significance of Soham. All creatures are breathing in and out. The adept yogis have told us that the number of breaths taken in a day is twenty-one thousand and six hundred. The inhalation generates the sound "So" and the exhalation generates the sound of "Ham." Thus the sound of "Soham" is being continuously generated in every creature, although very few are conscious of it. To consciously link up with this sound through the repetition of Soham in time with the breath–mentally intoning "So" when inhaling and "Ham" when exhaling–is the practice of Soham sadhana. Soham means I Am That, "That" meaning both our individual Self, the jivatman, and the Supreme Self, the Paramatman with which we are one. Soham sadhana reveals the oneness of the jiva (human spirit) and Shiva (Supreme Spirit). All knowledge has been centered in Soham. All the four Vedas, the Gita and the Gayatri Mantra tell us nothing except Soham. One can accomplish anything by meditating upon Soham: detachment from material bonds, the ending of all karma, release from the cycle of birth and death, and the realization of the Self. Everything can be obtained through Soham. This is the real dhyana yoga or raja yoga.

A worthy teacher of the Nath Pantha instructs an aspirant in the japa and meditation of Soham and thus puts him on the path of dhyana yoga. He tells him, "Where Light and Sound become one, there is the real Self. There is nothing more to be seen or told. Then consciousness of 'I am Brahman' also vanishes and only bliss, pure and simple, remains." In dhyana the sadhaka enters into the internal world which is inside himself. According to each disciple's efforts in practicing dhyana, he becomes easily accomplished in yoga. The spiritual experiences of various yogis differ. This is due to the differences in mental aptitude, intellect and practice already done in previous births. Ultimately the

"Soham" consciousness merges in the Supreme Self and the sadhaka attains perfection.

The dhyana Yoga taught by the Nath Panth is the path by which all great saints of old attained Self-realization.

WISDOM OF
SRI GAJANANA MAHARAJ

If you want to realize the sweetness of sugar or the bitterness of quinine, you must taste it yourself. Any amount of description in words will never make you realize it. Self-realization is similarly a matter of experience, and firm faith alone will enable one to get that experience.

Every human being is ceaselessly trying to acquire happiness or to increase his share in it and to avoid pain, or at least to lessen it as much as possible. But the experience is just the contrary. He is ever feeling the lack of something and is always plunged in misery. Things which are pleasant in the beginning end in sorrow, and misery is always on the increase and gets the upper hand. As man does not really understand wherein lies his happiness, he passes his days in the vain hope of securing happiness some time or other. Death catches him in its grip while his search for happiness is still going on. People do not profit by the example of their companions and fellow-beings, and so continue the same search and follow the same path. They, however, do not stop to think wherein lies real and lasting happiness. A man, if he thinks deeply about this, will come to know that all things in this world which appear pleasant are perishable and false like a mirage. They either cause pain or increase the pain which is already there. No one, however, acquires this insight. On the contrary, everyone is entangled more and more in this snare of misery and finds it difficult to see a way out of the maze.

It is therefore necessary that some royal road should be pointed out so that people going by that path might root out this unending sorrow and pain and reach the destination where there is everlasting peace and happiness. I am putting before the world my experiences in order that people might find an easy, short and sure way of reaching this goal of everlasting happiness. When you get experience for yourself, you will be sure that you are on the right path. You will yourself enjoy full, complete and everlasting happiness and also lead other forlorn and miserable fellow-beings to the same path.

There is a simple and royal road to obtain real happiness and bliss—a road which does not require the abandoning of worldly life and of our usual worldly activities. This path is known as Dhyana Yoga or Raja Yoga or Karma Marga.

If you follow this path you are sure to reach the goal. The series of difficulties which a person has to undergo in this worldly life in due course awakens a desire in him to find out this path leading to unchanging and everlasting happiness. He then tries his utmost to discover this path, but he is almost always groping in the dark. The main object in my writing this is to shed light in this darkness, and to illumine the path for the sake of these struggling human souls.

To thoroughly understand the "I," to seek for It and to catch hold of It, is the goal of this path. For a human being, whether man or woman, this is not an easy task. A keen desire to find out this "I," a firm determination to carry on the search for It, great perseverance in sticking to this pursuit and firm faith—these are the steps which an aspirant has to ascend if he wants to reach the goal. Once you reach the high pinnacle you can sit and cast a glance on the panorama of worldly existence spreading out below you.

A person who feels this urge to find out the "I" and thus to enjoy this unrivalled empire of complete and unchanging bliss, is known as a mumukshu [a seeker after liberation—moksha]. To complete this search and to be in the enjoyment of this everlasting happiness is known as obtaining moksha. The path which leads to this moksha is known as yoga. This yoga is merely a means leading to the end. There are different paths leading to moksha which are the different yogas and are known by different names. But the paths other than the one described here are difficult to follow.

Supposing you try to keep your mind pure and by continuous contemplation a feeling of detachment grows up in your mind. Still the question remains whether you, the sadhaka, can be said to have progressed. You can get a very satisfactory answer to this question.

Every aspirant must, with perseverance and firm faith, carry on the abhyasa (practice) until he becomes fit to be the recipient of the final experience. His progress will depend upon his practice in this life. But it goes without saying that he is sure to attain the goal sooner or later.

Just look back retrospectively. Consider what was the tendency of your thoughts before you began your practice, what were your defects and what were your merits then, and observe the tendency of your thoughts now. See whether your good qualities have increased and your defects have become less.

The following are some of the characteristics that accompany the stage of the realization of the final experience. Desire, hate, attachment and fondness for sensual enjoyments are conspicuously absent. A feeling of complete detachment reigns. The mind is, as it were, nullified. All disturbing waves of thought subside and the deep calm ocean of peace pervades everywhere. The real object of getting this human life is fulfilled. The real nature of "I" is thoroughly understood. The continuous practice of dhyana and japa leads to this stage. In that stage, the dhyata, dhyana and the dhyeya—the contemplator, contemplation and the object of contemplation—become one, and thereby the real object of devotion is fulfilled.

As the sadhaka progresses, he gets certain powers (siddhis) in the natural course. He, however, must not be attracted towards those powers, but must carry on the practice with firmness. If he allows himself to be attracted by them, he becomes their prey and various obstacles then arise in the path of his progress, which sometimes is altogether stopped.

As an illustration of comparing Dhyana Yoga with other yogas, let us take the case of the nine-fold path of Bhakti (Devotion). In this all the organs [jnanindriyas and karmindriyas] have to be utilized in the service of God. In the repetition of mantra or the contemplation of God, however, only the mouth, ear and mind are utilized. It is not necessary to make a comparison with all the other yogas. This illustration will convince anyone why Dhyana Yoga is by far the easiest. In the Yoga Sutras 1:28 we find: "Its japa and fixing one's attention on its meaning." Patanjali makes clear the method to be followed.

Now let us see how a man should act in worldly life so that he may progress spiritually while leading a life in the world. To him I say, "My good friend, do not leave your family. Continue to do your worldly duties as you are doing now. Only begin the practice of Dhyana Yoga and carry it on and stick to it with perseverance. You can thus kill two birds with one stone. You will be able to lead a worthy worldly life and also to progress spiritually. Try it and you will be convinced of the truth of what is said above from your own experience."

Now let us see how this can be accomplished. No human being can ever escape from the necessity of doing actions. There are, however, two different ways of doing these actions. In the one, we do all actions with the desire of achieving some object as a consequence of those actions. If our object is fulfilled, we become happy and full of joy. If, on the contrary, we fail in achieving our object and are unsuccessful, we are cast down and we become full of sorrow. Thus we see that the real cause of our happiness or sorrow is not the actions themselves, but the object or motive behind them. If we then abandon the object and do not pay any attention at all to the consequences of our actions, but do them from a sense of duty only, we shall never fall into the clutches of sorrow and our peace of mind will never be disturbed. Actions done with the desire of achieving some object are known as sakama and those done merely from a sense of duty without any object in view are known as nishkama.

Now if we cast a glance at the worldly experiences of our own and of others, what do we see? Do we find that all our actions are successful and that our desires are in every case fulfilled? Do the actual results of our actions correspond to the expectations entertained in our mind regarding them? No. On the contrary, we find that in the majority of cases we are unsuccessful and have to swallow the bitter pill of disappointment. There are various obstacles which intervene and frustrate our desires. We sometimes overcome some expected obstacles and triumph over the difficulties. But almost always we succumb before unexpected obstacles and difficulties. In such circumstances we get confounded, and getting submerged in the slough of despondency are completely at a loss to know what do. We are sometimes quite tired with our life and wish that it were ended. Why is it so? It is because when we do actions with some object in view, all our attention is directed towards the object, and once that is frustrated the equanimity of the mind is entirely disturbed and we become a prey to sorrow and despondency.

If on the other hand we do actions merely from a sense of duty without paying any attention to the result, and taste the fruit of those actions quite naturally as it comes, we shall not be affected either by joy or sorrow and our peace of mind will never be disturbed. This is because vasana (desire) which is the root cause of all sorrow is nullified. To do actions in this manner is known as Nishkama Karma Yoga. If a person follows this method while leading his life in the world he will surely attain Self-realization. Such a person need not renounce the world. Only he must follow this method with great perseverance and firm determination. He must only have the will to do so, and his efforts will surely be crowned with success.

All actions, therefore, which are done by us without any desire of obtaining the fruit, and simply from a sense of duty, are nishkama. Such a person is known as a Nishkama Karma Yogi. He easily achieves success in spiritual matters, and in course of time attains the bliss of the Self.

While practicing Nishkama Karma Yoga or Raja Yoga, many a time various miracles take place at our hands. This stage is known as the stage of siddhis (powers). There is a danger at this time of our becoming either afraid or triumphant or proud. Very great care must be taken at this time. Otherwise we shall become as blank as we were at the beginning of our spiritual career. If we make use of these powers for obtaining fame or wealth, our spiritual progress will be entirely stopped and we shall stray away far from our goal of acquiring the knowledge and realization of the Self. If we however consistently maintain the attitude that we are not the authors of these miracles, we are not responsible for them and they happened naturally, these siddhis will not operate as obstacles on our path and we shall easily attain our goal and gain complete peace and happiness.

I therefore humbly request you all, whether you are mumukshus or sadhakas: Think of all things with an independent and unbiased mind, through practice root out all likes and dislikes and acquire a sense of complete detachment. With Nishkama Karma Yoga carry on your worldly duties, and through meditation and practice become one with the universe and enjoy everlasting bliss.

Pure love is the real "I." It is the real sadguru. When a person becomes an embodiment of this pure love, he has really conquered the whole world. The same thought is expressed by Sri Tukaram when he says, "He who humbles himself before all creatures holds the unlimited (God) within himself." If you have unqualified pure love in your hearts you will really be blessed with this sadguru's grace. This love should be absolutely pure without the least malice towards anyone. A typical example of this love in worldly life is a mother's love. If that love which a mother feels for her child is felt by us towards all creatures, then God will surely come to dwell in our hearts. This love is awakened in our hearts by the words of saints and by coming in contact with them. It is this idea which Tukaram has expressed in the following words: "The nature of pure love is such that it loves without any motive of self-interest."

Maya was born from the Avyakta and the world was born from Maya. You may also say if you like that the world was born first and then Maya was born. It is just the same. Saints have said in their imperishable words that Maya is Brahman and Brahman is Maya. A sadhaka has to get an understanding of this principle at the feet of saints. When he does this, his whole samsara (worldly life) becomes full of bliss. Whatever actions he then does, his mind is always steeped in bliss. That action may be sakama or nishkama. He becomes absolutely detached. In that stage the thoughts expressed by him are of great benefit to all, whether they are ignorant or learned. If people listen to these thoughts and act to bring them into practice, they become full of love for him. Then, their egotism, kama, krodha and lobha (avarice) become as if dead. Their kama, krodha, etc., produce no reaction in others or in themselves.

This is the true path of progress for a mumukshu. A mumukshu must carry on this practice with great devotion and selfless love for at least twelve years. He will then be able to reach Self-realization. This faithful sadhaka then reaches the stage of vijnana. If a sadhaka feels true and selfless love, he later on reaches the stage when his own Atman (Self) becomes his guru. This love was born from the Avyakta; saints were born from love. Maya was born from the saints and the world was born from Maya. In order to reach the Avyakta we have to go back by the reverse process. God is enshrined in the hearts of saints who are full of love. It is the saints alone who teach how to look upon samsara as Brahman, and Brahman is nothing but Atmic bliss.

To trouble the saints regarding our worldly affairs is detrimental to our spiritual progress, because this shows that we attach undue importance to them. And when our worldly desires are not fulfilled, our faith in the saints becomes shaky. Some persons come to me and ask me to remove their worldly troubles. "I have incurred a debt of four thousand rupees. This makes my mind uneasy. Kindly shower your grace upon me and make me free from care." Such are some of the complaints which are often brought to me by people. They desire that I should ward off their difficulties and troubles. A real saint will never do this.

Therefore when people come to me for the redress of their worldly troubles I plainly tell them that every person must patiently bear the troubles sent to him by his fate, and that the best way of solving worldly difficulties is to follow worldly and practical methods.

There are some persons who come to me solely with the object of achieving their worldly objects. They have nothing to ask in spiritual matters. To such I say, "This is not my business. You should go to those saints who happen to possess such powers." It is the mission of real saints to point out the path which leads to sure and everlasting peace and happiness to persons who, being extremely harassed by worldly troubles, are in urgent need of finding out a way which will take them out of all troubles and establish them in everlasting peace. Real saints have this power of granting boundless happiness and complete peace of mind.

[That which is known as Paramartha is the highest attainment, purpose, or goal in our life, for it is itself the Absolute Reality. Gajanana Maharaj had the following to say regarding this:]

To obtain this Paramartha is the goal of human life, and you can obtain it by your own persistent and honest effort. Efforts are necessary to obtain any object in the world. Are we not required to make strong efforts to obtain money or learning? And are our efforts always crowned with success? But do we on that account abandon efforts to obtain these things? Similarly, we must continually make strong efforts to obtain the realization of the real "I." The various difficulties and obstacles which arise in this path must be removed by following the advice of experts, just as we do in worldly matters. Hence Saint Ramdas has said, "First a person should learn to make his prapancha (worldly life) all right, and then should have recourse to Paramartha. Oh, thoughtful persons, do not be careless regarding these important matters."

To make his prapancha all right does not mean that a person should try to secure a monthly income of a thousand rupees or should keep a motor car. It means that he must devote careful attention to each and every detail of worldly life, must have faith in the efficacy of his efforts and the advice given to him, and should have recourse more to policy than to force in his dealings. These very qualities are also extremely useful in spiritual matters. The answer to the question as to whether a person's prapancha is all right or not will depend upon the angle of vision which we adopt in looking at his life, our own attitude towards life in general, and the stage of mental development at which we ourselves have arrived. Hence, how can any general standard be fixed for all? Thus it should be clearly borne in mind that the solution of worldly things should be sought for by worldly means, and of spiritual matters by spiritual methods.

All human beings are the children of God. And it has been said that if a human being makes strong efforts he can even become Narayana (God). It has been said by a Western philosopher that God is what man can be. If it is so, how can you condemn yourselves as sinners?

In my opinion, there are three kinds of great men in the world. I do not say that there are no real saints at present. Some perform miracles by making use of their siddhis. People take them to be great saints and bow before them. These saints obtain some powers by the practice of hatha yoga and perform miracles. As ordinary people in the world want the fulfillment of some desires, or the averting of some calamities, they naturally go to such saints and become their followers. These great men, if they are at all great, are of the lowest order of the three kinds mentioned above. Just as in a village where all other people are illiterate, a person who has learned to read and write is considered wise and learned, similarly these saints are respected by worldly people who themselves know nothing about real spiritual matters. The happiness obtained through such siddhis is transitory. These siddhis merely create a false show of happiness for a time, and then disappear leaving the saint completely bankrupt.

The second kind of great men are those who being filled with the desire to serve mankind, shine as great leaders of men and patriots. Their ambition is to make all their fellow beings or fellow-countrymen prosperous and happy. They sacrifice their personal comfort, and sometimes even their lives, in trying to achieve the good of their fellowmen. They try to weld all their countrymen into one homogenous whole, preach to the people the good which is derived from unity, arouse the consciousness of their rights as subjects, and make them worthy of putting up a fight for their rights and for the redress of their wrongs. Their lives serve as an ideal for ordinary people to follow, and they represent in their lives the sum total of the good qualities of the world. These great men at least do not mislead people by exhibiting miracles by means of siddhis. But these great men are of no use to a human soul striving to attain Self-realization. It does not lie in their power to grace human beings and to lead them to the path of realizing the highest bliss.

The great men who can do this are different. They are the great saints who take pity on all troubled souls who are floundering in the mire of worldly pains and pleasures, and who are at a loss to find a way out. They call such persons their own. They do not lead them to the search of worldly happiness which is illusory, but show them the path which will ultimately take them to the source of all happiness, the path which will clearly show to them the real nature of their Self, and illumine their whole being with the all-pervading light of Self-knowledge. They say to the human soul: "The source of happiness is within you. The treasure is hidden within you. Only you have forgotten the place where it is hidden," and they point out that place, and show the way to reach it. Such great men are the real mahatmas, and they are the best of all great men. Sometimes miracles happen at the hands of such mahatmas also, but they happen naturally. They themselves are not conscious of having wrought them. They are always immersed in the atmic bliss, and whatever actions happen at their hands are natural and automatic.

A few days ago, a gentleman from Poona came to see me. While talking on various topics, he incidentally said: "Maharaj, some years ago a Santa Parishada (a meeting of saints) was held at Poona. Many maharajas, some having matted hair, some who had practiced penance and austerities, some sannyasins, some heads of maths, etc., had all assembled together at that meeting. From the name given to that meeting, 'Santa Parishada,' it was very natural to think that all these men were saints. Ordinary people think that saints are persons who, having realized the Self, are always immersed in the bliss of the Paramatman, and all of whom are directed towards leading other human beings to the path of everlasting happiness. A doubt, however, arose in my mind whether all these men were saints as understood in this sense.

"At the present, meetings of 'Nathas' often take place at Poona. Some say that they met Sri Matsyendranath, while some say they actually had the darshana of Sri Gorakshanath, and had received orders from him. It has been rumored that the famous Nine Nathas have been issuing orders through these various persons for spreading the doctrines of the Nath Pantha. If any one approaches any of these persons with the desire of knowing whom he should make his sadguru, he gets an order from these persons evidently inspired by one of the Nine Nathas, and he then exactly knows who is his destined sadguru. When I hear about these things, my mind gets confused and I ask myself, 'Are all these things true?' Everywhere we hear about these Nathas and their messages.

"In addition, we hear about various other saints. There are also different maths, temples, and different gods and goddesses. I am at a loss to know whether any of these things are true—or none are. My mind is absolutely confused. Hence, I request you to tell me in what I should believe, and how I should set my mind at rest?"

To this, I answered as follows: "You have asked a very good question. This question often troubles many thoughtful people, especially when they find saints and Nathas sprouting up like mushrooms on all sides.

"Paramartha (spirituality) is a subject regarding which various misconceptions hold full sway in our present-day society. Sri Ramdas has said: 'There is a bazaar of shastras, various gods and deities are crowding in it, and people are performing various religious ceremonies for securing the fulfillment of their desires. Various tenets and opinions clash with each other. Everybody thinks his own view to be correct, and anybody else's wrong. There is no agreement anywhere, and all are contradicting each other.' Under these circumstances, how to find out the truth is a very difficult question. Sri Tukaram says: 'There are so many gods. Where should I place my faith?'"

If a sadhaka thinks that seeing of divine visions is the ultimate goal, that it is Self-realization, that he has attained the highest stage, and nothing further remains to be done or achieved, it is sheer ignorance on his part. Because as long as there is duality, the flow of pain and pleasure continues unabated, and everlasting happiness is as far away as ever. If you think carefully, you will see that whatever is seen and heard is bound to disappear. But the knowledge of the Self is permanent and imperishable. This argument, I think, will appeal to all whether they are theists or atheists. Seeing of lights or visions and hearing of divine sounds, do not indicate the achieving of Atma Sakshatkara. To realize that the One Eternal Being on which these visions and sounds play and move is none other than our own Self, is the real Atma Sakshatkara. To be one with the everlasting Being is the real Sakshatkara.

When a person attains this oneness, his mind entirely becomes devoid of sankalpa (desire) and vikalpa (doubts), and it becomes absolutely indifferent. It goes beyond pleasure and pain. Actions are then automatically performed according to the prakriti dharma (promptings of nature). He becomes absolutely fearless, and is entirely devoid of egotism. When this state of mind is attained, then only can it be said that there is Atma Sakshatkara or Atmajnana. He is, as it were, merely sporting as a child while doing any actions. He is entirely detached from them. This is what is known as Sakshi Awastha (the state of being merely a witness of one's actions). Progress means the gradual attainment of this state of mind. We can ourselves get a clear idea of our progress. There is no necessity to ask anyone else about it.

In that state, although passions may be there according to the original nature of the aspirant, still the passions come and go automatically, without taking effect in the form of wrong actions. Right actions are naturally and automatically done. This state is known as Atmajnana. When this stage is reached, never-ending bliss and peace are attained. This is what is known as the sahaja state. This is merely another word expressing the same idea as Atmajnana. Merely defining Atmajnana, Brahmajnana, bliss, or samadhi is of very little use.

In short, I wish to emphasize that he who has no attachment for worldly objects, who is perfect, has completely controlled his senses, and whose mind is entirely devoid of any desire of sensual pleasures, who remains in the world but is, as it were, out of it—because of his entire detachment—he alone obtains the sovereign kingdom of everlasting atmic bliss. He becomes one with Soham. His mind is pure like the water of the Ganges, which moves in its course purifying all who come in contact with it. All bad thoughts entirely disappear, and his actions are quite naturally done. He is externally, as well as internally, quite calm and at peace.

In this stage, it is difficult to distinguish him from other ordinary persons. In this stage, he naturally attains the power of knowing the past, present and future. He becomes a Trikalajna. With all that, he never tells others of what is to happen, nor does he make use of this knowledge for his own benefit. It may happen that his words may at times be prophetic, but this takes place automatically. Never, never does the Atma Sakshatkari (*i.e.* one who has realized his soul) tell others of their past or future on his own initiative. In this stage he sees Brahman in all things; in other words, he is entirely immersed in the experience that everywhere there is nothing but all-pervading joy and bliss. His joy and peace are not dependent upon anything else, and hence they are everlasting. They are not disturbed under any circumstances, however adverse. His experience tells him that he himself has taken the form of the biggest as well as the minutest things. This is the real meaning of Soham. This is the real Atmajnana. Without this Atmajnana, all actions are useless. This is the meaning of Sri Krishna's words.

A person gets pleasures and pains in this world according to the good or bad actions of his previous lives. Though saints and mahatmas have all powers, still everyone has to suffer the results of his own previous karma. Saints do not interfere with the working of this law. Their mission in this world is to point out the way leading to everlasting happiness and thus to make persons going to them blessed in the real sense of the term. They pay very little heed to worldly pleasures and pains which are after all of an ephemeral nature.

Whenever a person, big or small, male or female, feels the want of anything, whether worldly or spiritual, he approaches God and begs Him for granting his desire. We go to a temple. The idol there is of stone. But we, through faith, attribute to it the divine powers of Sri Rama or Sri Krishna and pray to the idol to grant our desires. And we get the fruit of these prayers at some time or other. This is true in the case of all human beings. Whenever a person entertains a desire to obtain some worldly object or to attain spiritual progress, he obtains the fruit of his desire as a result of his efforts in this life or of his karma in previous lives, or owing to fate or destiny, call it anything you like. No astrologer or saint or God is required for that.

Men and women go to a saint, whether a true one or a false one, for getting their desires fulfilled. Some want employment, some are in want of progeny and some want the curing of their diseases. An aspirant on the spiritual path desires to obtain the bliss of the Self or the vision of God.

It is difficult to know who is a real sadguru. We find that even many educated men have fallen into the clutches of self-seeking pseudo-saints. The ways of outward conduct, too, of even really great saints differ on account of the difference of surroundings and of prarabdha (karmic destiny). Hence superficial observers are not likely to recognize the greatness of even real saints. Some persons posing as saints are very clever in giving learned and impressive discourses on Vedanta, while internally they are seeking opportunities to cheat their gullible followers. Real aspirants meeting such saints are ultimately disappointed, because they find that they asked for bread and got a stone instead. Hence it has been said in the Yoga Vashishtha that without the grace of God, it is not possible to meet with a real sadguru. A sadguru must teach yoga not merely by words, but must lead an aspirant to the path of Self-experience. The disciple, too, must know what questions to ask and how to ask them, otherwise everything will be futile.

Raja Yoga is the best of all Yoga practices. The practice of Raja Yoga can control the impressions produced in the mind and wipe them out. All this control is possible only through two things: practice [abhyasa] and vairagya [non-attachment]. A person who merely carries on practice without having vairagya, does not persevere to the end but has to abandon it in the middle. This is because every now and then he is attracted by sensual objects, gets tired of trying again and again to free himself from such attraction, and so he drops any practice. Hence perfect control can be accomplished only with the help of both practice and vairagya. Only those who have left off attachment to sensual objects can be the recipients of this knowledge. He alone who first of all subdues the desires of the mind regarding sensual objects, understands their comparative importance or unimportance and keeps his mind in a state of quietude, succeeds in ascending to the summit of yoga. He who understands how to dispel thoughts which arise in succession in the mind succeeds in going to the end of yoga and becoming a master.

Many persons think that bhakti (devotion) is easier than yoga, but Sri Jnaneshwar says, "Is there anything as easy as Yoga?" I also think that bhakti which depends upon some external object is not so easy as yoga which depends on one's own Self. If a person thinks on these questions deeply, gets explanations for himself and then turns away from the things which bind him and contemplates upon the opposite, he will succeed in putting an end to all pain and obtain the highest bliss. He should fix his mind upon and thoroughly grasp the principle that the Self is absolutely free from attachments, and then by means of Yoga he should practice meditation.

Ordinarily no one likes pain, hence every one desires to end it. We ourselves are dearer to us than any other thing. Things which come in the way of our happiness are disliked by us. We, however, have never any dislike respecting ourselves. Hence it is clear that real bliss lies in ourselves and not in any extraneous thing.

Suppose a person sees a rope in the darkness and thinking it to be a serpent, runs away from that place. He will not then be able to see it, but the impression will still remain upon his mind that he had seen a serpent. If, however, he stays at the place, brings a lamp and satisfies himself that it is a rope and not a serpent, all fear vanishes and no impression of the fear remains on his mind. Thus knowledge alone is capable of dispelling the fear of worldly existence. For obtaining this knowledge it is necessary to read religious books, to listen to discourses on them, to think over them in solitude, and when the mind is thoroughly satisfied about the truth of the principles, to ponder over them again and again.

Suppose you have a lighted lantern in your house and I ask you to bring and show its light to me here. Will you be able to bring the light here and show it to me? No. Then you would say to me, "I shall at the most be able to tell you what particular means are required and what particular action is to be done in order to generate the light." You would ask me to purchase a lantern, fix a wick in it, put kerosene oil in it, strike a match, ignite the wick etc. Then there would be light.

Similarly it is not an easy thing to show God. I may tell you in what way you should conduct yourself. When you will be endowed with all the four sadhanas, or when your desires have vanished, or when you are full of devotion or when your mind is fully detached from all worldly objects and you get knowledge of spiritual matters, you will be able to realize the presence of God who is really without form. You will then be able to see the light of the Self and be one with that Being which is self-existent, which is Life and which is Bliss. That is the real God.

God is not an external object which can be shown by simply pointing a finger towards it. A person's egoism must entirely disappear, his desires must all vanish, he must have complete vairagya and he must feel that he is one with God. Then quite naturally he attains everlasting peace and joy. His whole worldly life will be nothing but Brahman. He will go beyond pain and pleasure.

Suppose some night you get very sound sleep. When you get up the next morning you say to others, "For the last month or so I did not get good sleep. But last night I got such a sound and deep sleep that I was greatly delighted." Now just see. If you were in deep sleep, how can you say that you got sound sleep? Who was awake in that state? Had you seen who was awake in that state? Who enjoyed the bliss of sleep and who is now describing his feelings in that state? You yourself.

Do not, like the musk-deer, wander about seeking outside for what is really in yourself. You have now only to get Self-experience by carrying on the practice of meditation steadily.

Visions of Sri Krishna, or of the goddess or of any other deity is not of any real benefit. As long as the mind is not turned inwards and as long as desires have not entirely vanished, these external appearances are of very little use. All these appearances are illusory like a mirage.

When asked the meaning of Satchidananda: "Sat" means that which is never destroyed, which always exists. It is nothing but Brahman. "Chit" means that it is self-illumined in all the three states of waking, dreaming and sleeping. "Ananda" means bliss. A thing is dear to us not for the sake of that thing but for the sake of our Self, which is the real object of all our love and is therefore the only entity which is dear to us. The Self is, therefore, bliss—Ananda. You are the Self and the Self is Brahman. This principle should be thoroughly grasped by means of arguments, the authority of the Vedas and lastly through Self-experience. Some Vedantins say that "I" (the Self) is present always at the time when passions rise as well as when there are no passions. This principle, "I," exists independently of the passions. Hence the "I" is really not fettered but is mukta (free).

But the true Vedantic doctrine is that at the time of death only all thoughts become entirely merged in the Self. This sort of merging of thoughts cannot be brought about merely by self-control. If that is so, then how would the doctrine that the "I" is present both at the time when passions rise as well as when they are absent help a sadhaka in catching hold of the Self which can be grasped only when the flow of thoughts has altogether stopped? On the contrary when the sadhaka is in the waking–and therefore in the discriminating–state, he will surely be conscious of the existence of "this" and "that."

Although the mind always has a tendency to leave the object of meditation and run away to other things, the only remedy is to bring it back again and fix it on the object of meditation. If we try to give a bend to the branch of a tree, in the beginning as soon as we remove our hand from it, it again becomes straight and assumes its original position. But by continuous efforts of bending it and also by tying the bent parts by means of a rope etc., we succeed in giving it a permanent bend. Similarly, if a person while repeating his japa finds that his mind has wandered away, the only remedy is to forcibly bring it back and fix it again on the japa. Control over the mind is obtained not merely by such practice. Vairagya (detachment) is also necessary. The mind naturally runs towards those objects for which it has an attraction. By abhyasa (practice) the fickleness of the mind may be controlled. But its attachment cannot be done away with by mere practice. It has been said by Sri Krishna in the Sixth Chapter of the Gita, verse 26: "Wherever the fickle and unsteady mind runs away it should be brought back there from and made to fix itself on the Self."

If a sadhaka commits a sinful act once, in a way it might be explained away as the result of his karma in previous life or lives designated as prarabdha or sanchita. But if such sinful acts are committed over and over again and he tries to explain them away by attributing them to his prarabdha, he should certainly be considered a base man.

Just take a homely illustration. Suppose there is a live charcoal. You see it and although you are warned by your friend not to place your foot upon it, you out of a feeling of pride and arrogance do not heed the warning and place your foot upon it. You are sure to suffer pain. This is something like prarabdha. But would you ever again place your foot upon a fire even if you are asked to do so by a friend? No. Where has prarabdha gone now? That means that when a person is full of repentance he does not commit the sin again, nor does he quote shastras and the doctrines of prarabdha and sanchita for justifying the commission of the sin.

A sadhaka, therefore, should exercise his powers of reasoning and discrimination at the time of doing acts and should lead his life in accordance with the advice of his guru. Gradually all his fetters will fall off as he progresses in the practice of meditation.

I shall just tell you what Sri Gulabrao Maharaj says on this point. "Look at our present-day saints. Their 'jivanmukti' consists in not doing anything for their maintenance. They have therefore to practice tricks for getting their livelihood. They practice more deceits and do more degraded acts than persons who maintain themselves by labor ever dream of doing. These so-called saints have thrown off all social restrictions. If I, for instance, find some other saint is more respected as a guru and has more disciples, I am sure to spread scandals about him among my disciples and his disciples also. Even if these saints do not know anything, they can conceal their ignorance by assuming an attitude of being above discussions and arguments and of being merged in everlasting peace.

"I therefore say that in my opinion there is no class of scoundrels in this world worse than such saints who profit themselves by deceiving their followers. Whenever such saints are actually observed doing a sinful act, they attribute their sin to their prarabdha and seek protection under its wings. This prarabdha many a time saves them, because they do not suffer for their sins in this world. Of course, the punishment meted out to them hereafter will be beyond the knowledge of people in this world. All this argument of prarabdha has been trotted out from the inexhaustible store of Vedanta. All actions which a follower of Charvaka [an atheist] would do can safely be done by these saints on the authority of the doctrine that saints are beyond sin and virtue, and that they are above all principles of morality which are meant for ordinary people. The wonder is that these saints have learnt no real lessons from reading works on Vedanta.

"I do not mean to say that Vedanta is to be blamed for this. I should not be considered as belonging to that class of social reformers who have attacked Vedanta and have attributed many of the evils in our social system to its pernicious doctrines. What I want to say is this. Without performing the duties of his varna [caste] and ashrama [stage of life], without devotion and without acquiring the four sadhanas, a person can study books on Vedanta like a school or college student and repeat its doctrines like a parrot. What is the use of all this? But if a person acquires all the four sadhanas and then begins to think about Vedanta, a sentence or two from all these works will be quite sufficient to illuminate his mind and to enable him to attain moksha.

"Many of the present-day saints are similarly followers of Vedanta only partially. They conceal the fact that they have passions and remain unmarried. When, however, their passions are exposed in the case of the sisters or wives of their disciples, they explain them away and give them a garb of virtue by resorting to the argument of prarabdha. They represent that that particular woman was their wife in their previous life and that it had been predetermined by prarabdha that they should have sexual connection with her.

"Those who are real followers of Vedanta, however, are always sorry for any sinful action that occurs at their hands, even though it might have been brought about by the force of prarabdha, and they are always prepared to make a full admission of their faults. They always pray to the Almighty that they might be freed from the clutches of their passions without having been required by prarabdha to do bad actions. They generally never find fault with others who might have succumbed to their passions. If, however, they blame others, they also blame themselves.

"Although it is very difficult to define in words as to who should be regarded a saint, still it can be very easily understood that a person who comes forward as a guru must at least not be a man whose actions are without any moral restrictions. If saints are of different sorts and their external actions are also of different kinds, it is but natural that people also should treat different saints in different ways. If a saint's outward actions are morally bad, there is nothing to complain of if people blame him or treat him with disrespect. The present day saints pose as if they are divine sages as long as their passions are not exposed, and when they are exposed they represent that they are, like Sri Krishna, beyond all moral restrictions and that they are quite detached from all sense of enjoyment."

I look upon all human beings as being equal. All living creatures bear a spark of the Divine Spirit and hence every human being is fitted to follow the spiritual path. I do not look upon any one as wicked or unfit to follow the spiritual path. Whoever comes to me, I tell him what I know.

If you want to attain the goal of human life and therefore want to put your faith in some saint, remember that if that saint shows you the path of Self-experience, only then should you put your faith in him. If, however, you put your faith in a saint on account of the miracles performed or reported to be performed by him, you may perhaps obtain the fulfillment of some of your worldly desires, but you will never thereby attain the real aim of human life.

I am absolutely sure that saints can never change anyone's fate. Whatever is fated to happen is sure to happen. Do we not see hundreds of people rolling in wealth who have never gone to a saint or never even remembered God? They are enjoying the blessings of wealth and progeny according to their actions in previous births. If this is true then why should saints profess to change anybody's fate?

When we sleep, we sometimes dream and after that go into complete unconsciousness. In that state nothing is felt, we go into the Avyakta. When we awake, if somebody asks us, "How did you sleep?" we reply, "I got very good sleep and was full of bliss." Thus, when a person is awake, he begins to speak about his experience in words. That is, when he comes out of the Avyakta he begins to describe his experiences in words. Every person, be he learned or ignorant, saint or an ordinary person, is required to have recourse to words in order to express his ideas.

Saints like Sri Ramakrishna Paramahansa have given the illustration of a doll made of salt. They say if a salt doll enters water it is turned into water. Can it then describe its experience of water? If it wants to describe the experience, it must keep one foot in water and the other on land. Hence, saints who have been one with the Avyakta come out of the Avyakta by assuming bodies full of light, and are born into this world for the deliverance of other human beings. By their own acts and advice they teach the world how to make this Maya full of bliss, how to go beyond pleasure and pain and how to obtain eternal peace and happiness. They say to the people in the world, "Your treasure (of bliss) is with you; only you have forgotten the place where it is hidden." The saints neither give anything to the world nor do they take anything from the world. They carry out their mission and remain aloof and at peace with themselves.

If the mumukshus follow implicitly the advice of the saints without entertaining the least doubt, with full faith and real love, by continued practice they will succeed in curbing all evil tendencies and in resisting all temptations of lust and greed. They will then get realization of the bliss of the Self, and attain the stage which was attained by such immortal saints as Sri Jnaneshwar or Sri Tukaram. There is not the least doubt about this.

I have given expression to these ideas which have arisen in my innermost heart, and as such they are not my words but the words of the Paramatman dwelling in my heart. Whether they are true or false, I leave it to the world to judge.

We can in course of time succeed in getting control over our mind, and the whole tendency of our thoughts can be turned into a good channel. Thus we become our own guru. "The guru should turn away our mind from the various vices to which we are addicted. Everything is in the hands of a guru. If he means it, he alone will be able to develop good tendencies in my mind." Such thoughts are weak and misleading and would be of no use to anyone. The Gita says, "We alone are our friend and we alone are our enemy."

An external object may cause pleasure or pain according to circumstances. The pleasure that is felt from the enjoyment of external objects is evanescent owing to the perishable nature of all external objects. Hence, if your desire to obtain an external object is fulfilled, you get pleasure; if it is not fulfilled, you experience pain. The joy experienced in Paramartha, the realization of the Self, on the contrary, is not due to the obtaining of any external object. This joy is thus absolutely independent of anything else. Hence its nature has been described as being niramaya (without any disease or defect). The real "I" which dwells in the heart of everyone is the sole abode of this unchanging happiness and bliss. He who becomes one with this "I" gets hold of this sole source of happiness, and therefore feels no need of any pleasure which is derived from the enjoyment of external objects.

The path which leads to the true knowledge of this "I" and to the realization of oneness with it, is the path of spiritual progress. He who desires to go by this path must naturally practice self-restraint and keep himself detached from material pleasures. Abandoning of material pleasures outwardly, or abandoning them by merely forcibly curbing the mind, is of very little use. The renunciation must be mental—the mind must gradually develop a dislike for these material pleasures. If you will try to immerse your mind in the continuous contemplation of the sound of Soham, this renunciation becomes easy. The mind becomes one with Soham, and then the ajapa japa begins. In this stage our whole worldly existence becomes full of happiness. The mind of a person who attains this stage goes beyond pleasure and pain. It becomes full of universal love, and he feels nothing but love in this material world which to others is full of pleasure and pain.

The ultimate responsibility of obtaining success in worldly or spiritual matters rests upon ourselves. It is through intense devotion and persistent efforts that we have to achieve success. As we progress, we shall ourselves come to know the stage we have acquired in our previous life. Through incessant practice, desires for sensual pleasures slowly become less and less and ultimately disappear, and the aspirant reaches the final goal of everlasting happiness.

One is a friend or an enemy of one's Self, and one has to reach the goal of life by one's own efforts only.

With these words I stop and enter into the deep and changeless love and joy of the ajapa japa of Soham.

Breath And Sound
In Meditation

When we meditate we do not sit in silent blankness because that would not return us to our eternal consciousness of Spirit. Instead we have to have the right inner environment for the return to take place. This is provided by two things: the sound of Soham and the breath. The breath and Soham are like two firesticks. Fire is inherent in both, and when the two are brought together in friction the fire comes forth. The fire we are wanting to bring forth is the spirit-consciousness that is our real Self.

Swami Vivekananda, writing on Raja Yoga, points out that according to the philosophers of India the whole universe is composed of two materials: akasha and prana. "Just as Akasha is the infinite, omnipresent material of this universe, so is this Prana the infinite, omnipresent manifesting power of this universe." Sound rises directly from akasha, and breath rises directly from prana. Since they arise from the spirit-center, when their right joining is done they free and enable us to return and merge our consciousness with that center. Joining the two, we go straight to the heart of ourselves and the universe. That is, we go directly to the Heart of Brahman.

In Indian mythology it is said that the realm of Vishnu is guarded by two doorkeepers who escort the questing soul into the Divine Presence. This is a symbol of the breath and Soham which when united bring the yogi into the world of higher consciousness. In the realm of meditation, the doorkeepers/companions conduct the seeker into the throne room and then stand at the door to guard against intruders. That is, the breath and Soham lead us into the realm of the Chidakasha, the Space of Consciousness, and keep guard there against the intrusion of distracting thoughts and states of mind, seeing that nothing disturbs our inner quest. These two companion-friends deserve our careful study.

The Role of Breath in Meditation

The reversed shakti rises to Brahmand [Sahasrara];
The breath plays throughout the body, from the toes to the topknot.
The reversed Moon eclipses Rahu.
This is a sign of success, says the sage Gorakh.
(Gorakh Bani 27)

Breath, the universal factor

The Sanskrit word prana means both "breath" and "life." Breath is the single universal factor of life: all that lives, breathes. Therefore meditation practices involving the breath are found in many mystical traditions. The process of breath is identical in all beings, consisting of inhalation and exhalation, expansion and contraction. It is the most immaterial factor of our existence, the body-mind-spirit link. For this reason, the breath is a natural and logical factor in meditation.

Yoga and the breath

In fourteenth-century Kashmir, Lalleshwari sang:

Some leave their home, some the hermitage,
But the restless mind knows no rest.
Then watch your breath, day and night,
And stay where you are.

The breath is a dominant factor on all the planes of existence. It is necessary for the vitalization and functioning of all vehicles of consciousness, physical or superphysical. It possesses the essential qualities of both energy and consciousness and is thus able to serve as an instrument for their actions and reactions on each other.

The purpose of being aware of the physical breath is to enable us to become aware of the breath of the breath, the inner movement of consciousness that manifests as the physical breath. The more attention we give to the breath, the subtler it becomes until it reveals itself as an act of the mind, not of the body, and finally as consisting of mind-stuff (chitta) itself. The breath, like an onion, has many layers. In the practice of Soham Yoga meditation we experience these layers, beginning with the most objective, physical layer and progressing to increasingly subtle layers that are rooted in pure being.

Since it is natural for the breath to become increasingly refined as you observe it, you need not attempt to deliberately make this happen. Your attention and intonations of Soham will automatically refine it. As we become more and more aware of the subtle forms or movements of the inner breaths, it naturally happens that the breath movements on all levels become slower. This is the highest form of pranayama–cultivation of the breath. All authentic yoga practice involves the breath to some degree, because the breath truly is life, is everything. And Soham is the breath itself, the impulse, the vibration, of life. Outwardly it is sound, a mantra, but inwardly it is the breath, the consciousness of That Am I.

One of the cardinal virtues of Soham sadhana–especially in its aspect of pranayama–is its capacity to be practiced every waking hour of the day.

Breath and Yoga

The reason why breath plays such an important part in the technique of classical Yoga lies in the close relation existing between breath and mind. "Breath and mind arise from the same source," the Self, according to Sri Ramana Maharshi in *Day By Day With Bhagavan.* One of the most profound texts on the philosophy behind yoga, the Shiva Sutras, says: "The connection of pure consciousness with breath [prana] is natural" (Shiva Sutras 3:43). Breath is the meeting place of body, mind, and spirit.

The breath and the *body* are completely interconnected and interrelated, as is seen from the fact that the breath is calm when the body is calm, and agitated or labored when the body is agitated or labored. The heavy exhalation made when feeling exhausted and the enthusiastic inhalation made when feeling energized or exhilarated establish the same fact.

The breath and the *emotions* are completely interconnected and interrelated, as is seen from the fact that the breath is calm when the emotions are calm, and agitated and labored when the emotions are agitated or out of control. Our drawing of a quick breath, when we are surprised, shocked, or fearful, and the forceful exhalation done when angry or annoyed demonstrate this.

The breath and the *mind* are completely interconnected and interrelated, as is seen from the fact that the breath is calm when the mind is calm, and agitated, irregular, and labored when the mind is agitated or disturbed in any way. Our holding of the breath when attempting intense concentration also shows this.

Breath, which exists on all planes of manifestation, is the connecting link between matter and energy on the one hand and consciousness and mind on the other. It is necessary for the vitalization and functioning of all vehicles of consciousness, physical or superphysical.

We start with awareness of the ordinary physical breath, but that awareness, when cultivated correctly, leads us into higher awareness which enables us to perceive the subtle movement behind the breath. Ultimately, we come into contact with the breather of the breath, our own spirit.

Everything in the universe is vibration. A mantra is a vibratory sound formula that produces a specific effect. A mantra can enliven and direct the prana, and a subtle form of prana can enliven and direct the consciousness. A repetition of a mantra can be the exact point at which realization occurs or is produced. Ultimately the yogi discovers that mantra and prana are the same thing. This is an important insight, a key to very real mastery.

In many spiritual traditions the same word is used for both breath and spirit, underscoring the esoteric principle that in essence they are the same, though we naturally think of spirit as being the cause of breath(ing). The word used for both breath and spirit is: In Judaism, *Ruach.* In Eastern Christianity (and ancient Greek religion), *Pneuma.* In Western Christianity (and ancient Roman religion), *Spiritus* (which comes from *spiro*, "I breathe"). In Hinduism and Buddhism, *Atman* (from the root word *at* which means "to breathe"), and *Prana.*

Breath is the rope which either elevates or lowers our level of awareness. Breath is a manifestation of consciousness, and therefore the means to mastery of consciousness. Sound and breath conjoined is the path to Self-realization. The true breath is inside the outer, physical breath. It is already eternal. But when tied to the body it is agitated and struggles against its feeling of bondage and alienation. Many think that breath itself is the problem, but it is the state of being tied to the body that is the problem. When the inner breath is contacted and made to pervade our experience, then we move onward to freedom and our natural state.

Genuine Raja Yoga is concerned with the internal breath, the unitary breath. Just as a circle is unbroken, so the advanced yogi finds that inhalation and exhalation are moving internally in a circular manner and are not divided at all or opposing one another, but are the same impulse. He also perceives that he is perpetually inhaling and exhaling at all times. That is, even when he inhales he is aware of subtle exhalation, and when he exhales he is aware of subtle inhalation. Thus he comes to know that the breath is one, indivisible.

Arthur Avalon

The books of Arthur Avalon (Sir John Woodruffe) are unparalleled in their value regarding the many aspects of yoga. Here are three quotations from them regarding breath in the context of yoga.

321

"The ultimate reality is Saccidananda which, as the source of appearances, is called Shakti. The latter in its Sat (Being) aspect is omnipresent-indestructible (eternal) Source and Basis both of the Cosmic Breath or Prana as also of all vital phenomena displayed as the individual Prana in separate and concrete bodies" (*The Garland of Letters*, p. 140).

"The individual breath is the Cosmic Breath from which it seems to be different by the forms which the latter vitalizes" (*The Garland of Letters*, p. 157).

"Breathing is a manifestation of the Cosmic Rhythm to which the whole universe moves and according to which it appears and disappears" (*Shakti and Shakta*).

Breath, then, is an essential ingredient of liberating yoga because the breath is the spirit-Self in extension, and through it we can become established in the consciousness that is the Self.

The identity of the breath with the individual spirit, the Atman (Self)

"The Self is the breath of the breath" (Kena Upanishad 1:2).

"As a spider moves along the thread, as small sparks come forth from the fire, even so from this Self come forth all breaths, all worlds, all divinities, all beings. Its secret meaning is the truth of truth. Vital breaths are the truth and their truth is It (the Self)" (Brihadaranyaka Upanishad 2.1.20).

"Verily, the vital breath is truth, and He is the truth of that" (Brihadaranyaka Upanishad 2.3.6).

"He who breathes in with your breathing in is the self. He who breathes out with your breathing out is the self" (Brihadaranyaka Upanishad 3.4.1).

The identity of the breath with the Supreme Spirit, Brahman

But breath is much more than an individual matter, it is also a bridge to the infinite consciousness, being the living presence and action of God (Brahman).

"O prana, creatures here bring offering to thee who dwellest with the vital breaths" (Prashna Upanishad 2.7).

"When breathing he is called the vital force" (Brihadaranyaka Upanishad 1.4.7).

"This shining, immortal person who is breath (in the body), he is just this Self, this is immortal, this is Brahman, this is all" (Brihadaranyaka Upanishad 2.5.4).

"Which is the one God? The breath. He is Brahman" (Brihadaranyaka Upanishad 3.9.9).

"They who know the breath of the breath… have realized the ancient, primordial Brahman" (Brihadaranyaka Upanishad 4.4.18).

The Role of Sound in Meditation

Liberating sound

Why do we use sound in meditation? "By sound one becomes liberated [*Anavrittih shabdai*]," is the concluding verse of the Brahma Sutras (4.4.22). How is this so? Why not use one of the other senses or faculties, since touch, sight, taste, and smell must also possess increasingly subtler forms until they reach the point of their emerging? It is true that these four faculties do have subtle forms, but only sound reaches to the ultimate point of emergence.

The five senses correspond to the five elements of which all things consist. Those elements are ether [akasha], air [vayu], fire [agni], water [apah], and earth [prithvi]. That is, their grossest forms are those of sound [shabda], sight [drishti], touch [sparsha], taste [rasa], and smell [gandha] as perceived by the bodily senses. Because of this we use these terms to refer to them. But the water element is not just the liquid we call water, it is much more, having roots in the astral and causal planes. The same is true of the other elements.

When relative existence, individual or cosmic, begins, there is a chain of manifestation. First there is the out-turning of the consciousness itself.

This modification on the cosmic level is the emerging of the Mahat Tattwa, the Great Element, that is the Personal or Saguna Brahman, spoken of in Christianity as "the Only-begotten of the Father" or Son of God. In the individual this is the sense of *asmita*: I-am-ness. Then the Pradhana [Prakriti] modifies itself into the five elements, beginning with ether, and each succeeding element contains within itself some of the preceding elements. That is, air is mixed with some ether. Fire possesses some of the ether and air element. Water has some fire, air, and ether. Earth has some water, fire, air, and ether. So only ether is unmixed, and only ether is touching the principle of consciousness, only ether is in direct contact with the spirit. Yet ether (akasha) pervades all the other elements as their prime constituent–actually as their source and core element. Sound is the quality (or faculty) of ether; touch is the quality of air; sight is the quality of fire; taste is the quality of water; and smell is the quality of earth. Sound, then, is the only thing that reaches back to the principle of consciousness. The other elements stop somewhere along the way. Sound, then, can affect all the elements.

The five elements also correspond to the five levels or bodies known as koshas: the anandamaya, jnanamaya, manomaya, pranamaya, and annamaya bodies. These are the will, intellectual, mental (sensory), biomagnetic, and physical bodies. The highest (most subtle) body is the etheric body (anandamaya kosha) which is the seat of sound or speech.

There is more. The other four elements have only one faculty or power, but akasha has two faculties or powers: Vak and Shabda: Speaking and Hearing. The faculties of the four other elements are all passive. The faculty of smell cannot generate smells, the faculty of taste cannot generate tastes, etc., though the memory or imagination of them is possible. Ether, on the other hand, has the capacity to both generate and hear sound on the mental levels. The etheric faculty both speaks and hears what it speaks, is both active and passive. This is unique among the elements. Akasha alone possesses the creative power, the power of sound.

Consciousness is the root of sound—is innate in sound. Sound, then, is the direct means to return our awareness to the inmost level of our being and put us into touch with consciousness itself. At the same time, sound rules all the levels of our being and has the ability to infuse all those levels with the highest spiritual consciousness, to spiritualize every bit of us. Soham, then, is both energy and consciousness. Listening to our inner intonations of Soham during japa and meditation right away centers our awareness in the highest, etheric level of our being. It returns our awareness to its source and gathers up and centers every other aspect of our being in spiritual consciousness.

Through japa and meditation, Soham pervades all our bodies, corrects, directs, and empowers them to perfectly and fully manifest all their potentials—which is the root purpose of our relative existence. Through Soham Yoga practice all the aspects of our being are brought into perfect fruition and then enabled to merge back into their Source in the state of absolute liberation. Soham Yoga, then, embraces all the aspects of our existence—not only the highest part—and is supremely practical. Soham, through Its japa and meditation, perfects our entire being.

When we inwardly intone Soham and become absorbed in that sound, by centering our awareness in the act of intoning Soham and listening to It, we become centered in the Chidakasha, the Consciousness that is our Self.

Experiencing the Chidakasha to greater and greater degrees within meditation is the highest experience for the yogi. The more we meditate the more we penetrate into the infinite consciousness of which we are an eternal part. The process of meditation takes place within the Chidakasha, the seat of the spirit-Self that is itself the Chidakasha.

Internal sound

We use sound in Soham Yoga—but it is not just any form of sound. It is sound that is produced (generated) in the mind, not sound that is passively heard either through the ears or through the memory of auditory sound. This generation of sound is the process known as thinking. So yoga is accomplished by the generation and observation of a thought in the mind. This is why Shankara, commenting on Yoga Sutra 2:20, says that the activity of pure consciousness in the individual is "observation of thoughts in the mind.... Purusha, looking on at thought in the mind alone, sees only that, and never fails to see thought which is his object.... To witness is natural to him, in the sense that his essence is awareness of the mind's ideas." ("Mind is by definition the object of the purusha," said Vyasa.)

Now this is extremely profound. *The only thing we ever do in our real nature as pure consciousness is to observe thoughts in the intellect (buddhi).* That is why when Sri Ramakrishna was asked: "What is the Self?" he simply replied: "The witness of the mind." Sense impressions are perceived a step away from that in the lower mind (manas). Perceiving thought is the sole activity of the spirit-consciousness. Perception of thought is also a perpetual—truly an inescapable—activity of the purusha. It is only reasonable then to conclude that to discover the true Self or to cause the Self to become established in its real nature we must employ the faculty of thought. Yet it is thought that is tangling us up all the time in false identities. So it is not just thought in general that we need, but a special kind of thought—one that turns the awareness back upon itself and eventually merges itself into the pure consciousness that is spirit. That unique thought is Soham. Our eternal nature ensures our success.

The genealogy of sound

The cosmos and the individual are manifested by the same process: ever-expanding sound-vibration, Spanda. First there comes the most subtle expansion-movement or vibration on the causal level where rather than an objective sound it is a *bhava*, the slightest differentiation of primal consciousness. This is known as *dhvani*. Dhvani then expands and mutates into *nada*, which is sound, but in such a subtle form that it is more an *idea* of sound rather than actual sound. Nada develops into *nirodhika*, a kind of focussing of the energy so it becomes potential sound. This expands and becomes *ardha-indu* (*ardhendu*), the half-moon which is the crescent shape seen on the head of Shiva. This is both thought and sound, but sound that can only be heard as the faintest of inner mental sounds. Ardhendu then expands and becomes *bindu*, the vibratory source-point. This bindu is fully sound, but on the interior level only. It cannot be spoken aloud, it cannot be spoken at all, but only perceived and entered into as the first step back to the source consciousness that is Spirit. Yet, from bindu comes all the permutations that are the various sounds which are combined to form words, including mantras.

According to the yoga scriptures there are three basic forms of sound or speech: 1) *pashyanti*, that which can only be intuited or felt rather than heard, even within; 2) *madhyama*, that which can be heard in the mind as thought; and 3) *vaikhari*, that which is physically spoken and heard outwardly by the ear through the vibration of the air. But beyond even these is the transcendental sound, *para-vak* or supreme speech, which is soundless sound, consciousness itself. Soham encompasses all three.

"When men sent out Vak's [Speech's] first and earliest utterances, all that was excellent and spotless, treasured within them, was disclosed.... the trace of Vak they followed, and found her harboring within" (Rig Veda 10.71.1, 2). This hymn of the Rig Veda speaks of Vak, the creative Sound from which all things came. This Sound both manifested all things and revealed them: produced the consciousness capable of perceiving them. The sages, the hymn tells us, traced Vak back to the source and discovered it was within themselves as both Power and Consciousness.

Meditation is the process of tracing discovered by the sages, the procedure by which the yogi enters into the inner levels of Soham, tracing it to its very source which is consciousness. As he does so, he experiences within the depths of his awareness the subtle states of consciousness, or bhava, inherent in Soham. For this reason the word frequently translated meditation in texts relating to yoga is *bhavanam*, the experiencing of the inner states of consciousness called bhavas. Meditation leads us right into the heart of Soham as we trace its sound back through its many permutations to its original bhava or impulse of consciousness that expanded outward to manifest as its outermost form of the mental thought: Soham.

Reversing consciousness

As we enter into relative consciousness through the expansion of sound, just so can we enter back into transcendent consciousness through the intentional contraction of sound that occurs in meditation. Tracing Soham back to its source, the Soham yogi discovers it within himself as both Power and Consciousness, experiencing the subtle states of Soham and the subtle consciousness inherent in Soham.

This procedure is spoken of in the Katha Upanishad: "The Self, though hidden in all beings, does not shine forth but can be seen by those subtle seers, through their sharp and subtle intelligence. The wise man should restrain speech into the mind; the latter he should restrain into the understanding Self. The understanding Self he should restrain into the great Self. That he should restrain into the tranquil Self" (Katha Upanishad 1.3.12,13). By "mind" is meant the manas, the sensory mind; by "understanding Self" is meant the buddhi, the intellect; by "the great Self" is meant the will; and by "tranquil Self" is meant the subtlest level, the Chidakasha, the witness-link between our pure consciousness and our perceptions.

In *Viveka Chudamani* (verse 369) Shankara expresses it this way: "Restrain speech in the manas, and restrain manas in the buddhi; this again restrain in the witness of the buddhi [the chidakasha], and merging that also in the Infinite Absolute Self, attain to Supreme Peace."

In the subtle sound of Soham the consciousness of the yogi is resolved into its pure, divine state.

The subtle sound of Soham

The way to the pure, unalloyed consciousness that is the Self, is to enclose the mind in the subtle sound of Soham as you intone in time with the breath. I do not mean that you strain or force, but that you relax and let your awareness merge in the sacred sound. Relax and listen–not "fix the mind" or "concentrate." Listen to and savor and feel and enjoy the subtle sound vibrations of Soham along with the sensations of any kriyas that may be occurring–experience the subtle vibrations moving in your various bodies. Enjoy it. Love it. As Kabir wrote:

> There is a land where no doubt nor sorrow have rule: where the terror of Death is no more.
> There the woods of spring are a-bloom, and the fragrant scent "Soham" is borne on the wind:
> There the bee of the heart is deeply immersed, and desires no other joy.

The breeze of Soham is the subtle sound which bears the heavenly perfume of spiritual experience. Listen to the sound of Soham but also be aware of the state of consciousness, the Soham Bhava, to which it leads. It does not produce it, but rather it reveals it by centering the yogi's awareness in it.

A warning

As we all know, the mind is able to do more than one thing at a time. We often are doing something and at the same time having a conversation. The driver of a car does many things at a time just to drive, including listening to the radio and talking. So we definitely have the ability to do japa and do or think of something at the same time. This is good, because that enables us to keep up the flow of Soham in time with the breath. But at the same time, including during meditation, we can do japa of Soham while the mind roves here and there in thoughts, memories and other trivia when really we could and should be intent on Soham. When possible and practical, fill the mind with Soham alone.

And when you need to think of something else, do so along with your Soham repetition. Naturally you cannot talk and repeat Soham. Therefore break the habit of useless and trivial talk. But do not neglect sensible and friendly speech. Being a yogi is not being an indrawn spook.

I. K. Taimni on japa and meditation

In *The Science of Yoga* I. K. Taimni says this regarding japa and meditation:

"Japa begins in a mechanical repetition but it should pass by stages into a form of meditation and unfoldment of the deeper layers of consciousness.

"The efficacy of japa is based upon the fact that every jivatman is a microcosm thus having within himself the potentialities of developing all states of consciousness and all powers which are present in the active form in the macrocosm. All the forces which can help this Divine spark within each human heart to become a roaring fire are to be applied. And the unfoldment of consciousness takes place as a result of the combined action of all these forces.... A mantra is a sound combination and thus represents a physical vibration which is perceptible to the physical ear. But this physical vibration is its outermost expression, and hidden behind the physical vibration and connected with it are subtler vibrations much in the same way as the dense physical body of man is his outermost expression and is connected with his subtler vehicles. These different aspects of *Vak* or speech are called *Vaikhari, Madhyama, Pashyanti* and *Para.* Vaikhari is the audible sound which can lead through the intermediate stages to the subtlest form of *Para Vak.* It is really through the agency of these subtler forms of sound that the unfoldment of consciousness takes place and the hidden potentialities become active powers. This release of powers takes a definite course according to the specific nature of the mantra just as a seed grows into a tree, but into a particular kind of tree according to the nature of the seed."

The Unity of the Breath and Soham

As already cited, commenting on Yoga Sutra 1:34, Vivekananda says: "The whole universe is a combination of prana and akasha." Practically speaking we, too, are formed of prana and akasha, of breath and sound which are the manifestation of prana and akasha. Yoga is a combining of breath and sound.

Soham is the essential sound-energy form that manifests in living beings as the breath itself. Soham is the sound-form of the subtle power of life which originates in the pure consciousness, the spirit, of each one of us and extends outward to manifest as the inhaling and exhaling breaths. Hence, through the intoning of Soham in meditation we can become attuned to the essential Breath of Life and aware of its subtle movements within. Joined to our breath, the mantric formula Soham will lead us to the awareness of Breath and Life in their pure state. For Soham is both the breath and the Source of the breath. When joined to Soham, the breath becomes a flowing stream of consciousness.

In the beginning

In the beginning, there arose in the ocean of Divine Consciousness, a point (bindu) from which began flowing the stream of creative energy that manifested as all things, and back into which all things return. That Primal Point became dual upon the very moment of its arising. That duality manifested as Prana/Breath and Sound–specifically, Soham. The same thing happened with us. We came into manifestation on the twin streams of subtle breath and Soham.

Originally we were unmanifest, as transcendental as our Source. But just as the Source expanded into relative manifestation, so did we. In our undifferentiated being, the state of perfect unity, there manifested a single stress point (bindu or sphota). This did not upset or disrupt the original unity but it did just what I said: it stressed it. Then, so imperceptibly and subtly as to hardly have even occurred, that stress point became dual and began to move internally, producing a magnetic duality so subtle it was really more an idea than an actual condition. Then the halves or poles of that duality began alternating in dominance and a cycling or circling began. This cycling expanded ever outward, manifesting in increasingly more objective manners until at last the full state of relativity was reached complete with a set of complex bodies of infinitely varying levels of energy–everything we consider to be us. The same thing had already happened to our Source on a cosmic level so we found a virtually infinite environment for our manifestation. This is the process known as samsara.

The two original poles of the primal unity are prana (life force) which manifests in us most objectively as breath, and shabda (sound) which manifests in us most objectively as the mantra Soham–and secondarily that of hearing. These seemingly two creative streams of manifestation are in reality one, inseparable from one another, and together are capable of leading us back to their–and our–source. One or the other can do a great deal toward returning us to Unity, but the ultimate, full return can occur most easily when they are joined in the practice of Soham Yoga. Like the cosmos, we came into manifestation on the twin streams of subtle breath and Soham. Together these two wings have carried us upward into the heights of evolution.

The return

Soham is the essence of the breath and the breath is the essence of Soham–particularly in their most subtle forms. Speech and breath are manifested and reunited in Soham by mentally intoning it in time with the breath. "May you be successful in crossing over to the farther shore of darkness" (Mundaka Upanishad 2.2.6).

To turn back from samsara and return to our original unity we must grasp hold of that primal impulse to duality which manifested in the stress point from which all has occurred. Right now that original impulse is manifesting most objectively in the process of our physical inhaling and exhaling and in our inner power of speech as we intone Soham.

The breath and Soham together comprise the evolutionary force which causes us to enter samsara and manifest therein until–also through the breath and sound–we evolve to the point where we are ready to discard the evolutionary school of samsara and return to our original status with a now-perfected consciousness. By joining Soham and the breath in japa and meditation we begin moving back to the state where they are one.

In japa and meditation we join intonations of Soham to the breath because on the subtle levels the breath is always producing the sound of Soham. We can even say that the soul *breathes* Soham. When our intonations of Soham become subtle and whisper-like they are the actual breath sounds, the real sounds of the etheric breath. So by joining Soham to our breathing we can link up with our soul-consciousness and enter into it. That is the point of Unity where the breath and Soham are not two extensions, but a single unit. Here, too, the breath is one, moving in a circular manner or expanding and contracting rather than extending and moving in and out or back and forth. Joining our intonations of Soham to the breath in a fully easeful manner attunes us to that level of breath and sound.

One-pointedness

Many aspiring yogis struggle to make the mind one-pointed and mostly tire and frustrate themselves in the trying. This is because they think of one-pointedness as a condition of the mind, something it can be forced or moulded into. But one-pointedness is a matter of mental orientation. The more inward (internal) our awareness, the more one-pointed it will be. So it is a matter of directing our mind, which is a major reason for linking japa with the breath. Since the breath originates at the core of our being it is the most accessible means to lead the mind inward in meditation. And breath awareness along with japa outside meditation keeps the mind tending inward. After all, the word Atman comes from the root word *at* which means "to breathe." So the Self is the original Breather.

Whenever our attention is not as one-pointed as we wish, it is because the mind is not fully turned inward. That is why breath awareness and absorption of the mind in listening to the mental intonations of a mantra are so necessary. Those two factors will take care of everything in time.

Breath and sound are the oil and flame in the lamp of meditation. Not only is the body unable to move without breath, there is no movement upward of consciousness in meditation without the union of breath and mantra.

The evolving breath

Life and evolution are synonymous. Just as Brahman has clothed Itself in creative, evolutionary energy–Prakriti–and is actively engaged in cosmic progression toward perfection, in the same way the individual spirit (Atman) is encased in its own energy-prakriti and is evolving it toward perfection. This is life within Life. Both the cosmic and the individual life-force are known as prana–vital energy–which manifests as breath. All that exists is formed of prana-breath, which acts as a mirror for the individual and cosmic spirits, changing and modifying itself as they change and modify–as they evolve. The original Impulse which begins, sustains, and completes all evolution is Soham. The dance of creation is the moving of prana-breath to the directing sound-vibration of Soham.

Relativity evolves through the alternating cycles of creation and dissolution–outward movement and inward movement–and in the same way the simple act of breathing evolves all sentient beings, whose fundamental common trait is that of breathing. This is because the breath is always sounding Soham in the process the yogis call *ajapa japa*–involuntary/automatic repetition. (This is also true on the cosmic level. The cosmos is breathing Soham.) Thus merely living and breathing is a process of ascent in consciousness *if* the individual does nothing to counteract that process, which we all do, retarding our progress and causing ourselves to become bound to the wheel of continual birth and death. So it is necessary to live in the manner that allows this automatic development to go forward and manifest.

In time, however, a profound point of evolution is reached in which the individual becomes capable of consciously evolving himself and thereby speeding up the process of unfolding his consciousness. He does this by consciously doing what he has heretofore done only unconsciously: linking the repetition of Soham to his breath, merging It with the breath movements.

The original purpose of the original duality–breath and Soham–was to enable us to descend into the plane of relativity and begin evolving therein until we could develop the capacity for infinite consciousness. They not only moved us downward into material embodiment, they also began to impel us upward on the evolutionary scale so we might finally develop or evolve to the point where we can finally share–actually participate–in the infinity of God. If unhindered, they would accomplish this evolutionary movement. But in our present state we are always thwarting their purpose, especially by keeping their action bound and buried in the subconscious rather than resurrecting them into our conscious life, applying them and cooperating with them and thereby accelerating our growth. When awareness of the breath is consciously cultivated, and the sacred mantra Soham is joined to every breath, the two currents become united and oriented toward their original purpose, which they then accomplish. In this way every single breath and intonation of Soham become a step forward and upward on the path of spiritual evolution.

Through our attention focussed on the process of intoning Soham in time with our inhalation and exhalation, we can become immersed in the subtler levels of that alternating cycle, sinking into deeper and deeper levels until we at last come to the originating point and then transcend that dual movement, regaining our lost unity. By continual practice of that transcendence in meditation we will become established in that unity and freed forever from all forms of bondage, having attained nirvana–permanent unbinding. This is why both sound and breath must be the focus of our internal cultivation.

When we examine their nature, we see that the breath and the sound of Soham are not things, but *processes* which have the power to draw us into the core point from which they arise–the individual spirit itself whose nature is consciousness. In this way the pure Self manifests and works its will, changing all the levels of our being. The breath and our intonations of Soham become increasingly refined as we observe them, and as a result our awareness also becomes refined.

Rumi says: "In my heart rings as a harp-song that we must return to him." Soham is that harp-song. So when we join the repetition of Soham to the breath we are not merely entering the breath, but reaching that One Step Beyond into the eternal Soham which is inseparable from the Atman. Soham Yoga is the movement back into Original Consciousness that is enlightenment.

Literally we are initiated into Soham Yoga by God. This is why Patanjali says that God (Ishwara) "is Guru even of the Ancients" (Yoga Sutras 1:26). By ancients he means the very first spirits who so many creation cycles ago embarked on the path which we are now ourselves traversing. From that point onward our spirit-Self, our Atman, has been perpetually vibrating Soham in unison with God, who is eternally seated in the heart of our spirit. Soham is the impulse which begins, develops, perfects, and completes the entire process of evolution.

The inner and the outer

There are two breaths, the outer breath and the subtle inner breath which produces it. And there is the outer speech and the subtle inner speech from which it arises. By centering our awareness on the outer breath and sound and merging them we make ourselves aware of the inner Breath and Sound of Life. They occur at the same time and are of the same duration. By attuning ourselves to them we attune ourselves to the spirit from which they take their origin. The more attention we give to the breath and Soham, the subtler they become until they reveal themselves as acts of the mind, and finally as consisting of mind-stuff (chitta) itself.

The Self and the Supreme Self

In the Kena Upanishad we find this statement: "The Self is the breath of the breath" (Kena Upanishad 1:2). Beyond the Self is the Supreme Self–Brahman.

Pranayama

Within the yogic system the breath is considered an actual body within the body material. It is called the *pranamaya kosha*–the body formed of breath or prana. And working with it is known as *pranayama*. Pranayama can mean restraint of prana, and it can also mean control [yama] of the breath, but *ayama* also means length, expansion, and extension. Thus pranayama can also mean the lengthening, expansion, and extension of the breath as occurs spontaneously in Soham meditation. For Patanjali's Yoga Sutra 2:50 says that pranayama is "external, internal or suppressed modification [of breath], and it becomes measured or regulated [*paridrishto*], prolonged [*dirgha*] and subtle or attenuated [*sukshmah*]." Sutra 51 says: "That pranayama which goes beyond the sphere of internal and external is the fourth"–that which directly relates to turiya or pure consciousness, beyond the three states of waking, dreaming, and dreamless sleep. Also, internal and external can refer either to: 1) inhaling and exhaling, 2) the outer breath accompanied by movement of the lungs, or 3) the internal movement of the subtle prana or breath that has no outer manifestation. It is our steady attention to the breath that is the practice of pranayama. For Shankara says: "Pranayama is caused by a *mental activity* deriving from a restraining effort inherent in the Self."

Vyasa says that during meditation the breath becomes, "prolonged and light [fine]." In time a meditator becomes aware that there is an internal breath that is the support and stimulus of the bodily breathing.

Behind that breath is an even subtler force, and so on back to utter stillness at the core of his being. It is the experiencing of all such subtle forms of breath that is pranayama. Through meditation we effect the inner pranayama and achieve the inner breathlessness that is a state of pure awareness.

There is more to this pranayama: "From that [pranayama] is dissolved the covering of light" (Yoga Sutras 2:52). The inner pranayama dissolves the veil which covers the light of the knowledge of the Self. Yet this veil is itself light–the light of subtle matter or energy, the substance of which the most subtle bodies are formed. They are the light that veils the ultimate Light. "The covering of light referred to in this sutra is obviously not used in reference to the light of the soul, but to the light or luminosity associated with the subtler vehicles associated with and interpenetrating the physical vehicle," according to Taimni in *The Science of Yoga*.

Vyasa expands on this, saying: "It [pranayama] destroys the karma which covers up the light of knowledge in the yogi. As it is declared: 'When the ever-shining [Self] is covered over by the net of great illusion, one is impelled to what is not to be done.' By the power of pranayama, the light-veiling karma binding him to the world becomes powerless, and moment by moment is destroyed. So it has been said [in *The Laws of Manu* 6:70, 72]: 'There is no tapas higher than pranayama; from it come purification from taints and the light of knowledge [of the Self].'" Subtle pranayama, then, is the direct way to dissolve karma and be free, for "it is karma by which the light is covered," says Shankara. And both he and Vyasa explain to us that karma not only binds us to material experience, it also impels us to create even more karma–and more bondage–in a self-perpetuating circle. But by yoga the karma "becomes powerless, and moment by moment is destroyed." That is, the karmic seeds are roasted and rendered incapable of creating future experience or births and are ultimately completely annihilated. The more we do meditation, the more karma is dissolved.

In a conversation regarding his instructions on breath observation given in the book *Maha Yoga*, Sri Ramana Maharshi remarked: "Pranayama is of two kinds: one of controlling and regulating the breath *and the other of simply watching the breath*." The purpose of working with the breath is simple: "From that comes the dissolving of the covering of light and the fitting of the mind for meditation" (Yoga Sutras 52 and 53). When by this process the breath is refined, so also is the mind; and eventually so is the nervous system and the entire body. Since the body is a vehicle of the mind this is a very important effect.

But the breath does not accomplish this on its own. It must be joined to intonations of Soham. By joining the repetition of Soham to the breath the Soham Yogi causes pranayama to go on perpetually throughout the day as well as in meditation.

Breath and brain

The yogis knew ages ago what Western science has taken a long time to realize. In the fourth century an anatomist named Oribasius said that the brain literally moves in harmony with respiration. In 1690 a researcher named Slevogt published a book in which he said the same. But it was the mystic Emmanuel Swedenborg who wrote about this as both a physical and a metaphysical phenomenon in his *Oeconomia Regni Animalis* which contains a section titled *De Motu Cerebri*. That was in 1741, and in 1750 J. Daniel Schlichting, a physician of Amsterdam, declared that at each expiration the whole brain becomes elevated or expanded, while during inspiration it subsides and collapses. He showed that this motion is due neither to the contraction of the *dura mater*, nor to a pulsation of the sinuses or of the arteries, but is an intrinsic motion of the entire mass of the brain; that this motion continues during the whole existence of life, and that it is rendered possible by an empty space between the cranium and the brain.

In light of this we see why the yogis regarded the breath with amazement and awe, considering it to be a key to higher states of consciousness.

In modern times it has been demonstrated that every cell of the body is affected by the breath, that the entire body contracts and expands in a virtually imperceptible manner in time with inhalation and exhalation. The breath, then, is a major factor in the physical, mental and spiritual alchemy of yoga.

DID YOU ENJOY READING THIS BOOK?

Thank you for taking the time to read *Soham Yoga*. If you enjoyed it, please consider telling your friends or posting a short review at Amazon.com, Goodreads, or the site of your choice.

Word of mouth is an author's best friend and much appreciated

GET YOUR FREE MEDITATION GUIDE

Sign up for the Light of the Spirit Newsletter and get
Learn How to Meditate Effectively.

Get free updates: newsletters, blog posts, and podcasts, plus exclusive content from Light of the Spirit Monastery.

Visit: https://ocoy.org/signup

GLOSSARY

Abhanga: A devotional song in the Marathi language of Maharashtra.

Abhisheka(m): Bathing–the ritual pouring of various items over a sacred image or personage in homage and worship.

Abhyasa: Sustained (constant) spiritual practice.

Adesha: A divine command from within the being; teaching, as is upadesha–teaching received while sitting near (upa).

Adhara: A reservoir of pranic energies, storage units for the energies that flow into the subtle bodies through the chakras, therefore often mistaken for a chakra.

Adhimatra: The degree of vairagya when worldly enjoyment becomes a source of pain.

Adhishthana(m): Seat; basis; substratum; ground; support; abode; the body as the abode of the subtle bodies and the Self; underlying truth or essence; background.

Adhyatma: The individual Self; the supreme Self; spirit.

Adhyatmika: Adhyatmic; pertaining to the Self (Atman or Jivatman), individual and Supreme (Paramatman).

Adinath (Adi Nath): The first teacher of the Nath Panthi, or Nath Yogi Sampradaya, usually believed to be Shiva himself.

Advaita: Non-duality; literally, "not two."

Aghora: Not terrifying (ghora); benevolent; a title of Shiva.

Aghora Pantha: An order or sect of worshippers of Shiva (Shaivites).

Aham: I; I-awareness; the ego; the individual soul; self-consciousness; the pure inner Self.

Aham Brahmasmi: "I am Brahman." The Mahavakya (Great Saying) of the Brihadaranyaka Upanishad.

Ahamkara: See Ahankara.

Ahankara: Ego; egoism or self-conceit; the self-arrogating principle "I," "I" am-ness; self-consciousness.

Ahata: Natural sound.

Ahimsa: Non-injury in thought, word, and deed; non-violence; non-killing; harmlessness.

Aishwarya: Dominion, power; lordship; divine glory; majesty; splendor; attribute(s) of Ishwara.

Ajapa Gayatri: Soham.

Ajapa japa: The natural japa (mantric sounds) made by the breath as it flows in and out: Soham.

Ajna chakra: "Command Wheel." Energy center located at the point between the eyebrows, the "third eye." The medulla center opposite the point between the eyebrows.

Akarma: Inaction; non-doing.

Akasha: "Not visible;" ether; space; sky; the subtlest of the five elements, from which the other four elements arise; the substance that fills and pervades the universe; the particular vehicle of life and sound; the element from which the sense of sound (shabda)–both speech and hearing–arises.

Akhanda: Unbroken (literally: "not broken"); indivisible; undivided; whole.

Amanitwam: Humility; absence of pride.

Amrita: That which makes one immortal. The nectar of immortality that emerged from the ocean of milk when the gods churned it.

Anahata: "Unstruck;" "unbeaten." Continuous bell-like inner resonance; the heart; the heart chakra; the inner divine melody (mystic sounds heard by the Yogis); supernatural sound; Soham.

Anahata chakra: "Unstruck." Energy center located in the spine at the point opposite the center of the chest (sternum bone). Seat of the Air element.

Ananda: Bliss; happiness; joy.

Anandamaya kosha: "The sheath of bliss (ananda)." The causal body. The borderline of the Self (Atman).

Anna: In the old currency, there were sixteen annas in a rupee. In the modern currency, twenty-five and fifty pice coins are called four and eight annas, respectively, but it is not really so.

Annamaya kosha: "The sheath of food (anna)." The physical–or gross–body, made of food.

Antardrishti: Inner vision; inner sight.

Antahkarana: Internal instrument; the subtle bodies; fourfold mind: mind, intellect, ego and subconscious mind.

Anugraha: Divine grace; attraction; favor; kindness, conferring benefits; assistance.

Apana: The prana that moves downward, producing the excretory functions in general; exhalation.

Aparigraha: Non-possessiveness, non-greed, non-selfishness, non-acquisitiveness.

Arati: A ceremony of worship in which lights, incense, camphor, and other offerings representing the five elements and the five senses–the totality of the human being–are waved before an image or symbol of the Divine.

Arghya: Offering of water made in ritualistic worship. Sometimes an offering of flowers, bel leaves, sandal paste, durva grass, and rice together.

Arishadvarga: In Hindu theology, the Six Passions, Arishadvarga, are the six enemies of the mind, which are: kama (lust), krodha (anger), lobha (greed), moha (delusive, often emotional, attachment or temptation), mada (pride), and matsarya (jealousy): the negative characteristics of which prevent man from attaining moksha or salvation.

Arjuna: The third of the five Pandava brothers. A famous warrior and one of the heroes of the Indian epic, the Mahabharata. Friend and disciples of Krishna, it was to Arjuna that Krishna imparted the knowledge of the Bhagavad Gita.

Arta: Pained; distressed; afflicted; one who is seeking/asking for relief from personal troubles or suffering.

Asana: Posture; seat; Hatha Yoga posture.

Ashram(a): A place for spiritual discipline and study, usually a monastic residence. Also a stage of life. In Hinduism life is divided ideally into four stages (ashramas): 1) the celibate student life (brahmacharya); 2) the married household life (grihasta); 3) the life of retirement (seclusion) and contemplation (vanaprastha); 4) the life of total renunciation (sannyasa).

Asmita: I-ness; the sense of "I am;" "I exist."

Ashtanga Yoga: The "eight-limbed" Yoga of Patanjali consisting of yama, niyama, asana, pranayama, pratyahara, dharana, dhyana, and samadhi (see separate entries for each "limb").

Asteya: Non-stealing; honesty; non-misappropriativeness.

Asura: Demon; evil being (a-sura: without the light).

Atma(n): The individual spirit or Self that is one with Brahman. The true nature or identity.

Atmabala: Soul-force.

Atmajnana: Direct knowledge of the Self; Brahma-Jnana.

Atmajnani: One who has atmajnana.

Atmaprabha: Light of the Self; shining by one's own light; self-illuminated or Self-illuminated: illuminated by one's own true Self.

Atmarama: Satisfied–delighted–in the Self.

Atmasakshatkara: "Direct sight of the Self;" realization of the true nature of the Self; Self-realization.

Atmasakshatkari: One who possesses atmasakshatkara.

Atmic: Having to do with the atman–spirit or self.

Avadhuta: "Cast off" (one who has cast off the world utterly). A supreme ascetic and jnani who has renounced all worldly attachments and connections and lives in a state beyond body consciousness, whose behavior is not bound by ordinary social conventions. Usually they wear no clothing. They embody the highest state of asceticism or tapas.

Avatar(a): A fully liberated spirit (jiva) who is born into a world below Satya Loka to help others attain liberation. Though commonly referred to as a divine incarnation, an avatar actually is totally one with God, and therefore an incarnation of God-Consciousness.

Avidya: Ignorance; nescience; unknowing; literally: "to know not." Also called ajnana.

Avyakrita: Undifferentiated; undefined; unexpounded; inconceivable; unanswerable questions; the elementary substance from which all things were created, considered as one with the substance of Brahman.

Avyakta(m): Unmanifest; invisible; when the three gunas are in a state of equilibrium' the undifferentiated.

Baba: A title often given to sadhus, saints and yogis, meaning "father."

Bal(a)krishna: The child/boy Krishna.

Bandha: "Lock;" bond; bondage; tie or knot; a Hatha Yoga exercise.

Bhagavad Gita: "The Song of God." The sacred philosophical text often called "the Hindu Bible," part of the epic Mahabharata by Vyasa; the most popular sacred text in Hinduism.

Bhagavatam/Srimad Bhagavatam: One of the eighteen scriptures known as Puranas which are attributed to Vyasa.

Bhairava: Shiva.

Bhajan: Devotional singing; a devotional song; remembrance (of God).

Bhakta: Devotee; votary; a follower of the path of bhakti, divine love; a worshipper of the Personal God.

Bhakti: Devotion; love (of God).

Bhakti Marga: The path of devotion leading to union with God.

Bhasma: Ash; ash from a sacrificial fire; sacred ash smeared on the body—on the forehead, between the eyebrows or on the entire body.

Bhashya: Commentary.

Bhati: Shining; self-luminous; light; splendor; intelligence, consciousness.

Bhava: Subjective state of being (existence); attitude of mind; mental attitude or feeling; state of realization in the heart or mind.

Bhavanam: Meditation. "Bhavanam is setting the heart on the Lord Who is designated by Soham and brought into the mind by It." (Shankara, *Commentary on the Yoga Sutras*)

Bhuta: A spirit. Some bhutas are subhuman nature spirits or "elementals," but some are earthbound human spirits: ghosts. Bhutas may be either positive or negative.

Bija: Seed; source.

Bija Mantra: A "seed" mantra from which realization grows as a tree from a seed; usually a single-syllable mantra.

Bindu: Point; dot; seed; source; the point from which the subtle Soham arises that is experienced in meditation.

Brahma: God as creator (Prajapati) of the three worlds of men, angels, and archangels–bhur, bhuwah, and swah; the first of the created beings; Hiranyagarbha or cosmic intelligence.

Brahma Sutras: A treatise by Vyasa on Vedanta philosophy in the form of aphorisms. Also called the Vedanta Sutras or Vedanta Darshana.

Brahmacharya: Continence; self-restraint on all levels; discipline.

Brahmajnana: Direct, transcendental knowledge of Brahman; Self-realization.

Brahman: The Absolute Reality; the Truth proclaimed in the Upanishads; the Supreme Reality that is one and indivisible, infinite, and eternal; all-pervading, changeless Existence; Existence-knowledge-bliss Absolute (Satchidananda); Absolute Consciousness; it is not only all-powerful but all-power itself; not only all-knowing and blissful but all-knowledge and bliss itself.

Brahmanishtha: Remaining steadfast in the Absolute (Brahman). One who is firmly established in the Supreme being, in the direct knowledge of Brahman, the Absolute Reality.

Brahmarandhra: "The hole of Brahman," the subtle (astral) aperture in the crown of the head. Said to be the gateway to the Absolute (Brahman) in the thousand-petaled lotus (Sahasrara) in the crown of the head. Liberated beings are said to exit the physical body through this aperture at death.

Brahmavidya: Science of Brahman; knowledge of Brahman; learning pertaining to Brahman or the Absolute Reality.

Brahmin (Brahmana): A knower of Brahman; a member of the highest Hindu caste traditionally consisting of priests, pandits, philosophers, and religious leaders.

Brindaban: The place where Krishna was born and where he lived until the age of twelve. Today it is a city of devotees and temples. Many agree with a friend who once said to me in a very matter-of-fact way: "Brindaban is my life." Its actual name is Vrindavan, but so many Bengali devotees and saints for centuries have called it "Brindaban" in their dialect, it has become common usage throughout India.

Buddhi: Intellect; understanding; reason; the thinking mind.

Chaitanya: Consciousness; intelligence; awareness; the consciousness that knows itself and knows others; Pure Consciousness.

Chetana: Consciousness. Whereas chaitanya is the principle of pure consciousness, chetana is consciousness occupied with an object. It is this "consciousness" that Buddha rejected as an obstacle.

Chakra: Wheel. Plexus; center of psychic energy in the human system, particularly in the spine or head.

Charvaka: The Indian materialistic school, also known as Lokayata ("restricted to the world of common experience"). Its central teaching is that matter is the only reality, and sense perception is the only valid means of knowledge or proof. Therefore sense satisfaction is the only goal.

Chidabhasa: Reflected consciousness; the reflection of intelligence which resides in the internal organ (anthakarana).

Chidakasha: "Conscious ether" or "conscious space." The infinite, all-pervading expanse of Consciousness from which all "things" proceed; the subtle space of Consciousness in the Sahasrara (Thousand-petalled Lotus). The true "heart" of all things.

Chitta: The subtle energy that is the substance of the mind.

Collyrium (Khol): A black substance put around the eyes. Though used cosmetically, it is considered to have medicinal properties that protect the eyes from infection or disease. It is often put around children's eyes for this purpose.

Crore: Ten million.

Dada: Uncle.

Daityas: Demons who constantly war with the gods. Sometimes "races" or nationalities who acted contrary to dharma and fought against the "aryas" were also called demons (daityas or asuras); giant; titan.

Dakshina: Gift; priestly gift; sacrificial fee; donation; an offering given as a gift of gratitude; guru dakshina is that given at the time of initiation.

Damaji (Damaji Pant): A fifteenth-century Marathi saint who risked his life for the sake of others by distributing grain from the royal granaries to the people in famine.

Darshan: Literally "sight" or "seeing." Darshan is the seeing of a holy being as well as the blessing received by seeing such a one.

Darshana: "Seeing" in the sense of a viewpoint or system of thought. The Sad-darshanas are the six orthodox systems of Indian philosophy: Nyaya, Vaisheshika, Sankhya, Yoga, Mimamsa, and Vedanta.

Dattatreya: A famous sage, son of the Rishi Atri and Anasuya. His birth was a divine boon, hence his name: Datta–"given"–and atreya–"son of Atri." Considered a divine incarnation and known as the Lord of Avadhutas, he is often revered as the embodiment of the Supreme Guru. He is credited with the authorship of the *Avadhuta* Gita, the *Jivanmukti Gita*, and the *Tripura Rahashya*.

Deva: "A shining one," a god–greater or lesser in the evolutionary hierarchy; a semi-divine or celestial being with great powers, and therefore a "god." Sometimes called a demi-god. Devas are the demigods presiding over various powers of material and psychic nature. In many instances "devas" refer to the powers of the senses or the sense organs themselves.

Dharana: Concentration of mind; fixing the mind upon a single thing or point. "Dharana is the confining [fixing] of the mind within a point or area" (Yoga Sutras 3:1).

Dharma: The righteous way of living, as enjoined by the sacred scriptures and the spiritually illumined; characteristics; virtue.

Dharmashala: A place for pilgrims to stay, either free of charge or at a minimal cost.

Dhruva: A child who performed intense tapasya to attain the vision of Vishnu; permanent; fixed; steady.

Dhvani: Tone: sound; word; the subtle aspect of the vital shakti or the jiva in the vibrations.

Dhyana(m)/Dhyana Yoga: Meditation; contemplation.

Dhyatri: Meditator.

Dhyata: Meditator.

Dhyeya: Object of meditation or worship; purpose behind action.

Divyadrishti: Divine vision.

Diwali: The Hindu autumnal Festival of Lights celebrated everywhere in India and abroad.

Dosha drishti: Seeing defects; especially the defects in samsara and samsaric life.

Durbar: A royal court; a divine court of a god or goddess.

Duta: Messenger; ambassador; envoy; one who has been sent by another.

Dvaita: Dual; duality; dualism.

Dwapara Yuga: See Yuga.

Dwija: "Twice born;" any member of the three upper castes that has received the sacred thread (yajnopavita).

Ekagrata: One-pointedness of the mind; concentration.

Eknath: A renowned Vaishnava saint of Western India (Maharashtra).

Gadi: Throne; seat; head (of a monastery).

Gajanana Maharaj: Sri Gajanana Maharaj (Gajanan Murlidhar Gupte) of Nashik in western India (Maharashtra state) was a saint of the Nath Sampradaya in the first half of the twentieth century.

Ganapati: "Lord of the Ganas" (the spirits that always accompany Shiva). See Ganesha.

Gandharva: A demigod—a celestial musician and singer.

Ganesha: The elephant-headed son of Shiva and Parvati; the remover of obstacles; lord (pati) of the ganas (spirits that always accompany Shiva); god of wisdom; god of beginnings; the granter of success in spiritual and material life; in ritual worship he is worshipped first, and is therefore known as Adi-deva, the First God.

Gayatri Mantra: A Rig Vedic mantra in the gayatri meter invoking the solar powers of evolution and enlightenment, recited at sunrise and sunset.

Gita: The Bhagavad Gita.

Gokul(a): The place of Krishna's childhood; Brindaban (Vrindavan).

Gokulashtami: Birthday of Krishna.

Gorakhnath/Gorakshanath: A master yogi of the Nath Yogi (Siddha Yogi) tradition. His dates are not positively known, but he seems to have lived for many centuries and travelled throughout all of India, Bhutan, Tibet, and Ladakh teaching philosophy and yoga.

Guru: Teacher; preceptor; spiritual teacher or acharya.

Guru Dakshina: Gift given to the guru at the time of initiation.

Hamsah: "I am That;" swan.

Hansa: Swan; see Hamsah.

Hanuman: A powerful monkey chief of extraordinary strength and prowess, whose exploits are celebrated in the epic Ramayana, the life of Rama. He was an ideal devotee (bhakta) and servant of Lord Rama.

Hari: Vishnu; "thief" in the sense of stealer of hearts.

Hatha Yoga: A system consisting of physical exercises, postures, and breathing exercises for gaining control over the physical body and prana.

Hiranyagarbha: Cosmic intelligence; the Supreme Lord of the universe; also called Brahma, cosmic Prana, Sutratma, Apara-brahman, Maha-brahma, or karya-brahman; Samasti-sukshma-sarirabhimani (the sum-total of all the subtle bodies); the highest created being through whom the Supreme Being projects the physical universe; cosmic mind.

Ida: The subtle channel that extends from the base of the spine to the medulla on the left side of the spine.

Indra: King of the lesser "gods" (demigods); the ruler of heaven (Surendra Loka); the rain-god.

Ishta-devata: Beloved deity. The deity preferred above all others by an individual. "Chosen ideal" is the usual English translation.

Ishwara: "God" or "Lord" in the sense of the Supreme Power, Ruler, Master, or Controller of the cosmos. "Ishwara" implies the powers of omnipotence, omnipresence, and omniscience.

Ishwarapranidhana: Offering of one's life to God (Ishwara).

Jagrita samadhi: Samadhi experienced in the waking state.

Jamuna: A sacred river, tributary of the Ganges, which flows through Brindaban, the home of Lord Krishna in his childhood.

Janaka: The royal sage (raja rishi) who was the king of Mithila and a liberated yogi, a highly sought-after teacher of philosophy in ancient India. Sita, the wife of Rama, was his adopted daughter.

Janardan Swami: A renowned saint of Western India (Maharashtra), a devotee of Lord Dattatreya.

Jani Janardan: God present in all human beings.

Janmashtami: Birthday of Krishna.

Japa: Repetition of a mantra.

Japa Mala: A string of beads, usually one hundred and eight, on which repetitions (japa) of a mantra are kept count of, or used just to help the yogi remember to do japa. Though one hundred and eight is the usual number of beads, smaller malas can be used when more convenient, especially since they can be put around the wrist when not in use. The beads can be of any substance, whatever is convenient or preferred.

Jijnasu: One who aspires after knowledge; spiritual aspirant.

Jiva: Individual spirit; embodied spirit; living entity; life.

Jivanmukta: One who is liberated here and now in this present life.

Jivanmukti: Liberation in this life.

Jivatma(n): Individual spirit; individual consciousness.

Jnana: Knowledge; wisdom of the Reality or Brahman, the Absolute.

Jnana Marga: The path of discriminative knowledge leading to union with God.

Jnana Yoga: The path of knowledge; meditation through wisdom; constantly and seriously thinking on the true nature of the Self as taught by the upanishads.

Jnanamaya kosha: "The sheath of intellect (buddhi)." The level of intelligent thought and conceptualization. Sometimes called the Vijnanamaya kosha. The astral-causal body.

Jnandev: See Jnaneshwar.

Jnanendriyas: The five organs of perception: ear, skin, eye, tongue, and nose.

Jnaneshwar: A thirteenth-century saint of Maharashtra, a poet, philosopher and yogi of the Nath Yogi Panth or tradition.

Jnani: A follower of the path of knowledge (jnana); one who has realized–who knows–the Truth (Brahman).

Jyoti: Light; flame; illumination; luminosity; effulgence.

Kabir: An Indian mystic of the fifteenth and sixteenth centuries.

Kaivalya-mukti (moksha): Liberation in which the yogi becomes one with Brahman while living (jivanmukti); final emancipation.

Kali Yuga: See Yuga.

Kaliya: A monstrous serpent (cobra) that was killed by Krishna in his childhood.

Kama: Desire; passion; lust.

Kapila: The great sage who formulated the Sankhya philosophy which is endorsed by Krishna in the Bhagavad Gita. (See the entry under Sankhya.)

Karana sharira: The causal body (where the individual rests during sound, deep, dreamless sleep, the intellect, mind and senses being reduced to an unmanifested potential condition), also known as the anandamaya kosha, the "sheath of bliss."

Karma: Karma, derived from the Sanskrit root *kri*, which means to act, do, or make, means any kind of action, including thought and feeling. It also means the effects of action. Karma is both action and reaction, the metaphysical equivalent of the principle: "For every action there is an equal and opposite reaction." "Whatsoever a man soweth, that shall he also reap" (Galatians 6:7). It is karma operating through the law of cause and effect that binds the jiva or the individual soul to the wheel of birth and death.

There are three forms of karma: sanchita, agami, and prarabdha. Sanchita karma is the vast store of accumulated actions done in the past, the fruits of which have not yet been reaped. Agami karma is the action that will be done by the individual in the future. Prarabdha karma is the action that has begun to fructify, the fruit of which is being reaped in this life.

Karma Marga: The path of selfless knowledge leading to union with God.

Karma Yoga: The Yoga of selfless (unattached) action; performance of one's own duty; service of humanity.

Karma Yogi: One who practices karma yoga.

Karmabhumi: Land of action; the earth-plane; the world of karma, where karma is sown and reaped.

Karmendriyas: The five organs of action: voice, hand, foot, organ of excretion, and the organ of generation.

Karmic: Having to do with karma.

Kashaya: Attachment to worldly objects; passion; emotion; the subtle influence in the mind produced by enjoyment and left there to fructify in time to come and distract the mind from samadhi; hidden impressions.

Katha: Tale or story; history or narrative.

Kayastha: A kayastha is a member of the Kayastha caste that is traditionally believed to be been keepers of public records and accounts, writers and state administrators. Yet their actual place in the caste system has never been really determined. In north central India the term "kayastha" is a polite and non-commital term used to refer to non-Brahmins.

Kevala kumbhaka: Sudden restraint of breath, not preceded by either inhalation or exhalation. Spontaneous breath retention, the kumbhaka which occurs during samadhi.

Kirtan(a): Singing the names and praises of God; devotional chanting.

Klesha: Literally, taints or afflictions; pain. The kleshas are: ignorance, egotism, attractions and repulsions towards objects, and desperate clinging to physical life from the fear of death. (See Yoga Sutras 2:2-9.)

Kosha: Sheath; bag; scabbard; a sheath enclosing the soul; body. There are five such concentric sheaths or bodies: the sheaths of bliss, intellect, mind, life-force and the physical body–the anandamaya, jnanamaya, manomaya, pranamaya and annamaya bodies respectively.

Krama mukti: Attainment of liberation in stages; gradual liberation; passing from this world to a higher world beyond rebirth and from there attaining liberation.

Krishna: A Divine Incarnation born in India about three thousand years ago, Whose teachings to His disciple Arjuna on the eve of the Great India (Mahabharata) War comprise the Bhagavad Gita.

Krishnarpana: That which has been offered to Krishna, to God.

Kriya: Purificatory action, practice, exercise, or rite; action; activity; movement; function; skill. Kriyas purify the body and nervous system as well as the subtle bodies to enable the yogi to reach and hold on to higher levels of consciousness and being.

Kriyamana: Literally: "what is being done;" the effect of the deeds of the present life to be experienced in the future; same as Agami.

Krodha: Anger, wrath; fury.

Kukarma: Negative, bad or evil action.

Kulakundalini: The primordial cosmic energy located in the individual.

Kumbhaka: Retention of breath; suspension of breath.

Kundalini: The primordial cosmic consciousness/energy located in the individual; it is usually thought of as lying coiled up like a serpent at the base of the spine.

Lahiri Mahasaya: Shyama Charan Lahiri, one of the greatest yogis of nineteenth-century India, written about extensively in *Autobiography of a Yogi*.

Lakh: One hundred thousand.

Lila: Play; sport; divine play; the cosmic play. The concept that creation is a play of the divine, existing for no other reason than for the mere joy of it. The life of an avatar is often spoken of as lila.

Lalla Yogeshwari: A fourteenth-century yogini of Kashmir whose hymns and verses are still regarded as among the greatest treasures of Kashmiri literature and yogic lore.

Lalleshwari: See Lalla Yogeshwari.

Linga: Mark; gender; sign; symbol. Usually a reference to a column-like or egg-shaped symbol of Shiva.

Lobha: Greed; covetousness.

Loka: World or realm; sphere, level, or plane of existence, whether physical, astral, or causal. There are seven lokas: Bhuloka: The material plane of atomic matter. Bhuvaloka: The lesser astral world, similar to the material plane (Bhuloka). Swa(r)loka: The median astral world. Mahaloka: The higher astral world. Those who attain this world need never be reborn in the three lower worlds of Bhur, Bhuvah, and Swah. Janaloka: The world that embraces both the highest astral levels and the lower causal levels. Tapoloka: The median causal world exclusively inhabited by advanced spirits who perpetually engage in meditation–tapasya. Satyaloka: The highest causal world inhabited by those who have attained liberation (moksha).

Lota: A metal water vessel used for drinking, carrying, or pouring water.

Mahabharata: The world's longest epic poem (110,00 verses) about the Mahabharata (Great Indian) War that took place about three thousand years ago. The Mahabharata also includes the Bhagavad Gita, the most popular sacred text of Hinduism.

Mahabhava: Supreme love and yearning for God, exemplified by Sri Radha.

Mahabodha: The Great Awakening.

Mahadeva: "The Great God;" a title of Shiva.

Mahapralaya: The final cosmic dissolution; the dissolution of all the worlds of relativity (Bhuloka, Bhuvaloka, Swaloka, Mahaloka, Janaloka, Tapaloka, and Satyaloka), until nothing but the Absolute remains. There are lesser dissolutions, known simply as pralayas, when only the first five worlds (lokas) are dissolved.

Mahaprana: The undifferentiated, intelligent cosmic life-force that becomes the five pranas; all things contain the mahaprana and are manifestations of the mahaprana; the dynamic aspect of universal Consciousness; the superconscious Divine Life in all things.

Maharaj(a): "Great king;" lord; master; a title of respect used to address holy men.

Maharashtra: One of the largest–and the wealthiest–states in India, whose capital is Mumbai (Bombay).

Mahasamadhi: Literally "the great union [samadhi]," this refers to a realized yogi's conscious departure from the physical body at death.

Mahashivaratri: "The Great Night of Shiva." The major, night-long festival of the worship of Shiva that occurs on the fourteenth day of the dark half of the lunar month known as Phalguna (usually in February, but every third year when an extra month is added to the lunar calendar, it may occur in March).

Mahatma: Literally: "a great soul [atma]." Usually a designation for a sannyasi, sage or saint.

Mahavakya: Literally: "Great Saying." The highest Vedantic truth, found in the Upanishads expressing the highest Vedantic truths or the identity between the individual soul and the Supreme Soul.

Mahat Tattwa: The Great Principle; the first product from Prakriti in evolution; intellect. The principle of Cosmic Intelligence or Buddhi; universal Christ Consciousness, the "Son of God," the "Only Begotten of the Father," "the firstborn of every creature."

Maheshwara: The Great Ishwara (Lord); Shiva.

Manana: Thinking, pondering, reflecting, considering.

Manas: The sensory mind; the perceiving faculty that receives the messages of the senses.

Manasarovar: A sacred lake near Mount Kailash the abode of Shiva. Pilgrims not only bathe in the lake on the way to Kailash, they often see visions in its water, hence the name "Lake of the Mind." The present Dalai Lama was found through visions seen in Manasarovar.

Manipura chakra: Energy center located in the spine at the point opposite the navel. Seat of the Fire element.

Manomaya kosha: "The sheath of the mind (manas–mental substance)." The level (kosha) of the sensory mind. The astral body.

Mantra: Sacred syllable or word or set of words through the repetition and reflection of which one attains perfection or realization of the Self.

Literally, "a transforming thought" [*manat trayate*], or more exactly, "a *transubstantiating* thought."

Manu: The ancient lawgiver, whose code, *The Laws of Manu* (*Manu Smriti*) is the foundation of Hindu religious and social conduct.

Mara: The embodiment of the power of cosmic evil, illusion, and delusion.

Marathi: The language of Maharashtra.

Math: A monastery.

Matsyendranath: Guru of Gorakhnath and the first publicly known Nath Yogi, having become a disciple of Adinath who is considered an avatar of Shiva. As with Gorakhnath, we have no dates for him.

Maya: The illusive power of Brahman; the veiling and the projecting power of the universe, the power of Cosmic Illusion.

Mayic: Having to do with Maya.

Moksha: Release; liberation; the term is particularly applied to the liberation from the bondage of karma and the wheel of birth and death; Absolute Experience.

Mudhavastha: State of ignorance or forgetfulness of one's real nature.

Mudra: A position–usually of the hands/fingers–which inherently produces a desired state in the subtle energy levels (prana) according to the Tantric system. A Hatha Yoga posture. A position of the eyes in meditation.

Mukta: One who is liberated–freed–usually in the sense of one who has attained moksha or spiritual liberation.

Mukti: Moksha; liberation.

Mulachaitanya: Root consciousness; seed of the creation.

Muladhara chakra: "Seat of the root." Energy center located at the base of the spine. Seat of the Earth element.

Mulaprakriti: The Root [Basic] Energy from which all things are formed. The Divine Prakriti or Energy of God.

Mulashakti: Root power or energy; Mulaprakriti.

Mumukshu: Seeker after liberation (moksha).

Mumukshutwa: Intense desire or yearning for liberation (moksha).

Nada: Sound; the resonance of sound; mystic inner sound; the primal sound or first vibration from which all creation has emanated; the first manifestation of the unmanifested Absolute or Shabda Brahman. The inner sound of Soham experienced in meditation.

Nadi: A channel in the subtle (astral) body through which subtle prana (psychic energy) flows; a physical nerve.

Naivedya: Edible offerings to the deity in a temple or household shrine.

Nama: Name. The Divine Name.

Namasmarana: Remembrance (repetition) of the Name of God. Remembrance of the Lord through repetition of His name.

Narada: A primeval sage to whom some of the verses of the Rig Veda are attributed. Narada) is a Vedic sage, famous in Hindu traditions as a traveling musician and storyteller, who carries news and enlightening wisdom. He appears in a number of Hindu texts, notably the Mahabharata and the Ramayana, as well as in the Puranas.

Narayana: A proper name of God–specifically of Vishnu. The term by etymology means a Being that supports all things, that is reached by them and that helps them to do so; also one who pervades all things. He Who dwells in man. Literally: "God in humanity." Sadhus often address one another as Narayana and greet one another: "Namo Narayanaya"–I salute Narayana [in you].

Nashik: An ancient holy city in Western India (the state of Maharashtra) on the banks of the Godavari river.

Nath Pantha (Nathas): Various associations of yogis who trace their roots back to Matsyendranath and the Nath Yogi Sampradaya.

Nath Yogi: A member of the Nath Yogi Sampradaya.

Nath Yogi Sampradaya: An ancient order of yogis claiming Matsyendranath, Gorakhnath, Patanjali, Jnaneshwar and Jesus (Isha Nath) among their master teachers.

Nath Yogis: An ancient order of yogis, sometimes called Siddha Yogis, claiming Patanjali and Jesus (Isha Nath) among their master teachers.

Nididhyasana: Meditation; contemplation; profound and continuous meditation. It is a continuous, unbroken stream of ideas of the same kind as those of the Absolute. It removes the contrariwise tendencies of the mind.

Nine Nathas: Nine great Masters of the Nath Yogi Sampradaya, including Matsyendranath and Ghoraknath.

Nirakara: Without form.

Niramaya: Without disease, defect or deficiency; health; complete; entire; pure.

Niranjana: Without blemish; spotless; stainless; untainted; pure; simple; void of passion or emotion; a title of Brahman.

Nirguna: Without attributes or qualities (gunas).

Nirguna Brahman: The impersonal, attributeless Absolute beyond all description or designation.

Nirvana: Liberation; final emancipation; the term is particularly applied to the liberation from the bondage of karma and the wheel of birth and death that comes from knowing Brahman; Absolute Experience. See Moksha.

Nirvana chakra: Energy center located at the middle of the forehead–about an inch above the Ajna chakra.

Nirvikalpa: Indeterminate; non-conceptual; without the modifications of the mind; beyond all duality.

Nirvikalpa samadhi: Samadhi in which there is no objective experience or experience of "qualities" whatsoever, and in which the triad of knower, knowledge and known does not exist; purely subjective experience of the formless and qualitiless and unconditioned Absolute. The highest state of samadhi, beyond all thought, attribute, and description.

Nishkama: Free from wish or desire; desirelessness; selfless, unselfish.

Nishkama Karma Yoga: Action without expectation of fruits, and done without personal interest or egoism.

Nishkama: Without desire.

Nishkama karma: Desireless action; disinterested action; action dedicated to God without personal desire for the fruits of the action; selfless action.

Niyama: Observance; the five Do's of Yoga: 1) shaucha–purity, cleanliness; 2) santosha–contentment, peacefulness; 3) tapas–austerity, practical (i.e., result-producing) spiritual discipline; 4) swadhyaya–Self-study, spiritual study; 5) Ishwarapranidhana–offering of one's life to God.

Nityananda (Paramhansa): A great Master of the nineteenth and twentieth centuries, and the most renowned Soham yogi of our times. His *Chidakasha Gita* contains some of the most profound statements on philosophy and yoga.

Panchanga: The traditional Indian (Hindu) calendar. "It provides precise information about astrological factors, planets, and stars which influence and alter the nature of the subtle environment" (*A Concise Dictionary of Indian Philosophy*).

Pandharpur: The major pilgrim city for Vaishnavas in Maharashtra, site of the famous Vithoba (or Vithala) Temple of Lord Krishna.

Pandit: Scholar; pundit; learned individual.

Panduranga: Krishna, in the form worshipped in the Vithoba Temple in Pandharpur.

Parabrahman: Supreme Brahman.

Para(ma): Highest; universal; transcendent; supreme.

Paraloka: The world beyond this world; the future life. Not a technical term for a particular level or loka, but just a general term for a/the world we go to after death.

Paramananda: Supreme (param) bliss (ananda).

Paramartha: The highest attainment, purpose, or goal; absolute truth; Reality.

Paramatma(n): The Supreme Self, God.

Parameshwara: The Supreme (Param) Lord (Ishwara).

Paramhansa: Literally: Supreme Swan, a person of the highest spiritual realization, from the fact that a swan can separate milk from water and is therefore an apt symbol for one who has discarded the unreal for the Real, the darkness for the Light, and mortality for the Immortal, having separated himself fully from all that is not God and joined himself totally to the Divine, becoming a veritable embodiment of Divinity manifested in humanity.

Parasamvit: Supreme knowledge or consciousness.

Patala: Nether world; hell. In ancient Sanskrit texts the Western Hemisphere is called Patal Desh, the Underworld.

Patanjali: A yogi of ancient India, the author of the Yoga Sutras.

Pativrata: A chaste woman devoted to her husband.

Pice: A monetary unit. There were sixty-four pice in the old rupee, but now there are one hundred.

Pinda: Part of the whole; individual; the body–either of the individual jiva or the cosmic body of Ishwara. It can also mean an organized whole or a unity of diversities.

Pingala: The subtle channel that extends from the base of the spine to the medulla on the right side of the spine.

Prabhu: Lord.

Prabodha: Awakening; becoming conscious; consciousness; manifestation; appearance; knowledge; understanding; intelligence.

Pradhana: See Prakriti.

Prahlada: A daitya prince who rejected his daitya heritage and became a devotee of Vishnu. His father, the evil Hiranyakashipu, tortured him and attempted his life because of his devotion and his speaking to others of divine matters, yet he remained steadfast.

Prajapati: Progenitor; the Creator; a title of Brahma the Creator.

Prajna: Consciousness; awareness; wisdom; intelligence.

Prakash(a): Shining; luminous; effulgence; illumination; luminosity; light; brightness. Pure Consciousness, from the root kash (to shine) and pra (forth); cognition.

Prakriti: Causal matter; the fundamental power (shakti) of God from which the entire cosmos is formed; the root base of all elements; undifferentiated matter; the material cause of the world. Also known as Pradhana.

Prana: Vital energy; life-breath; life-force; inhalation.

Pranamaya kosha: "The sheath of vital air (prana)." The sheath consisting of vital forces and the (psychic) nervous system.

Pranavayu: The

Pranayama: Control of the subtle life forces, often by means of special modes of breathing. Therefore breath control or breathing exercises are usually mistaken for pranayama. It also means the refining (making subtle) of the breath, and its lengthening through spontaneous slowing down of the respiratory rate.

Prarabdha: Karma that has become activated and begun to manifest and bear fruit in this life; karmic "seeds" that have begun to "sprout."

Prasad(am): Grace; food or any gift that has been first offered in worship or to a saint; that which is given by a saint. It also means tranquility, particularly in the Bhagavad Gita.

Prashanta: Calmed; quiet; tamed; intensified peace.

Prashanta-vahita: Continuity of a tranquil state of mind.

Pratiti: Perception; apprehension; insight; complete understanding; conviction; faith, confidence, belief, trust, credit; fame, respect; delight.

Pratyahara: Abstraction or withdrawal of the senses from their objects, the fifth limb of Patanjali's Ashtanga Yoga.

Pratyaksha: Perception; direct perception; intuition.

Prayaschitta: Atonement (through various prescribed acts); expiation; mortification.

Pundit: Scholar; pandita; learned individual.

Punya: Merit; virtue; meritorious acts; virtuous deeds.

Purana: Literally "The Ancient." The Puranas are a number of scriptures attributed to the sage Vyasa that teach spiritual principles and practices through stories about sacred historical personages which often include their teachings given in conversations.

Purusha: "Person" in the sense of a conscious spirit. Both God and the individual spirits are purushas, but God is the Adi (Original, Archetypal) Purusha, Parama (Highest) Purusha, and the Purushottama (Best of the Purushas).

Rajasa: See Rajasic.

Rajasic: Possessed of the qualities of the raja guna (rajas). Passionate; active; restless.

Rakshasa: There are two kinds of rakshasas: 1) semidivine, benevolent beings, or 2) cannibal demons or goblins, enemies of the gods. Meat-eating human beings are sometimes classed as rakshasas.

Rama: An incarnation of God–the king of ancient Ayodhya in north-central India. His life is recorded in the ancient epic Ramayana.

Rama Nama: The name of Rama–both of the Absolute Brahman and of the incarnation, Rama of Ayodhya–used in devotional singing, japa and meditation.

Rama Tirtha (Swami): A renowned monk born in Maharashtra who came to America in 1902 and for two years taught philosophy and yoga, especially in San Francisco, before returning to India.

Ramakrishna: Sri Ramakrishna lived in India in the second half of the nineteenth century, and is regarded by all India as a perfectly enlightened person–and by many as an Incarnation of God.

Ramana Maharshi: A great sage of the twentieth century who lived in Arunachala in South India. He taught the path of Self-Inquiry (Atma Vichara) wherein, whatever the mode of spiritual practice, the yogi keep focussed on the fundamental attitude, "Who am I?" until the Self (Atman) is revealed.

Rasakrida: Transcendental sport that Lord Krishna played with the gopis and gopas of Brindaban.

Rig Veda: The oldest scripture of India, considered the oldest scripture of the world, that consists of hymns revealed in meditation to the Vedic Rishis (seers). Although in modern times there are said to be four Vedas (Rig, Sama, Yajur, and Atharva), in actuality, there is only one Veda: the Rig Veda. The Sama Veda is only a collection of Rig Veda hymns that are marked (pointed) for singing. The Yajur Veda is a small book giving directions on just one form of Vedic sacrifice. The Atharva Veda is only a collection of theurgical mantras to be recited for the cure of various afflictions or to be recited over the herbs to be taken as medicine for those afflictions.

Sadagati: Everlasting happiness; final beatitude.

Sadguru: True guru, or the guru who reveals the Real (Sat–God).

Sadhaka: One who practices spiritual discipline–sadhana–particularly meditation.

Sadhana: Spiritual practice.

Sadhana-chatushtaya: The fourfold aids to spiritual practice: 1) Viveka: the ability to discriminate between the transient and the eternal (nitya-anity-astu-viveka); 2) Vairagya: the absence of desire for securing pleasure or pain either here or elsewhere (iha-anutra-artha-phala-vairagya); 3) Shad-sampat: the attainment of calmness, temperance, spirit of renunciation, fortitude, power of concentration of mind, and faith (shama-damadi-sadhana-smaptti); 4) Mumukshutva: an intense desire for liberation (mumukshutwa).

Sadhu: Seeker for truth (sat); a person who is practicing spiritual disciplines. Usually this term is applied only to monastics.

Saguna: With attributes or qualities (gunas).

Saguna Brahman: The supreme Absolute conceived of as endowed with qualities like mercy, omnipotence, omniscience, omnipresence, etc., as distinguished from the undifferentiated Absolute–Nirguna Brahman.

Sahaja: Natural; innate; spontaneous; inborn.

Sahaja Nirvikalpa Samadhi: Natural, non-dual state of Brahmic Consciousness.

Sahaja samadhi: See Sahaja Nirvikalpa Samadhi.

Sahajavastha: Superconscious state that has become natural and continuous.

Sahasrara: The "thousand-petalled lotus" of the brain. The highest center of consciousness, the point at which the spirit (atman) and the bodies (koshas) are integrated and from which they are disengaged.

Sahasr(ar)adala: The Sahasrara chakra located in the center of the brain according to the Nath Panth tradition.

Sakshatakara: Self-realization; direct experience; experience of Absoluteness; Brahmajnana.

Sakshiavastha: Permanent establishment in the Witness State.

Sakshitwa: Establishment in the consciousness of being the Witness Self; looking upon oneself as merely the observer.

Samadhi: The state of superconsciousness where Absoluteness is experienced attended with all-knowledge and joy; Oneness; here the mind becomes identified with the object of meditation; the meditator and the meditated, thinker and thought become one in perfect absorption of the mind. See Samprajñata Samadhi, Asamprajñata Samadhi, Savikalpa Samadhi, and Nirvikalpa Samadhi.

Samarth Ramdas: A renowned saint and poet of Maharastra; guru of the great warrior-king Shivaji; rishi of the mantra: Sri Ram Jai Ram Jai Jai Ram.

Samata: Balanced state of mind.

Sampradaya: Tradition; philosophical school; literally: "handed-down instruction;" also a line of initiatic empowerment.

Samprajnata: A stage in samadhi wherein one is conscious of an object; that mind functions in this stage and concentrates on an object of knowledge (perception).

Samprajñata samadhi: State of superconsciousness, with the triad of meditator, meditation and the meditated; lesser samadhi; cognitive samadhi; samadhi of wisdom; meditation with limited external awareness. Savikalpa samadhi.

Samsara: Life through repeated births and deaths; the wheel of birth and death; the process of earthly life.

Samsarin: One who is subject to samsara–repeated births and deaths–and who is deluded by its appearances, immersed in ignorance.

Samyama: Self-control; perfect restraint; an all-complete condition of balance and repose. The combined practice of the last three steps in Patanjali's Ashtanga Yoga: concentration (dharana), meditation (dhyana), and union (samadhi). See the Vibhuti Pada of the Yoga Sutras.

Sanatana Dharma: "The Eternal Religion," also known as "Arya Dharma," "the religion of those who strive upward [Aryas]." Hinduism.

Sanchita: Sanchita karma.

Sanchita karma: The vast store of accumulated actions done in the past, the fruits of which have not yet been reaped.

Sankalpa: A life-changing wish, desire, volition, resolution, will, determination, or intention–not a mere momentary aspiration, but an empowering act of will that persists until the intention is fully realized. It is an act of spiritual, divine creative will inherent in each person as a power of the Atman.

Sankhya: One of the six orthodox systems of Hindu philosophy whose originator was the sage Kapila, Sankhya is the original Vedic philosophy, endorsed by Krishna in the Bhagavad Gita (Gita 2:39; 3:3, 5; 18:13, 19), the second chapter of which is entitled "Sankhya Yoga." *A Ramakrishna-Vedanta Wordbook* says: "Sankhya postulates two ultimate realities, Purusha and Prakriti. Declaring that the cause of suffering is man's identification of Purusha with Prakriti and its products, Sankhya teaches that liberation and true knowledge are attained in the supreme consciousness, where such identification ceases and Purusha is realized as existing independently in its transcendental nature." Not surprisingly, then, Yoga is based on the Sankhya philosophy.

Sanskrit: The language of the ancient sages of India and therefore of the Indian scriptures and yoga treatises.

Santosha: Contentment; peacefulness.

Sarada Devi ("Holy Mother"): The virgin-wife of Sri Ramakrishna, and a great teacher in her own right, considered by many to be an incarnation of the Mother aspect of God.

Sarvajña(twa): Knowing everything; omniscience.

Sat: Existence; reality; truth; being; a title of Brahman, the Absolute or Pure Being.

Sat Chakras: The six chakras: Muladhara, Swadhishthana, Manipura, Anahata, Vishuddha and Ajna, located at the base of the spine, in the spine a little less than midway between the base of the spine and the area opposite the navel in the spine, the point in the spine opposite the navel, the point in the spine opposite the midpoint of the sternum bone, the point in the spine opposite the hollow of the throat, and the point between the eyebrows, respectively.

Satchidananda: Existence-knowledge-bliss Absolute; Brahman.

Satguru: True guru, or the guru who reveals the Real (Sat–God).

Satsang(a): Literally: "company with Truth." Association with godly-minded persons. The company of saints and devotees.

Sattwa: Light; purity; harmony, goodness, reality.

Sattwic: Partaking of the quality of Sattwa.

Satya: Truth; the Real; Brahman, or the Absolute; truthfulness; honesty.

Satya Loka: "True World," "World of the True [Sat]", or "World of Truth [Satya]." This highest realm of relative existence where liberated beings live who have not entered back into the Transcendent Absolute where there are no "worlds" (lokas). From that world they can descend and return to other worlds for the spiritual welfare of others, as can those that have chosen to return to the Transcendent.

Satya Yuga: See Yuga.

Savikalpa Samadhi: Samadhi in which there is objective experience or experience of "qualities" and with the triad of knower, knowledge and known; lesser samadhi; cognitive samadhi; samadhi of wisdom; meditation with limited external awareness. Samprajñata samadhi.

Sayujya: Closely united with; united with God; becoming one with God.

Sayujyata: The state of being in Sayujya.

Shabda: Sound; word.

Shabda Brahman: Sound-God; Brahman in the Form of Sound; Omkara, or the Veda.

Shad-Sampat: The sixfold virtue: 1) Sama: serenity or tranquillity of mind which is brought about through the eradication of desires; 2) Dama: rational control of the senses; 3) Uparati: satiety—resolutely turning the mind away from desire for sensual enjoyment; 4) Titiksha: the power of endurance. An aspirant should patiently bear the pairs of opposites such as heat and cold, pleasure and pain, etc.; 5) Shraddha: intense faith, lasting, perfect and unshakable; 6) Samadhana: fixing the mind on Brahman or the Self, without allowing it to run towards objects.

Shaiva/Shaivite: A worshipper of Shiva; pertaining to Shiva.

Shakti: Power; energy; force; the Divine Power of becoming; the apparent dynamic aspect of Eternal Being; the Absolute Power or Cosmic Energy.

Shankara: Shankaracharya; Adi (the first) Shankaracharya: The great reformer and re-establisher of Vedic Religion in India around 300 B.C. He is the unparalleled exponent of Advaita (Non-Dual) Vedanta. He also reformed the mode of monastic life and founded (or regenerated) the ancient Swami Order.

Sharira: Body; sheath; literally: "that which perishes," from the root shri which means "to waste away."

Shastra: Scripture; spiritual treatise.

Shastri: One who is a scholar and teacher of the scriptures (shastras).

Shastric: Scriptural or having to do with the scriptures.

Shaucha: Purity; cleanliness.

Shesha: The endless; the infinite; The name of the snake (naga) upon which Vishnu reclines.

Shiva: A name of God meaning "One Who is all Bliss and the giver of happiness to all." Although classically applied to the Absolute Brahman, Shiva can also refer to God (Ishwara) in His aspect of Dissolver and Liberator (often mistakenly thought of as "destroyer").

Shivatma: The Paramatman who is the root cause of all the activities in the Universe.

Shodhana: Process of cleansing (purifying) in Hatha Yoga.

Shraddha: Faith; confidence or assurance that arises from personal experience.

Shravana: Hearing; study; listening to reading of the scriptures or instruction in spiritual life.

Shruti: That which is heard; revealed scripture in the sense of divine communication. Usually applied to the Vedas, Shankara also spoke of the Upanishads as Shruti.

Shuddha-chaitanya: Pure intelligence; pure consciousness.

Shyama Charan Lahiri: See Lahiri Mahasaya.

Siddha: A perfected–liberated–being, an adept, a seer, a perfect yogi.

Siddha Nama: The Perfect Name; an title of the Soham Mantra.

Siddhi: Spiritual perfection; psychic power; power; modes of success; attainment; accomplishment; achievement; mastery; supernatural power attained through mantra, meditation, or other yogic practices. From the verb root sidh–to attain.

Siddhaloka: The highest realm of existence in which the fully liberated (siddhas) live. (However, wherever a siddha is, that place is siddhaloka.)

Sivananda (Swami): A great twentieth-century Master, founder of the world-wide Divine Life Society, whose books on spiritual life and religion are widely circulated in the West as well as in India.

Smriti: Memory; recollection; "that which is remembered;" code of law. In this latter sense, Smriti is used to designate all scriptures except the Vedas and Upanishads (which are considered of greater authority: Shruti).

Soham: "I am That," the Ajapa Gayatri formula of meditation in which *So* is repeated mentally during natural inhalation and *Ham* is repeated mentally during natural exhalation.

Soham Bhava: The state of being and awareness: "I am That." Gorakhnath says that Soham Bhava includes total Self-comprehension (ahamta), total Self-mastery (akhanda aishwarya), unbroken awareness of the unity of the Self (swatmata), awareness of the unity of the Self with all phenomenal existence–as the Self (vishwanubhava), knowledge of all within and without the Self–united in the Self (sarvajñatwa).

Spanda: Vibration; flutter; throb; movement; creative shakti; pulsation; creative pulsation; apparent motion in the motionless Shiva which brings about the manifestation, maintenance, and withdrawal of the universe; the principle of apparent movement from the state of absolute unity to the plurality of the world.

Sphota: The Sanskrit original of our English word "spot;" manifester; the idea which bursts or flashes–including the Pranava which burst or flashes forth from the Absolute and becomes transformed into the Relative.

Sphurana: Vibration.

Sri: Holy; sacred; excellent; venerated (venerable); revered; a term of respect similar to "Reverend." Also: prosperity, glory, and success–and therefore an epithet for Lakshmi, the goddess of wealth and abundance, the consort of Vishnu. It is often used as an honorific prefix to the name of deities and holy persons to indicate holiness (Sri Krishna, Sri Swami N., etc.).

Also used as the equivalent of the English "Mr." (Srimati would be the equivalent of "Mrs.")

Sthirattwa: Steadiness or firmness of body or mind; the steady tranquillity born of meditation.

Stotra: A hymn or verse in praise of God.

Sudarshana: Sudarshana Chakra.

Sudarshana Chakra: The invincible weapon of Lord Vishnu which is able to cut through anything, and is a symbol of the Lord's power of cutting through all things which bind the jiva to samsara. Thus it is the divine power of liberation (moksha).

Sukarma: Good action; good deed; virtuous; diligent.

Sushumna: A subtle passage in the midst of the spinal column, corresponding to the spinal cord, that extends from the base of the spine to the medulla oblongata in the head.

Sushupti: The dreamless sleep state.

Sutra: An aphorism with minimum words and maximum sense; a terse sentence.

Swadhishthana chakra: Energy center located in the spine a little less than midway between the base of the spine and the area opposite the navel. Seat of the Water element.

Swadhyaya: Introspective self-study or self-analysis leading to self-understanding.

Swami Maharaj of Akalkot (Swāmi Samarth Mahāraj; Akkalkot Swami): A nineteenth century guru of the Dattatreya tradition (sampradaya), widely respected in the Indian states of Maharashtra, Karnataka and Andhra Pradesh. He lived in the Akkalkot village in Maharashtra for about twenty-two years.

Swapna: The dream state; a dream.

Swapna samadhi: Samadhi that occurs in a dream—that is, the dream passes into a superconscious state.

Swarupa: "Form of the Self." Natural–true–form; actual or essential nature; essence. A revelatory appearance that makes clear the true nature of some thing.

Swarupajnana: Knowledge which is of the nature of the Self; knowledge of one's essential nature; knowledge of pure consciousness, which is the highest end in life.

Taimni, I. K.: A professor of chemistry in India. He wrote many excellent books on philosophy and spiritual practice, including *The Science of Yoga*, a commentary on the Yoga Sutras. For many years he was the spiritual head of the Esoteric Section of the Theosophical Society headquartered in Adyar, Madras (Tamilnadu), and traveled the world without publicity or notoriety, quietly instructing many sincere aspirants in the path to supreme consciousness.

Talu chakra: Energy center located at the root of the palate opposite the tip of the nose.

Tantra: A manual of, or a particular path of, sadhana laying great stress upon japa of a mantra and other esoteric practices relating to the powers latent in the human complex of physical, astral, and causal bodies in relation to the cosmic Power usually thought as the Divine Feminine.

Tanumanasa: Threadlike (extremely subtle and attenuated) state of mind, indicating that impurities and impediments are lessening.

Tapas (tapasya): Austerity, practical (i.e., result-producing) spiritual discipline; spiritual force. Literally it means the generation of heat or energy, but is always used in a symbolic manner, referring to spiritual practice and its effect, especially the roasting of karmic seeds, the burning up of karma.

Taraka: Deliverer.

Taraka Mantra: From the root word *tara*–that which crosses. The Taraka Mantra is that which enables its invokers to cross over the ocean of samsara and attain liberation.

Tattwa: "Thatness." Principle; element; the essence of things; truth; reality.

Tirtha: A sacred place of pilgrimage; a river or body of water in which it is auspicious and spiritually beneficial to bathe; the water offered in ritual worship and then sprinkled on or drunk by the devotees. Also, a name of a Dasanami Sannyasin belonging to the Dwarka Math.

Tola: Three-eights of an ounce.

Trikalajnana: Knowledge of the past, present and the future.

Trikalajnani: One who knows the past, present and the future.

Tukaram: A poet-saint of seventeenth century India (Maharashtra) devoted to Krishna in his form of Panduranga (Vittala).

Turiya: The state of pure consciousness. *A Ramakrishna-Vedanta Wordbook* defines it as: "The superconscious; lit., 'the Fourth,' in relation to the three ordinary states of consciousness–waking, dreaming, and dreamless sleep–which it transcends."

Tyaga: Literally" leaving; separation; abandonment; renunciation in the sense of dissociation of the mind from worldly objects and the seeds of desire; in the Gita, the relinquishment of the fruit of action.

Tyagi: A renouncer, an ascetic.

Unmana: "That which transcends the mind;" the "mindless" state of a yogi that is really the state beyond the mind.

Unmani: One who is in the state of unmana.

Upadesha: Spiritual instruction; the instructions given by the guru at the time of initiation; initiation itself.

Upanishads: Books (of varying lengths) of the philosophical teachings of the ancient sages of India on the knowledge of Absolute Reality. The upanishads contain two major themes: (1) the individual Self (Atman) and the Supreme Self (Paramatman) are one in essence, and (2) the goal of life is the realization/manifestation of this unity, the realization of God (Brahman). There are eleven principal upanishads: Isha, Kena, Katha, Prashna, Mundaka, Mandukya, Taittiriya, Aitaryeya, Chandogya, Brihadaranyaka, and Svetashvatara, all of which were commented on by Shankara, thus setting the seal of authenticity on them.

Upasana: "Sitting near" or "drawing near;" worship; adoration; contemplation of God or deity; devout meditation; both teaching and learning.

Vachaka: That which is denoted by speech.

Vairagya: Non-attachment; detachment; dispassion; absence of desire; disinterest; or indifference. Indifference towards and disgust for all worldly things and enjoyments.

Vak: Speech.

Upasana: "Sitting near" or "drawing near;" worship; adoration; contemplation of God or deity; devout meditation; both teaching and learning.

Vairagya: Non-attachment; detachment; dispassion; absence of desire; disinterest; or indifference. Indifference towards and disgust for all worldly things and enjoyments.

Vani: Speech; voice; sound; music; language; words.

Varna: Caste. (Literally: color.) In traditional Hindu society there were four divisions or castes according to the individual's nature and aptitude: Brahmin, Kshatriya, Vaishya, and Shudra.

Varnashrama: Related to the four castes and the four stages (ashramas) of Hindu life; the laws of caste and ashrama.

Varnashram dharma: The observance of caste and ashram.

Vasana: Subtle desire; a tendency created in a person by the doing of an action or by experience; it induces the person to repeat the action or to seek a repetition of the experience; the subtle impression in the mind capable of developing itself into action; it is the cause of birth and experience in general; an aggregate or bundle of samskaras–the impressions of actions that remain unconsciously in the mind.

Vasana(s): A bundle or aggregate of such samskaras.

Vedanta: Literally, "the end of the Vedas;" the Upanishads; the school of Hindu thought, based primarily on the Upanishads, upholding the doctrine of either pure non-dualism or conditional non-dualism. The original text of this school is Vedanta-darshana or the Brahma Sutras compiled by the sage Vyasa.

Vedas: The oldest scriptures of India, considered the oldest scriptures of the world, that were revealed in meditation to the Vedic Rishis.

Vedic: Having to do with the Vedas.

Vibhu: All-pervading; great.

Vichara: Subtle thought; reflection; enquiry; introspection; investigation; enquiry/investigation into the nature of the Self, Brahman or Truth; ever-present reflection on the why and wherefore of things; enquiry into the real meaning of the Mahavakya Tat-twam-asi: Thou art That; discrimination between the Real and the unreal; enquiry of Self.

Videha: Bodiless.

Videhakaivalya mukti: Disembodied salvation.

Videhi: One who is bodiless.

Vidya: Knowledge; both spiritual knowledge and mundane knowledge.

Vijnana: The highest knowledge, beyond mere theoretical knowledge (jnana); transcendental knowledge or knowing; experiential knowledge; a high state of spiritual realization–intimate knowledge of God in which all is seen as manifestations of Brahman; knowledge of the Self.

Vikalpa: Imagination; fantasy; mental construct; abstraction; conceptualization; hallucination; distinction; experience; thought; oscillation of the mind.

Viraj: The macrocosm; the manifested universe; the world man–the masculine potency in nature in contradistinction to the feminine potency.

Virat: Macrocosm; the cosmic form of the Self as the cause of the gross world; the all-pervading Spirit in the form of the universe.

Vishnu: "The all-pervading;" God as the Preserver.

Vishuddha: Supremely pure; totally pure.

Vishuddha chakra: "Supreme purity." Energy center located in the spine opposite the hollow of the throat. Seat of the Ether element.

Vishwaprana: The universal life force (prana).

Vithoba: See Vitthala.

Vitthala: A title of Krishna, meaning "the one standing on a brick," a reference to the image of Krishna worshipped in Pandharpur in Western India.

Vivarta: Illusory appearance; a doctrine of the Nondualistic school of Vedanta philosophy explaining creation as an illusory appearance of the Absolute; apparent variation; illusory manifestation of Brahman; apparent or unreal or seeming change; superimposition; appearance.

Viveka: Discrimination between the Real and the unreal, between the Self and the non-Self, between the permanent and the impermanent; right intuitive discrimination.

Vivekananda (Swami): The chief disciple of Sri Ramakrishna, who brought the message of Vedanta to the West at the end of the nineteenth century.

Vritti: Thought-wave; mental modification; mental whirlpool; a ripple in the chitta (mind substance).

Vyakta: Manifest(ed); revealed.

Vyasa: One of the greatest sages of India, commentator on the Yoga Sutras, author of the Mahabharata (which includes the Bhagavad Gita), the Brahma Sutras, and the codifier of the Vedas.

Vyatireka: Separate; negation; distinguishing the non-Self from the Self.

Yaksha: There are two kinds of yakshas: 1) semidivine beings whose king is Kubera, the lord of wealth, or 2) a kind of ghost, goblin, or demon.

Yama: Yamaraja; the Lord of Death, controller of who dies and what happens to them after death.

Yama: Restraint; the five Don'ts of Yoga: 1) ahimsa—non-violence, non-injury, harmlessness; 2) satya—truthfulness, honesty; 3) asteya—non-stealing, honesty, non-misappropriativeness; 4) brahmacharya—continence; 5) aparigraha—non-possessiveness, non-greed, non-selfishness, non-acquisitiveness.

Yama Duta: A messenger of Yama; who who comes to take the soul from the body at the time of death.

Yamuna: A sacred river, tributary of the Ganges, which flows through Brindaban, the home of Lord Krishna in his childhood.

Yantra: Geometrical designs of the energy patterns made by mantras when they are recited or which, when concentrated on produce the effects of the corresponding mantras. Though often attributed to deities, they are really the diagrams of the energy movements of those deities' mantras.

Yashoda: The foster-mother of Krishna in Brindaban where Krishna was taken by his father Vasudeva on the night of his birth for his protection from his mother Devaki's brother, Kansa, the king of Mathura. His foster-father was Nanda.

Yoga: Union; abstract meditation or union with the Supreme Being; the name of the philosophy by the sage Patanjali, teaching the process of union of the individual with the Universal Soul; union with God; any practice that makes for such union.

Yoga Darshan(a): Hinduism embraces six systems of philosophy, one of which is Yoga. The basic text of the Yoga philosophy–Yoga Darshana–is the Yoga Sutras (also called Yoga Darshana), the oldest known writing on the subject of yoga, written by the sage Patanjali, a yogi of ancient India. Further, the Yoga Philosophy is based on the philosophical system known as Sankhya, whose originator was the sage Kapila.

Yoga Nidra: A state of half-contemplation and half-sleep; light yogic sleep when the individual retains slight awareness; state between sleep and wakefulness.

Yoga Shastra: The scriptures and writings of various authorities dealing specifically with the theory and practice of yoga, especially the Yoga Sutras (Yoga Darshan) of Patanjali.

Yoga Sutras: The oldest known writing on the subject of yoga, written by the sage Patanjali, a yogi of ancient India, and considered the most authoritative text on yoga. Also known as *Yoga Darshana*, it is the basis of the Yoga Philosophy which is based on the philosophical system known as Sankhya.

Yoga Vashishtha: A classical treatise on Yoga, containing the instructions of the Rishi Vashishtha to Lord Rama on meditation and spiritual life.

Yogananda (Paramhansa): The most influential yogi of the twentieth century West, author of *Autobiography of a Yogi* and founder of Self-Realization Fellowship in America.

Yogi: One who practices Yoga; one who strives earnestly for union with God; an aspirant going through any course of spiritual discipline.

Yogic: Having to do with Yoga.

Yogini: A female practicer of yoga.

Yogiraj: "King of Yogis," a title often given to an advanced yogi, especially a teacher of yogi.

Yuga: Age or cycle; aeon; world era. Hindus believe that there are four yugas: the Golden Age (Satya or Krita Yuga), the Silver age (Treta Yuga), The Bronze Age (Dwapara Yuga), and the Iron Age (Kali Yuga). Satya Yuga is four times as long as the Kali Yuga; Treta Yuga is three times as long; and

Dwapara Yuga is twice as long. In the Satya Yuga the majority of humans use the total potential–four-fourths–of their minds; in the Treta Yuga, three-fourths; in the Dwapara Yuga, one half; and in the Kali Yuga, one fourth. (In each Yuga there are those who are using either more or less of their minds than the general populace.) The Yugas move in a perpetual circle: Ascending Kali Yuga, ascending Dwapara Yuga, ascending Treta Yuga, ascending Satya Yuga, descending Satya Yuga, descending, Treta Yuga, descending Dwapara Yuga, and descending Kali Yuga–over and over. Furthermore, there are yuga cycles within yuga cycles. For example, there are yuga cycles that affect the entire cosmos, and smaller yuga cycles within those greater cycles that affect a solar system. The cosmic yuga cycle takes 8,640,000,000 years, whereas the solar yuga cycle only takes 24,000 years. At the present time our solar system is in the ascending Dwapara Yuga, but the cosmos is in the descending Kali Yuga. Consequently, the more the general mind of humanity develops, the more good can be accomplished by the positive, and the more evil can be accomplished by the negative. Therefore we have more contrasts and polarization in contemporary life than previously before 1900.

ABOUT THE AUTHOR

Swami Nirmalananda Giri (Abbot George Burke) is the founder and director of the Light of the Spirit Monastery (Atma Jyoti Ashram) in Cedar Crest, New Mexico, USA.

In his many pilgrimages to India, he had the opportunity of meeting some of India's greatest spiritual figures, including Swami Sivananda of Rishikesh and Anandamayi Ma. During his first trip to India he was made a member of the ancient Swami Order by Swami Vidyananda Giri, a direct disciple of Paramhansa Yogananda, who had himself been given sannyas by the Shankaracharya of Puri, Jagadguru Bharati Krishna Tirtha.

In the United States he also encountered various Christian saints, including Saint John Maximovich of San Francisco and Saint Philaret Voznesensky of New York. He was ordained in the Liberal Catholic Church (International) to the priesthood on January 25, 1974, and consecrated a bishop on August 23, 1975.

For many years Swami Nirmalananda has researched the identity of Jesus Christ and his teachings with India and Sanatana Dharma, including Yoga. It is his conclusion that Jesus lived in India for most of his life, and was a yogi and Sanatana Dharma missionary to the West. After his resurrection he returned to India and lived the rest of his life in the Himalayas.

He has written extensively on these and other topics, many of which are posted at OCOY.org.

Atma Jyoti Ashram
(Light of the Spirit Monastery)

Atma Jyoti Ashram (Light of the Spirit Monastery) is a monastic community for those men who seek direct experience of the Spirit through yoga meditation, traditional yogic discipline, Sanatana Dharma and the life of the sannyasi in the tradition of the Order of Shankara. Our lineage is in the Giri branch of the Order.

The public outreach of the monastery is through its website, OCOY.org (Original Christianity and Original Yoga). There you will find many articles on Original Christianity and Original Yoga, including *The Christ of India*. *Foundations of Yoga* and *How to Be a Yogi* are practical guides for anyone seriously interested in living the Yoga Life.

You will also discover many other articles on leading an effective spiritual life, including *Soham Yoga: The Yoga of the Self* and *Spiritual Benefits of a Vegetarian Diet*, as well as the "Dharma for Awakening" series–in-depth commentaries on these spiritual classics: the Bhagavad Gita, the Upanishads, the Dhammapada, the Tao Teh King and more.

You can listen to podcasts by Swami Nirmalananda on meditation, the Yoga Life, and remarkable spiritual people he has met in India and elsewhere, at http://ocoy.org/podcasts/

Reading for Awakening

Light of the Spirit Press presents books on spiritual wisdom and Original Christianity and Original Yoga. From our "Dharma for Awakening" series (practical commentaries on the world's scriptures) to books on how to meditate and live a successful spiritual life, you will find books that are informative, helpful, and even entertaining.

Light of the Spirit Press is the publishing house of Light of the Spirit Monastery (Atma Jyoti Ashram) in Cedar Crest, New Mexico, USA. Our books feature the writings of the founder and director of the monastery, Swami Nirmalananda Giri (Abbot George Burke) which are also found on the monastery's website, OCOY.org.

We invite you to explore our publications in the following pages.

Find out more about our publications at
lightofthespiritpress.com

BOOKS ON MEDITATION

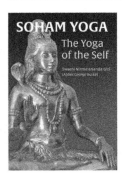

Soham Yoga
The Yoga of the Self

A complete and in-depth guide to effective meditation and the life that supports it, this important book explains with clarity and insight what real yoga is, and why and how to practice Soham Yoga meditation.

Discovered centuries ago by the Nath yogis, this simple and classic approach to self-realization has no "secrets," requires no "initiation," and is easily accessible to the serious modern yogi.

Includes helpful, practical advice on leading an effective spiritual life and many Illuminating quotes on Soham from Indian scriptures and great yogis.

"This book is a complete spiritual path." –Arnold Van Wie

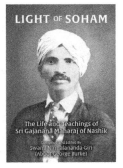

Light of Soham
The Life and Teachings of Sri Gajanana Maharaj of Nashik

Gajanan Murlidhar Gupte, later known as Gajanana Maharaj, led an unassuming life, to all appearances a normal unmarried man of contemporary society. Crediting his personal transformation to the practice of the Soham mantra, he freely shared this practice with a small number of disciples, whom he simply called his friends. Strictly avoiding the trap of gurudom, he insisted that his friends be self-reliant and not be dependent on him for their spiritual progress. Yet he was uniquely able to assist them in their inner development.

The Inspired Wisdom of Gajanana Maharaj
A Practical Commentary on Leading an Effectual Spiritual Life

Presents the teachings and sayings of the great twentieth-century Soham yogi Gajanana Maharaj, with a commentary by Swami Nirmalananda.

The author writes: "In reading about Gajanana Maharaj I encountered a holy personality that eclipsed all others for me. In his words I found a unique wisdom that altered my perspective on what yoga, yogis, and gurus should be.

"But I realized that through no fault of their own, many Western readers need a clarification and expansion of Maharaj's meaning to get the right understanding of his words. This commentary is meant to help my friends who, like me have found his words 'a light in the darkness.'"

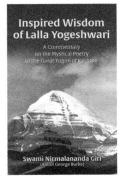

Inspired Wisdom of Lalla Yogeshwari
A Commentary on the Mystical Poetry
of the Great Yogini of Kashmir

Lalla Yogeshwari was a great fourteenth-century yogini and wandering ascetic of Kashmir, whose mystic poetry were the earliest compositions in the Kashmiri language. She was in the tradition of the Nath Yogi Sampradaya whose meditation practice is that of Soham Sadhana: the joining of the mental repetition of Soham Mantra with the natural breath.

Swami Nirmalananda's commentary mines the treasures of Lalleshwari's mystic poems and presents his reflections in an easily intelligible fashion for those wishing to put these priceless teachings on the path of yogic self-transformation into practice.

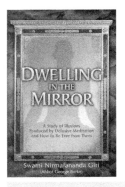

Dwelling in the Mirror
*A Study of Illusions Produced By Delusive Meditation
And How to Be Free from Them*

Swami Nirmalananda says of this book:

"Over and over people have mistaken trivial and pathological conditions for enlightenment, written books, given seminars and gained a devoted following.

"Most of these unfortunate people were completely unreachable with reason. Yet there are those who can have an experience and realize that it really cannot be real, but a vagary of their mind. Some may not understand that on their own, but can be shown by others the truth about it. For them and those that may one day be in danger of meditation-produced delusions I have written this brief study."

BOOKS ON YOGA & SPIRITUAL LIFE

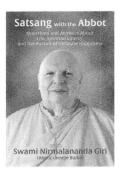

Satsang with the Abbot
*Questions and Answers about Life, Spiritual Liberty,
and the Pursuit of Ultimate Happiness*

The questions in this book range from the most sublime to the most practical. "How can I attain samadhi?" "I am married with children. How can I lead a spiritual life?" "What is Self-realization?" "How important is belief in karma and reincarnation?"

In Swami Nirmalananda's replies to these questions the reader will discover common sense, helpful information, and a guiding light for their journey through and beyond the forest of cliches, contradictions, and confusion of yoga, Hinduism, Christianity, and metaphysical thought.

Foundations of Yoga
Ten Important Principles Every Meditator Should Know

An introduction to the important foundation principles of Patanjali's Yoga: Yama and Niyama

Yama and Niyama are often called the Ten Commandments of Yoga, but they have nothing to do with the ideas of sin and virtue or good and evil as dictated by some cosmic potentate. Rather they are determined by a thoroughly practical, pragmatic basis: that which strengthens and facilitates our yoga practice should be observed and that which weakens or hinders it should be avoided.

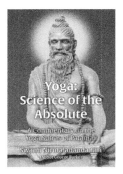

Yoga: Science of the Absolute
A Commentary on the Yoga Sutras of Patanjali

The Yoga Sutras of Patanjali is the most authoritative text on Yoga as a practice. It is also known as the Yoga Darshana because it is the fundamental text of Yoga as a philosophy.

In this commentary, Swami Nirmalananda draws on the age-long tradition regarding this essential text, including the commentaries of Vyasa and Shankara, the most highly regarded writers on Indian philosophy and practice, as well as I. K. Taimni and other authoritative commentators, and adds his own ideas based on half a century of study and practice. Serious students of yoga will find this an essential addition to their spiritual studies.

The Benefits of Brahmacharya
A Collection of Writings About the Spiritual,
Mental, and Physical Benefits of Continence

"Brahmacharya is the basis for morality. It is the basis for eternal life. It is a spring flower that exhales immortality from its petals." Swami Sivananda

This collection of articles from a variety of authorities including Mahatma Gandhi, Sri Ramakrishna, Swami Vivekananda, Swamis Sivananda and Chidananda of the Divine Life Society, Swami Nirmalananda, and medical experts, presents many facets of brahmacharya and will prove of immense value to all who wish to grow spiritually.

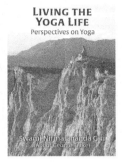

Living the Yoga Life
Perspectives on Yoga

"Dive deep; otherwise you cannot get the gems at the bottom of the ocean. You cannot pick up the gems if you only float on the surface." Sri Ramakrishna

In *Living the Yoga Life* Swami Nirmalananda shares the gems he has found from a lifetime of "diving deep." This collection of reflections and short essays addresses the key concepts of yoga philosophy that are so easy to take for granted. Never content with the accepted cliches about yoga sadhana, the yoga life, the place of a guru, the nature of Brahman and our unity with It, Swami Nirmalananda's insights on these and other facets of the yoga life will inspire, provoke, enlighten, and even entertain.

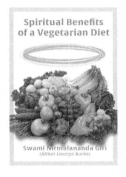

Spiritual Benefits of a Vegetarian Diet

The health benefits of a vegetarian diet are well known, as are the ethical aspects. But the spiritual advantages should be studied by anyone involved in meditation, yoga, or any type of spiritual practice.

Diet is a crucial aspect of emotional, intellectual, and spiritual development as well. For diet and consciousness are interrelated, and purity of diet is an effective aid to purity and clarity of consciousness.

The major thing to keep in mind when considering the subject of vegetarianism is its relevancy in relation to our explorations of consciousness. We need only ask: Does it facilitate my spiritual growth—the development and expansion of my consciousness? The answer is Yes.

BOOKS ON THE SACRED SCRIPTURES OF INDIA

The Bhagavad Gita for Awakening
A Practical Commentary for Leading a Successful Spiritual Life

Drawing from the teachings of Sri Ramakrishna, Jesus, Paramhansa Yogananda, Ramana Maharshi, Swami Vivekananda, Swami Sivananda of Rishikesh, Papa Ramdas, and other spiritual masters and teachers, as well as his own experiences, Swami Nirmalananda illustrates the teachings of the Gita with stories which make the teachings of Krishna in the Gita vibrant and living.

From *Publisher's Weekly*: "[The author] enthusiastically explores the story as a means for knowing oneself, the cosmos, and one's calling within it. His plainspoken insights often distill complex lessons with simplicity and sagacity. Those with a deep interest in the Gita will find much wisdom here."

The Upanishads for Awakening
A Practical Commentary on India's Classical Scriptures

The sacred scriptures of India are vast. Yet they are only different ways of seeing the same thing, the One Thing which makes them both valid and ultimately harmonious. That unifying subject is Brahman: God the Absolute, beyond and besides whom there is no "other" whatsoever. The thirteen major Upanishads are the fountainhead of all expositions of Brahman.

Swami Nirmalananda illumines the Upanishads' practical value for spiritual seekers from the unique perspective of a lifetime of study and practice of both Eastern and Western spirituality.

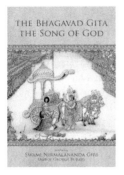

The Bhagavad Gita–The Song of God

Often called the "Bible" of Hinduism, the Bhagavad Gita is found in households throughout India and has been translated into every major language of the world. Literally billions of copies have been handwritten or printed.

The clarity of this translation by Swami Nirmalananda makes for easy reading, while the rich content makes this the ideal "study" Gita. As the original Sanskrit language is so rich, often there are several accurate translations for the same word, which are noted in the text, giving the spiritual student the needed understanding of the fullness of the Gita.

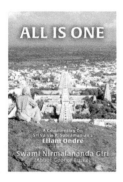

All Is One
A Commentary On Sri Vaiyai R. Subramanian's Ellam Ondre

"I you want moksha, read and practice the instructions in Ellam Ondre." –Ramana Maharshi

Swami Nirmalananda's insightful commentary brings even further light to Ellam Ondre's refreshing perspective on what Unity signifies, and the path to its realization.

Written in the colorful and well-informed style typical of his other commentaries, it is a timely and important contribution to Advaitic literature that explains Unity as the fruit of yoga sadhana, rather than mere wishful thinking or some vague intellectual gymnastic, as is so commonly taught by the modern "Advaita gurus."

A Brief Sanskrit Glossary
A Spiritual Student's Guide to Essential Sanskrit Terms

This Sanskrit glossary contains full translations and explanations of hundreds of the most commonly used spiritual Sanskrit terms, and will help students of the Bhagavad Gita, the Upanishads, the Yoga Sutras of Patanjali, and other Indian scriptures and philosophical works to expand their vocabularies to include the Sanskrit terms contained in these, and gain a fuller understanding in their studies.

BOOKS ON ORIGINAL CHRISTIANITY

The Christ of India
The Story of Original Christianity

"Original Christianity" is the teaching of both Jesus and his Apostle Saint Thomas in India. Although it was new to the Mediterranean world, it was really the classical, traditional teachings of the rishis of India that even today comprise the Eternal Dharma, that goes far beyond religion into realization.

In *The Christ of India* Swami Nirmalananda presents what those ancient teachings are, as well as the growing evidence that Jesus spent much of his "Lost Years" in India and Tibet. This is also the story of how the original teachings of Jesus and Saint Thomas thrived in India for centuries before the coming of the European colonialists.

May a Christian Believe in Reincarnation?

Discover the real and surprising history of reincarnation and Christianity.

A growing number of people are open to the subject of past lives, and the belief in rebirth—reincarnation, metempsychosis, or transmigration—is commonplace. It often thought that belief in reincarnation and Christianity are incompatible. But is this really true? May a Christian believe in reincarnation? The answer may surprise you.

"Those needing evidence that a belief in reincarnation is in accordance with teachings of the Christ need look no further: Plainly laid out and explained in an intelligent manner from one who has spent his life on a Christ-like path of renunciation and prayer/meditation."—Christopher T. Cook

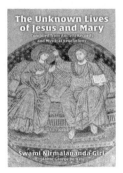

The Unknown Lives of Jesus and Mary
Compiled from Ancient Records and Mystical Revelations

"There are also many other things which Jesus did, the which, if they should be written every one, I suppose that even the world itself could not contain the books that should be written." (Gospel of Saint John, final verse)

You can discover much of those "many other things" in this unique compilation of ancient records and mystical revelations, which includes historical records of the lives of Jesus Christ and his Mother Mary that have been accepted and used by the Church since apostolic times. This treasury of little-known stories of Jesus' life will broaden the reader's understanding of what Christianity really was in its original form.

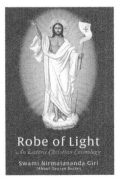

Robe of Light
An Esoteric Christian Cosmology

In *Robe of Light* Swami Nirmalananda explores the whys and wherefores of the mystery of creation. From the emanation of the worlds from the very Being of God, to the evolution of the souls to their ultimate destiny as perfected Sons of God, the ideal progression of creation is described. Since the rebellion of Lucifer and the fall of Adam and Eve from Paradise flawed the normal plan of evolution, a restoration was necessary. How this came about is the prime subject of this insightful study.

Moreover, what this means to aspirants for spiritual perfection is expounded, with a compelling knowledge of the scriptures and of the mystical traditions of East and West.

The Gospel of Thomas for Awakening
A Commentary on Jesus' Sayings as Recorded by the Apostle Thomas

When the Apostles dispersed to the various area of the world, Thomas travelled to India, where evidence shows Jesus spent his Lost Years, and which had been the source of the wisdom which he had brought to the "West."

The Christ that Saint Thomas quotes in this ancient text is quite different than the Christ presented by popular Christianity. Through his unique experience and study with both Christianity and Indian religion, Swami Nirmalananda clarifies the sometimes enigmatic sayings of Jesus in an informative and inspiring way.

The Odes of Solomon for Awakening
A Commentary on the Mystical Wisdom of the Earliest Christian Hymns and Poems

The Odes of Solomon is the earliest Christian hymn-book, and therefore one of the most important early Christian documents. Since they are mystical and esoteric, they teach and express the classical and universal mystical truths of Christianity, revealing a Christian perspective quite different than that of "Churchianity," and present the path of Christhood that all Christians are called to.

"Fresh and soothing, these 41 poems and hymns are beyond delightful! I deeply appreciate Abbot George Burke's useful and illuminating insight and find myself spiritually re-animated." –John Lawhn

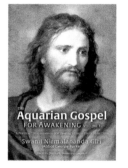

The Aquarian Gospel for Awakening (2 Volumes)
A Practical Commentary on Levi Dowling's Classic Life of Jesus Christ

Written in 1908 by the American mystic Levi Dowling, The Aquarian Gospel of Jesus the Christ answers many questions about Jesus' life that the Bible doesn't address. Dowling presents a universal message found at the heart of all valid religions, a broad vision of love and wisdom that will ring true with Christians who are attracted to Christ but put off by the narrow views of the tradition that has been given his name.

Swami Nirmalananda's commentary is a treasure-house of knowledge and insight that even further expands Dowling's vision of the true Christ and his message.

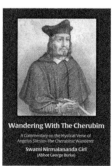

Wandering With The Cherubim
A Commentary on the Mystical Verse of Angelus Silesius–The Cherubinic Wanderer"

Johannes Scheffler, who wrote under the name Angelus Silesius, was a mystic and a poet. In his most famous book, "The Cherubinic Wanderer," he expressed his mystical vision.

Swami Nirmalananda reveals the timelessness of his mystical teachings and The Cherubinic Wanderer's practical value for spiritual seekers. He does this in an easily intelligible fashion for those wishing to put those priceless teachings into practice.

"Set yourself on the journey of this mystical poetry made accessible through this very beautifully commentated text. It is text that submerges one in the philosophical context of the Advaita notion of Non Duality. Swami Nirmalananda's commentary is indispensable in understanding higher philosophical ideas, for Swami's language, while readily approachable, is rich in deep essence of the teachings."–Savitri

The Dhammapada for Awakening
A Commentary on Buddha's Practical Wisdom

Swami Nirmalananda's commentary on this classic Buddhist scripture explores the Buddha's answers to the urgent questions, such as "How can I find find lasting peace, happiness and fulfillment that seems so elusive?" and "What can I do to avoid many of the miseries big and small that afflict all of us?" Drawing on his personal experience and on parallels in Hinduism and Christianity, the author sheds new light on the Buddha's eternal wisdom.

"Swami Nirmalananda's commentary is well crafted and stacked with anecdotes, humor, literary references and beautiful quotes from the Buddha. I found it to be entertaining as well as illuminating, and have come to consider it a guide to daily living." –Rev. Gerry Nangle

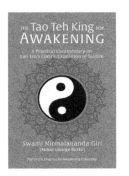

The Tao Teh King for Awakening
A Practical Commentary on Lao Tzu's Classic Exposition of Taoism

"The Tao does all things, yet our interior disposition determines our success or failure in coming to knowledge of the unknowable Tao."

Lao Tzu's classic writing, the Tao Teh King, has fascinated scholars and seekers for centuries. His presentation of the Tao which is the Eternal Reality, and the Way of the Sage that is the path to the realization of and dwelling in this Reality is illuminating, but its deeper meanings and practical applications remain obscure to many, especially in the West.

Swami Nirmalananda offers a commentary that makes the treasures of Lao Tzu's teachings accessible and applicable for the sincere seeker.

More Titles

The Four Gospels for Awakening

Light on the Path for Awakening

How to Read the Tarot

Light from Eternal Lamps

Vivekachudamani: The Crest Jewel of Discrimination for Awakening

Magnetic Therapy: Healing in Your Hands

Printed in Great Britain
by Amazon

25954823R10229